FROM THE DEPTH OF THE WELL

From the Depth of the Well

An Anthology of Jewish Mysticism

EDITED BY
Ariel Evan Mayse

FOREWORD BY
Arthur Green

Paulist Press
New York / Mahwah, NJ

The Scripture quotations contained herein are from *Tanakh: The holy Scriptures: The new JPS Translation According to the Traditional Hebrew Text* (New Jewish Publication Society, 1985). Used by permission. All rights reserved.

Cover image copyright © by dendurda/123RF
Cover design by Cynthia Dunne, www.bluefarmdesign.com
Book design by Lynn Else

Library of Congress Cataloging-in-Publication Data

From the depth of the well : an anthology of Jewish mysticism / edited by Ariel Evan Mayse ; foreword by Arthur Green.
pages cm
Includes bibliographical references.
Summary: "From Abraham Isaac Kook to Zeitlin, Jewish spirituality has a rich mystical tradition. This volume gathers the most significant and treasured writings from the Jewish mystics"— Provided by publisher.
ISBN 978-0-8091-4879-0 (pbk. : alk. paper) — ISBN 978-1-58768-367-1 (ebook)
1. Mysticism—Judaism. I. Mayse, Ariel Evan. II. Green, Arthur.
BM723.F76 2014
296.7`12—dc23

2014012791

ISBN 978-0-8091-4879-0 (paperback)
ISBN 978-1-58768-367-1 (e-book)

Published by Paulist Press
997 Macarthur Boulevard
Mahwah, New Jersey 07430

www.paulistpress.com

Printed and bound in the
United States of America

For my father Mark, exemplar of resilience and determination

And for my teacher Stuart, who lived with knowledge in the mind, strength in the body, and courage and honesty in the heart

May their memories ever be a blessing

Contents

Contents

Foreword

by Arthur Green

It is now a thousand years since the teachings of Jewish mystics began to appear in writing. These traditions, which may stretch back yet another millennium into the obscurity of Late Antiquity, were passed down largely by word of mouth as the closely guarded secrets of practitioners and their followers. When they were finally committed to writing, the protective shell of esotericism took the forms of elliptical style, unexplained symbolism, and extended treatises emphasizing letters rather than words, especially various permutations of the names of God. Outsiders to the mystics' circles, both the curious and the hostile, were kept away by these devices. Manuscripts of esoteric texts were distributed cautiously, widening the formerly oral privacy of transmission at a gradual and controlled pace.

When Hebrew printing began (ca. 1470), mystical texts were not included in the output of the presses. It took nearly one hundred years for this ban to be broken by the printing of the *Zohar* (Mantua, 1558–60; Cremona, 1660), the masterwork of medieval Kabbalah. When it did appear, it was introduced by a legal opinion of Rabbi Isaac De Lattes, who, after great hesitation, permitted its publication only because messiah was about to be revealed and it was urgent to raise the spiritual quality of Jewish life preceding his arrival. This letter of approbation is reprinted in every traditional edition of the *Zohar* to this day.

Alas, we who select, translate, and comment on Jewish mystical texts today—and in English translation, at that!—have no such excuse. Indeed, perhaps it is redemption's long delay rather than its imminent arrival that motivates us. It is because so many Jews—and others—are in need of inspiration and comfort that will help us live in this unredeemed universe and seek motivation to move that redemptive process forward inch by inch, that we have come to feel a new urgency to make the secrets available, dressed up in the finery of readable translations with explanatory introductions and footnotes.

Nothing less than a reclamation of the Jewish mystical tradition is taking place before our eyes. A Western-looking Jewry that two hundred years ago created a notion called "mainstream Judaism" mainly for the purpose of excising and burying the mystical part of our legacy is now in the midst of a complete about-face. Today we are seeking to understand and appreciate our mystical sources, then asking what aspects of their deep and complex teachings might enhance a Judaism of the twenty-first century and what might better be left behind. Different circles within world Jewry have varied answers to these questions, but the sense that there is profound wisdom to be learned from the study of these sources is widely shared.

In this effort to rediscover the mystical tradition, Jewry has no better friend than the Paulist Press and its Classics of Western Spirituality series. From the very inception of the series in 1978, its editors have enthusiastically welcomed volumes of Jewish sources. In the early years, when few other publishers, either Jewish or general, saw any profit in publishing such works, the forward-looking post–Vatican II Catholics at Paulist Press, inspired by my late friend Ewert Cousins, appreciated the importance of spiritual teachings from many traditions and the effort to make them accessible to a new generation of seekers.

Perhaps I will be permitted two brief personal stories to illustrate my gratitude for this openness and generosity. During my years as a rabbinical student at the Jewish Theological Seminary, I had the great privilege of studying closely with my teacher Abraham Joshua Heschel, of blessed memory. Among the texts he taught was a treatise called *'Amud ha-Tefillah*, the collected teachings of the Ba'al Shem Tov on prayer. In 1969 my friend Barry Holtz and I translated selections from that text in poetic format, a little book we called *Your Word Is Fire*. I tried to market it to the three or four well-known Jewish publishers, but could evince no interest. "We don't publish prayer books," I was told by one. "Nobody's interested in this stuff," said another. Disappointed, I left the manuscript in a bottom drawer. About four years later, I received a call from Richard Payne of Paulist, who said they were about to publish a series to be called "The Spiritual Masters," including brief poetic selections from each of the great mystical traditions. Might I know an appropriate Jewish text, he wondered. "It's in my desk; I've been waiting for your call," was my response. And so began a long and fruitful relationship.

As plans for the Classics developed, I was asked to join an advisory board. Richard and I discussed several times the question of whether Jews would buy Judaic sources published by a Catholic press, or whether old fears and suspicions would carry the day. I assured him that, while some would hesitate at first, the excellent content and the names of well-known Jewish editors would counter the residual bias. But then the first volume of the Classics series, Julian of Norwich, appeared in 1978. As a member of the board, I received a copy. My heart sank when I opened to the verso of the title page and read "Copyright by the Missionary Society of St. Paul the Apostle," the legal name of the order that owns the press. I immediately telephoned Richard and told him we had a dilemma. "Paulist" alone we might get away with, I told him. But Jews will surely be suspicious of anything published by "The Missionary Society...." So began the custom of all Jewish books in the series being listed as "Copyright by the author." This immediate willingness to give up a claim to rights and potentially to money in order to include these volumes made a great impression on me.

Now, some thirty-five years and 128 volumes later, Paulist Press has called upon my dear student Ariel Mayse to edit a Jewish mystical reader with contents culled from the rich offerings included in this series. He has made wise if difficult choices, having to leave many great gems behind, but offering students and seekers a chance to "enter the orchard" of Jewish mystical literature in a rich and diverse one-volume sourcebook. I am confident that it will be widely used and appreciated, leading some of its readers back to the volumes from which it was culled, from there back to the original sources, and from them back to the Source of it all. May God bless the work of this young scholar's hands, in this and in many more works to come.

Acknowledgments

Finding the words to convey my appreciation concisely and adequately has been without a doubt the most difficult part of this book.

It is my pleasure to begin by thanking the translators and editors of the previous volumes of Jewish thought in the Classics of Western Spirituality series. Many of them took the time to correspond with me personally and offered helpful advice regarding selections and notes. This book belongs to them as well. I owe a great debt to Paulist Press, and to my friend and editor Nancy de Flon in particular, for having placed their trust in a young scholar and inviting me to contribute to this great series.

Several of my students read earlier drafts of this manuscript and studied the texts with me over the past year and a half. I greatly appreciate their comments and insights. I must also thank my friends and colleagues of the Scholem Collection of the National Library in Jerusalem, where much of my work was carried out. This unique reading room is a home for study where the spiritual and academic can meet.

Thanks are due to the exceptional scholars who have guided me over the years. My undergraduate advisor David Biale gave me my start in the world of Jewish thought, and my progress since those early days is thanks to his continued friendship and support. Bernard Septimus, my advisor at Harvard University, has shown me how rigorous and felicitous intellectual history grows out of reading texts patiently and attentively. Luis Giron-Negron opened my eyes to the beauty and difficulties of the study of mystical literature from different religious traditions.

I can only begin to thank my teacher and mentor Arthur Green. Over the past six years, he has taught me what it means to be an uncompromising scholar and a sensitive theologian. He gave me careful feedback and criticism on every section of this manuscript, often more than once, and has helped me formulate many of the points herein. In addition to my academic training, he has welcomed me as a disciple and made me a part of his lifelong quest to draw forth new inspiration from the sublime wellsprings of Jewish mysticism. The only fitting expression of gratitude can be in carrying forward this project.

This volume is dedicated to two of my earliest and most beloved mentors, both of whom died far too young. My father was a man devoted to science and deeply suspicious of religion. Yet he valued truth, honesty, and the human spirit above all, and I know this book would bring a smile to his face. My teacher of martial arts, Sensei Stuart Quan, taught me the path of the warrior. It was from him that I learned how a physical discipline can teach the spirit to fly.

To my family: My mother made me aware of the possibility of spirituality in my youth, and has given me such loving support throughout my religious quest across these many years. My father-in-law, Nehemia Polen, has shared his profound wisdom with me on countless occasions. He has taught me so much of what it means to read and teach the texts of our mystical tradition with integrity and presence.

Significant portions of this manuscript were written with our dear son, Ezra Elimelech Meir, sitting on my lap. I discerned much critical insight in his playful babbling, and bless him with many more years of joyful bliss. But our friend Rachel Bickel took care of Ezra during many of my working hours, and I could not have completed this work without her help.

To you, my loving wife, Adina Ora Naama, I extend my deepest of thanks. Your constant support and encouragement have carried me forward in every way. Equally valuable has been your practical and sagacious advice throughout the process. This work would have remained but a smoldering ember without the illumination you bring to every moment of my life.

I conclude with thanks to the compassionate One to whom all thanks are due. No life is certain, especially for those who live in the shadow of illness. Our days are a gift, and we may choose to do with them what we will. I ask only for the continued strength to write and to teach, to study and to do, and to fulfill all the words of Your Torah with love.

To the Reader

This anthology brings together a collection of Jewish mystical texts spanning nearly a millennium. The passages have been selected from among the earlier volumes in the Classics of Western Spirituality series and were chosen for their historical importance, theological richness, relative accessibility, and potential interest to the contemporary seeker. Yet reading mystical works is no easy task, even in translation. These texts cannot simply be skimmed; they must be read slowly and studied mindfully. It will often prove helpful to look up references to biblical and rabbinic citations and read them in their original context. Be alert to the shared symbolic language of Kabbalah, but remember that each author uses mystical terminology and symbols in a unique way. After you have read the text and are satisfied that you understand its meaning, think about the deeper existential and religious questions with which the author is engaging. Some of these teachings are more theological and others are more focused on actual practice, but all engage with enduring questions of the spirit. It is my hope that the reader will find them to be a source of both intellectual and personal growth.

The chapter and section introductions provide historical context and offer some basic guidance to help the reader through the passages. The endnotes refer to important works of contemporary scholarship and will help clarify some of the more complicated texts, but, for the most part, this book may be studied without recourse to these points. The notes to the selections themselves are those of the original translators, though in some cases they have been shortened or slightly adjusted to ensure stylistic consistency throughout the volume; my own addenda are designated by square brackets. Most academic scholarship on Jewish mysticism takes place in Hebrew, only a small part of which is translated. English alternatives have been cited whenever possible, and studies in Hebrew are referenced only when absolutely necessary. Students who have been inspired or intrigued by a certain selection should return to the volume from which it was taken. Suggestions for further reading, which represent some of the most important and accessible works in the field, appear at the end of each introduction. Together with the original volumes of translations, these works will prove an enriching next step for readers who wish to deepen their journey.

The Ten Sefirot

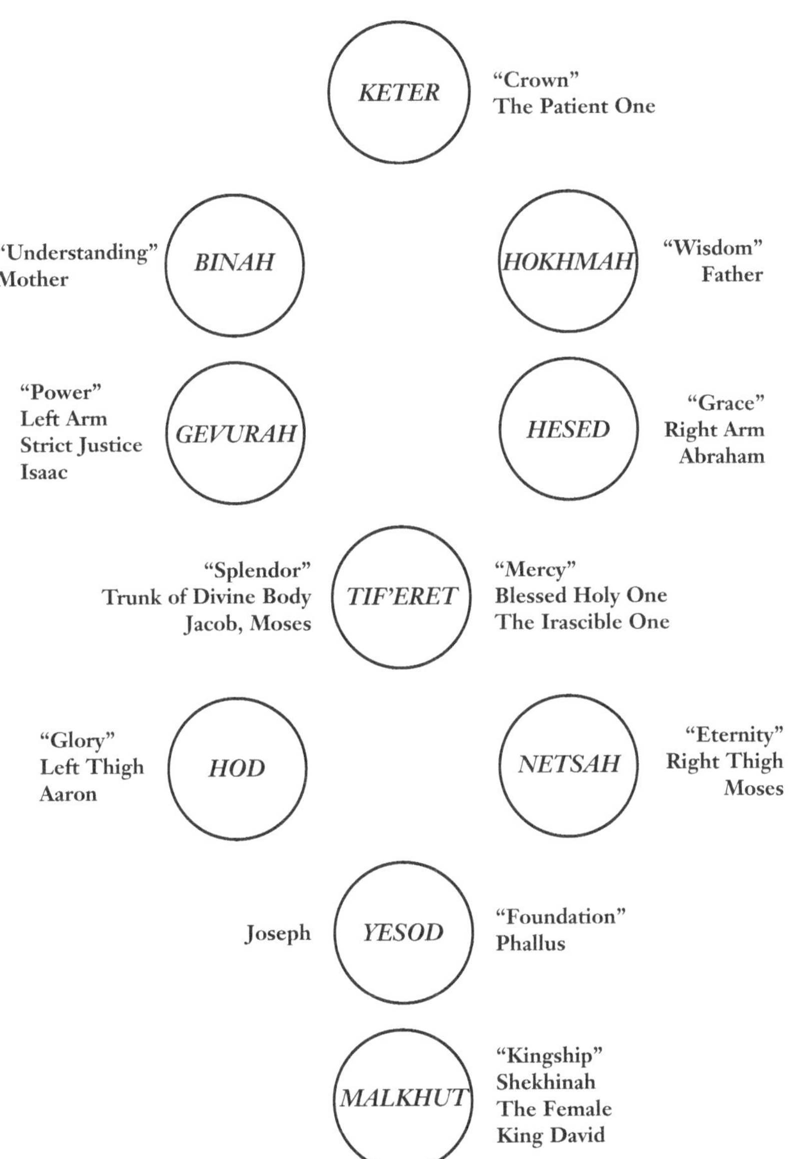

Introduction

It was once accepted as fact that Judaism had no authentic mystical tradition. The scholars of the nineteenth-century *Wissenschaft des Judentums* ("the Science of Judaism"), the pioneers of academic study of Jewish thought and culture, were deeply embarrassed by Kabbalah. These western European intellectuals hoped to inspire religious reform and dispel the regnant prejudice against Judaism (and Jews) by presenting it as a rational tradition of ethical monotheism fully congruent with the principles of the Enlightenment. Jewish mysticism did not fit these criteria, and with few exceptions they caricatured it as backward, superstitious, and aberrant. Heinrich Graetz (1817–91) was among the greatest spokesmen of this school. His landmark *History of the Jews* portrays mysticism as a peculiar parasite that had been grafted onto the trunk of rational Judaism.[1]

This claim has been reversed in the twentieth century, and scholarship has now demonstrated that the mystical tradition has been an integral part of Judaism's vital core since ancient times. The paradigm shift was largely the result of the work of the German-born Gershom Scholem (1897–1982), who rebelled against the patent rationalism of the *Wissenschaft* and chose to become an expert in Kabbalah. Scholem criticized the *Wissenschaft* scholars for having allowed their agenda to blunt their analytic tools, and he argued that Jewish mysticism had been a living and creative force at the heart of Judaism for thousands of years.[2] Throughout his long and influential career in Israel, Scholem published unknown manuscripts, authored critical and insightful studies of mystical thinkers that had been previously neglected, and painstakingly drew up a detailed history of Jewish mysticism from its earliest origins in antiquity until the Hasidic movement of the nineteenth century.[3] The burgeoning academic interest in

Kabbalah in the second half of the twentieth century rests firmly on his shoulders.[4]

Scholem focused almost exclusively on the historical and philological analysis of mystical texts. He contextualized Kabbalah within the diachronic history of Jewish thought and assumed that each major stage or "trend" was directly related to those immediately preceding it. Scholem trained several generations of important disciples, who continued largely within the boundaries of his methodology. But Moshe Idel (b. 1947), another prominent Israeli scholar, has done much to demonstrate the weaknesses of Scholem's approach by qualifying and, at times, overturning his linear mapping of the history of Kabbalah. Idel's work demonstrated that the assumption of what he calls "proximism," or the necessary connection between historically contiguous events, is not always correct. In fact, just the opposite may be true: mystical traditions were often transmitted orally, making their influence very difficult to chart, and therefore two geographically and temporally disparate groups might indeed be connected.

Idel has also suggested that the historian must embrace the tools of phenomenology, or the study of subjective religious experience, in order to explore the conceptual similarities among mystical texts written in different times and places. This is indicative of Idel's belief that many important works of Jewish mysticism reflect actual experiences, thus penetrating a level of understanding largely neglected by Scholem, who remained an academic less than comfortable in dealing with such phenomena. It is not up to the scholar to judge the veracity of such experiences, argues Idel, but being cognizant of this element reminds us that Jewish mysticism is not abstract sophistry; it is a theology embodied in devotional practices.[5]

The structure of the present anthology reflects the methodologies of these two great scholars. The chapters are arranged chronologically, allowing the reader to see that Jewish mystics have continuously engaged with certain core themes over the course of many generations. The introductions contextualize the texts within their original cultural milieus, both Jewish and non-Jewish, since knowing their provenance is critical for understanding them correctly. Yet we should not assume that subsequent stages of Jewish mysticism are built on top of one another like bricks in a pyramid. It may be the case that mystical groups with little or no direct historical contact share much in common, just as there have been mystics who were not influenced by those that preceded them. It should also be remembered that these religious texts reflect human phenomena and perceived spiritual experiences, and should not be analyzed only as literary creations that may be reduced into a combination of cultural and historical influences.

We have noted that mysticism is part of the vital core of the Jewish tradition, but some discussion of the term *mysticism* and its implications for the study of religion will help us better understand this claim. To be clear, mysticism does not exist in a vacuum as a religion of its own.[7] It is a helpful category that we may use when speaking about the similarities between certain types of religious experiences, spiritual writings, and theological systems. But the Jewish mystical tradition cannot be disentangled from Judaism itself, and treating them as two separate phenomena is misleading. Jewish mystics have been shaped by the cultural environments in which they lived, and their experiences and writings reflect the symbols and values of their religious tradition. The noun *mysticism* is not an indigenous Jewish term, nor does it have any precise Hebrew cognate.[8] The words *sod* ("secret") or *raz* ("mystery") refer to hidden doctrines or an esoteric interpretation of a particular text, but they do not describe an overall approach to the spiritual life that parallels the term *mysticism.*

The term *Jewish mysticism* refers to far more than a closed body of esoteric teachings, and it is applied to a wide range of spiritual paths and religious experiences. The Jewish mystical library includes many thousands of volumes as well as countless smaller works and unpublished manuscripts. These represent a broad spectrum of literary genres, including poetry, prose, scriptural commentary, liturgy, law, fictional stories, spiritual autobiographies, and letters. Given this variety, what defines Jewish mysticism as a distinctive subcategory of Jewish piety? What does a withdrawn and ascetic Kabbalist who pores over pages of labyrinthine theology have in common with the Hasidic mystic who serves God through the physical world and longs to be fully reunited with the Infinite One? What does the Israelite of Late Antiquity, who uses mantra-like hymns to escape the physical world by ascending into the heavenly palaces and gazing upon the throne of glory, share with a twentieth-century eastern European writer who is conversant in modern romantic philosophy and sees nature as saturated with divine energy?

Surely no single definition of Jewish mysticism can fully describe all texts associated with this literature. In place of an unrealistic panacea, I propose the following working definition: Mysticism refers to the quest for a direct or immediate experience of God's presence, and the longing to grasp the mysteries of the human soul and know the inner dynamics of the divine realm. These goals lie at the very heart of Jewish mysticism, and are shared by all of the texts included in this volume. But the similarities between them extend far beyond this single axis. Reflecting on the other important elements common to most, if not all, of the various manifestations of Jewish mysticism will help us answer a second part of this question: What makes these mystical texts specifically Jewish?

Jewish mystics are united by their relationship to canonical Jewish texts. First and foremost this means interpreting the Torah and Hebrew Bible, and to a lesser extent the Talmud and rabbinic Midrashim. In the eyes of the mystic, the Torah is no mundane book of wisdom or law. It is a vessel that holds God's wisdom itself, and the Torah is composed of divine names, expressed in narrative form. As later Jewish mystics will put it, Scripture is divinity expressed in the language of humanity. Its words were revealed on Mount Sinai, but the Torah is a fountain from which all religious truth flows; any authoritative teaching must be derived from (or anchored in) its text. Rabbinic laws and lore (*aggadah*) are open to constant reinterpretation, but only the Torah has truly infinite layers of meaning.[9] Even mystical works that are not primarily exegetical, such as *Sefer Yetsirah* or the *Heikhalot* literature, are deeply influenced by the themes, imagery, and theology of the Hebrew Bible.

This unfailing commitment to a common body of sacred literature has allowed Jewish mystics to develop a shared symbolic language rooted in their canonical texts. The writings of Jewish mystics employ a rich matrix of associations and symbols inspired by biblical verses and rabbinic teachings, which have been expanded and refined over the years. Some of these symbols are found in very early mystical works, but the symbolic language began to take on a recognizable, relatively stable form in early medieval Kabbalah. Starting in the twelfth and thirteenth centuries, the *sefirot* (sing. *sefirah*) form the core of this language. As will become clear in the following chapters, the *sefirot* are a series of emanations that bridge between the abstract, unknowable Deity and the immanent Presence in this world. But the *sefirot* have also become the anchors to which the vast array of symbols adhere. This vibrant language of linguistic and conceptual associations is one of the mystical tradition's greatest contributions to Jewish religious thought.[10]

To be a mystic is to struggle with the boundaries of words and the limited capacity of the human mind to conceive of God. Yet Jewish mysticism has generally maintained a positive view of language, rarely retreating into purely apophatic or negative theology.[11] This is in no small part due to the great flexibility and richness of its symbolism, which offers the mystic a way of speaking about divine matters that extends beyond the literal meaning of words. But Jewish mystics also believe that language itself has a divine origin. God formed the world by means of letters and words, and the language of human beings retains this tremendous creative power as well. In many cases, but by no means all, this sanctity is restricted to Hebrew, commonly referred to as the "holy tongue" (*leshon ha-kodesh*). Nowhere is the positive vision of language more manifest than in the mystical understanding of Scripture and prayer. The Hebrew text of the Torah shimmers with divine Presence, accessed through reading and intoning its words carefully in order to explore their symbolic associations. The words of prayer also afford an opportunity for mankind to reach out toward God, an act described as both a spiritual ascent and a contemplative inner journey. The transcendent divine Being may be ineffable and unknowable, but language is a gift that lessens the gap between humanity and God.[12]

Jewish mystics also share a commitment to embodying their spiritual life in religious praxis. For most, this means at least the proscriptions of normative *halakhah* (Jewish law) that provide the concrete ritual framework for their inner devotional activities. Mystics have also developed a wealth of supererogatory rituals, pathways for spiritual expression beyond the letter of the law. Prayer and the study of Torah are often devotional highpoints of Jewish religious life, but all commandments are imbued with deeper cosmic and personal significance.[13] Some mystics argue that humankind's actions have great theurgic power, for pious deeds increase the divine glory and draw spiritual vitality into the world by aligning the various elements of the Godhead. In an even more daring formulation common in mystical literature, God *needs* human actions.[14] This aspect of their religious lives almost always takes place in the public arena. With rare exceptions, Jewish mystics are part of communities, though at times they may belong primarily to highly elite, quasi-monastic fellowships. They rarely live alone or cultivate a devotional life in permanent solitude. Occasionally, this proximity puts mystics at odds with more orthodox elements of the Jewish community, but it has meant that mystics have had a profound influence on Jewish intellectual and social life.[15]

Jewish mystics employ symbols of their tradition and are deeply influenced by their cultural heritage and its assumptions. However, they also share much in common with the great spiritual masters of other religious traditions. The present anthology appears in the Classics of Western Spirituality series, and while this is not the place for an extensive discussion of the merits and perils of comparative religion, some brief words on the subject are in order. As noted above, there is no mysticism independent of religious traditions, and the writings of all mystics are shaped by their own intellectual and spiritual contexts. Reading their works in translation masks some of their uniqueness, which is more clearly visible in the nuances of their original language. It is hard, however, to ignore conceptual affinities found in the clusters of ideas and experiences that are shared by mystics from across different religions.[16] In some cases this may be attributed to influence from one mystical tradition to another, yet at other times this explanation is unlikely or impossible. Even granted that there is no ineffable core common to all mystical experiences, the similarities in the poetic outpourings of mystical souls and their yearnings to draw near to God transcend denominational and religious boundaries.[17] The reader is invited to examine the following texts carefully, pondering their words and sitting with them, and then to compare these teachings of the Jewish mystics with the wisdom of other great spiritual classics.

The Beginnings of Jewish Mysticism: A Historical Overview

Our volume explores the developments of Jewish mysticism after the emergence of Kabbalah in early medieval France and Spain. However, important elements of the mystical tradition are found far earlier in Jewish history. Its earliest echoes may indeed already be heard in the Hebrew Bible, where God's interaction with the physical world is taken for granted. Ancient Israelites were not mystics, but they surely possessed a rich devotional life. The words of the psalmist evocatively articulate the longing of one who seeks to dwell in God's presence and to gaze upon his majestic glory. In Exodus 40, the divine Indwelling literally fills the tabernacle, and other biblical accounts of direct, often anthropomorphic visions of God abound: Moses and the elders' vision of God and the sapphire beneath his feet (Exod 24); Isaiah's encounter with God seated on the throne (Isa 6); Ezekiel's terrifying confrontation with the divine chariot (Ezek 1, 10); and Daniel's apocalyptic fantasies (Dan 7, 9).[18]

Yet these traditions are complemented by biblical voices claiming that it is impossible to see God's face and live (Exod 34), and by strong prohibitions against creating any sort of images of the Divine. Even the moment of revelation is remembered by some sources as being primarily linguistic rather than visual, with only fire and clouds accompanying the pronouncement of the Ten Commandments.[19] The Jewish tradition has continued to struggle between the poles of anthropomorphism and aniconism, and both are given their due, even side by side, in the later works of Kabbalah.[20]

The first genre of Jewish literature with recognizable elements that may rightly be called "mystical" emerged in the final centuries before the Common Era.[21] These works, called apocalypses, describe the ascent of an individual into the heavens. Sometimes the mystic enters into the supernal temple, where he is granted a direct vision of God. In some cases, the journey culminates with the mystic being transformed into one of the angels, or more rarely, even becoming deified. This ascent on high is often accompanied by the revelation of strange, symbolic prophecies that require extensive interpretation. Apocalypses were inspired by the great biblical prophets and wisdom literature, but they also incorporate motifs taken from Hellenistic and Roman culture.

We know nothing about the authors of these texts, since most apocalypses are pseudepigraphic, purporting to be the work of biblical figures such as Noah, Abraham, Ezra, and Daniel. Enoch, who appears briefly in Genesis 5:18–24 and is mysteriously "taken by God," was a particular favorite; a broad and influential corpus of ascent texts was attributed to him.[22] Apocalypses share a set of literary conventions, and their narrative elements seem to have been just as meaningful for those who studied them as the revelatory visions they preserve. While scholars debate whether they were based on mystical experiences or are purely literary creations, it is clear that they seemed real to many generations of readers, both Jewish and Christian.[23] The research into apocalypses has been further enriched by the discovery of the Dead Sea Scrolls. Manuscripts of several well-known apocalyptic texts were found among this priceless collection, and many other Dead Sea works distinctly resemble the apocalypses in style and content. This has sparked a lively debate regarding the existence of mystical texts and practices in the Qumran community near the turn of the millennium.[24]

The destruction of the Jerusalem Temple in 70 CE and the emergence of rabbinic Judaism ushered in a time of monumental change for Jewish piety and theology. The biblical model of God's indwelling presence was razed along with the temple, and Jews were forced to rethink the concept of divine immanence in light of their new reality.[25] For the architects of the rabbinic tradition, God was now to be encountered primarily through the nexus of sacred words. The synagogue and study hall superseded the holy space of the temple as the central loci of religious devotion, and prayer and the interpretation of Torah took the place of sacrificial ritual. Thus it was in the rabbinic period that Judaism was truly transformed into a scriptural religion.[26]

Much in keeping with biblical conceptions of piety, the project of rabbinic Judaism articulated a model of religious service defined by action and deeds. The rabbinic ideal is the performance of *halakhah*, a word that may be translated as both "law" and "way."[27] Some have argued that early Jewish mysticism represents an alternative to the ordered legalism and transcendent theology of the rabbis, one that recaptured the spiritual dynamism and living creativity of the biblical myths.[28] Yet recent scholarship has suggested that there are indeed concepts and experiences described in foundational rabbinic texts that anticipate later Jewish mysticism. Despite warnings about the dangers of engaging in the study of the esoteric traditions referred to as *ma'aseh bereshit* ("Works of Creation") and *ma'aseh merkavah* ("Works of the Chariot"), theological speculations about God and quasi-prophetic visions of the Divine abound in rabbinic literature.[29] It is surely no coincidence that it was in this period that the Song of Songs was reread as a passionate love song between the Jewish people and God, setting the stage for the later mystics' captivation with this brilliant work of biblical poetry.[30] Early rabbinic reflections on the process of studying and interpreting sacred texts are another excellent illustration of this point. Biblical exegesis is perhaps the most fundamental rabbinic activity, and some early rabbinic texts describe scriptural interpretation as a revelatory and prophetic act. The goal is not to achieve a mystical experience cordoned off from their primary focus of legal interpretation, but rather to enter into the deepest divine realms in order to explore and clarify the law.[31]

The short but influential *Sefer Yetsirah* (*Book of Formation*) is by all accounts an inscrutable work.[32] This obscure text is very difficult to date, but its overall worldview and finely balanced literary structure suggest that it was roughly contemporaneous with the Mishnah (ca. 200 CE).[33] *Sefer Yetsirah* describes God's creation of the universe by means of the "thirty-two pathways of wisdom;" namely, the ten *sefirot* and the twenty-two letters of the Hebrew alphabet. This work thus introduces the term *sefirot* into the Jewish lexicon for the first time. In this context, however, the *sefirot* refer to something very different from the complex web of symbols they will represent in medieval Kabbalah. Here the *sefirot* are simply the numerical (*mispar*) elements used by God to fashion the world. The first four *sefirot* are divine elements that emanate one from the other, and the latter six correspond to the directions of physical space.[34] This account of Creation assures the reader that unity and near-mathematical order undergird the apparent multiplicity and chaos of the material world.[35]

The power of language is one of the central themes of *Sefer Yetsirah*.[36] God forms the world through speech in the Genesis narrative as well, but *Sefer Yetsirah* builds upon this notion by explaining that Creation was accomplished by combining the Hebrew letters with one another. Letters are the very foundations of the world as well as the most basic elements of language. It is interesting to note that *Sefer Yetsirah* does not examine the shapes of the letters nor their numerical values, techniques that were to become quite popular in later Jewish mysticism.[37] Nor does this work assign a special status to Hebrew language as the "holy tongue" vis-à-vis other languages. This election may be implied, but nowhere is it stated explicitly, and there is at least a possibility that *Sefer Yetsirah* assigns the same creative power to all languages.[38] This positive relationship to language and preoccupation with the creative power of the letters was one of its greatest contributions to the Jewish mystical tradition.[39]

The elliptical style of *Sefer Yetsirah* sets this work apart from most other Jewish mystical texts. It rarely quotes the Bible, though, at times, its words echo the language of key scriptural passages.[40] Unlike the earlier apocalypses (or the later *heikhalot* texts), *Sefer Yetsirah* is not framed within a pseudepigraphic narrative and devotes relatively little space to personal mystical experience. This work does suggest, however, that the secrets of Creation are being revealed in order that human beings might be able to emulate them. The biblical figure of Abraham appears in this capacity at the very end of *Sefer Yetsirah*. Through his contemplative efforts, he attains divine wisdom, and he too is able to create as an act of *imitatio Dei*.[41] This quasi-magical element of *Sefer Yetsirah* was embellished in later traditions of the Golem, an inanimate being formed from the earth and imbued with life through the letters of the divine name.[42]

Sefer Yetsirah contains the earliest kernels of the symbolic language that was to become the heart of later kabbalistic works, and this short treatise had a great impact on Jewish mysticism. Its traditions were likely available to the sages of the Talmud in some form,[43] and it was frequently cited by Jewish thinkers beginning in the tenth century. *Sefer Yetsirah* was also the subject of a great number of commentaries. Later mystics and philosophers interpreted this epigrammatic work in accord with the religious ideas of their own day, thus giving their ideas great antiquity and authority. These plentiful commentaries, together with the many other mystical explanations of Creation produced by early medieval Kabbalists, constitute a category of Jewish mystical literature unto themselves.[44]

Rabbinic Judaism crystallized at the same time as nascent Christianity. These two traditions have a shared heritage in the Hebrew Bible, but their theological connections extend beyond that. Early Jewish and Christian mystical traditions were influenced by a common pool of ideas and texts circulating in the first few centuries of the Common Era.[45] Also flourishing at this time were the "gnostic" circles, which held that secret knowledge (*gnosis*) of God had the power to save one from the inherent corruption of the physical world.[46] These groups fused ideas from ancient Jewish texts with those adopted from Greco-Roman pagan religion, especially the popular mystery cults. Some believed in two deities, a beneficent god that created the universe and another, lesser god that ruled over the world. Many believed that God's divine *pleroma* ("fullness") was composed of emanated divine powers (*aeons*). The vectors of influence between these groups went in all directions, and one may speak of Jewish gnostics, Christian gnostics, and elements of Gnosticism that were incorporated into both of these religions.

The apocalypses of Late Antiquity have much in common with the journeys through supernal *heikhalot* ("palaces") and visions of the heavenly *merkavah* ("chariot") described in a body of Hebrew and Aramaic works popular in the post-Talmudic period.[47] Ascent texts, both apocalyptic and *heikhalot*, are predicated on a perceived rift between humanity and the Divine, which the mystic hopes to bridge through his heavenly journey.[48] However, the *heihkalot* works differed in a number of important ways. In classical apocalypses, individuals were overtaken by a moment of prophetic rapture, but, in these texts, the mystic sought to induce his own experience by repeating names of God, mantras, and adjurations; fasting; and reciting liturgical hymns, some of which are similar to the liturgical poems developed for use in synagogues.[49]

The goals of the journey in the *heikhalot* texts are many and varied. In some, the mystic descends (*yored*) before the *merkaveh* in order to gaze upon the throne of glory resting upon the chariot, perhaps even glimpsing the divine Figure itself. The most audacious of these anthropomorphic visions is found in *Shi'ur Komah* (*The Measure of the Form*).[50] The mystic's journey is quite hazardous, and along the way he is confronted by myriads of angels, many of which are terrifying specters indeed. The very intensity of his vision of the divine Presence can lead to the mystic's demise.[51] But dangerous though it may be, this journey offers a unique opportunity to join the heavenly chorus in reciting songs of glory before God. In this the *heikhalot* literature builds upon a much older Jewish tradition of God's coronation through the hymns of people (and angels).[52] In some cases, the ascent is a means of accomplishing more magical or mundane goals. Yet, in many of these texts, the mystic undertakes his heavenly journey in order to gain a deeper understanding of Torah; heavenly secrets are revealed as the mystic steps into the presence of God.[53]

The early sages Rabbi Akiva and Rabbi Yishma'el appear frequently as the protagonists of *heikhalot* texts, but these attributions are pseudepigraphic. Scholem contended that the origins of *heikhalot* literature are in the early rabbinic period, particularly from circles informed by Gnosticism,[54] but scholars now believe that *heikhalot* and *merkavah* texts only became a genre of their own sometime closer to the codification of the Talmud (c. 500 CE).[55] The works of *heikhalot* or *merkavah* mysticism are linked to one another by their common themes, but they display great variety and are in no way a monolithic literature. In fact, most of the texts are not books in the formal sense. Even classics like *Heikhalot Rabbati* and *Heikhalot Zutartei* (the "Greater" and "Lesser Palaces") are composites of many textual strata, the editing and redaction of which continued well into the Early Middle Ages.[56]

There is no evidence to suggest that mystical texts were studied with any great enthusiasm in the Talmudic academies of the Geonim in the ninth to eleventh centuries, though they were aware of these traditions.[57] Some type of mystical creativity must have continued in the Near East, but by the turn of the millennium the center of gravity of Jewish mysticism was shifting to the West. A similar change was taking place in Jewish intellectual culture more broadly, as the hegemony of the Babylonian Geonim started to falter and sages of the Iberian Peninsula and Ashkenaz (Germany) began their rise to prominence. Mystical ideas and literature were brought first to Italy, which remained a kabbalistic center well into the Renaissance, and, from there, they spread to the Jewish heartlands of the European continent.[58]

The high medieval Rhineland was the home of the next important development in Jewish mysticism. In the twelfth and thirteenth centuries, small circles of intense ascetics formed around members of the illustrious Kalonymous family, a few of whom are known to us by name. Foremost among them was Rabbi Yehudah ha-Hasid (ca. 1150–1217), author of the immensely popular *Sefer Hasidim* (*Book of the Pious*).[59] His student Rabbi Eleazar of Worms (ca. 1165–1230) was a poet and Talmudist as well as a mystic. He was the author of *Sefer ha-Roke'ah* (*Book of the Perfumist*), a book of law and ethics. Rabbi Eleazar also wrote many other shorter, more esoteric works, a great number of which have yet to be published. These fiery mystics, referred to as the *Hasidei Ashkenaz* ("German Pietists"), were consumed by the search for ever more exacting standards for upright behavior and devotional expression. The *Hasidei Ashkenaz* emerged in the turbulence left in the wake of the Crusades. Their rigorous penitential practices were likely informed by the surge of pietism in both Christian and Jewish circles, as well as by the examples of martyrdom in the massacres at the hands of the Crusaders.[60]

The German Pietists developed a rich esoteric theology that was inspired by the *Heikhalot* literature, neo-Platonism, and early Jewish philosophical works.[61] Like many other mystics, their religious lives were driven by a longing to draw nearer to God. The Pietists believed the Deity was utterly transcendent and incorporeal, and their writings sought to purge the tradition of all anthropomorphism. Yet, an interesting conception of divine immanence came to them from the teachings of Rabbi Saadya in Hebrew paraphrase. God's essence may be forever unattainable, but the emanated divine glory (*kavod*, also called *shekhinah*) and the intermediary powers that stand between humanity and God could indeed be known. The writings of the Pietists are perhaps the first to mention the *sefirot* as creations that bridge between the human and the Divine. Their God, though ineffable and unknowable, was also omnipresent. God could be known through observing the patterns and machinations of the natural world, an idea similar to those found in medieval Christianity.[62] Gone was the rift between man and God that so defined *heikhalot* and *merkavah* mysticism. The *Hasidei Ashkenaz* never attempted to reconcile this perplexing tension between immanence and transcendence.[63]

The Pietists believed it was incumbent on humankind to act in accordance with the divine will (*retson ha-Bore*) at all times. However, the limits of God's desires were not expressed in the proscribed legal norms of the Torah, the later works of Jewish law, or the Midrashic *aggadah*. The Pietists must have sensed a disconnect between the requirements outlined in the canonical texts and their own religious experiences, and believed that these works must be reexamined in order to uncover the divine will concealed within them. The will discovered by the *Hasidei Ashkenaz* demanded tremendous new levels of religious stringency and higher degrees of moral perfection. The wicked, and indeed the multitudes of people around them, were inescapably led into sin by their ignorance of these demands. But instead of closing ranks and forsaking the broader Jewish community, the Pietists hoped to save their brethren by enlightening them to the demands of *retson ha-Bore*. This quest to reveal and fulfill God's deeper will fueled their mystical and social agenda.[64]

Living in conformity with the divine will meant that the Pietists advocated a new set of spiritual values. Dissatisfied with a simplistic model of religious observance, they sought mystical rationale for the commandments.[65] Judaism has long venerated the act of learning Torah, but in the teachings of the *Hasidei Azhkenaz*, sacred study took on a decidedly mystical valence. For them the Torah was a manifestation of the divine glory and the *shekhinah*, and its study could even induce an ecstatic experience. Scripture is encoded with a host of divine names that must be teased forth from amidst the narrative and laws, and according to some of their writings, the Torah itself *is* the Tetragrammaton, the four-letter divine name. Reading its words aloud was likened to intoning God's most sacred name.[66] The *Hasidei Ashkenaz* emphasized the importance of mystical prayer, which replaced the ascent to the throne of glory as the engine of mystical experience. They offered complex mystical interpretations of the liturgy, tallying the number of letters in various prayers, or reading its text as full of acronyms referring to other words.[67] The Pietists had no doctrine similar to the notion of *kavvanot* ("intentions") found in later Kabbalah, but their teachings did attribute special significance to one's inner state while performing on the commandments. The ideal Hasid was an ascetic who lived with absolute fear of God and served him with loving devotion, but not necessarily someone who had perfected his intellect. It is likely that the *Hasidei Ashkenaz* were reacting to the emergence of the Tosafistic school of Talmudic interpretation. These scholars had replaced traditional modes of learning with the flashy methods of dialectics. The Pietists decried this new technique as shallow, since it did not require one to undergo years of ethical refinement through carefully regimented study.[68]

The theology of the German Pietists represents a crucial step in the transition from the rabbinic paradigm of Late Antiquity to the new worldview of the Middle Ages.[69] The groups around the Kalonymous family were small, and the social and religious revolution of which they dreamed never came to be. In fact, their bitter critique and attempts at reform were met with significant opposition. But their ideas spread through living teachers and in manuscripts, and they had a subtle impact on Jewish communities in western Europe. As the Jews began to move into eastern Europe in the thirteenth century, they brought many ideas from the *Hasidei Ashkenaz* along with them. Of course, not all later pietists and penitents were inspired by Rabbi Yehudah and his disciples, but their works are an important stage in the development of Jewish mysticism.[70]

Concurrently with the German Pietists, and perhaps even in dialogue with them, a mystical renaissance was quietly taking place to the west in Provence. Like the *Hasidei Ashkenaz*, this new form of Jewish mysticism began in small circles of intensely devoted spiritualists. It did not remain esoteric for long, however, and it swiftly erupted into public discourse, forever changing the face of Jewish mysticism. It was in this dynamic region of southern France that the story of Kabbalah truly begins.

Further Reading

Ariel, David. *The Mystic Quest: An Introduction to Jewish Mysticism.* New York: Schocken Books, 1988.

Dan, Joseph. *Jewish Mysticism,* 4 vols. Northvale, NJ: Jason Aronson, 1998/1999.

Green, Arthur, ed. *Jewish Spirituality.* 2 vols. New York: Crossroad, 1986/7.

Idel, Moshe. *Kabbalah: New Perspectives.* New Haven: Yale University Press, 1988.

Scholem, Gershom. *Kabbalah.* Jerusalem: Keter, 1974.

Scholem, Gershom. *Major Trends in Jewish Mysticism.* New York: Schocken Books, 1995.

CHAPTER 1

The Dawn of Kabbalah

Introduction

Provence was home to a creative and multicultural Jewish community in the late twelfth and early thirteenth centuries. Talmudists, philosophers, and other Jewish intellectuals lived and taught in close proximity, and their works were enriched by fresh ideas absorbed from the non-Jewish culture surrounding them. This vibrant region was the scene for the next great movement in Jewish mysticism. It began with a small group of Provençal scholars whose teachings eventually spread west into Spain. These mystics articulated a radical conception of God and the inner workings of the divine structure, reinterpreted the story of Creation as a process of divine emanations, and offered a theological worldview that redefined the relationship between God and the physical world.[1] Deep spiritual significance was attributed to traditional rituals such as prayer and Torah study, and these scholars emphasized the centrality of *devekut*, or the radical experience of God's presence.[2] In order to convey their theology, the Provençal mystics employed a new type of symbolism in which certain keywords were associated with an increasingly vast array of mystical concepts. The theological writings and symbolic language developed by these mystics represent the first appearance of Kabbalah.[3]

Lack of reliable historical data has led to disagreements about nearly every aspect of the origins and early stages of Kabbalah, including dating, location, attribution, and influence. Gershom Scholem argued that the Kabbalah evolved in a linear fashion. It began with the mysterious *Sefer ha-Bahir* and moved from the Provence circle to the Spanish cities of Gerona and then to Castile. More recent scholarship has suggested that Kabbalah emerged from a number of contemporaneous groups who influenced one another in subtle ways that are difficult to chart.[4] It has been claimed that the theology of Kabbalah was entirely the invention of the Provençal mystics. However, even the earliest Kabbalists already had a vast and surprisingly well-developed pool of mystical symbols. Therefore it is reasonable to entertain the Kabbalists' own claim that they were writing down and transmitting ideas received from their own teachers; they had inherited *kabbalot* ("traditions," sing. *kabbalah*) in the strictest sense of the word, based on oral teachings that they considered ancient. These mystics creatively engaged with older traditions by reinterpreting them, but we need not assume that they invented the entire theology of Kabbalah out of whole cloth.[5]

It is unlikely that we will ever definitively answer the question of *why* Kabbalah first emerged into writing and public discourse in late twelfth- and early thirteenth-century Provence. However, there are a number of important historical factors that may have influenced this mystical awakening. Provence stands at the crossroads of the Ashkenazi heartland and Spain, and its unique cultural milieu was fertile ground for the synthesis of different intellectual traditions.[6] Only there could the esotericism of the German Pietists meet the philosophy, especially the mystically tinged neo-Platonism, inherited from Muslim Spain. Indeed, the twelfth century was also a period of great creativity in the Islamic and Christian majority cultures of Western Europe.[7] Kabbalah may also be seen as a paradoxical internal response to the rise of Jewish philosophy. The anti-rationalist mystics took an active role in the Maimonidean controversy, but they too had assimilated philosophical concepts and terminology.[8]

Sefer ha-Bahir (*The Book of Brightness*) is perhaps the oldest extant work of Kabbalah. In this text, which appeared in late twelfth- or early thirteenth-century Provence, we see Jewish mystical symbolism beginning to crystallize. The enigmatic *Bahir*, however, is markedly different from the other kabbalistic texts of Provence and Gerona. Some have explained this by arguing that its oldest stratum originated somewhere in the Middle East and only later traveled to Provence via the German Pietists.[9] Others place more emphasis on the editorial (and perhaps even authorial) role of the *Hasidei Ashkenaz*.[10] There is no clear evidence that the first Provençal mystics were directly influenced by this work,[11] but though they never quote its words, the earliest Kabbalists were clearly in possession of a symbolical language similar to that found, albeit in variant form, in the *Bahir*.

The *Bahir* fuses elements of many earlier intellectual traditions, including classical rabbinic literature, *Sefer Yetsirah*, German Pietism, and perhaps elements of ancient esoteric teachings that have been referred to as Jewish Gnosticism.[12] The work is a textual composite with no single author, though it is pseudepigraphically attributed to the early sage Rabbi Nehuniyah ben ha-Kanah.[13] It is difficult to discern any sustained conceptual order in the *Bahir*, possibly due to its fragmentary preservation, and even the divisions between sections are subject to editorial discretion.[14] Its structure is much closer to the associative style of rabbinic midrash than to a linear work of biblical exegesis.[15] However, the *Bahir* is distinguished from its rabbinic antecedents by its matrix of mystical symbols. Biblical verses are not deployed simply as proof texts, but are rather interpreted as being embedded with keywords that refer to kabbalistic concepts.

These symbols and their accompanying motifs and parables are the most significant contribution of the *Bahir* to the development of Jewish mysticism. They include the metaphor of an inverted tree (roots above, branches below) to describe the genesis of multiplicity out of divine unity;[16] the role of God's wisdom in creation;[17] the relationship between the many divine names; the nature and origins of evil;[18] and the place of the feminine in the divine superstructure.[19] The term *sefirot* briefly appears here for the first time since *Sefer Yetsirah*. Their number, structure, and the names associated with them remain obscure, however, and we should not confuse them with the more fully defined *sefirot* of later Kabbalah. In the *Bahir*, they are divine powers, manifestations of interacting forces with the Godḥead. In the kabbalistic works of Provence and Gerona, however, the *sefirot* are hypostatic elements emanating forth from a dynamic Deity that lies mysteriously beyond them. The *sefirot* and the symbolic language of the *Bahir* were absorbed by later mystical literature, especially the *Zohar*, and the *Bahir* itself was consistently cited from the thirteenth century into the modern era.

The *'Iyyun* ("Contemplation") Circle refers to a loosely associated group of scholars and texts about which very little is known.[20] The anonymous texts they left behind reveal that they were influenced by the ideas of *Heikhalot* literature, neo-Platonic philosophy, and German

Pietism, but we have little information about the individuals who made up these groups or precisely when they were active. Even their geographic location is a subject of dispute: while it was long assumed that they lived in Provence sometime between 1200 and 1225, more recent scholarship places the *'Iyyun* Circle in 1230–79 Castile.[21] This means that they may have been roughly contemporaneous with the Provençal and the Gerona kabbalistic schools, to whom we shall turn shortly. However, the doctrines and style of the *'Iyyun* literature are radically different from those of *Sefer ha-Bahir* and Yitshak the Blind, and they should be considered a theologically independent circle of scholars. Their writings remained influential and were cited with reverence by the sixteenth-century Kabbalists such as Rabbi Moshe Cordovero and Rabbi Hayyim Vital. The *'Iyyun* works also piqued the interest of post-Renaissance Christian Kabbalists such as Johann Reuchlin (1455–1522) and Athanasius Kircher (ca. 1602–80).[22]

Rabbi Yitshak "the Blind" of Provence is one of the first Kabbalists we know by name.[23] His commentary to *Sefer Yetsirah* is the earliest kabbalistic treatise attributed to a contemporary author.[24] Rabbi Yitshak was the son of Rabbi Avraham ben David (RaBaD) of Posquieres, the mighty Talmudist famous for his critical glosses to Maimonides's *Mishneh Torah*. We know little of his father's involvement in Kabbalah, though it is possible that RaBaD may have passed down some mystical traditions to Rabbi Yitshak.[25] His teachings are even more cryptic than *Sefer ha-Bahir* or the *'Iyyun* literature, due in part to the laconic, fragmentary manner in which his teachings have been preserved. Their difficulty is compounded by the fact the he seems to be drawing upon an assumed knowledge of symbols to which we have no immediate access. He is the first to associate the *sefirot* with the list of divine attributes in 1 Chronicles 29:11, a mapping adopted by most later Kabbalists. His mystical system is deeply contemplative, and his writings are rich in aural and linguistic metaphors as well as in visual imagery. Rabbi Yitshak emphasized *kavvanah* ("intention") in prayer, during which the mystic is to turn inward and ascend through the words of the liturgy to the realm of divine thought. The ultimate aspiration is to reach the *Ein Sof*, a term that was used first by Rabbi Yitshak to designate the unknowable, infinite Deity.

Rabbi Yitshak's direct influence upon the development of Jewish mysticism was profound. Many of his students were important members of the kabbalistic school in Gerona, which formed in the 1220s and 1230s. This Catalonian center in northeast Spain was home to a large and established community with close connections to the intellectual centers of Provence.[26] Members of this school included the famed Rabbi Moshe Nahmanides (RaMBaN, 1194–1270),[27] and Rabbi Asher ben David (mid-thirteenth century), the nephew and disciple of Yitshak the Blind. Rabbi Asher lived with his uncle for a number of years before making his home in Spain, thus forging another important link between Provence and Gerona.[28] Indeed, many others of this group of mystics had been students of Yitshak the Blind as well. The Gerona mystics knew of the *Bahir* and may have been aware of *'Iyyun* literature, but these works were less influential than the teachings of Rabbi Yitshak.

It was in Gerona that Kabbalah first moved into the public sphere. Unlike the anonymous circles that produced the *Bahir* and the *'Iyyun* literature, the Gerona mystics wrote without resorting to pseudepigraphy. And unlike the terse references to Kabbalah in RaMBaN's commentary on the Torah or the elliptical teachings of Yitshak the Blind, the latter's disciples authored mystical tracts that exposed kabbalistic ideas to a broader audience. This transition was met with significant resistance, both internal and external. Rabbi Yitshak the Blind, who believed the ideas should be kept secret, discharged a fiery letter of protest and deployed his nephew Rabbi Asher to help stem the tide.[29] His protests were unsuccessful, and Jewish mysticism began to shift away from esotericism, a process that began at the end of the twelfth century and was to continue in a dialectical fashion for the next eight hundred years.[30]

The mystics also faced opposition from some of the rabbinic elite, who accused them of heresy and idolatry. The Kabbalists took to the attack, and their works include explicit polemics against the Jewish rationalist tradition. The mystics portrayed themselves as bastions of tradition, defending orthodox faith and praxis against the insidious spiritualizing of the philosophers. Yet even though they were critical of Jewish philosophy, the mystics shared in its project of reinterpreting Jewish theology and absorbed some of its new concepts.[31]

Rabbi Ezra ben Shlomo and Rabbi 'Azriel were two of the most important Kabbalists from the Gerona school. Rabbi Ezra (d. circa 1245), the elder of the two, wrote a mystical commentary on Song of

Songs that was long misattributed to RaMBaN and a shorter interpretation of the legendary material in the Talmud. His commentary on Song of Songs brought this text into the world of mystical interpretation, where it provided extraordinary fertile ground for later Kabbalists.[32] Rabbi 'Azriel (dates uncertain) was a younger contemporary of Rabbi Ezra. He too wrote a commentary to the talmudic legends, but more influential was his *Explanation of the Ten Sefirot* (*Sha'ar ha-Sho'el*). This short treatise was written in the form of question and answer, a literary structure never used by a Kabbalist before him. Rabbi 'Azriel's didactic choice reflects his goal of introducing kabbalistic ideas to a public as yet unversed in their mysteries. He may have been motivated to defend Kabbalah against its increasingly vociferous critics, or perhaps he wished to inspire others and recruit them to his cause.[33] Rabbi 'Azriel describes the ten *sefirot* in great detail, justifying the orthodoxy of this belief by responding to the inquiries of his foil. Rabbi 'Azriel's writings are the first fully developed description of God as divine Naught (*ayin*), an idea central to later Kabbalah.[34]

Rabbi Ya'akov ben Sheshet (dates unknown) was one of the most innovative kabbalistic scholars of Gerona. He was a fierce antirationalist and decried what he saw as the dangerous heresies of philosophy. His important work *Meshiv Devarim Nekhohim* (*Response to Correct Answers*) offers sustained criticism of Maimonidean rationalism. Yet Rabbi Ya'akov's writings also articulate a value not found in the writings of his contemporaries: freedom and creativity in mystical interpretation of the Bible. Ya'akov ben Sheshet did not simply rely on the traditions passed down to him, and he offered new symbolic interpretations of Scripture and religious rituals. This type of original exegesis had an important place in later Jewish mysticism.[35]

The thirteenth century witnessed another mystical renaissance to the west in the region of Castile.[36] Unlike the adepts of Provence and Gerona, who were talmudic scholars as well as Kabbalists, the Castilian mystics seem to have devoted themselves solely to the study of Kabbalah. Their theology was influenced by German Pietism and earlier streams of Provençal Kabbalah, including the *'Iyyun* literature. But the Castilian Kabbalists developed a rich and largely innovative symbolism of their own. Two of the foremost members of this circle were the brothers Rabbi Ya'akov and Rabbi Yitshak ha-Kohen. Their works had a particularly strong impact upon the next generation of great Castilian mystics, including Rabbi Avraham Abulafia, Rabbi Yosef Gikatilla,[37] and the author(s) of the *Zohar*.[38]

Further Reading

Dauber, Jonathan. *Knowledge of God and the Development of Early Kabbalah*. Leiden and Boston: Brill, 2012.

Scholem, Gershom. *Origins of the Kabbalah*. Edited by R. J. Zwi Werblowsky. Translated by Allan Arkush. Philadelphia: Jewish Publication Society, 1987.

Verman, Mark. *The Books of Contemplation: Medieval Jewish Mystical Sources*. Albany: State University of New York Press, 1992.

Sefer ha-Bahir

Editor's introduction: The following is one of the *Bahir*'s more thematically cohesive passages.[39] The fifteen short sections explain the mystical significance of the priestly blessing (Num 6:24–26) and the biblical verses at the heart of the liturgical unit known as the *kedushah*. Using an abundance of parables, the *Bahir* interprets the words of Scripture as symbols that shed light on the various divine powers (*sefirot* or *middot*), God's relationship with the created world, the nature of the Torah, and the spiritual dimensions of prayer.

124. And what is the reason for the raising of the hands and blessing them with a benediction?[40] This is because there are ten fingers on the hands, a hint to the ten *sefirot*[41] by which the sky and the earth were sealed.[42] And those ten correspond to the Ten Commandments, and within these ten all 613 *mitsvot* are included.[43] If you count the number of letters of the Ten Commandments you will find that there are 613 letters, comprising all 22 letters of the alphabet, except for the letter *tet*, which is absent. What is the reason for that? To teach you that the *tet* represents the *beTen* (stomach, abdomen), and not the *sefirot*.[44]

125. And why are they called *sefirot*? Because it is written: "The heavens declare (*mesaprim*) the Glory (*kavod*) of God" (Ps 19:2).[45]

126. And what are they [i.e., the *sefirot*]? They are three,[46] and they include three armies and three realms.[47] The first realm is light, and the living light of water. The second realm is the holy beasts and the *ofanim* and the wheels of the chariot.[48] And all the hosts of God bless and praise and glorify and magnify and sanctify the King who is extolled in sanctity and praised in the innermost great sanctity, a terrible and terrifying King, and they crown him with "three holy's."[49]

127. And why are there "three holy's" and not four? This is because celestial sanctity is always expressed in threes, as it is written: "Y-H-V-H is King, Y-H-V-H was King, Y-H-V-H will be King forever and ever."[50] And it is written: "Y-H-V-H will bless you...He will give you light...He will raise His face" (Num 6:24–26).[51] And it is written: "Y-H-V-H, Y-H-V-H" (Ex 34:6) and the rest of the *middot*. And the third is which? It is "God is a merciful God"—the thirteen *middot*.[52]

128. And what are *holy, holy, holy* and then "Y-H-V-H of hosts whose Glory fills the earth" (Is 6:3)?[53] They are *holy*—the Supreme Crown;[54] *holy*—the root of the tree;[55] *holy*—united and special in all of them:[56] *Y-H-V-H of hosts, whose glory fills the earth.*

129. And what is that *holy* which is united and special?[57] This can be explained by a parable: A king had sons, and to his sons—grandsons. When the grandsons fulfill his wishes he enters among them and makes everything exist and provides them with food and pours goodness upon them, so that both the fathers and the sons will be satisfied. But when the grandsons do not fulfill his wishes he provides for no more than the needs of the fathers.[58]

130. And what is *the whole earth is full of his glory*? It is all that land which was created in the first day, which is above, corresponding to the Land of Israel, full of the divine Glory. And what is it? Wisdom, as it is written: "Honor (*kavod*, "Glory") of the wise will inherit" (Prov 3:35),[59] and it is said: "Blessed be the Glory of Y-H-V-H from Its place" (Ezek 3:12).[60]

131. And what is this divine Glory? This can be explained by a parable: A king had a great lady in his room.[61] She was loved by all his knights, and she had sons.[62] They all came every day to see the face of the king, and they blessed him. They asked him: "Our mother, where is she?" He said to them: "You cannot see her now." They said: "Blessed is she wherever she is."[63]

132. What is the meaning of that which is written *from its place*?[64]

Because no one knows Its place. This is like a king's daughter who came from afar, and nobody knew where she came from. When they saw that she was a fine lady, beautiful and just in all that she did,[65] they said: "She undoubtedly was taken from the side of the light, for her deeds give light to the world."[66] They then asked her: "Where are you from?" She answered: "From my place." They said: "If so, the people of your place must be great! Blessed are you and blessed is your place!"

133. But is not this divine Glory one of God's hosts? Why is it the subject of a special blessing?[67] This can be explained by a parable: A man had a beautiful garden, and outside the garden but very near to it there was a beautiful piece of land, a field. He planted a garden there. When he watered his garden, the water flowed over the whole garden but did not reach that piece of land, which is not united, even though it is all one.[68] Therefore he opened a place for it, and watered it separately.[69]

134. Rabbi Rehumai said: "*Glory* and *Heart* are one,[70] but the Glory is called by a name corresponding to a celestial action, while heart is called by a name corresponding to a lower one. But they are one and the same—the Glory of God is the same as the heart of heaven."[71]

135. Rabbi Yohanan said: "What is the meaning of that which is written: 'When Moses lifted his hand Israel was victorious, and when he dropped it Amalek became more powerful' (Ex 17:11)?[72] This is to teach that the world exists because of the lifting of the hands in prayer, in the priest's benediction. Why? Because of that power which was given to our patriarch Jacob, whose name is Israel."[73]

Abraham, Isaac, and Jacob were given powers, one to each one of them, and it was given to each of them according to the character of his ways. Abraham performed acts of Lovingkindness to the whole world, for he used to invite all the people of the world and all the passers-by on the roads, provide them with food and run to welcome them, as is written: "And he ran toward them" (Gen 18:2), and it is written: "and he bowed down to the earth" (Gen 18:2). This was a perfect act of Lovingkindness, and God bestowed upon him according to his measure and gave him the measure of Lovingkindness, as it is written: "You shall give Truth to Jacob and Lovingkindness to Abraham which you swore to our forefathers in ancient days" (Micah 7:20).

What is the meaning of *in ancient days*? This is to teach that if Abraham had not performed acts of Lovingkindness and not merited the measure (*middah*)[74] of Lovingkindness, Jacob would not have merited the measure of Truth,[75] for it is because Abraham was worthy of the measure of Lovingkindness that Isaac merited the measure of Fear, as it is written: "And Jacob swore in the fear of his father Isaac" (Gen 31:53).[76] Is there a man who will swear in this way in the faith of his father's fear? But at that point Jacob did not yet receive his own power, so he swore by the power which was given to his father, as it is said: *and he swore in the fear of his father Isaac*.

And what is [Isaac's fear]? This is the *tohu*[77] from which the evil which confuses (*ha-matheh*) people proceeds. And what is it? It is that about which is written: "And fire fell and burnt the sacrifice and the wood and the stones and the earth and the water which were in the canal it touched" (1 Kings 18:38), and it is written: "For your God is a consuming fire, a jealous God" (Deut 4:24).

136. And what is Lovingkindness? It is the Torah, as it is written: "All who are thirsty go to the water" (Is 55:1).[78] And to him who does not have money, it is money, as it is written: "Go and take and eat, go and take it without money and without price, wine and milk" (ibid.). He will feed you and teach you Torah for you already have become worthy of it because of the merit of Abraham who used to do charitable deeds, and used to feed without pay and give drinks of *wine* and *milk* free of charge.

137. What are wine and milk? And what is the connection between them? This is to teach us that the wine is Fear, and the milk is Love. Why did he mention wine first? Because it is nearer to us.[79] Do you really think they are wine and milk? But it is the image of wine and milk. And because of the worthiness of Abraham who won the measure of Lovingkindness, Isaac won the measure of Fear. And because Isaac was worthy of the measure of Fear, Jacob won the measure of Truth, which is the measure of Peace.[80]

And God gave Jacob a measure which is his own measure, as it is written, "And Jacob was innocent and dwelt in tents" (Gen 25:27). "Innocent" means Peace, as it is written: "You should be innocent with your God" (Deut 18:13). This verse is translated as: "You should be in Peace." "Innocent" means the Torah, as it is written: "Torah of Truth was in his mouth" (Mal 2:6). And what is written after that? "In peace and justice he went with me," and "justice" is really peace, as it is written: "Innocence and justice" (Ps 28:21). This is why: "When Moses raised his hand Israel was victorious." It teaches us that the measure called Israel includes in it the *Torah of Truth*.

138. And what is the *Torah of Truth*? This is that power which represents the truth of the worlds, and He operates by Thought.[81] And He gives existence to Ten Utterances by which the world exists, and He is one of them.[82] And He created in man ten fingers on the hands to correspond to the Ten Utterances, and when Moses raised his hands with the minimum of his heart's intention to that measure which is called Israel in which there is the true Torah, and points out to Him his ten fingers to signify that he makes the ten exist, and if He will not assist the people of Israel the Ten Utterances will not exist every day—this is why Israel was victorious. And when Moses let his hand down Amalek would win. Did Moses cause Amalek to win, as it is written "When he let his hands down Amelek would be victorious" (Ex 13:11)? But it is forbidden for a person to stay for three hours with his hands turned toward heaven.

The *'Iyyun* Circle

Editor's introduction: The widely circulated *Sefer ha-'Iyyun* (*Book of Speculation*, ca. 1230) is the earliest work of the *'Iyyun* literature. It is framed as a commentary to an unknown *Heikhalot* text. God is portrayed as an unknowable, singular deity that preexisted the world. While his unity cannot be comprehended, the mystic may indeed contemplate its expression in the thirteen emanated divine powers (they are ten in some early versions). They begin with Primordial Wisdom (*hokhmah kedumah*), from which all others subsequently emerge. Other versions of the *Book of Speculation* were influenced by later conceptions of the *sefirot*, but the present text preserves an older account of the emanations. The selection below is devoted to this exercise of meditating on the divine unity of God hidden within the matrix of the powers.

Ma'ayan ha-Hokhmah (*Fountain of Wisdom*) was written after *Sefer ha-'Iyyun* and together they are the foundational texts of the *'Iyyun* school. This work claims to be a record of mystical secrets delivered to Moses by an angel. It is an extremely difficult text, further complicated by scribal errors in nearly all manuscripts and printings. Its content may be roughly divided into two sections, the first of which examines the relationship between the Hebrew language and divine names. The second, translated in part below, explores the creation of the cosmos and the emergence of primordial matter from its divine source. Since God is manifest through the works of Creation, contemplating the world's formation becomes a method for studying the Divine.[83] *Explanation of the Four-Lettered Name* (*Perush Shem ben Arba Otiyyot*) is a popular *'Iyyun* work describing the mystical and creative power of words. Language ultimately originates in the names of God, specifically the four and forty-two letter names. The centrality of language is a theme that stretches back to the pre-kabbalistic *Sefer Yetsirah* and forward through the history of Jewish mysticism in every age, including our own.

The *Book of Speculation*

This is the *Book of Speculation* of the great Rabbi Hamai,[84] foremost expositor of the Innermost. In it he revealed the essence of the entire reality of the revealed Glory, whose source of existence and quintessence no living being can accurately fathom, for He is in a state of balanced unity. In His perfection the upper and lower worlds unite one to another, and He is the foundation of all, both hidden and revealed. From Him pours forth all that is emanated from the wondrousness of the Unity. Rabbi Hamai has explained all these matters by way of the Chariot and interpreted the prophecy of Ezekiel, peace be upon him.[85] Here begins the book in the proper order.

Blessed and exalted is God, glorious in power. He is one, united in all His powers as the flame is united in its colors. The powers which emanate from His unicity are like the light of the eye which springs forth from the pupil.[86] [These powers] are emanated one from the other, as a fragrance from a fragrance or a candle from a candle. One emanates from the other, and from that another. The power of each resides in that which is emanated from it, yet the emanator lacks for nothing. Thus, before creating any entity, the Holy One, blessed be He, was one and eternal, beyond examination and boundary, without compound or distinction, without change or movement, concealed through existence itself.

When the thought arose in His mind to bring objects into being, His glory became visible. Then were His Glory and Splendor revealed together.

Knowledge of Him is made explicit through five means: restoration (*tikkun*), utterance (*ma'amar*), combination (*tseruf*), grouping (*mikhlal*), and calculation (*heshbon*).[87] Knowledge of these five matters is unique in the branches of the root of change and it increases in the course of the thirteen sorts of transformation (*temurah*). What is restoration? [One] removes a thing from utterance, and utterance from the thing; grouping from calculation, and calculation from grouping; so that [one] causes all things to resemble a flaming fount. The flame is unfathomably and immeasurably within the fount. Infinite light lies hidden within the mysterious darkness. To truly know oneness is to know this blackness....

In this order are all the forms of the divine Name in the *Book of Creation*[88] to be explained. These are revealed counsels of the highest hidden mystery called "Artisan" (*oman*),[89] which means the source of faith (*emunah*), for faith emerges by His power. He, may He be blessed, is united in His powers, yet He remains completely beyond and transcendent to them, elevated endlessly. These are the thirteen powers with which He is united, and each has its own name, each one higher than the former. The first is called "primeval wisdom"; the second, "wonderful light"; the third, "electrum"; the fourth, "mist"; the fifth, "throne of light"; the sixth, "the wheel of greatness," also called *hazhazit*—meaning the place of vision for visionaries (*hezyon ha-hozim*). The seventh is called "cherub"; the eighth, "the wheels of the Chariot"; the ninth, "the surrounding ether"; the tenth, "the curtain"; the eleventh, "the Throne of Glory"; the twelfth, the dwelling of the souls called "the chambers of splendor"; and the thirteenth, the secret of the supernal structure, called "the outer palace of holiness." These thirteen powers are revealed as one from the highest hidden mystery called "Artisan"—the source of faith—from which faith emerges.... When He began to bring His deeds into existence He created the two products of mystery and faith, while maintaining unicity and essence. For no one may grasp knowledge of the world's Creator.[90]

The *Fountain of Wisdom*

...And now behold and direct your heart to the first attribute, long and true and straight like a scepter. Regarding these matters, each of the attributes is called a flame. Now these flames are scepters, and the scepters are eyes, and each of the eyes themselves divide into five matters. Now these matters divide into sources, the sources into a structure, and the structure congeals. This congealment becomes a glowing ember, and it is to the ember that the five matters cling. For this reason the flame is linked to the ember.[91] From the flame the ether springs forth, and the ether is the principle which informs structure, action, restoration, mechanics, calculation, utterance, and grouping: These together are the essentials of all being.

Now we must think and understand, contemplate and examine in the hidden depths of our heart and thoughts, in our logic and our vision, in our spiritual vicissitudes and in the whisper of our tongues and the utterances of our mouths until we achieve clarity and certainty and comprehension in all these subjects. We will begin with the first matter, since it is foremost among all firsts, the restoring of all restorations. It will lead us along the true path.

Know that the Holy One, blessed be He, is the First Existent. He is called "Existent" for no other reason than that He brought Himself into existence. And since He brought Himself into existence, it is incumbent for us to understand and contemplate an examination of His reality, and how He began creation, and in what way did He step and stand. In which path did [He emanate]? Was it one path or many paths? Did they divide into parts or extended entities? Or should one say "road" or "path" or "channel"? For "channels" are narrow and short while "paths" are excessive and "roads" are wide. Also, channels are like children while paths are akin to mothers, and roads are engraved with the archetypes of male and female.

Regarding this issue, wonders abound and are clarified. The wonders become more wonderful, and from them [come] the flames, and from the flames the thread extends outwards, and the threads thicken, and in this thickened state they grow stronger until they become scepters. This, then, is the point: Everything is again and again dissolved and then returns to the ether as it once was, and the ether is the essential element....

Know and comprehend that before all the above-mentioned entities there was nothing but this ether. And this ether darkened because of two things, each having different sources. The first issued an infinite, inexhaustible and immeasurable light. The gushing forth was sudden, not unlike the sparks which fly and burst forth when the craftsman forges with a hammer.[92]

After [the first light] another fountain was drawn out from which flows darkness. Now this darkness is itself a combination of three hues. The first is a darkness like that of dawn, a kind of green. The second was combined from green and light blue, and the third is a white darkness, composed of green, light blue, and red. And this is the primeval darkness which springs out of the ether. Do not try to perceive or examine it or investigate it scientifically for even Moses our teacher, peace be upon him, was unable to ask about it. If he was unable to inquire, then how much more so would be our investigation!

Everything that Moses stated (Ex 33:12–23) was said so that his knowledge of the image of the Holy One, blessed by He, would be unchanged in his heart, and that the knowledge regarding Him would be true and unified. That is to say, at the moment when the matter became clear to [Moses], knowing the true knowledge, he intended in his mind—even though there was no need—to examine and gaze and inquire into the higher levels. When he apprehended His secret thoroughly and the image of his understanding of the Holy One, Blessed be he, remained unchanging within his heart, he rejoiced and asked his intended question.

At this point [Moses] requested "Show me now your ways" (Ex 33:13). The Holy One, blessed be He, responded to this request, saying, "You cannot see My face" (Ex 33:20). That is to say: This darkness, about which you have requested knowledge, is all from Me alone and is My own source, and you cannot comprehend it with any studious clarity. Therefore God said, "You shall see My back, but My face shall not be seen" (Ex 33:23). This means that that which preceded the existence of the universe you cannot apprehend, so that you will not be unable to say that I [God] am like all other entities, having a particular origin or place. Therefore you cannot apprehend knowledge of this darkness which was parallel to My existence. But from that point on you may know all: everything from and below the darkness, even My essence, the power of My Name, and My Glory.

At that moment Moses began to observe the primeval light, the root of all. And he found it to be a darkness composed of two entities stemming from two sources, one flowing with light, the second with darkness. Now this flow extends and gushes forth by way of channels, and the flow again becomes weak like a stream, and the stream again becomes minute, turning into a thread. And in this exiguity it extends and is directed until it becomes small, tiny droplets. These droplets grow and become fragmented entities, and the fragments continue to grow until they burst forth in great strength, mingling and interacting one with another, expanding and enjoining until a sap pours forth from them. Now this sap flows and extends and is congealed; and through this coagulation they are polished, purified, and clarified such that the original fragments that we mentioned are utterly disintegrated. From them come forth a kind of foam which floats on the water, and it transforms everything into a juice, and from this juice comes forth a wind, that is, the Holy Spirit. Therefore it is written hintingly, "And the Spirit of God hovered upon the water" (Gen 1:2). This means that the Spirit grew stronger in holiness and transformed into many blades, each blade transforming into a branch, and each branch transforming into a root from which came forth a myriad of powers, entities, and objects....

Explanation of the Four-Lettered Name

We have found in the *Book of Reliance* composed by Rabbi Judah ben Beteirah that the prophet Jeremiah—peace be upon him—was studying the *Sefer Yetsirah* on his own. A heavenly voice came forth and declared: "Find yourself a companion!" He went to Sira his son and they together submerged themselves in the *Sefer Yetsirah* for three years, to uphold that which is written: "Then they that feared the Lord spoke one with another" (Mal 3:16).

At the end of three years, when they set about combining the alphabets by means of combination, grouping, and word formation, a man was created for them on whose forehead was written Y-H-V-H *Elohim emet.*[93] But there was a knife in the hand of this created being, and he erased the *alef* of *emet*, leaving only *met.*[94] Jeremiah rent his garments and said, "Why have you erased the *alef* from *emet*?"

He replied, "I shall tell you a parable. To what may this be compared? An architect built many houses, cities, and courts, and no one could copy his style and no one understood his knowledge nor possessed his skill. Then two men forced themselves upon him. He taught them the secret of his trade, and they knew every aspect of the craft. When they had learned his trade and his secret and his skills, they began to argue with him until they broke away from him and became independent architects, charging a lower price for the same services. When people noticed this, they ceased to honor the craftsman and instead came to the newcomers and honored them and gave the commissions when they required to have something built.

"So too has God made you in His image, shape, and form. But now that you have created a man like Him, people will say: 'There is no God in the world another than these two!'"

Then Jeremiah said, "What solution is there?"

He answered, "Write the alphabets with intense concentration backwards on the earth you have strewn. Only do not meditate with the intention of honor and restoration, but rather the complete opposite."

So they did, and the being turned to dust and ashes before them. Then Jeremiah, peace be upon him, said, "Truly, one should study these matters only to know the power and omnipotence of the Creator of the universe, but not to practice them, for it is written, 'You shall not learn to do' (Deut 18:9)...

The School of Rabbi Yitshak the Blind

Editor's introduction: *The Process of Emanation* rereads the opening of Genesis as a description of the origins of the *sefirot*. Creation begins with *keter*, followed by the emergence of Wisdom (*hokhmah*). The Torah itself proceeds from Wisdom, which God then uses to create the world. This process culminates in the final *sefirah 'atarah* ("Diadem," also referred to as "Kingdom," or *malkhut*). *The Mystical Torah—Kabbalistic Creation*[95] also reinterprets the ancient tradition that the world was created by means of the Torah.[96] God's Will (the *sefirah keter*) awakens divine Thought, which then sparks a chain of emanation in which divine names and powers are drawn forth from the primordial Torah.

The Process of Emanation

In the beginning (*be-reshit*): The letter *bet* is the most elevated Crown (*keter*) and therefore this *bet* is larger than all the other *bets*.[97] The word "beginning" (*reshit*) is in fact Wisdom (*hokhmah*). In truth, then, two *sefirot* are encompassed in one word.

From whence do we know that Wisdom is called "beginning"? It states: "The *beginning* of *wisdom* is fear of the Lord" (Ps 111:10). With both Crown and Wisdom He created *the heavens and the earth*—that is: Beauty (*tif'eret*) and Diadem (*'atarah*). He also created the [two] *ets*: and these are the supernal powers which are Lovingkindness (*hesed*) and Fear (*pahad*).[98] All of creation is summarized in this. Afterward, he explained the entire matter, beginning with the result of creation, Diadem, through which the entire Structure is made complete. And it states:

And the earth was unformed and void (*tohu va-bohu*): First is Diadem. Before it was emanated from the Cause of causes, it was *tohu*, something that is astounding (*mathe*), for it has nothing substantial within it, nor does it possess any form. But when it was emanated it then became a substance more ethereal than Spirit.

Void (*bohu*): This means "in it" (*bo*)—when it was emanated, something substantial was made in it. And our Rabbis, may their memories be blessed, explained that these [two] are called collectively "the foundation stone."[99]

And the darkness over the surface of the deep: This is the depth of above and the depth of below.[100] *And a wind from God sweeping over the water*: Wisdom envelops everything, as in "sweeping over her young" (Deut 32:11).

Over the water: Everything was called water, for Lovingkindness—the summit of five *sefirot*[101]—is water. More precisely, [Wisdom] is the power of water, for water pours forth from its overflow.

God (Elohim) said, "Let there be light." God—This is Repentance (*teshuvah*).[102] And thus He, may his memory be blessed, said: "To wrap oneself—to wrap oneself in a prayer shawl, and this means to wrap oneself in Wisdom."[103] And it states: *Let there be light*: This means Beauty, for the Torah came forth from Wisdom.[104] From Nothing (*me-ayin*) spread forth the thirty-two paths which stem from Wisdom. These [paths] are the source and the derivatives of the Torah and all other sciences. And He wraps Himself [with the Torah] and peers into it and builds worlds and destroys worlds. He saw that all things were hidden and He said, "Let all these things expand from potentiality to actuality, that they be actuated and uncovered," "they" being the now actualized Beauty and Diadem....

And God saw the light, that it was good (*tov*): This is derived from "when he tends (*be-hetivo*) the lamps" (Ex 30:7). The matter is ignited as if one lights a candle one from the other. Thereby He grants a power to the essences to expand and draw forth....

The Mystical Torah—Kabbalistic Creation

Legend:[105] It is written, "God by wisdom founded the earth" (Prov 3:19). Wisdom (*hokhmah*) is nothing other than Torah. It is called Torah due to the number of its commandments.[106] Also, its name was Amon before the world was created, as it is written, "I was by him, as an architect (*amon*)" (Prov 8:30). And if you were to say that the Torah was [written] on something or other: on a tree?—it had not yet been created; or parchment?—it had not yet been created; or silver or gold?—they had not yet been created. If this be the case, then on what was the Torah [inscribed]? The Sages, may their memory be blessed, said: The world was created in the right side of the Holy One, blessed be He, as it says, "But He is unchangeable, and who can turn Him?" (Job 23:13). What did He do? He took the Torah and drew from it a single name, and drew there from three droplets of water...and due to [His] abundant love for Israel, He gave them the Torah.

Up to this point is the text of the legend that I found, and what follows is its commentary written next to it.

In the right side of the Holy One, blessed be He, was engraved all the inscriptions which were destined to change from potentiality to actuality, due to the emanation of the all the crowns which are inscribed, pressed, and formed in the degree of Lovingkindness (*hesed*).[107] Its image is inward and esoteric, beyond all scrutiny. Thus it is called the beginning of the thought of the Torah, and it includes the Torah of Lovingkindness. In general, all the engravings which are inscribed on it are of two types. The image of the first engraving is the Written Torah and the other image is the Oral Torah. The image of the Written Torah is of the colors of a white-hot fire, while the image of the Oral Torah is the color of a kind of black fire. And all the engravings and even the very Torah which encompasses them all existed in potentia and were not visible, neither spiritually nor sensibly visible. But then the Will arrived which awakened Thought (*mahshavah*)[108] into actuality by means of primordial Wisdom and hidden Knowledge (*da'at*).

Prior to any action there existed [this] Torah—which is the right arm [of God]—encompassing all the impressed inscriptions hidden therein. This is what he meant to say: The Holy One, blessed be He, *took* the primordial *Torah*, which is derived from the quarry of repentance[109] and from the source of Wisdom. He emanated by spiritual activity this encompassing Torah to render permanent the foundations of the world from this very inscription, which is the beginning of the emanation of the Holy One, blessed be He. When [this Torah] was actualized, *he drew from it a single name*. He hewed from it one name whose essence and name are from one quarry and one essence and He called it by one spiritual name, [and that name is] Lovingkindness....

He brought forth a second name—this is a second grade which is the mammoth inferno called the attribute Strength (*gevurah*)....[110] He drew forth a third name called the image of the Written Torah, and it is the hue of a white fire. He brought forth from it three droplets of one light which divided and transformed itself into three powers of light: Urpani'el changed to Pani'uri'el changed to Re'upani'el.[111] From the first light the Throne of Glory was created. This throne itself is a throne to the upper Throne and in it is encompassed all the crowns which are below the upper Throne of Glory, established on the basis of Lovingkindness, Strength, Mercy (*rahamim*). From the second light the world to come was created, a world of Severity (*din*) and Mercy, these being the qualities of Kingdom (*malkhut*), where punishment and reward are found. From the third light this world was created.[112]...

The World to Come, which we have already stated is the world of Severity—either as punishment or as reward, is the crown of Kingdom, the Oral Torah. It is the hue of a black fire on white fire, which is the Written Torah. Now the forms of the letters are not vowelized nor are they shaped except through the power of black, which is like ink. So too the Written Torah is unformed in a physical image, except through the power of the Oral Torah. That is to say, one cannot be explained fully without the other.[113] So too, the attribute of Mercy is not comprehended nor seen except by means of the attribute of Severity. Now the hues of the mark of black (which are the hues of the attribute of Severity) rise and expand and spread over the hues of white (which are the colors of the attribute of Mercy) that rise and cover the blackness. This is similar to the image of the light of a glowing ember, for the force in the colors of the flame rises and strengthens until the light of the ember is invisible due to the intensity of the flame which envelops it. When the colors of the flame increase and spread out one from another then the physical eye rules over the essence of the ember [by] physical, sensible sight.

So too [we find] that in the grade of the crown of Mercy the hues of the luminaries are absolutely hidden and secret. [These luminaries] surround [Mercy] with a great intensity so that [Mercy] is not perceived by any worldly creature. But with the advent of Will (*ratson*), the shades of blackness are weakened and dissipated and dispersed from the unreflecting mirror above the white hues which illuminate and sparkle and shine like the splendor of a white sapphire.[114] Then a few of the prophets, peace be upon them, were able to perceive this splendor by means of the crown of Kingdom, each according to their merit: a spiritual perception and vision appropriate to each prophet. The shades of blackness which spread forth and sparkle from it are similar to the image of the flame which sparkles from the light of the ember, like the intensity of the hues of the small luminary in the midst of the intensely strong light of the sun, and [the small luminary] shines because of [the sun's] strength. It darkens the face of one who peers into it and blinds anyone who persists and continues his gaze. And if he escapes the blindness by distancing himself from the rays of the sun he [still] cannot see the light of the ether until he calms down and rests nearly an hour or two. And due to the abundant intensity of its light and splendor, it is called the reflecting mirror. It illuminated the greatest of the prophets, peace be on him. For no other prophetic eye viewed it or united with it, save Moses our teacher, peace be upon him....[115]

And due to [His] abundant love for Israel, He gave them the Torah. And this is like, "For His love for us is great" (Ps 117:2).

Up to this point I have acquired and found the interpretation of this legend, transmitted in the name of the venerable Rabbi Yitshak, may his memory be blessed. And I do not know who he is.[116]

Rabbi Ezra ben Shlomo of Gerona

Commentary on the Song of Songs

The Song of Songs, which is Solomon's (Song 1:1).

The Song of Songs: The most pleasant of canticles, the choicest of songs; words of might recited by the Throne of Glory,[117] day to day expressing utterance, standing in prayer in good order arrayed, its speech lucid, in all things well ordered and sure.

Which is Solomon's: This is a name designated the Holy One, blessed be He. As it is written: "Gideon built there an altar to the Lord and called it 'the Lord of peace'" (Judg 6:24). This is the meaning of the statement of our sages of blessed memory: "The Song which the Holy One blessed be He recites daily."[118]

Oh, let him kiss me with the kisses of his mouth; for your love is more delightful than wine (Song 1:2).

Oh let him kiss me: These are the Glory's[119] words, full of longing, desiring to make its ascent, to adhere to the light of the supernal luminescence to which nothing else is like. It ascends in thought and idea and thus speaks in third person. The kiss symbolizes the joy attained by the soul in its adhesion to the source of life and the additional infusion of the holy spirit.[120] Thus the verse specifies "kisses." For each and every sefirotic power[121] receives consciousness and a superabundance from that sweet light and pure refulgence. When it speaks to the Glory, gateway to the entities [i.e., the *sefirot*], it speaks in third person.

For your love is better (tovim) than wine: This emanated light expands over me because it comes from You, that is to say, it is derived from "wine," from divine Wisdom called "I," the rung of supernal luminescence. All desire and will is to ascend and adhere to Wisdom.

For your love is better (tovim) than wine: The phrase "is better" (*tovim*) refers to the outpouring and amplification of that clear light, which divides and shines in all directions.[122] As it says: "when Aaron lights (*be-hetivo*) the lamps" (Ex 30:8)—which the Aramaic translation renders as "kindles." Such also is the meaning of "God saw that the light was good" (Gen 1:4).[123]

We will add wreaths of Gold to your points of silver (Song 1:11)

...*To your points*[124] *of silver:* Oral Torah is emanated from the written and it sustains her, just as the spirit upholds the body. Thus written Torah has been compared to points (*nekudot*), since the vowels (*nekudot*) function among the consonants like the spirit in the body, as our sages say.[125] Both Torahs, oral and written, were given through *shekhinah* as they state in the Midrash to Psalms, "the Lord gives a command; the women who bring the news are a great host" (Ps 68:12).[126] From here it is clear that the innermost voice was not differentiated and rendered audible until it reached the end of the chain of emanation, the tenth *sefirah*.

Sweetness drops from your lips, O bride; honey and milk are under your tongue; and the fragrance of your robes is like the fragrance of Lebanon (Song 4:11).

Honey and milk: The allusion is to the two modalities of Torah (written and oral) and the fact that *shekhinah* is situated between the two cherubim.

And the fragrance of your robes: The robe is not an entity distinct from Her. Rather, it is the overflow of Wisdom's brightness which surrounds her. Our sages state in *Bereshit Rabbah* (21:5) concerning the verse "I looked and saw a man dressed in linen" (Dan 10:5): "He was comparable to a snail whose shell is inseparable from his body." Since Wisdom's brightness, encompassing thirty-two paths, surrounds the Glory, as in "your faithful ones surround You" (Ps 89:8), it is called "the garment of God," as it says: "You are garbed in splendor and majesty" (Ps 104:1).

In order to fulfill the verse "You shall walk in His ways" (Deut 28:9), Israelites were commanded to wrap themselves in the *tallit*,[127] which possesses thirty-two fringes. Concerning the tallit it is written: "You shall gaze upon them and remember all of God's commandments" (Num 15:39). Now Wisdom encompasses and is crowned with six hundred and thirteen precious gems. For each of the thirty-two paths within is divisible into two portions: good and evil, the positive and negative commandments. This division finds allusion in the ten divine statements (revealed directly at Sinai) in the words "remember" and "keep" the Sabbath Day.[128] Thus there are sixty-four paths. And as each and every one contains the ten [*sefirot*], their sum is six hundred and forty. If one deletes the twenty-seven letters of the Torah, the final sum is six hundred and thirteen. Thus concerning the fringes, Scripture states: "You shall gaze upon them and remember all of God's commandments." Therefore our sages said in the tractate Shevu'ot (29a): "The precept of fringes equals all of the commandments."

It is incumbent upon us to engage in a detailed inquiry concerning all the commandments, to find an allusion pointing to them in the ten divine statements revealed at Sinai. This is comparable to the manner in which the sages of Israel sought an allusion in the Torah for every aspect of fundamental ethics and courtesy which was not included within the commandments (b. Ta'anit 9a.)....

We should interpret each and every commandment in accord with our path, determining from which *sefirah* it derives and finding allusion to all of the reasons for the commandments which are not explicitly stated in the Torah.... You should realize that all of the precepts depend upon two fundamental principles: the positive and negative commandments. The positive commandments are born of the quality of remembrance (*zakhor*); the negative commandments of the quality of observance (*shamor*). It is also well known that the remembrance and observance correspond to two of the attributes of the Holy One, blessed be He. Consequently, an individual who performs the command of his master and fulfills it, does so as a consequence of the quality of love. This constitutes the highest degree [of service] and the most excellent virtue, and corresponds to the category of positive commandments. An individual who desists from performing a deed out of fear of his master, does so as a consequence of the quality of awe. This stands on a lower rung than the quality of love, just as negative commandments occupy a gradation lower than the positive....

Since these two qualities, the inclination to the good and the inclination to evil, which correspond to the positive and negative commandments, are impressed upon human nature, the Torah was given with positive and negative commandments to direct an individual and habituate him towards positive qualities. The inclination towards evil would be drawn after the good and annihilated within it. Concerning this our sages said: "'You shall love the Lord your God with all your heart' (Deut 6:5)—with your two inclinations, towards good and evil" (b. Berakhot 54a). This is the purpose of the commandments, the acts and worship, prayers, and fasting. They serve to subjugate the evil inclination so that it might be rendered and subordinate to the impulse towards good. Thus the body, whose foundation is dust and nature evil and which descends below, will be drawn after the faculty of the soul, whose foundation is life, whose nature is wholly for the good and ascends upwards. Give careful heed and listen to my wondrous words, let them always be present and before your eyes, for they are pleasant and should be stored inside you....[129]

You should know that the Torah is entirely clear, spoken by the divine dynamis,[130] containing not a single letter or vowel point that is not needed. All of it is a divine structure, hewn out in the name[131] of the blessed Holy One. There is no difference between "Timna was the concubine of Eliphaz" (Gen 36:12) or "the chieftain of Magdiel, the chieftain of Eram" (Gen 36:43) and the Ten Commandments or "Hear O Israel"[132] (Deut 6:4). Whoever deletes a single letter is like one who deletes God's whole name and a whole world. Therefore it was necessary that the letters and words be counted, that *plene* and *lene*[133] spellings be recorded, forms written but not pronounced, as well as forms pronounced but not written, open and closed beginnings of sections [i.e., paragraph divisions], larger and smaller letters. Let this be implanted in our heart and inscribed within you. Take care to your soul and lend no ear to [those who] say that Ezra the Scribe added things of his own accord as he copied it....

Because the commandments are the very body of purity and holiness, and the one concerned with them becomes purified and holy, Scripture said, *The fragrance of your robes is like the fragrance of Lebanon*, for that fragrance is the life of both worlds.

A garden locked is my own, my bride, a fountain locked, a sealed up spring (Song 4:12).

A garden locked is my own, my bride: *Shekhinah* is compared to a garden, since a person plants and fences it, bringing in water to irrigate it and producing all manner of lovely herbage and plants. *Shekhinah*'s fence is the cherubim, the plants are the seventy nations, the trees are the angels. All these are supplied by that spring which proceeds from Wisdom's paradise, within which souls flower in joy. It flows forth without ceasing either day or night; on its account the world is sustained. As our sages said in tractate Yoma (38b): "On account of the righteous one is the world created and sustained, as it says: 'The Righteous one is the world's foundation'" (Prov 10:25)....[134]

"A river goes forth from Eden to water the garden" (Gen 2:10). The garden constitutes the beginning of the differentiated universe. As it says: "from there it divides and becomes four branches" (ibid.). The verse is in present tense, the process is eternal. Thus it says: "There is a river whose streams gladden God's city, the holy dwelling-place of the Most High" (Ps 46:5). And "You make springs gush forth in torrents; they make their way between the hills, giving drink to all the wild beasts" (Ps 104:10–11).

Concerning this spring, it states: "a garden spring, a well of fresh water, flowing streams from Lebanon" (Song 4:15). Our sages of blessed memory said: "'a garden spring': this is Jacob who is a spring for the garden. 'A well of fresh water': this is Isaac. 'Flowing streams': this is Abraham."[135] Everything is sated from that Lebanon which is divine Wisdom.[136]

Contemplate the wonders of this symbolism and you will know and understand what our sages wrote, the manner in which their words constitute the height of completeness and perfection. Such truly befits sages like these, whose every word was uttered through the holy spirit in allegorical allusion, so as to arouse the consciousness of the kabbalistic illuminati, rather than the fools, idiots and confused who treat their words as if they were fox fables! Thus we find in the tractate Sanhedrin (38b): "'As I looked upon, thrones were set down...' (Dan 7:9)—one for God and one for David: these are the words of R. Akiva. R. Yose the Galilean said to him: 'Akiva, how long are you going to profane the *shekhinah*!? Rather, one throne is for justice and one is for righteousness.' R. El'azar ben 'Azaryah said to Akiva: 'What are you doing occupying yourself with words of *uggadah*!? Desist from your discourse and occupy yourself with the laws of leprosy and tents.'[137] Rather one is a throne and one is a footstool: a throne upon which to sit, a footstool to rest the feet." Surely these sages had no essential argument with one another, but they differed on whether it was appropriate to reveal the secret meaning. This occurs in several places where the rabbis are in dispute.

A garden locked: A closed gate.

A fountain sealed: The light lacks nothing for it is preserved in its "grapes" from the seven days of creation.[138]

My beloved has gone down to his garden, to the beds of spices, to browse in the gardens, and to pick lilies (Song 6:2).

My beloved has gone down to his garden: An all-encompassing entity does not differentiate between such distinctions as "above" and "below." Descent is equivalent to ascent; ascent to descent. Because exile has caused it to be occulted amidst its sefirotic manifestations, Scripture refers to it as engaging in an act of "descent."[139] Whence has it [descended] to the garden?

To the beds of spices: That is to say, [from] transcendent Wisdom, the locus from which this aroma and emanative energy spread forth.

To browse in the gardens: To provide nurturance for itself and to pour forth its luminescence to the gardens and *shekhinah*.[140]

And to gather the lilies: This is Thought, the luminescence of Wisdom flowing forth to the six cosmic boundaries (*ketsavot*). All this takes place during the period of exile, a time bereft of festal offerings, sacrifices of thanksgiving and the meal offerings. The spiritual entities ascend and are drawn to that place from which they nurse. This is the meaning of: "on evil's account, the righteous one dies" (Is 57:1).[141] For this reason, one must strive to invoke and emanate an outflow of blessing to the Fathers,[142] so that the sons too be imbued with emanative energy. In this verse the process of emanation and outpouring is referred to as "gathering...."

Rabbi 'Azriel of Gerona

Explanation of the Ten *Sefirot*

If a questioner asks: Who can compel me to believe that the world has a Ruler?

Answer: Just as it is inconceivable that a ship be without a captain, so too is it impossible that the world be without a ruler. This Ruler is infinite (*ein sof*) in both His Glory and Word, as in the matter that is written: "I have seen an end to every purpose, but Your commandment is exceedingly immense" (Ps 119:96), and it is written: "For God shall bring every act into judgment—every *hidden* thing whether good or bad" (Eccl 12:14). That which is *hidden* is without end and limit; it is unfathomable and nothing exists outside it.

The philosophers admit to this fact that the Cause of all causes and the Origin of origins is infinite, unfathomable, and without limit. According to the way of the Ruler we see that the end of every act is hidden from the probing of an investigator, as in the matter that is written: "So that no man can find out the work which God has made from the beginning to the end" (Eccl. 3:11). And it is further recorded: "Should the wise man say that he knows, even he will not be able to find it" (ibid. 8:17)....

If a questioner asks: Who can compel me to believe in *Ein Sof*?

Answer: Know that everything visible and perceivable to human contemplation is limited, and that everything that is limited is finite, and that everything that is finite is insignificant. Conversely, that which is not limited is called *Ein Sof* and is absolutely undifferentiated in a complete and changeless unity. And if He is [truly] without limit, then nothing exists outside Him. And since He is both exalted and hidden, He is the essence of all that is concealed and revealed. But since He is hidden, He is both the root of faith and the root of rebelliousness. Regarding this it is written: "In his faith a righteous man shall live" (Hab 2:4). Furthermore, the philosophers are in agreement with these statements that our perception of Him cannot be except by way of negative attribution.[143] And that which radiates forth from *Ein Sof* are the ten *sefirot*. [And this is sufficient for the enlightened.]

If the questioner persists: By what necessity do you arrive at the assertion that the *sefirot* exist? I rather say that they do not exist and that there is only *Ein-Sof*!

Answer: *Ein Sof* is perfection without any imperfection. If you propose that He has unlimited power and does not have finite power, then you ascribe imperfection to His perfection. And if you claim that the first limited being that is brought into existence from Him is this world—lacking in perfection—then you ascribe imperfection to the force which stems from Him.

Since we should never ascribe imperfection to His perfection, we are compelled to say that He has a finite power which is unlimited. The limitation first existentiated from Him is the *sefirot*, for they are both a perfect power and an imperfect power. When they partake of the abundant flow stemming from His perfection they are perfected power, and when the abundant flow is withdrawn they possess imperfect power. Thus, they are able to function in both perfection and imperfection, and perfection and imperfection differentiate one thing from another.

Now if you were to claim that He alone willed the creation of the world without [recourse to] the *sefirot*, the response to this [assertion] is that the intention indicates an imperfection in the intender. Alternatively, if you claim He did not intend His creation—if such were the case, then creation was a random accident. All things which are the outcome of a random accident have no order. Yet we witness that creation is ordered, with the sun during the day and the moon and stars at night. They exist by an order and by order they are generated and pass away. This order by which they exist and pass away is called the *sefirot*, for they are the force behind every existent being in the realm of plurality. Since the existentiation of created beings is brought about by means of the *sefirot*, each one differs one from the other; some are elevated, some are lowly, while others are intermediate. This is the case despite the fact that they are all derived from one principle. Every being is from *Ein Sof*, and nothing exists outside of Him.

4. If the questioner persists and asks: Agreed, you have demonstrated the necessity of *sefirot*, but by what [argument] do you establish that they are ten and yet one power?

Answer: I have already informed you that the *sefirot* are the beginning and commencement of all that is subject to limitation. Everything subject to limitation is bounded by substance and place, for there is no substance without place and there is no place except by means of substance. There is at least a third force in substance, and this third force is manifest in length, width, and depth. Thus there are nine. Since substance cannot exist without place and since there is no space except by means of substance, the number is not complete regarding substance and place with anything less than ten. Thus it states: "ten and not nine."[144] And since we cannot complete the number without taking into account substance—itself bounded by substance and place—it states: "ten and not eleven."[145] Just as the three produce nine; the fourth—which is place—when added to the three, produces sixteen. But it is sufficient for us to use ten in order to hint to the fact that place is derived from substance, and substance is but one power.

5. If the inquirer continues to ask: How can you say that the *sefirot* are emanated? I say they were created like all the other created beings!

Answer: I have already informed you that *Ein Sof* is perfect without any imperfection, and that the agent which initially is brought forth from Him must also be perfect. Thus, the dynamic of emanation is fittingly the beginning of all creation, for the potency of emanation is the essence of the creation of all things. Had there been no emanative potency extracted form *Ein Sof*—lacking in nothing—how would we recognize the abundant perfection stemming from *Ein Sof*? How would the dynamic of the *sefirot* properly receive and subsequently circulate [the abundant flow] to all the needy beings without being diminished? For, when one draws from something in creation it is decreased and diminished. Since the *se*firot are the first act existentiated from *Ein Sof*, it is appropriate that He be their dynamic, perfect without imperfection. Yet they are the ones who flow upon the impoverished, receiving from *Ein Sof*.

6. About this the inquirer persists: How can we possibly say that He is One and the multiplicity of ten unites within Him? By this we may preserve the truth in our hearts but certainly not in our statements.

Answer: I have already informed you that the One is the foundation of the many and that in the many no power is innovated—only in Him. He is more than them and each of them is superior to its antecedent, and the potency of one is in the other. Nevertheless, the first is the dynamic of all the others. Though this first is the dynamic of the other, it is not so specifically but only generally. The metaphor for this is the fire, the flame, the sparks, and the aura. They are all of one essence even though they are different one from the other and divisible into separate components.

7. If the inquirer persists after you have established that there are *sefirot* and that they are ten and they were emanated and not created and their multiplicity is derived from unity and asks: Now answer me, why should I [not] ascribe to them measure, limit, and corporeality?

Answer: I have already informed you that *Ein Sof* is perfection without imperfection, and that He has a finite power which is unlimited and that the limitation emanating from Him which delimits all existent beings is the *sefirot*, having the power to act in perfection and imperfection. Had He not existentiated for them limits, we would be unable to recognize that He has the power to existentiate limitation. As a testimony to the fact that nothing exists outside of Him, He brought into existence limitation, so that the confined beings could recognize their own boundaries. And though there are no limits above, the musings stemming from *Ein Sof* suggest that He is above and beyond extension in boundaries.

All that is limited, whether apprehended by the pondering of the heart or hinted at in thought extending below, can be found in speech and vision. Further, anything subject to limitation has magnitude and corporeality, because anything existent that is grasped by contemplation of the heart is called "body," not only spiritual things but even the *sefirot*. For they are [part of] the rule of all limited entities: They are the root of limitation. This limitation which is unlimited is emanated, and thus it states: "Their measure is without end."[146] Finally, the philosophers stated that man's intellect is finite, and that from the way of the Ruler we see that everything has limitations, magnitude, and measure.

8. If the inquirer continues: Now you must answer me—these *sefirot*, when did they come into existence? If you now answer me that they were almost contemporaneous with the creation of the world, then it may be countered: Why did He intend their emanation at that precise moment and not some earlier point—would this not be a change of mind in Perfection? And if you answer that they are His eternality, then they would subsist in His answer that they are His eternality, then they would subsist in His undifferentiatedness; and if such were the case, what would be the difference between God and the *sefirot*?

Answer: Some of the *sefirot* existed in potentia within *Ein Sof* before they became actualized, like the first *sefirah* which is equal to all the others. There were some that were intelligible that were then emanated, like the second *sefirah* from which the preexistent Torah came forth. There were some that were perceived and some that were innate, such as those *sefirot* which were needed for this world and which were emanated almost contemporaneously with the creation of the world.

And since the existentiation of the first two *sefirot* the hidden and intelligible powers [of the two] were totally intermingled, their reality nourished the other [*sefirot*]. As the Sages, may their memories be blessed, said, "Could not [the world] have been created with one statement?"[147]

As to your other question, "That they would subsist in His undifferentiatedness"—

Answer: Even though we should avoid coining metaphors regarding *Ein Sof*, in order to help you understand let us compare the matter to a candle. The candle lights a myriad of other candles. Each lit candle shines more, yet they are all equal in comparison to the first candle and they all derive from one principle. But one must not liken the latter to the former. Their phylogenesis should not be compared to His ontogenesis, for He is greater than them and their energy is brought forth from Him, because of His supra-preeminence. Furthermore, no change takes place in Him. Rather the dynamic of emanation becomes revealed through the division of their existence. Thus, one cannot say that there was a change of mind in Him, even though nothing exists outside of Him.

9. If the questioner continues: What is the nature of [the *sefirot*]?

Answer: The nature the *sefirot* is the synthesis of every thing and its opposite. For, if they did not possess the power of synthesis, there would be no energy in anything. For that which is light is not-darkness and that which is darkness is not-light.

Therefore we should liken their nature to the will of the soul, for it is the synthesis of all the desires and thought stemming from it. Even though they be multifarious, their source is one, either in thesis or antithesis. This is the case with every function of the soul: intellect, esthetics, love, and mercy—even though they are all [created] *ex nihilo*, their existence is not absolute.

But, by embellishing substance with imagination, we can liken the first power to the concealed light. The second power [can be likened] to the light which contains every color. This light is like *tekhelet*,[148] the essence (*takhlit*) of all colors in which there is no known hue. The third power can be compared to green light. The fourth power can be likened to white light. The fifth power can be likened to red light. The sixth power is composed of whiteness and scarlet. The seventh power is the power of scarlet tending toward whiteness. The eighth power is the power of whiteness tending toward scarlet. The ninth power is composed of whiteness and scarlet and scarlet tending toward whiteness and whiteness tending toward scarlet. The tenth power is composed of every color.

10. If the inquirer persists and asks: What are their names, their order, and their rank?

Answer: The name of the first power is Elevated Height (*rom ma'alah*), for it is elevated above the probing of an investigator. The second is called Wisdom (*hokhmah*), for it is the beginning of conceptualization. The third is called Understanding (*binah*). Up to this point is the world of intelligence (*'olam ha-sekhel*).

The fourth is called Lovingkindness (*hesed*). The fifth is called Fear (*pahad*). The sixth is called Beauty (*tif'eret*). Up to this point, the world of the soul (*'olam ha-nefesh*). The seventh is called Victory (*netzah*). The eighth is called Majesty (*hod*). The ninth is called Righteous One, Foundation of the World (*tsaddik yesod 'olam*). The tenth is called Justice (*tsedek*). Up to this point is the world of the body (*'olam ha-guf*).

Following is the order of their activity. The first is the divine power. The second is for angelic power. The third is for prophetic power. The fourth extends lovingkindness to the heights. The fifth passes judgment with the fear of His strength. The sixth has compassion in fear upon the lower worlds. The seventh nurtures and strengthens the vegetative soul. The eighth weakens and infirms it. The ninth draws together all their powers, sometimes for one purpose, sometimes for another. The tenth is the lower attribute of severity. It is composed of the power of all the others in order to judge the lower worlds.

The energy of the human soul is drawn from them and their powers in the following way: Elevated Height exists as the power of that soul which is called "only one" (*yehidah*). Wisdom exists in the soul as the animative soul; Understanding exists in the power of spirit; Fear in the power called "animus" (*neshamah*); Beauty in the power of blood; Victory in the power of bone; Majesty in the flower of flesh; Foundation of the World in the power of the sinew; and Justice in the power of the skin.

And their placement above is as follows: Elevated height encompasses and encircles Wisdom and Understanding, which in turn surround all that is beneath them. Lovingkindness is drawn to Eternity, which is on the right side. Fear is drawn to Majesty, which are in the middle, and Justice is opposite them.

11. Should the questioner persist: You have now informed me as to their names, rank, and order. You have further informed me as to the position of Justice, which receives from all their power. Now tell me whether there is bestowing and receiving in each.

Answer: Know that no emanation is radiated forth except to proclaim the unity within *Ein Sof*. If the receptor did not unite with the bestower into one power, then it would not be possible to recognize that the two are really one. In their unity one knows that power of union. Upon seeing the uniting force made manifest, how much more should one not ruminate upon it in secret. Thus, everything is both receptor and bestower....[149]

Rabbi Ya'akov ben Sheshet

The Book of Faith and Reliance
(*Sefer ha-Emunah va'ha-Bitahon*)

CHAPTER FIVE: THE MYSTICAL PRAYER

...It is required that the benediction for redemption be joined to the standing prayer (b. Berakhot 9b), not because redemption is the outcome of prayer—prayer, after all, is in *Ein Sof* and redemption is the end (*sof*) of all that is—but rather because its end is inextricably contained within its beginning.[150]

[The Rabbis furthermore] instituted the recitation of "may the words of my mouth and meditation of my heart be according to Your will (*le-ratson*) before You, O God, my Rock and Redeemer" (Ps 19:15) after the standing prayer. The "to" (*le* of *le-ratson*) fulfills a variety of uses—you may choose the best one. I am of the opinion that the reason for the inclusion of "May the words…" is in order to unite everything into *Ein Sof*. Then one draws the divine emanation even while leaving [the standing prayer] so that one does not appear to be "cutting off the shoots."[151]

Furthermore, know that the Will is the cause of all things, and it is hidden and secreted, only comprehended by means of a meditation. Expanding forth from it is an entity which is perceptible. This is wisdom, which clarifies and refines Will. It is through Wisdom that Will is perceived, and not through itself….

The sage R. Ezra [ben Shlomo], may his memory be blessed, wrote: It does not say one prays in the south [will become wise] (b. Bava Batra 25b), but rather that one turns southward. This means he directs his heart to the southern attribute, the bright light. Because of this he who desires wealth should turn north to the northern attribute from which comes wealth. Therefore it states: "Why are [the prayers of Israel] not answered? Because they do not know how to pray with the Holy Name."[152] This means that it applies to that very entity and that very thought, and it derives from the unity of all. That is his statement.

But this doesn't appear to me to be its meaning whatsoever. For when [the Sages] said that [Israel] does not know how to pray with the Holy Name, they did not say it except for the fact that Israel, accompanied by the divine Presence, is in exile. They do not know how to awaken love, for the stirring fountains have been closed to Israel, as in [God's] promise not to incite the end of days when it says "I charge you, O daughters of Jerusalem, by the gazelles and by the hinds of the fields that you stir not up, nor awaken My love till it please" (Song 2:7).[153] But with regard to all other matters there can be no doubt that they are answered. For prayer has been efficacious for our patriarchs and ourselves since the exile from Jerusalem. Also, a covenant has been made by the thirteen attributes that [Israel] will not be turned away empty-handed.[154] With the increase of good deeds prayer becomes more effective with all things that are fit to be revealed….

Another aspect [of the statement] that we do not know how to pray: It is a well-known fact that every word of the Torah can change by the modification of its diacritical points even though the letters remain unaltered. If you vocalize some words one way, then all the letters are linked to the root. If you take these same words and vocalize them differently, its content changes and one of the letters becomes a connective. So we can say that the Tetragrammaton must be expressed with its correct vocalizations. If one knows how to construct its structure, he directs himself to the structure that this vocalization teachers. His prayer will be accepted and he will be answered from heaven. Do not regard this as far-fetched, for had I not discovered this in my heart I would have said it is a direct tradition from Moses at Sinai. It is quite likely that this was also the opinion of the sage R. Ezra, may his memory be blessed.

The Kohen Brothers

Editor's introduction: Two selections from the Kohen brothers appear below.[155] Rabbi Ya'akov's *Explanation of the Letters* explores the mystical dimensions of the Hebrew alphabet. While not innovative in doctrine, this fascinating text is an early example of Jewish mystics' consistent preoccupation with the Hebrew language as a focal point of meditation. Rabbi Ya'akov uses the shapes of the letters, their numerical values, and the means of their pronunciation to explain their spiritual meaning. Also of note is the explicit connection between letters and light. Rabbi Yitshak's *Treatise on the Left Emanation* represents a highly original development in the history of Kabbalah. He describes evil as an independent entity created by God. The demons Lilith and Sama'el, familiar specters in earlier Jewish mystical texts, are here described as a divinely emanated couple, a sadistic parallel to the biblical Adam and Eve.[156] The darkness generated by human sin will be healed only after an eschatological battle between the messianic hero and the forces of evil. Yitshak ha-Kohen's work brought this stark dualism, reminiscent of early Gnosticism, directly into Kabbalah, a notion that continued to reverberate in the words of the *Zohar*.

Explanation of the Letters

Concentrate on the image of the letter *alef* (א) with your eyes and understand it in your heart. You will find that many hidden truths concerning the shapes of other letters are depicted and encompassed in the shape of the *alef*—something you will not find in any other letter. Now we should seek out and investigate why all the shapes of all the letters of the alphabet are depicted in the *alef*.

You know full well that all the letters are pronounced in specific places in the mouth. The *alef* is the first letter pronounced in the mouth with air, without any strain or effort, to teach that the Holy One, blessed be He, is one with no other partner, and that He is hidden from all creatures. Just as the *alef* is pronounced in a hidden and concealed spot at the back of the tongue, so the Holy One, blessed be He, is hidden from visible sight. Similarly, just as the *alef* is ethereal and imperceptible, so the Holy One, blessed be He, denied to all creatures the ability to comprehend Him, save by means of thought, for thought is pure and unblemished and subtle as the ether. But not even thought can grasp the Holy One, blessed be He, so hidden that He is.

That you see all the letters depicted in the *alef* is because the powers of all created things are hidden within the power and awesomeness of the Holy One, blessed be He. Every single power emerges from the divine Will when He so desires. Thus we learn from the image of the *alef*, within which the shapes of all the letters are hidden, that there is no creature without a Creator, no handiwork without a Maker, and no depiction without an Illustrator.

Now you should examine the form of the *alef*, the inner white form and the external black form. You will discover that it is as if the inner [form] bears the external [form], and that the inner [form] is the abode of the external [form]. This teaches you that the inner [form] corresponds to the Holy One, blessed be He, completely hidden from the sight of all creatures and unbounded in His interiorness. The external form corresponds to the world, dangling from the arm of the Holy One, blessed be He, as a charm on the arm of a hero.[157] And just as the inner form is the abode of the outer [form], so too the Holy One, blessed be He, is the abode of the world, though the world is not His abode.[158]

When I said to you that the white form and not the black exterior form in the *alef* corresponds to the exaltedness of the Holy One, blessed be He, I said this to you as a principle and a great secret: The white form corresponds to the white robe. And the Sages, may their memories be blessed, said (*Bereshit Rabbah* 3:4): "From whence was the light created? It teaches that the Holy One, blessed be He, wrapped Himself in a white robe whose sparks shone forth from one end of the world to the other. As it is written, 'He wraps Himself with light as a garment' (Ps 104:2), and 'the light dwells with Him' (Dan 2:22)."[159] Thus, you cannot pronounce the word "light" (*or*) without the letter *alef* at the beginning.[160]

When we say that He "wrapped Himself in a white robe," do not take this literally. For it is known that the Holy One, blessed be He, is not a body nor does He wrap like one of flesh and blood. Rather, the Sages, may their memories be blessed, spoke in human terms, for this wrapping is mentioned solely to teach that there was nothing [standing] before Him except light. And this is what David, peace be upon him, said, "Even the darkness is not darkness for You" (Ps 139:12).

When you observe the four directions from which the letter *alef* extends forth from the center point, know that they correspond to the four directions of the heavens and the four letters of His great and holy name and the four holy animals and the four encampments of the Chariot.

As the inner white form encircles the four directions of the outer form, so the Holy One, blessed be He, encompasses all the degrees we have already mentioned, all resting upon His right hand. When you observe that all the shapes of the letters are included in the *alef*, it is to teach you that the Holy One, blessed be He, appears in various images and visions to His prophets and servants. This is what is meant when it is said, "To whom then will you liken me that I should be his equal, says the Holy One" (Is 40:25), meaning: "I can reveal myself to My prophets and worshipers in various guises, for the power of all the forms and images and similitudes, both the encompassed and depicted, are within my ability, power and strength." Even though Scripture states that the Holy One, blessed be He, reveals himself in various manifestations, do not think that such is the case. Rather there are at His disposal fluctuating forces which change into various manifestations. These are the powers of angels, as it is written, "He makes the winds His messengers, the flames of fire His ministers" (Ps 104:4). But the Holy one, blessed be he, is one and utterly unchangeable, as it is written, "For I the Lord do not change" (Mal 3:6). This (lesson) you can learn from the *alef*: for though the *alef* contains all the shapes, it never ceases to remain an *alef*. Similarly the Holy One, blessed be He, reveals Himself to His prophets in a variety of images and visions, yet He never varies in His unity. Therefore the numerical value of *alef* is one, since it partakes of the image of the unity of the Holy One, blessed be He.

Furthermore, the shape of *alef* acts as a witness to the name of the Holy One, blessed be He. The tip of the *alef* is in the shape of a *yod*, the middle stroke is in the shape of a *vav,* while the foot of the letter is shaped like *yod*. Now add *yod*, *vav*, *yod* (10+6+10) and you will get 26, which equals Y-H-V-H (10+5+6+5). The letter *alef* is established at the beginning of the word "one" (*ehad*), because it is a witness that the Lord our God is one....

Now look at the shape of *alef* and discover that it contains the shape of man with his head, his hands, and his feet. The tip resembles *yod*, which corresponds to the ten parts of the human head, namely: the four temples of the head, the two ears, two eyes, and two nostrils—behold ten, corresponding to the value of the shape *yod* (י) in the tip of *alef*. It also corresponds to the ten fingers in the human hand. The middle stroke resembles *vav* (ו), which corresponds to the six directions of man. For man is a microcosm, and just as the world possesses six directions, so too does man possess six directions. They are: front, back, left, right, head, and feet. The front corresponds to the east, the back to the west, left to north, right to south, the head corresponds to up and the feet to down—behold six directions in man, which equal the shape of *vav* in *alef*. The foot of *alef* resembles *yod* corresponding to the ten toes of man. Now you have discovered that the shape of *alef* is like the shape of man. Therefore the *alef* is placed in the world man (*adam*), is a great wonder (*pel'e*), as Scripture states: "terrible in wondrous deeds, doing wonder (*pel'e*)" (Ex 15:11)—reverse it to [read] *alef*....

Treatise on the Left Emanation

6. ...Now I shall allude to you the reason for all the jealousy between these latter princes and the former princes of these seven groups of holy angels which are called "the guardians of the walls."[161] A form destined for Sama'el stirs up enmity and jealousy between the heavenly delegation and the forces of the supernal army. This form is Lilith, and she is in the image of a feminine form. Sama'el takes on the form of Adam and Lilith the form of Eve. They were both born in

a spiritual birth as one, as a parallel to the forms of Adam and Eve above and below: two twinlike forms. Both Sama'el and [Lilith, called] Eve the Matron—also known as the Northern One—are emanated from beneath the Throne of Glory. It was the Sin which brought about this calamity, in order to bring her shame and disgrace to destroy her celestial offspring. The calamity was caused by the Northern One, who was created beneath the Throne of Glory and it resulted in a partial collapse and weakening of the legs of the Throne. Then, by means of Gamali'el and the primeval snake Nahashi'el, the scents of each intermingled: the scent of man reached the female, and the scent of woman reached the male. Ever since then the snakes have increased and have taken on the form of biting snakes. Thus it is written, "The Lord sent fiery snakes among the people" (Num 21:6). This requires a full explanation in a separate treatise for it is very deep—"no one can find it out" (Eccl 7:24)....[162]

19. In answer to your question concerning Lilith, I shall explain to you the essence of the matter. Concerning this point there is a received tradition from the ancient Sages who made use of the *Secret Knowledge of the Lesser Palaces*, which is the manipulation of demons and a ladder by which one ascends to the prophetic levels.[163] In this tradition it is made clear that Sama'el and Lilith were born as one, similar to the form of Adam and Eve who were also born as one,[164] reflecting what is above. This is the account of Lilith which was received by the Sages in the *Secret Knowledge of the Palaces*. The Matron Lilith is the mate of Sama'el. Both of them were born at the same hour in the image of Adam and Eve, intertwined in each other....

This is the exact text of what is written in *The Chapters of the Lesser Palaces* as we have received it, word for word and letter for letter.[165] And the scholars of this wisdom possess a very profound tradition from the ancients. They found it stated in those *Chapters* that Sama'el, the great prince of them all, grew exceedingly jealous of Asmodeus the king of the demons because of this Lilith who is called Lilith the Maiden (the young). She is in the form of a beautiful woman from her head to her waist. But from the waist down she is burning fire—like mother like daughter. She is called Mehatabel daughter of Matred, and the meaning is something immersed (*mahu tabal*). The meaning here is that her intentions are never for the good. She only seeks to incite wars and various demons of war and the war between Daughter Lilith and Matron Lilith. They say that from Asmodeus and his mate Lilith a great prince was born in heaven. He is the ruler of eighty thousand destructive demons and is called "the sword of king Asmodeus." His name is Alefpene'ash and his face is like a raging fire (*esh*). He is also called Gurigur, for he antagonizes and struggles with the prince of Judah, who is called Gur Aryeh Yehudah ("Lion-cub of Judah"). From the same form that gave birth to this war-demon another prince, a prince whose root is in Kingdom, was born in heaven. He is called "the sword of the Messiah." He too has two names: Meshihi'el and Kokhvi'el. When the time comes and when God wishes, this sword will leave its sheath and verses of prophecy will come true: "For My sword shall be drunk in the heavens; Lo, it shall come down upon Edom" (Is 34:5). "A star rises from Jacob" (Num 24:17). Amen. Soon in our days may we merit to see the face of the Messiah our righteous one; we and all our people…

CHAPTER 2

The *Zohar*

Introduction

Some fifty years after the emergence of Kabbalah in Provence, Gerona, and Castile, manuscripts of a previously unknown mystical book began to surface. Small sections circulated toward the end of the thirteenth century, first in the city of Guadalajara and then throughout Christian Spain. This work, structured as commentary to the Torah, wove together narrative, legal, and mystical interpretations of the biblical text. Its protagonists were the second-century sage Rabbi Shim'on bar Yohai and his students, and it was written in a strange Aramaic, perhaps meant to recall the language of the talmudic Galilee. What was this mysterious work? At first it was cited only by veiled reference, but for the generations to come it was known as the *Zohar*.

The *Zohar* (*Book of Splendor*) is an associative work of biblical exegesis similar in style to that of classical rabbinic midrash. Verses from all over Scripture are cited and interpreted in light of one another. However, the *Zohar* uses this literary form to elevate the symbolic language of earlier Kabbalah to an entirely different level. The *Zohar* builds on motifs found already in the Bahir, such as the cosmic tree, the divine Matron (*shekhinah*), and the *sefirot*, but they now reappear as part of a finely developed theosophical system, or one that offers secret teachings on the inner world of God. Yet attempting to reduce the *Zohar* to its symbolic (or esoteric) meaning alone, treating it like a cypher whose riddle may be disregarded once it has been cracked, will blind one to the beauty of its poetry. The richness of the *Zohar*'s language is neither accidental nor superfluously rhetorical, for it represents an effort to recapture the mythos of Jewish theology.[2] The *Zohar* is a romantic work in every sense of the term, and it uses sensual, often erotic imagery to describe the relationship between masculine and feminine elements of the *sefirot*, the dynamic between humanity and the Divine (and the Torah), and even interactions between the scholars of Rabbi Shim'on's mystical circle. Verses plucked from the Song of Songs, first introduced to the mystical canon by Rabbi Ezra of Gerona, are present on nearly every page, suffusing the text with an amorous vitality.[3]

The *Zohar* is not a book that may be read quickly from cover to cover, nor may its passages be perused lightly. To study the *Zohar* is to enter into its world of symbols, to immerse oneself in the poetry of its language. It is a delightful blend of theosophy and narrative, and reading its passages closely will reveal that the stories of Rabbi Shim'on and his mystical fellowship (*havrayya*, translated as "Comrades" below) are not simply a convenient frame for the theological teachings; their adventures mirror and amplify *Zohar*'s mystical ideas by giving them narrative expression.[4] The reader must consent to step inside the beauty and grandeur of its language, and be awakened by the *Zohar*'s mystical brilliance. As our first text makes clear, the *Zohar* teaches its readers "how to look at Torah."

The *Zohar* is also concerned with the mystical significance of the commandments. Occasionally it offers a surprising legal ruling or refers to an otherwise unknown custom,[5] but, more often, the *Zohar* explores the spiritual dimensions of the normative commandments. On this issue, the *Zohar* speaks with one voice: Jewish mysticism is a spirituality that must be embodied in physical practice. Indeed, portions of the *Zohar* are devoted to complicated and abstract theosophy, but its pages also contain rich descriptions of the mystical experience. Of all the commandments, the *Zohar* affords prayer and learning Torah a central place. As is found in earlier Kabbalah, the *Zohar* describes prayer as a contemplative journey to God through the various heavenly palaces and *sefirot*.[6] This type of intimacy with the Divine is perhaps second only to that achieved when engaging in Torah study. The interpretative movement is described as a revelatory experience, and creative exegesis of Scripture is extolled with the highest praises.[7] Much of the *Zohar* unfolds as Rabbi Shim'on and his disciples offer differing interpretations of a single biblical passage, one after another. As one contemporary scholar has put it, these assemblies are like mystical jazz sessions in which each Kabbalist presents his original variations on a theme.[8] The Kabbalists of

Provençal and Geronian Kabbalah were largely conservative, and except for the writings of Ya'akov ben Sheshet, they were ambivalent about the place of creativity. For the *Zohar*, however, the deeper meaning of a verse is not found in an inherited esoteric secret that must be safeguarded; the mystical dimensions of the biblical text are aroused by human imagination.

The authorship of the *Zohar* is a particularly thorny issue. The work was traditionally attributed to its hero Rabbi Shim'on, though nowhere does the *Zohar* refer to itself as a book written by this sage. Gershom Scholem confirmed the suspicions of earlier skeptics and argued that the *Zohar* is the original work of a Spanish Kabbalist by the name of Rabbi Moses de Leon (c. 1240–1305).[9] De Leon was the first to circulate its manuscripts, and Scholem claimed that he singlehandedly forged the *Zohar* and attempted to use psuedepigraphy to grant it authority.[10] For many reasons, this late dating is generally accepted. The *Zohar* has clearly been influenced by Jewish philosophy, its language reflects medieval Hebrew, and its context in the Jewish exile of Christian Spain is immediately evident. However, the thesis that Moses de Leon was the work's sole author has since been challenged. Yehuda Liebes has even suggested that the *Zohar* was written by an actual circle of Spanish Kabbalists whose own mystical lives mirrored the group around Rabbi Shim'on.[11]

The *Zohar* is not a single unified work. It is a marbled literary corpus with a dozen or more different layers. When the *Zohar* was printed for the first time in Mantua and Cremona (1558 and 1560, respectively), its editors were forced to choose what would be included on its pages. Some textual strata had already been woven together into what was printed as the main body of the *Zohar*, while others were printed as separate units. These include *Midrash ha-Ne'elam (The Hidden Midrash)*, the section of the *Zohar* written first, and the *Ra'aya Meheimna* (*The Faithful Shepherd*), a mystical commentary on the commandments composed after the rest of the *Zohar*. The extremely influential *Tikkunei Zohar (Embellishments on the Zohar)*, a series of mystical interpretations of the first verse of Genesis, was written a few decades after the main body of the *Zohar* and is published as a separate work. *Zohar Hadash* (*New Zohar*) was also printed in the sixteenth century. This work is an early body of authentic *Zohar* material gleaned from manuscripts that were left out of the original printing, including commentary on the scrolls of Ruth, Song of Songs, and Lamentations.[12]

The *Zohar*'s success is nothing short of remarkable. At first its study was restricted to relatively small, though important, kabbalistic groups in Spain, but within a short time after the expulsion of Jews in 1492, it had become the central text of an emerging Jewish mystical canon throughout Europe and the Middle East.[13] As we shall see, the kabbalistic revival in sixteenth-century Safed, the Sabbatian heretics of seventeenth century, the Hasidic masters of the eighteenth and nineteenth centuries, and mystics of the modern era were profoundly influenced by its teachings.

Further Reading

Giller, Pinchas. *Reading the Zohar: The Sacred Text of the Kabbalah.* Oxford and New York: Oxford University Press, 2001.

Green, Arthur. *A Guide to the Zohar.* Stanford: Stanford University Press, 2004.

Hellner-Eshed, Melila. *A River Flows From Eden: The Language of Mystical Experience in the Zohar.* Translated by Nathan Wolski. Stanford: Stanford University Press, 2009.

Matt, Daniel C. *The Zohar: Pritzker Edition.* Translation and commentary by Daniel C. Matt. 7 vols. to date. Stanford: Stanford University Press, 2003–present.

Scholem, Gershom. *Major Trends in Jewish Mysticism.* New York: Schocken Books, 1995.

Tishby, Isaiah. *The Wisdom of the Zohar: An Anthology of Texts.* Translated by David Goldstein. Oxford: Littman Library Of Jewish Civilization, 1989.

The Text

How to Look at Torah

Rabbi Shim'on said: "Woe to the human being who says that Torah presents mere stories and ordinary words![14] If so, we could compose a Torah right now with ordinary words and better than all of them! To present matters of the world? Even rulers of the world possess words more sublime. If so, let us follow them and make a Torah out of them! Ah, but all the words of Torah are sublime words, sublime secrets![15]

Come and see: The world above and the world below are perfectly balanced: Israel below, the angels above. Of the angels it is written: 'He makes His angels spirits' (Ps 104:4). But when they descend, they put on the garment of this world. If they did not put on a garment befitting this world, they could not endure in this world and the world could not endure them. If this is so with the angels, how much more so with Torah, who created them and all the worlds and for whose sake they all exist! In descending to this world, if she did not put on the garments of this world the world could not endure.

So this story of Torah is the garment of Torah. Whoever thinks that the garment is the real Torah and not something else—may his spirit deflate! He will have no portion in the world that is coming. That is why David said: 'Open my eyes so I can see wonders out of Your Torah!' (Ps 119:18), what is under the garment of Torah!

Come and see: There is a garment visible to all. When those fools see someone in a good-looking garment, they look no further. But the essence of the garment is the body; the essence of the body is the soul!

So it is with Torah. She has a body: the commandments of Torah, called 'the embodiment of Torah.'[16] This body is clothed in garments: the stories of this world. Fools of the world look only at that garment, the story of Torah; they know nothing more. They do not look at what is under that garment. Those who know more do not look at the garment, but rather at the body under that garment. The wise ones, servants of the King on high, those who stood at Mt. Sinai,[17] look only at the soul, root of all, real Torah![18] In the time to come they are destined to look at the soul of the soul of Torah!

Come and see: So it is above. There is garment and body and soul and soul of soul. The heavens and their host are the garment. The Communion of Israel[19] is the body who receives the soul, the Beauty of Israel.[20] So She is the body of the soul.[21] The soul we have mentioned[22] is the Beauty of Israel who is real Torah. The soul of the soul is the Holy Ancient One.[23] All is connected, this one to that one.

Woe to the wicked who say that Torah is merely a story![24] They look at this garment and no further. Happy are the righteous who look at Torah properly! As wine must sit in a jar, so Torah must sit in this garment. So look only at what is under the garment! So all those words and all those stories—they are garments!"

The Creation of *Elohim*

In the beginning...(Gen 1:1).

When the King conceived ordaining, He engraved engravings in the luster on high.[25] A blinding spark[26] flashed within the Concealed of the Concealed from the mystery of the Infinite, a cluster of vapor in formlessness, set in a ring, not white, not black, not red, not green, no color at all. When a band spanned,[27] it yielded radiant colors. Deep within the spark gushed a flow imbuing colors below, concealed within the concealed of the mystery of the Infinite. The flow broke through and did not break through its aura.[28] It was not known at all until, under the impact of breaking through, one high and hidden point shone.[29] Beyond that point, nothing is known. So it is called Beginning, the first command of all.[30]

"The enlightened[31] will shine like the *Zohar*[32] of the sky, and those who make the masses righteous will shine like the stars forever and ever" (Dan 12:3). *Zohar*, Concealed of the Concealed, struck its aura. The aura touched and did not touch this point. Then this Beginning emanated and made itself a palace for its glory and its praise. There it sowed the seed of holiness to give birth for the benefit of the universe.[33] The secret is: "Her stock is a holy seed" (Isa 6:13).

Zohar, sowing a seed for its glory like the seed of fine purple silk. The silkworm wraps itself within and makes itself a palace.[34] This palace is its praise and a benefit to all.

With the Beginning the Concealed One who is not known created the palace. This palace is called *Elohim*. The secret is: "With Beginning, ——— created *Elohim*."

Male and Female

This is the book of the generations of Adam. On the day that God created Adam, in the likeness of God He created him; male and female He created them. He blessed them and called their name Adam on the day they were created (Gen 5:1–2).

Rabbi Shim'on said: "High mysteries are revealed in these two verses. 'Male and female He created them' to make known the Glory on high, the mystery of faith.[35] Out of this mystery, Adam was created.

Come and see: With the mystery by which heaven and earth were created Adam was created. Of them it is written: 'These are the generations of heaven and earth' (Gen 2:4). Of Adam it is written: 'This is the book of the generations of Adam.' Of them it is written: 'when they were created.' Of Adam it is written: 'on the day they were created.' 'Male and female He created them.' From here we learn: Any image that does not embrace male and female is not a high and true image. We have established this in the mystery of our Mishnah.[36]

Come and see: The Blessed Holy One does not place His abode in any place where male and female are not found together. Blessings are found only in a place where male and female are found,[37] as it is written: 'He blessed them and called their name Adam on the day they were created.' It is not written: 'He blessed him and called his name Adam.' A human being is only called Adam when male and female are as one."[38]

Openings

He [Abraham] was sitting in the opening of the tent...Sarah heard from the opening of the tent (Gen. 18:1, 10).

Rabbi Yehudah opened: "'Her husband is known in the gates when he sits among the elders of the land' (Prov 31:23). Come and see: The Blessed Holy One has ascended in glory. He is hidden, concealed, far beyond. There is no one in the world, nor has there ever been, who can understand His wisdom or withstand Him. He is hidden, concealed, transcendent, beyond, beyond.

The beings up above and the creatures down below—none of them can comprehend. All they can say is: 'Blessed be the Presence of Y-H-V-H in His place' (Ez 13:12). The ones below proclaim that He is above: 'His Presence is above the heavens' (Ps 113:4); the ones above proclaim that He is below: 'Your Presence is over all the earth' (Ps 57:12). Finally all of them, above and below, declare: 'Blessed be the Presence of Y-H-V-H wherever He is!'[39] For He is unknowable. No one has ever been able to identify Him. How, then, can you say: 'Her husband is known in the gates'? Her husband is the Blessed Holy One![40] Indeed, He is known in the gates. He is known and grasped to the degree that one opens the gates of imagination![41] The capacity to connect with the spirit of wisdom, to imagine in one's heart-mind[42]—this is how God becomes known. Therefore 'Her husband is known in the gates,' through the gates of imagination. But that He be known as He really is? No one has ever been able to attain such knowledge of Him."

Rabbi Shim'on said: "'Her husband is known in the gates.' Who are these gates? The ones addressed in the Psalm: 'O gates, lift up your heads! Be lifted up, openings of eternity, so the King of Glory may come!' (Ps 24:7). Through these gates, these spheres on high, the Blessed Holy One becomes known. Were it not so, no one could commune with Him. Come and see: *Neshamah*[43] of a human being is unknowable except through limbs of the body, subordinates of *neshamah* who carry out what she designs. Thus she is known and unknown. The Blessed Holy One too is known and unknown. For He is *Neshamah* of *neshamah*,[44] Pneuma of pneuma, completely hidden away; but through these gates, opening for *neshamah*, the Blessed Holy One becomes known.

Come and see: There is opening within opening, level beyond level. Through these the Glory of God becomes known. 'The opening of the tent' is the opening of Righteousness,[45] as the Psalmist says: 'Open for me the gates of righteousness....' (Ps 118:19). This is the first opening to enter. Through this opening, all other high openings come into view. One who attains the clarity of this opening discovers all the other openings, for all of them abide here.

Now that Israel is in exile, this opening is unknown; all the openings have abandoned Her. It is impossible to know, impossible to grasp. But when Israel comes forth from exile, all the soaring spheres will touch down upon this opening, one by one. Then human beings will perceive wondrous, precious wisdom never known by them before, as it is written: 'The spirit of Y-H-V-H shall alight upon him: a spirit of wisdom and insight, a spirit of design and power, a spirit of knowledge and awe of Y-H-V-H' (Isa 11:4).

Therefore when Abraham received the good news, this sphere delivered it, as has been said, for it is written: 'Then one said, "I will return to you when life is due"' (Gen 18:10). 'One said'—who it was is not spelled out. It was the Opening of the Tent!

Now the same verse says: 'Sarah heard.' She heard this sphere speaking with her husband; someone she had never heard before. And so it is written: 'Sarah heard the Opening of the Tent' who was delivering the good news: 'I will return to you when life is due and your wife Sarah will have a son.'"

Seduction Above and Below

And it came to pass after these things that his master's wife cast her eyes upon Joseph and said, "Lie with me!" And he refused.... Though she urged Joseph day after day, he did not yield to her, to lie beside her, to be with her (Gen 39:7–8, 10).

Rabbi El'azar said: "When that evil side approaches to seduce a human being, he should pull it toward Torah and it will leave him.[46] Come and see what we have learned: When the evil side confronts the Blessed Holy One, accusing the world of evil doings, the Blessed Holy One feels compassion for the world and offers a device to human beings to save themselves from him, to neutralize his power over them and their actions. What is the device? Engaging in Torah! This saves them from him.

How do we know? Because it is written: 'A *mitsvah* is a lamp; Torah is light; rules of disciple lead to life' (Prov 6:23). What is written in the following verse? 'To guard you from the evil woman, the smooth-tongued alien.' This is the unclean side, the Other Side,[47] who constantly confronts the Blessed Holy One to press charges based on human sin, who constantly confronts human beings to pervert and mislead them below. He constantly presents himself above to report the sins of humans and accuse them of their doings so that they be delivered into his power, as was done to Job. At this same time he looms over humans below to mislead them and remind them of their sins, everything they have done.

Especially when the Blessed Holy One stands in judgment over them, he rises to indict them and enumerate their sins. The Blessed Holy One, however, felt compassion for Israel and gave them a device to save themselves from him. What? A *shofar* on Rosh ha-Shanah,[48] and on Yom Kippur a scapegoat to give to him so that he leave them alone and occupy himself with a portion of his. This has been established.[49]

Come and see what is written: 'Her feet lead down to death, her steps grasp the netherworld' (Prov 5:5). But of the mystery of faith,[50] it is written: 'Her ways are ways of delight, all her paths are peace' (Prov 3:17). These are the ways and paths of Torah. All is one, this peace and that death, reverse sides of each other.[51]

Come and see: When this evil side comes down and roams through the world and sees how human beings act, how they all stray from their paths in this world, he ascends and accuses them. If the Blessed Holy One did not feel compassion for the work of His hands, no one would survive!

What is written, 'Though she urged Joseph day after day'? She rises faithlessly every single day and uncovers for the Blessed Holy One so much evil news so that she can destroy mankind. What is written, 'He did not yield to her, to lie beside her, to be with her'? He does not yield to her request, because He feels compassion for the world. 'To lie beside her.' Why does she want Him to lie beside her? So she can take control and dominate the world! Her control does not prevail until she is given power...."[52]

Rabbi Abba said: "It is all one path,[53] but it is the Deviser of Evil who comes to seduce human beings to perfect their paths, to cling to them day after day. Time after time, he diverts one from the path of truth, to force him off the path of life and draw him on toward hell. A righteous person—what does he do? He watches his step on the path so the Deviser of Evil cannot cling to him, as it is written, 'Though she urged Joseph day after day, he did not yield to her,' to what she proposed day after day. For the unclean spirit, the Deviser of Evil, seduces a man every day 'to lie beside her' in hell, to be condemned there 'to be with her.'[54]

Come and see: When a person joins that side he is drawn to her more and more; he defiles himself with her both in this world and the other world. Come and see this unclean side: It is ugly, it is filth. '"Out!" you will call to it' (Isa 30:22), excrement! One who turns away from Torah is punished in excrement! Sinners of the world who do not believe in the Blessed Holy One are punished in excrement![55]

What is written? 'One such day, he came into the house to do his work. There was no man of the household there inside' (Gen 39:11). 'One such day,' a day when the Deviser of Evil is at large in the world, coming to lead humans astray. When is that day? The same day a person acknowledges his sins and begins to turn himself around,[56] or when he engages Torah and resolves to obey her commands. At that very moment, he descends to lead humans astray.

'He came into the house to do his work,' to engage Torah and obey her commands, for that is the work a person should do in this world. Now since a person's real work in this world is the work of the Blessed Holy One, he must be as strong as a lion on every side so that the Other Side will not overpower him or be able to seduce him.

What is written? 'There was no man,' no man to stand up against the Deviser of Evil and wage war with him as one should. How does the Deviser of Evil operate? Once he sees that no man stands in his way, ready to fight him, immediately 'she grabbed him by his coat and said, "Lie with me!"' (Gen 39:12). She grabbed him by his coat, because when the Deviser of Evil takes control of a person he dresses him up in beautiful clothes and curls his hair and says, 'Lie with me! Join me!'[57] One who is pure steels himself and wages war. What is written? 'But he left his coat in her hand and fled outdoors.' One should abandon him, harden oneself against him, flee from him to be safe from him. Then he cannot take control."

Jacob's Garment of Days

The days of Israel grew near to die. He summoned his son Joseph and said to him, "If I have found favor in your eyes, place your hand under my thing; act toward me out of true love: please do not bury me in Egypt. I will lie down with my fathers; then take me out of Egypt and bury me in their burial place" (Gen 47:29–30).

Rabbi Yehudah opened and said: "'Listen, you deaf ones! You blind ones, look up and see!' (Isa 42:18). 'Listen, you deaf ones!', you human beings who do not hear Torah speaking, who do not open your ears to let in the commands of your Master. 'You blind ones' who do not examine your own foundations, who do not seek to know why you are alive!

Every single day a herald comes forth and proclaims but no one hears his message![58] It has been taught: When a human being is created, on the day he comes into the world, simultaneously, all the days of his life are arranged above. One by one, they come flying down into the world to alert that human being, day by day. If, when a day comes to alert him, he sins on that day before his Master, then that day climbs up in shame, bears witness, and stands alone outside. It has been taught: After standing alone it sits and waits for that human to turn back to his Master, to restore the day. If he succeeds, that day returns to its place; if not, that day comes down to join forces with the outlaw spirit. It molds itself into an exact image of that human and moves into his house to torment him. Sometimes his stay is for the good if one purifies himself. If not, it is a horrible visitation. Either way, such days are lacking, missing from the total. Woe to the human being who has decreased his days in the presence of the Holy King, who has failed to reserve days up above—days that could adorn him in that world, days that could usher him in to the presence of the Holy King!

Come and see: When those days draw near to the Holy King,[59] if the person leaving the world is pure he ascends and enters into those days and they become a radiant garment for his soul![60] But only his days of virtue, not his days of fault. Woe to him who has decreased his days up above! For when he comes to be clothed in his days, the days that he ruined are missing and he is clothed in a tattered garment. It is worse if there are many such days; then he will have nothing to wear in that world! Woe to him! Woe to his soul! He is punished in hell for those days, days upon days, two days for every wasted day! For when he left this world, he found no days to wear, he had no garment for cover. Happy are the righteous! Their days are all stored up with the Holy King, woven into radiant garments to be worn in the world that is coming.

We have learned in the mystery of our Mishnah:[61] Why is it written: 'And they knew that they were naked' (Gen 3:7)? Adam and Eve knew the naked truth: the radiant garment woven from their days had faded away.[62] Not one single day was left to wear, as it is written: 'Your eyes saw my unformed limbs; in Your book they were all recorded. The days that were fashioned—not one of them is left' (Ps 139:16). Exactly! Not one of those fashioned days was left to be worn. And so it remained until Adam made the effort to turn back to God and mend his ways. The Blessed Holy One accepted him and made him different garments but not from his days, as it is written: 'Y-H-V-H *Elohim* made garments of skin for Adam and his wife and He clothed them' (Gen 3:21).[63]

Come and see: Abraham, who was pure, what is written of him? 'He came into days' (Gen 24:1).[64] When he left this world he entered into his very own days and put them on to wear. Nothing was missing from that radiant garment: 'He came into days.' But what is written of Job? 'He said, "Naked I came from my mother's womb and naked shall I return there"' (Job 1:21). No garment was left for him to wear..."[65]

Rabbi Yitshak said: "Happy is the destiny of Jacob! He had such faith that he could say, 'I will lie down with my fathers.' He attained their level, nothing less! He surpassed them, dressed in his days and in theirs."[66]

Manna and Wisdom

Come and see: Every single day, dew trickles down from the Holy Ancient One[67] to the Impatient One,[68] and the Orchard of Holy Apple Trees[69] is blessed. Some of the dew flows to those below; holy angels are nourished by it, each according to his diet, as it is written: "A human ate angel bread" (Ps 78:25).[70] Israel ate of that food in the desert.

Rabbi Shim'on said: "Some people are nourished by it even now! Who are they? The Comrades, who engage Torah day and night. Do you think they are nourished by that very food? No, by something like that very food; two balancing one.

Come and see: When Israel entered and joined themselves to the Holy King by uncovering the holy marking,[71] they were pure enough to eat another kind of bread, higher than at first. At first, when Israel went out of Egypt, they went into the bread called *Matsah*.[72] Now they were purer; they went in to eat higher bread from a high sphere, as it is written: 'I am about to rain down for you bread from heaven' (Ex 16:4)—literally, from Heaven![73] It was then that Israel discovered the taste of this sphere.

Comrades engaging Torah are nourished from an even higher sphere.[74] Which is that? That which is written: 'Wisdom gives life to those who have it' (Eccl 7:12), a very high sphere."

Rabbi El'azar said to him: "If so, why are they weaker than other human beings? Other human beings are stronger and more powerful; the Comrades should be the stronger ones."

He said to him, "A good question! Come and see: All human food comes from above. The food that comes from heaven and earth is for the whole world. It is food for all; it is coarse and dense. The food that comes from higher above is finer food, coming from the sphere where

Judgment is found. This is the food that Israel ate when they went out of Egypt.

The food found by Israel that time in the desert, from the higher sphere called Heaven—it is an even finer food, entering deepest of all into the soul, detached from the body, called "angel bread."

The highest food of all is the food of the Comrades, those who engage Torah. For they eat food of the spirit and the soul-breath; they eat no food for the body at all. Rather, from a high sphere, precious beyond all: Wisdom.

That is why a Comrade's body is weaker than a normal body: they do not eat food for the body at all. They eat food for the spirit and the soul-breath from someplace far beyond, most precious of all. So their food is finest of the fine, finest of all. Happy is their portion! As it is written: 'Wisdom gives life to those who have it.' Happy is the body that can nourish itself on food of the soul!"

Rabbi El'azar said to him, "Certainly that is true. But how can such food be found now?"

He answered, "Certainly a good question! Come and see: This is the clarity of the word.... The food of the Comrades engaging Torah is most precious of all. This food flows from Wisdom on high. Why from this sphere? Because Torah derives from Wisdom on high, and those who engage Torah enter the source of her roots; so their food flows down from that high and holy sphere."[75]

Rabbi El'azar came and kissed his hands. He said, "Happy is my portion! I understand these words! Happy is the portion of the righteous! Engaging Torah day and night entitles them to this world and the world that is coming, as it is written: 'That is your life and the expanse of your days'" (Deut 30:19–20).

All of Israel Saw the Letters

I (anokhi) am Y-H-V-H, your God. . . (Ex 20:2).

A secret of secrets for those who know wisdom: The moment these letters came forth, secretly circling as one, a spark flashed out to engrave.[76] A flowing measure extended ten cubits on this side, and out shot comets inside comets, seventy-one.[77] Sparks burst into flashes, up high and down below, then quieted down and rose up high, beyond, beyond. The flow measured out ten cubits on the other side, and comets shot out in colors like before. And so on every side.

The spark expanded, whirling round and round. Sparks burst into flashes and rose high above. The heavens blazed with all their powers; everything flashed and sparkled as one. Then the spark turned from the side of the South and outlined a curve from there to the East and from the East to the North until it had circled back to the South, as before. Then the spark swirled, disappearing; comets and flashes dimmed.

Now they came forth, these carved, flaming letters flashing like gold when it dazzles.[78] Like a craftsman smelting silver and gold: when he takes them out of the blazing fire, all is bright and pure; so the letters came forth, pure and bright from the flowing measure of the spark.[79] Therefore it is written: "The word of Y-H-V-H is refined" (Ps 18:31), as silver and gold are refined. When these letters came forth, they were all refined, carved precisely, sparkling, flashing. All of Israel saw the letters flying through space in every direction, engraving themselves on the tablets of stone.

The Old Man and the Beautiful Maiden

Rabbi Hiyya and Rabbi Yose met one night at the Tower of Tyre. They stayed there as guests, delighting in each other. Rabbi Yose said, "I am so glad to see the face of *Shekhinah*.[80] For just now, the whole way here, I was pestered by an old man, a donkey driver,[81] who kept asking me riddles the whole way:[82]

'What is a serpent that flies in the air and wanders alone, while an ant lies peacefully between its teeth? Beginning in union, it ends in separation.

What is an eagle that nests in a tree that never was? Its young who have been plundered, who are not created creatures, lie somewhere uncreated. When they go up, they come down; coming down, they go up. Two who are one, and one who is three.

What is a beautiful maiden who has no eyes and a body concealed and revealed? She comes out in the morning and is hidden all day. She adorns herself with adornments that are not.'

All this he asked on the way; I was annoyed. Now I can relax! If we had been together, we would have engaged in words of Torah instead of strange words of chaos."

Rabbi Hiyya said, "That old man, the donkey driver, do you know anything about him?"

He answered, "I Know that there is nothing in his words. If he knew anything, he should have opened with Torah; then the way would not have been empty."

Rabbi Hiyya said, "That donkey driver, is he here? For sometimes in those empty fools, you discover bells of gold!"[83]

He said to him, "Here he is! Fixing up his donkey with food."

They called to him; he came before them. He said to them, "Now two are three, and three are like one!"[84]

Rabbi Yose said, "Didn't I tell you that all his words are empty nonsense?"

He sat before them and said, "Rabbis, I turned into a donkey driver only a short time ago.

Before, I wasn't one. But I have a small son, and I put him in school; I want him to engage Torah. When I find one of the rabbis traveling on the road I guide his donkey from behind. Today I thought that I would hear new words of Torah. But I haven't heard anything!"

Rabbi Yose said, "Of all the words I heard you say, there was one that really amazed me. Either you said it out of folly, or they are empty words."

The Old Man said, "And which one is that?"

He said, "The one about the beautiful maiden."

The Old Man opened and said: "'Y-H-V-H is on my side; I Have no fear. What can any human do to me? Y-H-V-H is by my side, helping me.... It is good to take refuge in Y-H-V-H...' (Ps 118:6–8).[85]

How good and pleasant and precious and high are words of Torah![86] But how can I say them in front of rabbis from whose mouths, until now, I haven't heard a single word? But I should say them because there is no shame at all in saying words of Torah in front of everyone!"

The Old Man covered himself.... The Old Man opened and said, "'Moses went inside the cloud and ascended the mountain...' (Ex 24:18). What is this cloud? The one of which it is written: 'I have placed My bow in the cloud' (Gen 9:13). We have learned that Rainbow took off Her garments and gave them to Moses.[87] Wearing that garment, Moses went up the mountain; from inside it he saw what he saw, delighting in the All, up to that place."

The Comrades approached and threw themselves down in front

of the Old Man. They cried, and said, "If we have come into the world only to hear these words from your mouth, it is enough for us!"

The Old Man said, "Friends, Comrades, not for this alone did I begin the word. An old man like me doesn't rattle with just a single word. Human beings are so confused in their minds! They do not see the way of truth in Torah. Torah calls out to them every day, in love, but they do not want to turn their heads. Even though I have said that Torah removes a word from her sheath, is seen for a moment and then quickly hides away—that is certainly true—but when she reveals herself from her sheath and hides herself right away, she does so only for those who know her intimately.

A parable: To what can this be compared? To a lovely princess, beautiful in every way and hidden deep within her place. She has one lover, unknown to anyone; he is hidden too. Out of his love for her, this lover passes by her gate constantly, lifting his eyes to every side. She knows that her lover is hovering about her gate constantly. What does she do? She opens a little window in her hidden palace and reveals her face to her lover, then swiftly withdraws, concealing herself. No one near the lover sees or reflects, only the lover, and his heart and his soul and everything within him flow out to her. And he knows that out of love for him she revealed herself for that one moment to awaken love in him.

So it is with a word of Torah: She reveals herself to no one but her lover. Torah knows that he who is wise of heart hovers about her gate every day. What does she do? She reveals her face to him from the palace and beckons him with a hint, then swiftly withdraws to her hiding place. No one who is there knows or reflects; he alone does, and his heart and his soul and everything within him flows out to her. That is why Torah reveals and conceals herself. With love she approaches her lover to arouse love with him.

Come and see! This is the way of Torah: At first, when she begins to reveal herself to a human she beckons him with a hint. If he knows, good; if not, she sends him a message, calling him a fool. Torah says to her messenger: 'Tell that fool to come closer, so I can talk with him!' as it is written: 'Who is the fool without a heart! Have him turn in here!' (Prov 9:4). He approaches. She begins to speak with him from behind a curtain she has drawn, words he can follow, until he reflects a little at a time. This is *derashah*.[88] Then she converses with him through a veil, words riddled with allegory.[89] This is *haggadah*.

Once he has grown accustomed to her, she reveals herself face to face and tells him all her hidden secrets, all the hidden ways, since primordial days secreted in her heart.[90] Now he is a perfect human being, husband of Torah, master of the house.[91] All her secrets she has revealed to him, withholding nothing, concealing nothing.

She says to him, 'Do you see that word, that hint with which I beckoned you at first! So many secrets there! This one and that one!'

Now he sees that nothing should be added to those words and nothing taken away. Now the *peshat* of the verse, just like it is![92] Not even a single letter should be added or deleted.

Human beings must become aware! They must pursue Torah to become her lovers!…"

He was silent for a moment. The Comrades were amazed; they did not know if it was day or night, if they were really there or not….

"Enough, Comrades! From now on, you know that the Evil Side has no power over you. I, Yeiva Sava,[93] have stood before you to awaken your awareness of these words."[94]

They rose like one who is awakened from his sleep and threw themselves down in front of him, unable to utter a word. After a while they began to cry.

Rabbi Hiyya opened and said: "'Set me as a seal upon your heart, as a seal upon your arm' (Song 8:6).… Love and sparks from the flame of our heart will escort you! May it be the Will that our image be engraved in your heart as your image is engraved in ours!"

He kissed them and blessed them, and they left.

When they rejoined Rabbi Shim'on and told him everything that happened, he was delighted and amazed. He said, "You are so fortunate to have attained all this! Here you were with a heavenly lion, a powerful hero compared with whom many heroes are nothing, and you did not know how to recognize him right away! I am amazed that you escaped his punishment! The Blessed Holy One must have wanted to save you!"

He called out these verses for them: "The path of the righteous is like the light of dawn, growing brighter and brighter until the day is full. When you walk, your stride will be free; if you run, you will not stumble. Your people, all of them righteous, will inherit the land forever; a sprout of My planting, the work of My hands, making Me glorious!" (Prov 4:18, 12; Isa 60:21).

The Secret of Sabbath

The Secret of Sabbath: She is Sabbath! United in the secret of One to draw down upon Her the secret of One.[95]

The prayer for the entrance of Sabbath: The holy Throne of Glory is united in the secret of One, prepared for the High Holy King to rest upon Her. When Sabbath enters She is alone, separated from the Other Side,[96] all judgments removed from Her. Basking in the oneness of holy light, She is crowned over and over to face the Holy King. All powers of wrath and masters of judgment flee from Her.[97] There is no power in all the worlds aside from Her. Her face shines with a light from beyond; She is crowned below by the holy people,[98] and all of them are crowned with new souls.[99]

Then the beginning of prayer to bless Her with joy and beaming faces: *Barekhu ET Y-H-V-H ha-Mevorakh*, "Bless *ET* Y-H-V-H, the Blessed One," *ET* Y-H-V-H, blessing Her first."[100]

Korban and *'Olah*, Drawing Near and Ascending

He called to Moses. Y-H-V-H spoke to him from the Tent of Meeting, saying: "Speak to the Children of Israel and say to them: 'When any of you brings a korban *to Y-H-V-H…'"* (Lev 1:1–2).

Rabbi Hizkiyah was in the presence of Rabbi Shim'on. He said to him: "That which is called *korban* (sacrifice)—it should be called *kereivut*, drawing near, or *kereivut*, nearness. Why *korban*?"

Rabbi Shim'on replied: "This is well-known to the Comrades! *Korban*, their drawing near,[101] the drawing near of those holy crowns, drawing near to one another, connecting with each other, until all turn into one, complete oneness, to perfect the Holy Name,[102] as it is written: '*korban* to Y-H-V-H.' The drawing near of those holy crowns is to Y-H-V-H so that the Holy Name be perfected and united, so that compassion fill all the worlds and the Holy Name be crowned with its crowns and everything be sweetened.

All this is intended to arouse Compassion, not to arouse Judgment. Therefore 'to Y-H-V-H,' not 'to *Elohim*.' 'To Y-H-V-H' we must arouse compassion! Not 'to *Elohim*.' We need compassion, not Judgment!"[103]

Rabbi Hizkiyah said: "I am so happy that I asked and gained these words! This is the clarity of the word!"

Y-H-V-H spoke to Moses, saying: "Enjoin Aaron and his sons, saying: 'This is the torah (teaching) *of the* 'olah…'" (Lev 6:1–2).

Rabbi El'azar asked Rabbi Shim'on, his father: "The bond of *'olah*,[104] bound to the Holy of Holies, lighting up the joining of desire of priests, Levites, and Israel up above—how high does it ascend?"[105]

He replied: "We have already established this: to Infinity.[106] For all binding and union and wholeness are secreted in the secrecy that cannot be grasped and cannot be known, that includes the desire of all desires.

Infinity does not abide being known, does not produce end or beginning. Primordial Nothingness[107] brought forth Beginning and End. Who is Beginning?[108] The highest point, beginning of all, the concealed one abiding in thought. And It produces End, 'the end of the matter' (Eccl 12:13). But there, no end. No desires, no lights, no sparks in that Infinity. All these lights and sparks are dependent on It but cannot comprehend. The only one who knows, yet without knowing, is the highest desire, concealed of all concealed, Nothingness. And when the highest point and the world that is coming[109] ascend, they know only the aroma, as one inhaling an aroma is sweetened."

God, Israel, and *Shekhinah*

"I will place My *mishkan* in your midst…" (Lev 26:11). My *mishkan* is *shekhinah*,[110] My *mishkan* is My *mashkon*,[111] My dwelling is My pledge, who has been seized on account of Israel's sins.

"I will place *mishkan*." My *mashkon*, literally Mine! A parable: One person loved another, and said, "My love for you is so high I want to live with you!" The other said, "How can I be sure that you will stay with me?" So he took all his most precious belongings and brought them to the other, saying "Here is a pledge to you that I will never part from you."

So, the Blessed Holy One desired to dwell with Israel. What did He do? He took His most precious possession and brought it down to them, saying, "Israel, now you have My pledge; so I will never part from you."

Even though the Blessed Holy One has removed Himself from us,

He has left a pledge in our hands, and we guard that treasure of His. If He wants His pledge, let Him come and dwell among us![112] So "I will place My *mishkan* in your midst" means "I will deposit a *mashkon* in your hands to ensure that I will dwell with you." Even though Israel is now in exile,[113] the pledge of the Blessed Holy One is with them, and they have never forsaken it.

"And My soul will not abhor you." A parable: One person loved his friend and wanted to live together. What did he do? He took his bed and brought it to his friend's house. He said, "My bed is now in your house, so I will not go far from you or your bed or your things." So, the Blessed Holy One said, "I will place My Dwelling in your midst and My soul will not abhor you. Here, My Bed is in your house.[114] Since My Bed is with you, you know I will not leave you; my soul will not abhor you."...

One night, Rabbi Yitshak and Rabbi Yehudah were staying in a village near the Sea of Tiberias. They rose at midnight.[115] Rabbi Yitshak said to Rabbi Yehudah, "Let us converse in words of Torah, for even though we are in this place, we must not separate ourselves from the Tree of Life."

Rabbi Yehudah opened and said, "'Moses took the Tent and pitched it outside the camp...' (Ex 33:7). Why? Moses said to himself, 'Since Israel has dealt falsely with the Blessed Holy One and exchanged His Glory, let His pledge be placed in the hands of a trustee until we see with whom it remains.' What is written? 'And he [Moses] returned to the camp, but his attendant, Joshua the son of Nun, a youth, did not stir out of the Tent' (Ex 33:11). Why Joshua? Because he was to Moses as the moon is to the sun.[116] He was worthy to guard the pledge; so he 'did not stir out of the tent.'

The Blessed Holy One said to Moses, 'Moses, this is not right! I have given My pledge to them! Even though they have sinned against Me, the pledge must remain with them so that I will not leave them. Do you want Me to depart from Israel and never return? Return My pledge to them, and for its sake I will not abandon them, wherever they are.' Even though Israel has sinned against God, they have not abandoned this pledge of His, and the Blessed Holy One has not taken it from them. So wherever Israel goes in exile, *Shekhinah* is with them. Therefore it is written: 'I will place My *mishkan* in your midst.' This has been established."

Rabbi Yitshak opened and said: "'My beloved is like a gazelle, like a young deer. There he stands behind our wall, gazing through the windows, peering through the holes' (Song 2:9).

Happy of Israel! They are privileged to hold this pledge of the Supreme King! For even though they are in exile, every new moon and Sabbath and festival the Blessed holy One comes to watch over them and to gaze at His pledge which is with them, His treasure. A parable: There was a king whose queen offended him. He expelled her from the palace. What did she do? She took his son, his precious beloved. Since the king was fond of her, he let him go with her. When the king began to yearn for the queen and her son he climbed up on roofs, ran down stairs, scaled walls; he peered through the holes in the walls just to see them! When he caught a glimpse of them he started to cry from behind the wall. Then he went away.

So, with Israel:[117] Even though they have left the palace of the King, they have not abandoned that pledge. And since the King loves them, He has left it with them. When the Holy King begins to yearn for the Queen and for Israel He climbs up on roofs, runs down stairs, scales walls; He peers through the holes in the walls just to see them! When He catches a glimpse of them, He starts to cry. As it is written: 'My beloved is like a gazelle, like a young deer,' jumping from wall to roof, from roof to wall. 'There he stands behind our wall' in the synagogues and houses of study.[118] 'Gazing through the windows,' for indeed, a synagogue must have windows.[119] 'Peering through the holes' to look at them, to look after them. Therefore Israel should rejoice on that day, for they know this, and they say, 'This is the day Y-H-V-H has made—let us rejoice and be happy' (Ps 118:24)."

Threshing Out the Secrets

It has been told: Rabbi Shim'on said to the Comrades, "How long will we sit on a one-legged stand?[120] It is written: 'Time to act for Y-H-V-H! They have violated Your Torah!' (Ps 119:126).[121] The days are few, the Creditor is pressing, a herald cries out every day![122] The Reapers of the Field are few and only at the edge of the vineyard![123] They do not watch or know where they are going, as they should. Assemble, Comrades, at the threshing house,[124] wearing coats of mail, with swords and spears in your hands![125] Arm yourselves with your array: Design, Wisdom, Intellect, Knowledge, and Vision, the power of Hands and Feet.[126] Enthrone and acknowledge the King who has the power of life and death, that words of truth may be ordained, words followed by high holy ones, happy to hear them and know them!"

Rabbi Shim'on sat down. He cried, and said, "Woe if I reveal! Woe if I do not reveal!" The Comrades were silent. Rabbi Abba rose and said to him, "If it pleases the Master to reveal, it is written: 'The secret of Y-H-V-H is for those who fear Him' (Ps 25:14), and these Comrades are God-fearing. They have already crossed the threshold of the Dwelling. Some have entered; some have emerged."[127]

It has been told: The Comrades were mustered before Rabbi Shim'on. Present were: Rabbi El'azar, his son, Rabbi Abba, Rabbi Yehudah, Rabbi Yose son of Jacob, Rabbi Yitshak, Rabbi Hizkiyah son of Rav, Rabbi Hiyya, Rabbi Yose, Rabbi Yeisa. Giving hands to Rabbi Shim'on, raising fingers above, they entered the field and amidst the trees sat down.

Rabbi Shim'on rose and prayed his prayer. He sat down among them, and said, "Let everyone place his hands on my breast." They placed their hands, and he took them. He opened and said: "'Cursed be the one who makes a carved or molten image, the work of the hands of an artisan, and sets it up in secret!'" (Deut 27:15).[128] They all responded, "Amen!"

Rabbi Shim'on opened and said: "'Time to act for Y-H-V-H.' Why is it time to act for Y-H-V-H? Because 'they have violated Your Torah!' What does this mean? The Torah up above is nullified if this Name is not arrayed perfectly.[129] The verse is addressed to the Ancient of Days.[130] It is written: 'O happy Israel! Who is like you?' (Deut 33:29), and it is written: 'Who is like You among the gods, Y-H-V-H?' (Ex 15:11)."[131] He called Rabbi El'azar, his son, and sat him in front, and Rabbi Abba on the other side. He said, "We are the sum of the whole![132] Now the pillars stand firm!"[133] They were silent. They heard a sound, and their knees knocked, one against the other. What sound? The sound of the Assembly on High assembling. Rabbi Shim'on rejoiced, and said, "'Y-H-V-H, I heard of You, I was afraid!' (Hab 3:2). There it was right to be afraid;[134] for us the word depends on love, as it is written: 'Love your neighbor as yourself,' 'Love Y-H-V-H your God,' 'Because Y-H-V-H loved you,' 'I have loved you.'[135]...

It has been told: When the desire arose in the Will of the White

Head[136] to manifest Its Glory, It arrayed, prepared, and generated from the Blinding Flash one spark,[137] radiating in 370 directions. The spark stood still. A pure aura emerged[138] whirling and breathed upon the spark. The spark congealed and one hard skull emerged,[139] emanating to four sides.[140] Surrounded by this pure aura, the spark was contained and absorbed.[141] Completely absorbed, you think? No, secreted within. That is how this skull emanated to its sides. This aura is the secret of secrets of the Ancient of Days. Through the breath hidden in this skull fire emanated on one side,[142] and air on the other,[143] with the pure aura standing over this side and pure fire over the other. What is fire doing here? It is not fire, but the spark surrounded by the pure aura illuminates 270 worlds, and from its side, judgment comes into being.[144] That is why this skull is called the Hard Skull.

Inside this skull lie ninety million worlds moving with it, relying upon it. Into this skull trickles dew from the White Head, constantly overflowing. From this dew shaken from Its Head the dead are destined to come to life.[145] It is a dew composed of two colors: from the aspect of the White Head it is imbued with a white embracing all whites,[146] but when it settles upon the Head of the Impatient One red appears.[147] Like this crystal that is white: the color red appears within the color white. Therefore it is written: 'Many of those who sleep in the dust of the earth will awake; these to eternal life, those to shame and eternal horror!' (Dan 12:2). 'To eternal life' because they deserve the white that comes from the aspect of the Ancient of Days, the Patient One. 'To shame and eternal horror' because they deserve the red of the Impatient One. All is contained in that dew, as it is written: 'Your dew is a dew of lights' (Isa 26:19);[148] 'lights,' two of them! That dew that trickles, trickles every day to the Apple Orchard,[149] colored white and red. This skull lights up in two colors, on this side and that. From this pure aura one-and-a-half million worlds emanate through the skull to His face. That is why He is called the Impatient One. When necessary,[150] His face expands and becomes long-suffering, for then He is gazing into the Face of the Ancient of Ancients[151] and He feels compassion for the world...."

It has been told: Before they left that threshing place Rabbi Yose son of Jacob, Rabbi Hizkiyah, and Rabbi Yeisa died. The Comrades saw holy angels carrying them off in a canopy. Rabbi Shim'on said a word, and they settled down. He cried, and said, "Perhaps, God forbid, a decree has been issued for us to be punished because through us has been revealed something not revealed since the day Moses stood on Mt. Sinai, as it is written: 'He was there with Y-H-V-H forty days and forty nights…" (Ex 34:28).[152] What am I doing here? Were they punished because of this?" He heard a voice: "Happy are you, Rabbi Shim'on! Happy is your portion! Happy are the Comrades who stand with you! For something not revealed to all the powers above has been revealed to you! But come and see what is written: 'At the cost of his firstborn, he shall lay its foundations; at the cost of his youngest, he shall set up its gates' (Josh 6:26). All the more so, for by intense desire, their souls joined the Divine the moment they were taken. Happy is their portion! They rose in perfection!"

It has been told: While the worlds were being revealed, those above and those below were shaken, and a voice stirred through 250 worlds,[153] for ancient words were being revealed below! While the souls of these ones were being sweetened with those words, their souls departed by a kiss and were bound in that canopy.[154] The angels took them away and lifted them above. Why these ones? Because on a previous occasion they had entered and not emerged. All the others had entered and emerged. Rabbi Shim'on said, "How happy is the portion of these three! Happy is our portion in the world that is coming, because of this!" The voice resounded: "You who cleave to Y-H-V-H your God are alive, every one of you today!" (Deut 4:4).[155] They rose and walked on. Wherever they looked, aromas rose. Rabbi Shim'on said, "This proves that the world is being blessed because of us!" Everyone's face shone, and human beings could not look at them.

It has been told: Ten entered, seven emerged. Rabbi Shim'on was happy; Rabbi Abba was sad. One day Rabbi Shim'on was sitting, and Rabbi Abba was with him. Rabbi Shim'on said a word, and they saw these three. Angels were carrying them gloriously, showing them treasures and threshing houses in the sky,[156] bringing them to mountains of pure balsam.[157] Rabbi Abba's mind was eased.

It has been told: From that day on, the Comrades did not leave the house of Rabbi Shim'on. When Rabbi Shim'on revealed secrets, only they were present. Rabbi Shim'on called out to them: "The seven of us are the eyes of Y-H-V-H, as it is written, 'These seven are the eyes of Y-H-V-H' (Zech 4:10). This verse was said for us!"[158] Rabbi Abba said, "We are six lights shining from the seventh. You are the seventh of all! The six exist only because of the seventh. All depends on the seventh!"[159] Rabbi Yehudah called him "Sabbath, source of blessing for all six, as it is written: 'Sabbath for Y-H-V-H' (Ex 20:10), 'Holy to Y-H-V-H' (Ex 16:23). Just as Sabbath is holy to Y-H-V-H, so Rabbi Shim'on is Sabbath, holy to Y-H-V-H!"

The Rabbis Encounter a Child

Rabbi Yitshak and Rabbi Yehudah were out on the road. They reached the village of Sikhnin and stayed there with a woman who had one little son who went to school every day. That day he left school and came home. He saw these wise men. His mother said to him, "Approach these distinguished men; you will gain blessings from them!" He approached them and suddenly turned back. He said to his mother, "I don't want to go near them because they haven't recited *Shema'*[160] today, and I have been taught: 'Anyone who has not recited *Shema'* at its proper time is under a ban that entire day.'"[161]

They heard this and were amazed. Raising their hands, they blessed him. They said, "Indeed, it is so! Today we were engaged with a bride and groom who did not have what they needed and were delaying their union.[162] There was no one to engage in helping them, so we engaged, and we did not recite *Shema'* at its proper time. One who is busying doing a *mitzvah* is exempt from another *mitzvah*."[163] Then they said, "My son, how did you know?"

He said, "I knew by the smell of your clothes when I came near you." They were amazed. They sat down, washed their hands, and broke bread. Rabbi Yehudah's hands were dirty, and he blessed before he washed.[164] The boy said to them, "If you are students of Rabbi Shema'yah the *Hasid*,[165] you should not have blessed with filthy hands. One who blessed with filthy hands should be put to death."[166]

The child[167] opened and said: "'When they enter the Tent of Meeting, they shall wash with water so they will not die...' (Ex 30:20). We learn from this verse that one who is not careful and appears in the presence of the King with filthy hands should be put to death. Why? Because the hands of a human being inhabit the height of the world.[168]

There is one finger on the human hand: the finger that Moses raised.[169] It is written: 'You shall make bars of acacia wood: five for the planks of one side of the Dwelling, five for the planks of the other side of the Dwelling.'[170] And it is written: 'The center bar in the middle of the planks shall run from end to end' (Ex 26:26–28). Now you might say that the center bar is another one, not included in those five. Not so! That center bar is one of those five. Two on this side, two on that side, and one in the middle.[171] This is the Center Bar, Pillar of Jacob, Secret of Moses! Corresponding to this are the five fingers on the human hand. The center bar is in the middle, greatest and highest of all. All the others exist through it. Those five bars are the five hundred years through which the Tree of Life extends.[172] The Holy Covenant[173] is aroused by the five fingers of the hand. It is a secret word that I have spoken!

That is why all the blessings of the priest depend on the fingers.[174] Moses' hand was spread out because of this. If they embody all this, doesn't it follow that they must be clean when with them one blesses the Blessed Holy One? For by them and their paradigm, the Holy Name is blessed! You who are wise, how could you be so careless? Didn't you serve Rabbi Shema'yah the *Hasid*? He himself said: 'All filth and all dirt heighten the Other Side, for the Other Side feeds on filth and dirt.'[175] That is why washing after a meal is compulsory, a compulsory offering!"

They were amazed and could not speak. Rabbi Yehudah said, "My son, what is the name of your father?" The child was silent for a moment. He rose and went over to his mother and kissed her. He said, "Mother, these wise men have asked me about father. Should I tell them?" His mother said, "My son, have you tested them?" He said, "I've tested them and found them lacking!" His mother whispered to him, and he returned to them.

He said, "You have asked about father. He has departed from the world, but whenever holy devotees are walking on the road he appears as a donkey driver behind them. If you are so high and holy, how could you have missed him following you as a donkey driver? Ah, but right from the start I saw who you were, and now I see through you! For father never sees a donkey and fails to goad it from behind so he can share the yoke of Torah. Since you weren't worthy enough for father to follow you, I won't say who father is!"[176]

Rabbi Yehudah said to Rabbi Yitshak, "It seems that this child is not a human being!" They began to eat, and that child spoke words of Torah, new discoveries of Torah....

The Wedding Celebration

It has been told: On the day that Rabbi Shim'on was to leave the world, while he was arranging his affairs, the Comrades assembled at his house. Present were Rabbi El'azar, his son, Rabbi Abba, and the other Comrades. The house was full.

Rabbi Shim'on raised his eyes and saw that the house was filled. He cried, and said: "The other time I was ill,[177] Rabbi Pinhas son of Ya'ir was in my presence. I was already selecting my place in Paradise next to Ahiyah of Shiloh[178] when they extended my life until now! When I returned, fire was whirling in front of me; it has never gone out. No human has entered without permission. Now I see that it has gone out, and the house is filled!"

While they were sitting Rabbi Shim'on opened his eyes and saw what he saw;[179] fire whirled through the house. Everyone left. Rabbi El'azar, his son, and Rabbi Abba remained; the other Comrades sat outside.

Rabbi Shim'on said to Rabbi El'azar, his son, "Go out and see if Rabbi Yitshak is here, for I have been surety for him.[180] Tell him to arrange his affairs and sit by my side. Happy is his portion!" Rabbi Shim'on rose and laughed in delight. He said, "Where are the Comrades?" Rabbi El'azar rose and brought them in.

They sat in front of him. Rabbi Shim'on raised his hands and prayed a prayer. He rejoiced and said, "Those Comrades who were present at the threshing house will convene here!"[181] Everyone left. Rabbi El'azar, his son, Rabbi Abba, Rabbi Yehudah, Rabbi Yose, and Rabbi Hiyya remained.

Meanwhile, Rabbi Yitshak came in. Rabbi Shim'on said to him, "Your portion is so fine! So much joy will be yours today!" Rabbi Abba sat behind him and Rabbi El'azar in front. Rabbi Shim'on said, "Now is a time of favor! I want to enter without shame into the world that is coming. Holy words, until now unrevealed; I want to reveal in the presence of *Shekhinah*, so it will not be said that I left the world deficiently. Until now they were hidden in my heart as a password to the world that is coming. I will arrange you like this: Rabbi Abba will write; Rabbi El'azar, my son, will repeat; the other Comrades will meditate within."

Rabbi Abba rose from behind him; Rabbi El'azar, his son, sat in front. Rabbi Shim'on said, "Rise, my son, for someone else will sit in that place." Rabbi El'azar rose.

Rabbi Shim'on enwrapped himself and sat down.

He opened and said: "'The dead cannot praise *Yah*, nor any who go down to Dumah'[182] (Ps 115:17). 'The dead cannot praise *Yah*' the ones who are really dead! For the Blessed Holy One is alive and He dwells among the living, not with those called 'dead.' The verse concludes: 'nor any who go down to Dumah.' All those who go down to Dumah remain in hell. It is different with those called 'living,' for the Blessed Holy One wants them to be honored."

Rabbi Shim'on said: "It is so different now than at the threshing house. There the Blessed Holy One and His chariots convened. Now He is accompanied by the righteous from the Garden of Eden! This did not happen before! The Blessed Holy One wants the righteous to be honored more than He wants Himself to be honored! So it is written concerning Jeroboam. He offered incense to idols and worshiped them; yet the Blessed Holy One was patient. But as soon as he stretched out his hand against Ido the prophet, his hand dried up, as it is written: 'His hand dried up....' (1 Kgs 13:4). Not because he worshiped idols, but because he threatened Ido the prophet! Now the Blessed Holy One wants us to be honored and all of them are coming with Him! Here is Rav Hamnuna Sava surrounded by seventy of the righteous adorned with crowns, each one shining from the splendor of the luster of the Holy Ancient One, Concealed of all Concealed! He is coming to hear in joy these words I am about to speak."

He was about to sit down when he exclaimed: "Look! Here is Rabbi Pinhas son of Ya'ir! Prepare his place!" The Comrades trembled; they got up and moved to the outskirts of the house. Rabbi El'azar and Rabbi Abba remained with Rabbi Shim'on.

Rabbi Shim'on said: "In the threshing house, we were found to be: all the Comrades speaking, I among them. Now I alone will speak; all are listening to my words, those above and those below. Happy is my portion this day."

Rabbi Shim'on opened and said: "'I am my Beloved's, His desire is upon me' (Song 7:11). All the days that I have been bound to this world, I have been bound in a single bond with the Blessed Holy One.[183] That is why now 'His desire is upon me'! He and His holy company have come to hear in joy concealed words and praise for the

Holy Ancient One,[184] Concealed of all Concealed! Separate, separated from all, yet not separate! For all is attached to It, and It is attached to all. It is all! Ancient of all Ancients! Concealed of all Concealed! Arrayed and not arrayed. Arrayed in order to sustain all; not arrayed, for It is not to be found. When arrayed, It generates nine lights, flaming from It, from Its array. Those lights, sparkling, flashing, radiate, emanate to all sides.... Until now these words were concealed, for I was scared to reveal; now they have been revealed! Yet it is revealed before the Holy Ancient One that I have not acted for my own honor, nor for the honor of my family, but rather so I will not enter His palace in shame. Furthermore, I see that the Blessed Holy One and all these righteous ones approve: I see all of them rejoicing in this, my wedding celebration![185] All of them are invited, in that world, to my wedding celebration! Happy is my portion!"

Rabbi Abba said: "When the Holy Spark, the High Spark, finished this word he raised his hands and cried and laughed. He wanted to reveal one word. He said, 'I have been troubled by this word all my days and now they are not giving me permission!' Summoning up his courage, he sat and moved his lips and bowed three times. No one could look at his place, certainly not at him! He said, 'Mouth, mouth, you have attained so much! Your spring has not dried up! Your spring flows endlessly! For you we read: "A river issues from Eden" (Gen 2:10), and it is written: "Like a spring whose waters do not fail" (Isa 58:11).[186] Now I avow: All the days I have been alive, I have yearned to see this day! Now my desire is crowned with success. This day itself is crowned! Now I want to reveal words in the presence of the Blessed Holy One; all those words are adorning my head like a crown! This day will not miss its mark like the other day, for this whole day is mine! I have now begun revealing words so I will not enter shamefully into the world that is coming. I have begun! I will speak!...

I have seen that all those sparks sparkle from the High Spark,[187] Hidden of all Hidden! All are levels of enlightenment. In the light of each and every level there is revealed what is revealed. All those lights are connected: this light to that light, that light to this light, one shining into the other, inseparable, one from the other. The light of each and every spark, called Adornments of the King, Crowns of the King[188]—each one shines into, joins onto the light within, within, not separating without. So all rise to one level. All is crowned with one word; no separating one from the other. It and Its Name is one.[189]

The light that is revealed is called the Garment of the King. The light within, within is a concealed light. In that light dwells the Ineffable One, the Unrevealed. All those sparks and all those lights sparkle from the Holy Ancient One, Concealed of all Concealed, the High Spark. Upon reflecting, all those lights emanating—there is nothing but the High Spark, hidden and unrevealed!...'"[190]

Rabbi Abba said: "Before the Holy Spark finished saying 'life' (Ps 133:3), his words subsided. I was still writing, intending to write more but I heard nothing. I did not raise my head: the light was overwhelming; I could not look. Then I started trembling. I heard a voice calling: 'Length of days and years of life...' (Prov 3:2). I heard another voice: 'He asked You for life...' (Ps 21:5).

All day long, the fire in the house did not go out. No one reached him; no one could: light and fire surrounded him! All day long, I lay on the ground and wailed. After the fire disappeared I saw the Holy Spark, Holy of Holies, leaving the world, enwrapped, lying on his right, his face smiling.

Rabbi El'azar, his son, rose, took his hands and kissed them. As for me, I licked the dust from the bottom of his feet. The Comrades wanted to cry but could not utter a sound. Finally they let out a cry, but Rabbi El'azar, his son, fell three times, unable to open his mouth. Finally he opened and said, 'Father! Father! Three there were! Turned back into one! Now the animals will wander off![191] Birds are flying away, sinking into the Bowels of the Great Sea! All the Comrades are drinking blood!'"[192]

Rabbi Hiyya rose to his feet and said, "Until now the Holy Spark has looked after us; now is the time to engage in honoring him!" Rabbi El'azar and Rabbi Abba rose. They carried him in a truckle made out of a gangplank—who has seen the confusion of the Comrades?—and the whole house was fragrant. They lifted him onto his bed; only Rabbi El'azar and Rabbi Abba attended him. Truculent stingers and shield-bearing warriors from Sepphoris came and beset them.[193] The people of Meron ganged together and shouted, for they feared he would not be buried there.

After the bed emerged from the house it rose into the air; fire blazed before it. They heard a voice: "Come and enter! Assemble for the wedding celebration of Rabbi Shim'on! 'He shall come to peace; they shall rest on their couches'" (Isa 57:2).

As he entered the cave, they heard a voice from inside: "This is the man who shook the earth, who made kingdoms tremble! Many open mouths of accusation up in heaven subside today because of you, Rabbi Shim'on son of Yohai! His Lord prides Himself on him every day. Happy is his portion above and below! Many sublime treasures lie in store for him! Of him it is said: 'As for you, go to the end and take your rest; you will rise for your reward at the end of days'" (Dan 12:13).

Zohar Hadash: The Hidden Midrash to the Book of Lamentations

The inhabitants of Babylon sent this missive to the inhabitants of the Holy Land:

> Weeping befits us, eulogizing becomes us, for the destruction of God's house, since we are dispersed amongst the nations. Thus, we should be the first to lament, we should be the first to explicate the puzzle which the World's Master has sent to bewail the destruction of His House.

The inhabitants of the Holy Land responded, sending this missive to the Babylonians:

> It is surely right for you, dispersed among the nations, outside the borders of the Holy Land, to bewail yourselves. For you have gone forth from light to darkness, like a servant who has departed from his master's house. But it is we who should weep, we should eulogize, for the Blessed Holy One has sent us the Book of Lamentations. It is we who are the children of the Mistress divine; we the members of her household who know the glory of World's master...when we had sinned against our father, and the strap thrashed out to whip us, she stood before us and received the King's lashing, defending us, as it is written, "He was wounded on account of our sins, crushed because of our iniquities...by his bruises we were

healed" (Isa 53:5). Alas, now we no longer have a mother. Woe for us! Woe for you!...

"Alas! Lonely sits the city..." (Lam 1:1).

R. Pinhas opened his discourse: "'A cry is heard in Ramah, wailing, bitter weeping, Rachel weeping for her children. She refuses to be comforted, for her children who are gone' (Jer 31:15).

When the Temple was destroyed and set ablaze, a voice went and aroused itself over the graves of the primordial fathers. It said: 'Primordial fathers, you are slumbering in your sleep and are unaware of the world's suffering. The children whom you raised with great labor, and brought up with great faith in God, die and are slaughtered. They go forth into exile among their enemies, their hands tied behind their backs, perishing from starvation, their houses put to flame. Where is your compassion?! Where is your faith?! Come, arouse yourselves for their sakes!'

The fathers and mother woke immediately. They went before Moses, saying to him: 'Moses, faithful shepherd! Where are those children? Where did you leave them?' Moses aroused himself immediately and in their company went to Joshua. Moses said to him: 'The Children of these fathers, the children of Israel, whose charge God gave me, whom I left in your hand—where are they?'

Joshua answered, saying: 'Our Master Moses. I left them in the holy land. I left them, dividing the land for them in accord with a lottery as you commanded me. I left all of them, each in accord with his inheritance and lot.'

Immediately, all of them journeyed to the holy land. They found it destroyed, bereft of human voice. They entered the Sanctuary and found it consumed by flame. They lamented, producing a sound of bitter weeping so strong that it reached the heights of heaven and all of the celestial angels wept with them from on high.

The Blessed Holy One was himself aroused and came to them. He found them grieving bitterly, with crying voices amidst the dust of the Sanctuary. He said to them: 'My soul's beloved—what are you doing here? Why is my beloved in my house?'

Grandfather Abraham was the first to rise. He addressed the world's maker: 'You know how I walked before You in the path of truth. Ten times you tested me; I withstood them all. Where are my children? For I do not hear their voices within the land in which you promised to sustain them.'

The Blessed Holy One said to him: 'Alas, Abraham my soul's beloved! "Holy flesh has passed away from you" (Jer 11:15): your descendants annulled the holy covenant and engaged in idolatrous worship. For this reason my anger waxed against them. I was long suffering for your sake, but they did not return to me.'

When Abraham heard this, he said: 'May all of their sins against the holiness of Your Name be erased among the nations until You will to return them to You.' All of them acted thusly and departed.

Yet Rachel remained there and raised her voice in the most embittered of cries.

The Blessed Holy One said to her: 'Rachel, for what reason are you crying?' She said to him: 'Shall I not cry? Where are my children? How have they sinned against you?' God answered: 'They brought My rival before Me; they introduced it into My house!' Immediately Rachel retorted: 'Did I not do more than that? I brought my rival into my own house!' As it is taught, 'Jacob told Rachel that he was her father's kinsman...' (Gen 29:12). Jacob said, 'Marry me.' Rachel said, 'Yes. But I have a sister who is older than I. I fear my father for he is a trickster.' Immediately 'Jacob told Rachel that he was her father's kinsman': akin to him in trickery. He transmitted secret signs to her. When Leah entered that night, Rachel said: 'Now my sister will be shamed.' She went and taught her the signs. For this reason she said to God: 'Have I not done more? For I brought my rival into my house! And You, of whom it is written that You are compassionate, gracious and long-suffering. You should have overlooked their sins!'

She accepted no comfort from everything which He said to her, as it is written: 'A cry is heard in Ramah, wailing, bitter weeping. Rachel weeping for her children. She refuses to be comforted for her children who are gone.' She had no desire to receive comfort. Why? Because it was not like former days when He rested among them. But rather, He had ascended above. Because God was no longer among her children she refused consolation until He promised her: 'Restrain your voice from weeping, your eyes from shedding tears, for there is a reward for your labor...your children shall return to their country' (Jer 39:16).

As Rachel acted in the worlds below, so too *shekhinah* engaged in the worlds above. So the Aramaic translation renders our verse: 'In the celestial heights a voice is heard.'[194] The *shekhinah* cries for her children. At that time her lamentations aroused sixty myriads of heavenly angels. Before her all commenced to cry. At that moment a voice was heard piercing far, far to the Aravot heaven, shaking on a thousand worlds, hidden from creation's day, from their rest. To the height of heaven that voice penetrated. What is the height of heaven? It is that expanse, whose awe-inspiring gleam is like crystal, extending over the heads of the *hayyot* (Ezek 1:22).

Then Mother revealed herself to Daughter, saying to her: 'Restrain your voice from weeping...' (Jer 31:16). Then *shekhinah* departed that place, entering into exile with her troops, dispersing into multiple directions, so that all might experience banishment, *shekhinah* remaining alone."

"Alas!" said Rabbi Nehumia: "Who said this? That world-to-come, supernal, hidden within." *Eikhah*: Just a breathing out of air. For this reason the word is spirit-breath; neither tongue, teeth, nor lips participate in saying it. Mother inquired concerning her daughter—Is this the "crowing of Kir" (Isa 22:5), the great lord and master?

"[Lonely] sits...." Sits rather than stands. At first *shekhinah* stood, all of her troops standing with her. Now desolate, she sits. All alone, as it is written, "he shall sit alone" (Lev 13:46), like one defiled. "The maidservant inheriting her mistress" (Prov 30:23). The defiler assuming her place....

We have taught: "Every night, from the heights of heaven to the worlds below, from the worlds below to the heavens above, Zion's voice, embittered pain, makes itself heard." As it is written: "From on high the Lord roars; from His holy dwelling He makes Himself heard, He roars aloud over His earthly abode" (Jer 25:30).

At the onset of night, she [*shekhinah*] sets herself to weeping, roaring from the heavenly heights above. She descends below, to the place of the outer altar, views her place destroyed, utterly defiled, every place abandoned. Lowing, wailing, crying out in a bitter voice, she says: "O altar, My altar! My sustenance. Sating Me with oblations of water and wine, sacrifices pure and holy. From all of the holy people, the great multitudes of hosts, drew their delight and rejoiced, consuming the delicacies, sharing their portions with the heights of heavens. The enemies placed upon you, the corpses of pious saints, my children slaughtered upon you. Their blood desolates me!"...

From each of the world's four quarters, six thousand holy angels who consumed the sacrifices daily, descend with her, lamenting and mourning the altar of the burnt offerings. There had been more, but their numbers diminished. Even those forces which stood outside, within the dimension of that other spirit, who were nurtured from those limbs and fat particles burnt through the onset of night, cried, lowed and lamented that altar. "Woe to the donkey which has lost its crib, the place from which it drew its nourishment!"

Who has seen anything like the mourning of those holy servitors of the celestial Lady, spanning the worlds terrestrial to those celestial, from the worlds above to those below!

At midnight He enters into the point called "Zion," the place of the Holy of Holies. He sees it destroyed and defiled, Her dwelling-place and her bed. She breaks out in wailing, flying up from below, down from above. She looks at the place of the cherubim and calls out with a bitter cry: "My bed! My bed! The place of my dwelling!" Concerning this place it is written: "Upon My bed at night" (Song 3:1). "My bed": the bedstead of the celestial lady.

She utters a cry and says: "My bedstead! The place of my sanctuary! The locus of precious rubies! The inner sanctum's screen and the ark's cover! Sixty thousand myriads of precious gems were affixed within you, meticulously arrayed rows upon rows, all reflecting each other. You were plated with rows of pomegranates upon all four sides. For your sake the Master of the World sustained the universe. My husband would come to me, lie between my arms. At that time, he fulfilled my every wish, each and every desire. He would come to me, making me his dwelling-place, taking his pleasure between my breasts.

Oh my bed, my bed! Don't you remember when I would come to you in joy, in the heart's beauty, how myriads of youths would precede me, to receive me, their wings rustling in joy. Your very dust would rise from its place, they would view my exaltations. From the ark of the Torah placed there, sustenance would go out to the entire world, light and blessing for all. I look for my husband but he is not here. I search in every direction.

At that time, when my husband would come to me, surrounded by countless righteous sons, these angelic maidens prepared to greet him. From afar, I would hear the sound of the clustered bells ringing between his legs, so that his approach might be audible before he came to me. My maidens would praise and glorify the Blessed Holy One. Then they would depart, we would be alone, embracing in kisses of love.

My husband, O my husband! Where have you gone? Now is the time that I would gaze upon you. In every direction I seek you but you are not there. Where can I gaze upon you and not put my claim upon you. This is your place, your time, to come to me. Here I await you, but you have forgotten me. Don't you remember the days of our love, when I would lie with you so firmly that I was impressed with your image, your likeness impressed upon mine, and mine upon you, like a seal embossing its impression upon a document. So I left my image upon you so that you might delight in it, when I was among my host."

Crying, she moaned and called: "My husband, my husband, my eyes' light grows darkened. Don't you remember when you stretched your right hand under mine and I took my joy in that abundance of peace, your right hand embracing me like a brother's, and with kisses you swearing to me that your love would never cease? You swore to me: 'If I forget Jerusalem may my right hand wither!' (Ps 137:5). Yet by you I have been forgotten!

Don't you remember how I stood, six hundred thousand perfect individuals before you at Mt. Sinai accepting your kingship? With them I crowned you, more than with all the other nations, we followed you in accord with your will. That maidservant[195] killed them in their thousands and myriads; I protested not. All were lost in the desert, where you left them. Their small children I brought to stand before you in this land. I separated them to stand before you in accord with your will.

My husband! My husband! Remember how many holy children I brought before you in every generation. In the days of David and Solomon his son? Do you not remember how much good they did before you? Is it fitting for you to remember sins and not merits. How has it all been turned upon us? I seek you, but you are not; I inquire after my children, but they are not. I inquire after the sanctity of this place; it is defiled. On account of this place the world in its entirety attained peace. At that time the dogs did not howl, all was harmonious."

Shekhinah moans and laments, the inhabitants of the worlds celestial and the dogs below join her, at the onset of the third watch.

Departing, she comes to the place of the altar of incense, moaning, crying, she descends above, and finds one of the two cherubim who had served her before (for from the time of the destruction she had retained but one). From her that young child who remains nurses lamentations and tears.

> Then the Blessed Holy One encounters her, comes down and converses with her. As it is written: "Refrain from crying, your eyes from tears, for there is hope for your future" (Jer 31:15). Of this it is taught: "[During the third watch of night] an infant nurses at its mother's breast, a wife converses with her husband" (b. Berakhot 3a).

CHAPTER 3

The Safed Renaissance and Its Legacy

PART ONE: THE KABBALISTIC WORLD OF SAFED

Introduction

The tragic and shocking expulsion of Jews from Spain in 1492 ended a golden period of Iberian Jewish creativity that had slowly been eroding. The exiled Spanish Jews were dispersed throughout the Mediterranean and Europe, some as individuals and others as whole communities. Many took up residence within the borders of the Ottoman Empire. The recent Turkish conquest of the land of Israel allowed Jews to settle there for the first time in hundreds of years. While the economic situation in much of the land was rather poor, the small Galilean town of Safed boasted of financial opportunity and stable living conditions. Particularly attractive to Jewish mystics was the fact that this mountain city is located near the burial ground of several important sages, including Rabbi Shim'on bar Yohai, the illustrious hero of the *Zohar*. This confluence of conditions allowed sixteenth-century Safed to become the home of a great revival of Jewish spritiual disciplines, including *halakhah*, poetry, biblical interpretation, and above all, Kabbalah.[1]

The theology developed by the Safed Kabbalists is grounded in motifs and symbols inherited from earlier mystical traditions. These Kabbalists were particularly inspired by the *Zohar*, whose teachings on the *sefirot*, the process of creation, and the human soul lie at the very heart of the Safed renaissance. The works of the Safed Kabbalists, especially those of Rabbi Yitshak Luria, are distinguished by their theoretical complexity and abstraction.[2] Yet the intricacy of their theology should not imply that the contribution of the Safed Kabbalists is restricted to dry, intellectual speculation. Mystical acts of piety and religious rituals formed the core of their spiritual lives. For these mystics, correctly performing the commandments not only meant fulfilling their strict legal parameters; it also required one to know the appropriate contemplative intentions (*kavvanot*). All devotional activities were to be accompanied by the correct "unifications" (*yihudim*), or mystical meditations on that action's role in restoring the cosmos to a state of equilibrium and healing the intra-divine fracture between the *sefirot*. In addition to this universal goal, striving for the more personal experience of *devekut* through traditional mediums of prayer and study was also crucial for the Safed Kabbalists.[3] These two values were thoroughly intertwined in their religious lives.

The Safed mystics invented new rituals to express their devotional yearnings, and they revived old ceremonies that had been either abandoned or restricted to elite individuals. Their practices included rising each night at midnight to mourn the destruction of the Temple, remaining awake and studying Torah all night on Shavu'ot, special gatherings to celebrate *Rosh Hodesh* (the "New Moon"), frequent immersions in the *mikveh* to impart ritual purity, and confessional rites for all members of their mystical fellowships.[4] They formed close-knit fraternities intentionally modeled after the group surrounding Rabbi Shim'on bar Yohai in the *Zohar*. Ethical behavior and devotional commitment to one another were upheld as spiritual ideals. The Safed Kabbalists found particular inspiration in the rituals of the Sabbath table. It was they who established the custom of *kabbalat shabbat*, going into the fields on Friday evenings to welcome the Sabbath with liturgical song.[5] This practice has been adopted in some form by nearly all Jewish communities around the world. The spiritual customs of the Safed community are most visible in its conduct literature (*hanhagot*), a selection of which has been translated below.[6]

Acute messianic longing occupied a critical place in the worldview of the Safed Kabbalists. Integral to this process of redemption was uplifting the exiled and fallen *shekhinah*, accomplished through performing the commandments with the correct mystical intentions. The

Safed mystics even physically reenacted *shekhinah*'s plight by temporarily going into self-imposed exile. Some of these Kabbalists were also rigorous ascetics, perhaps a sublimated expression of deep feelings of guilt over Jewish exile. In addition to frequent fasting, as well as more intense acts of self-mortification, the material world was treated with great scorn and disdain. Drawing near to God required one to withdraw from all physical pleasures to the greatest degree possible, but it is interesting to note that this pietistic asceticism did not seem to conflict with the mandate for constant joy in all religious service.

A brief survey of the most important figures of the Safed circle will give the reader some context necessary for understanding the translations below:

RABBI YOSEF KARO (1488–1575) was a legal scholar par excellence. He authored the *Shulhan Arukh, an* authoritative and comprehensive legal code still revered as the last word in matters of Jewish law, as well as an enormously influential commentary on the *Arba'ah Turim* intended for scholars. In his mystical diary, *Maggid Mesharim*, Karo recorded a series of visitations by a heavenly spirit (*maggid*) that took place over several decades. He studied Torah with this spirit, who is sometimes described as the spirit of the Mishnah and other times as *shekhinah* herself, though these mystical experiences did not influence his legal rulings. While not published until the mid-1700s, *Maggid Mesharim* circulated in manuscript, and rumors and legends about Karo's visitations spread far and wide.[7] This type of *maggid* was not uncommon in sixteenth-century Safed, but Karo's was one of the best known cases.[8]

RABBI MOSHE CORDOVERO (1522–70) was the most prominent pre-Lurianic mystic in Safed.[9] His *Pardes Rimmonim* (1592) is a systematic treatment of the major issues of Kabbalah, including Creation, the structure of the *sefirot*, the divine names, and the mystical dimensions of language. His other works include *Or Ne'erav* (1587), a more accessible introduction to Kabbalah; *Or Yakar* (1965), an enormous commentary on the *Zohar* that remained in manuscript until recently; and the concise but influential *Tomer Devorah* (1589), a mystical guide to character development based on the *sefirot*.[10] Historically, Luria's system tended to dominate later kabbalistic discourse, but Cordovero's writings were also widely read by later Jewish mystics and were particularly influential on the Hasidic movement.[11]

RABBI SHLOMO ALKABETS (1505–76) was a close disciple of Cordovero. His mystical poem *Lekha Dodi* (*Come, My Beloved*), translated below, is a remarkable expression of lyrical talent and mystical symbolism. This work has several interwoven motifs: the longing for messianic future, the restoration of Jerusalem, and the unification of the blessed Holy One (*tif'eret*) with his female consort *shekhinah* (the *sefirah malkhut*) on the Sabbath. *Lekha Dodi* is now recited each Friday night as a part of *kabbalat shabbat* in nearly all Jewish congregations.[12]

RABBI MOSHE ALSHEKH (1508–93) was a student of Karo and, by his own description, an immensely popular preacher. He authored lengthy and involved commentaries on a number of biblical books. Alshekh was once the teacher of Hayyim Vital, who later excluded him from the Lurianic study circles.[13]

RABBI YITSHAK LURIA (1534–72) lived in Safed for less than three years, but his personality and teachings define the historical memory of the renaissance. Luria was born in Jerusalem but spent most of his young life in Egypt, where he received his religious training in Talmud, *halakhah*, and quite possibly Kabbalah. He underwent a period of self-imposed solitude in the Nile, during which he began to write his own mystical works. He arrived in Safed at the end of 1569 or early 1570 and immediately became a central figure in the kabbalistic community. Luria regarded Cordovero as his teacher, becoming a leader only after Cordovero's death. Luria's doctrines were largely original, and he claimed that they were based on new divine revelations. He fashioned himself as a mystical leader akin to Rabbi Shim'on bar Yohai, the hero of the *Zohar*.[14] In addition to being described as an extremely moral, pietistic figure, Luria was also remembered as a charismatic clairvoyant with access to esoteric knowledge. Sacred histories about his life and exploits began to emerge shortly after his death, and in later traditions he is generally referred to as *Ha-Elohi Rabbi Yitshak*, the Saintly Rabbi Yitshak, or by the acronym ARI (the holy "Lion").[15]

Yitshak Luria wrote very little, leaving behind only a few Sabbath hymns and short commentaries on parts of the *Zohar*. The vast majority of his teachings were preserved in the writings of his students. They reveal that Lurianic Kabbalah is perhaps the most complicated and abstract Jewish mystical system. As in the Kabbalah of Gerona and the *Zohar*, the process of creation is absolutely central to his worldview, but Luria describes the process of emanation in new terms. His creation myth begins with an infinite Deity, abstract and entirely boundless (*Ein Sof*). Yet, because of a desire to allow for a world with individuated existence, the Infinite One withdrew from a certain area and left a vacuum in which finite creation could formally take place.[16] This act of self-imposed divine contraction is known as *tsimtsum*. Into this void was projected a beam of light, refracted through an array of ten vessels—the *sefirot*, also referred to as *admon kadmon* (the "Primal Man").

Yet, in the tragic moment of *shevirat ha-kelim*, the vessels shattered and sparks of the light were scattered throughout the world. Their broken forms are the *kelippot* ("husks"), which obscure the sparks and must be broken by acts of devotion. After this tragedy, the *sefirot*/*adam kadmon* are emanated into the void once more, but are now recombined into five basic *partsufim*, or clusters of *sefirot* along with their various symbolic associations. These are: *arikh anpin* ("Long-faced" or "Compassionate One"), *abba* ("Father"), *imma* ("Mother"), *ze'ir anpin* ("Short-faced" or "Impatient One"), and *nukba* ("Feminine"). Luria grafted the map of the *partsufim* onto the well-established system of ten *sefirot* and four worlds. In this new configuration, every one of the *partsufim* contains all of the *sefirot*, multiplied by each of four worlds. The result is a nearly endless matrix of combinations of *sefirot* intricately woven together. Humankind is charged with the enormous responsibility of *tikkun*, fixing the discord between the *sefirot* caused by the initial *shevirah*, uplifting the scattered sparks and aligning the various elements of the Godhead, thereby ensuring the flow of blessing and effluence into the world.

Related to this understanding of Creation and the complicated array of *sefirot* is the Lurianic doctrine of "soul roots" (*shoreshei ha-neshamah*). Each human soul is a combination of three different parts that emerged from a specific location in one of the *partsufim*. All transgressions sully the various dimensions of the soul, and since sin carries over from one transmigration to the next, diagnosing his students' lingering "ailments" from a former life was one of the more important roles of the kabbalistic master. Only by correctly identifying someone's sin and its root in his soul can the correct *tikkun* (penitential rite or ceremony) be prescribed.[17]

RABBI HAYYIM VITAL (1543–1620) was originally a student of Cordovero, becoming Luria's devoted disciple sometime between six and twelve months after Luria arrived in Safed. However, Vital's writings are among our most important sources for Lurianic Kabbalah. He was a prolific author, but, of his many works, *Ets Hayyim* (1782) is the longest and most comprehensive anthology of Lurianic teachings. Vital was also a jealous guardian of Luria's teachings. After Luria's death, Vital claimed to have the only authentic Lurianic tradition, which he divulged only to those whom he deemed worthy.[18] Vital was also the author of a mystical autobiography entitled *Sefer ha-Hezyonot* (*The Book of Visions*). This fascinating text, selections of which appear below, was the first of its kind in the Jewish tradition. *Sefer ha-Hezyonot* includes many details about Vital's dreams and visions, and a substantial amount of it is devoted to explicating the root of his soul.[19]

RABBI ELIYAHU DE VIDAS (d. 1593) was a student of both Moshe Cordovero and Yitshak Luria. His magnum opus *Reshit Hokhmah* (*The Beginning of Wisdom*, 1579) was frequently reprinted and extremely popular. This book blends the mystical thought of both Cordovero and Luria with earlier traditions from the Talmud and midrashim; medieval pietistic books such as *Hovot ha-Levavot*, *Sefer Hasidim*, and *Sefer ha-Rokeah*; and kabbalistic works such as the *Bahir* and *Zohar*. The translations below are taken from the Italian scholar R. Ya'akov ben Mordecai Poyetto's more accessible recasting of de Vidas' work.[20]

The dramatis personae of the Safed renaissance in the sixteenth century represent some of the greatest minds in Jewish mystical thought. These mystics shared much in common with one another, and indeed they lived and studied in close-knit fellowships, but we should note that their kabbalistic systems are not all identical. Especially pronounced are the differences between works by the mystics who lived and wrote in Safed before the arrival of Rabbi Yitshak Luria, such as Karo and Cordovero, and those who were either among his disciples or influenced by his teachings after his death. Luria's students rarely denied the essential validity of the other mystical systems, but some, especially Vital, subtly undercut their validity by claiming that Luria's teachings represented the highest level of kabbalistic knowledge. In part because of the power of his charisma and the legends it generated, and in part because of the zealous efforts of his students, Luria's became the dominant voice in Jewish mysticism in the late sixteenth and early seventeenth century.

Further Reading

Fine, Lawrence. *Physician of the Soul, Healer of the Cosmos: Isaac Luria and his Kabbalistic Fellowship*. Stanford: Stanford University Press, 2003.

Magid, Shaul. *From Metaphysics to Midrash: Myth, History and the Interpretation of Scripture in Lurianic Kabbala*. Bloomington: Indiana University Press, 2008.

Sack, Bracha. *Be-Sha'arei ha-Kabbalah shel Rabbi Moshe Kordovero*. Be'er Sheva: Ben Gurion University Press, 1995 [Hebrew].

Schechter, Solomon. "Safed in the Sixteenth Century." *Studies in Judaism* 2. Philadelphia: Jewish Publication Society of America, 1908, 202–306.

Scholem, Gershom. "Isaac Luria and His School." In *Major Trends in Jewish Mysticism*, 244–86. New York: Schocken Books, 1995.

Werblowsky, R. J. Zwi. *Joseph Karo, Lawyer and Mystic*. Philadelphia: Jewish Publication Society of America, 1977.

Rules of Mystical Piety

The Pious Customs of Rabbi Moshe Cordovero

1. A person should not turn his heart away from meditating upon the words of Torah and holiness, so that his heart will not be empty and void of reflection upon the commandments, and in order that his heart may become a dwelling place for *shekhinah*.[21]

3. Let an individual always enjoy the company of others and behave toward them with a kindly spirit, even with respect to people who transgress the Torah.

8. One must never curse any fellow Jew, even in a moment of anger; on the contrary, let him bless him, and by doing so be blessed, as it is written: "I will bless those who bless you, and him who curses you I will curse" (Gen 12:3).

14. Let a person commune with one of the Associates every day for the purpose of conversing about devotional concerns.

15. A person ought to discuss with this same Associate, every

Sabbath eve, what he did each day of that past week. From there he should go forth to welcome the Sabbath Queen.

16. One ought to pray the *'amidah* in a contemplative way to the degree that he is able; at very least he should concentrate meditatively during the three opening blessings, the four bows, as well as the four places where one stands erect again. For with respect to one who fails to concentrate upon these, *shekhinah* cries out: "The Lord has delivered me into their hands against whom I am not able to stand" (Lam 1:14).[22]

20. Every night one ought to sit on the ground, mourn the destruction of the Temple, and weep on account of one's transgressions which delay the redemption.

25. A person should donate charity every day so as to effect atonement for his sins, as it says: "and break off thy sins with almsgiving" (Dan 4:24).[23]

29. An individual should be careful about confessing his transgression prior to eating and before going to sleep.

31. A person should fast in accordance with his capacity.

32. A person ought to meditate upon matters of Torah with each and every bite he eats in order that his food may serve as a sacrifice and his drinking of water and wine as drink-offerings.[24]

The Pious Customs of Rabbi Avraham Galante[25]

1. On the eve of the New Moon all the people fast, including men, women, and students.[26] And there is a place where they assemble on that day and remain the entire time, reciting penitential prayers, petitionary devotions, confessions of sins and practicing flagellation. And some among them place a large stone on their stomach in order to simulate the punishment of stoning. There are some individuals who "strangle" themselves with their hands and perform other things of a like nature. There are some persons who place themselves into a sack while others drag them around the synagogue.[27]

8. On the eve of Shavu'ot there are those who sleep one or two hours after completely preparing for the festival. This is because, at night, following the meal, every congregation assembles in its own synagogue and those present do not sleep the whole night long. They

read selected portions from the Torah, Prophets, and Hagiographa, the Mishnah, *Zohar,* and the rabbinic Homilies until the break of dawn. And then all the people ritually immerse themselves prior to the morning service, as it indicates in the portion *Emor* of the *Zohar* (3:97a–98b). This is in addition to the immersion which they practice on the eve of Shavu'ot.

9. Every Sabbath eve they go out into the field or to the courtyard of the synagogue and welcome the Sabbath. Everyone dresses in his Sabbath garments. They recite the Psalm "Give to the Lord, O heavenly beings" (Ps 29) and the Sabbath hymn, followed by the "Psalm for the Sabbath day" (Ps 92).

13. On the night of the Day of Atonement they do not sleep at all, thus following the example set by the nobility of Jerusalem who stayed awake throughout the night; they spend it studying the laws of the Day of Atonement and its prohibitions, as well as by singing songs, praises of God, and liturgical hymns.[28]

"Come, My Beloved"

"Observe" and "Remember," in a single command, the One God announced to us.
The Lord is One, and His name is One, for fame, for glory and for praise.[29]

Come, my Beloved, to meet the Bride; let us welcome the Sabbath.[30]

Come, let us go to meet the Sabbath, for it is a source of blessing.
From the very beginning it was ordained; last in creation, first in God's plan.

Come, my Beloved...

Shrine of the King, royal city, arise! Come forth from your ruins.
Long enough have you dwelt in the valley of tears! He will show you abundant mercy.

Come, my Beloved...

Shake off your dust, arise! Put on your glorious garments, my people, and pray:
"Be near to my soul, and redeem it through the son of Jesse, the Bethlehemite."[31]

Come, my Beloved...

Bestir yourself, bestir yourself, for your light has come; arise and shine!
Awake, awake, utter a song; the Lord's glory is revealed upon you.[32]

Come, my Beloved...

Be not ashamed nor confounded. Why are you downcast? Why do you moan?
The afflicted of my people will be sheltered within you; the city shall be rebuilt on its ancient site.

Come, my Beloved...

Those who despoiled you shall become a spoil, and all who would devour you shall be far away. Your God will rejoice over you as a bridegroom rejoices over his bride.

Come, my Beloved...

You shall extend to the right and to the left, and you shall revere the Lord.
Through the advent of a descendent of Perez we shall rejoice and exult.[33]

Come, my Beloved...

Come in peace, crown of God, come with joy and cheerfulness;
amidst the faithful of the chosen people come, O Bride; come; O Bride, come.
O Bride, O Queen Sabbath.

Come, my Beloved, to meet the Bride; let us welcome the Sabbath.

The Pious Customs of Rabbi Yitshak Luria

I. ETHICAL AND INTERPERSONAL RELATIONS

5. Before an individual begins to pray in the synagogue...he must take upon himself the precept "...and thou shalt love thy neighbor as thyself..." (Lev 19:18). And he should concentrate upon loving every member of the house of Israel as he loves himself, on account of which his prayer will ascend, bound up with all the prayers of Israel. By this means his soul will be able to rise above and effect *tikkun*.

And especially when it comes to the love for one's Associates who study Torah with one another, each and every person must bind himself to the others as if he were one limb within the body of this fellowship. This is particularly important when an individual possesses the knowledge and the mystical insight with which to understand and apprehend his friend's soul. And should there be one among them in distress, all must take it upon themselves to share his trouble, whether it has to do with some illness or with his children, God forbid. And they must all pray on his behalf. Likewise, in all one's prayers and petitions one should be mindful of his fellows. My teacher, of blessed memory, took great care to caution me about the love which we ought to bear toward our associates, the members of our brotherhood.

7. With respect to the wages owed a hired laborer, my teacher, may his memory be for an everlasting blessing, used to be exceedingly careful. He would sometimes delay in praying the afternoon service until he had paid someone his wages. And on occasion, he would not pray the afternoon service until after sundown when he did not have the money with which to pay what he owed; he would request money from this one and that one until he could pay what he owed to a hired laborer. Only afterwards would he pray the afternoon service. He would say: "How can I pray to God, may He be exalted, when I have an obligation such as this to fulfill and I have not yet done so? And how can I lift up my countenance to pray?"[34]

8. As regards the attribute of charitableness and generosity, I observed that my teacher, of blessed memory, was not concerned with his own vanity, as expressed [for example] in the wearing of especially

fine clothes. In his eating, as well, he would consume very little. However, when it came to his wife's apparel, he was exceedingly careful to honor her, and to clothe her well. He used to satisfy her every desire, even if it was not within his means.[35]

II. MYSTICAL INSPIRATION AND THE STUDY OF TORAH

14. My teacher, of blessed memory, used to tell me that the principal element of a person's contemplation—while studying Torah—which is directed at drawing upon him mystical inspiration and supernal holiness consists in this: All his mental concentration must be directed towards binding and uniting his soul to its supernal source by means of the Torah. He should do so in order that the restoration of the supernal Adam might be accomplished. For this is God's purpose in creating human beings and His intention in enjoining them to occupy themselves with Torah.[36] An individual must also be mindful never to forget about the fixed, daily study of Scripture, Mishnah, Talmud, and Kabbalah, accompanied by the proper devotional intentions, as will be explained in the appropriate place. One ought to be exceedingly careful about this.[37]

15. In addition, Rabbi Avraham ha-Levi,[38] may God protect and preserve him, related to me that my master, of blessed memory, gave him the following advice concerning the attainment of mystical inspiration: a person must not indulge in idle conversation; he must rise in the middle of the night and weep on account of our poverty of knowledge. He ought to study forty or fifty pages of *Zohar* each day with the exclusive goal of textual familiarity, without engaging in intensive investigation. He should read the *Zohar* frequently.

When I asked my teacher how he had merited all the esoteric wisdom in his possession, however, he told me that he had invested a great amount of effort studying. But I responded that Rabbi Moshe Cordovero, of blessed memory, had also done the same. Even I, Hayyim, devoted a tremendous amount of effort in acquiring this wisdom. He then told me that while it is true that we applied ourselves extremely diligently, to an extent greater than any of our contemporaries, we did not do as he had done. For how many nights had he remained awake, poring over a single passage of the *Zohar*? Sometimes he would seclude himself, sit and study only a single passage during the course of six weekday nights. And usually, he would avoid sleeping altogether during these nights…

17. My teacher, of blessed memory, also informed me that the source of inspiration is the intensive study of the law (*halakhah*). This is so, he said, because intensive legal study consists in concentrating one's attention upon the fact that every nut possesses a shell (*kelippah*) which protects its inner core, the part constituting its holy element. This protective shell corresponds to the difficult problem (*kushia*) in need of resolution in the particular legal question; for the shell shields the law, preventing an individual from comprehending it….

My master, of blessed memory, reported to me that he always used to interpret legal problems, in accordance with the exoteric meaning, in six different ways. The seventh interpretation would be in accordance with the esoteric meaning; this corresponds to the mystery of the six weekdays and the seventh day, the Sabbath….[39]

19. Additionally, in connection with the intensive study of rabbinic law with the Associates of our academy, I observed that my master, may his memory be for an everlasting blessing, used to gird up his strength like a lion to such an extent that he would become exhausted and break out in a great sweat. When I asked him why he exerted such tremendous effort, he replied that the purpose of such study was to destroy the evil, namely, those difficult problems connected with particular legal questions which are not easily understood. Therefore, an individual has to expend enormous effort and to exhaust his strength. Thus, the Torah may be called wisdom which exhausts the strength of one who engages in its study.

IV. SABBATH AND FESTIVALS

32. These were the practices of my teacher, of blessed memory: as soon as he had finished the morning service on Friday, he would walk to the synagogue or to his house of study. If there was a proper Torah scroll there, he would remove it from the Ark and read the portion for the coming Sabbath, twice in Hebrew and once in Aramaic translation.[40]…

After having read the portion he would ritually immerse himself in preparation for the Sabbath…. He used to say that having read the portion an individual already possesses the power with which to receive the extra sanctity of the Sabbath. And therefore, he desisted from immersing himself before reading the portion, unless he did so unwittingly.... Know that an individual must immerse himself twice in a row, first for the purpose of divesting his soul of its weekday "garments," and the second time in order to honor the Sabbath and receive its extra holiness....[41] When you climb out of the ritual bath avoid drying yourself off with a towel so as to permit the body to absorb the Sabbath's waters.

33. This is the order of *kabbalat shabbat*: Go out into an open field and recite: "Come and let us go into the field of holy apple trees[42] in order to welcome the Sabbath Queen."...Stand in one place in the field; it is preferable if you are able to do so on a high spot, one which is clean as far as one can see in front of him, and for a distance of four cubits behind him. Turn your face towards the West where the sun sets, and at the very moment that it sets close your eyes and place your left hand upon your chest and your right hand upon your left. Direct your concentration—while in a state of awe and trembling as one who stands in the presence of the King—so as to receive the special holiness of the Sabbath.

Begin by reciting the Psalm: "Give to the Lord, O heavenly beings" (Ps 29), singing it entirely in a sweet voice. Following this, recite three times: "Come, O Bride, Come O Bride, O Sabbath Queen." Next, recite: "A psalm, a song for the Sabbath day" (Ps 92) in its entirety, followed by "The Lord is King; He is robed in majesty" until "for all time" (Ps 93). Then open your eyes and return home. Enter and wrap yourself in a fringed prayer shawl.... Circle the table—prepared with the Sabbath loaves—walking around it several times until you have repeated everything which you had recited while in the field.

34. Upon returning home and entering the house, sing out with great joy: "Sabbath peace!" For such an individual may be compared to a bridegroom who greets his bride with tremendous happiness and warmth. If your mother is still living, go and kiss her hands. Then circle the table.... Following this take two bundles of myrtle...and holding them between your hands, join them together and recite over them the blessing: "Blessed are You, Y-H-V-H our God, King of the universe, who creates fragrant trees." After this, smell their fragrance. Following this, walk around the table once again with the bundles of

myrtle in silence.... The reason for taking two bundles is because one represents the obligation to "remember" the Sabbath while the other represents the obligation to "observe" the Sabbath.[43]...

Regarding devotional practices at the Sabbath table, I observed that my teacher, of blessed memory, used to take very great care to eat at a table which had four legs, after the pattern of the table which was used in the Sanctuary. Further, as to the bread with which the table is prepared, care must be taken to place twelve loaves upon the table at every meal, corresponding to the twelve loaves of show-bread.[44]... Having finished the meal, my master, of blessed memory, would sing a certain hymn in a sweet melody. He composed three special hymns of an esoteric character which include all the detailed contemplative intentions associated with the Sabbath, one for the evening meal, one for the morning meal, and one for the afternoon....

Following the song a person ought to recite several chapters from Mishnah Shabbat. If you want, read the first eight on Sabbath eve, and the eight middle chapters at the morning meal, and the final eight chapters in the afternoon....

36. Know that my teacher, of blessed memory, cautioned me.... that it is improper for a person to wear any of the clothes which he wore during the week on the Sabbath. It is wrong even to wear one's Sabbath cloak during the rest of the week. Moreover, on the Sabbath a person must wear white garments, not colored ones. My master reported to me that the color of the garment which one will wear in the world to come, following his death, will be the same color of the clothes which he wears on the Sabbath in this world. He told me that once, during *kabbalat shabbat*, he envisioned the soul of a certain sage who had recently died, and he saw that he was dressed in black. My teacher told me that because this person used to wear black clothes in this world on the Sabbath, they were punishing him in the world to come....

38. I observed that my teacher, of blessed memory, traveled to Meron once on the holiday of Lag be-'Omer, he and his entire household, remaining there for the first three days of that week. This occurred soon after he arrived from Egypt; but I do not know if he was already expert in the wonderful esoteric wisdom which he attained subsequently. Rabbi Johanan Sagis reported to me that during my master's first year in Safed—before I became his disciple—he brought his young son to Meron along with all his household. And there they

cut his hair in accordance with the well-known custom, and enjoyed a day of feasting and joyous celebration.[45]

Rabbi Yitshak Luria's Aramaic Invocations for the Sabbath Eve

SABBATH EVE

Prepare the meal of perfect faith
To rejoice the heart of the holy King,
Prepare the meal of the King.
This is the meal of the Field of holy apples,
And the Impatient and the Holy Ancient One.
Behold, they come to share the meal with Her.[46]

RABBI ISAAC LURIA'S HYMN FOR SABBATH EVE

I sing in hymns to enter the gates,
of the Field of holy apples.

A new table we prepare for Her,[47]
a lovely candelabrum sheds its light upon us.

Between right and left the Bride approaches,
in holy jewels and festive garments.

Her Husband embraces Her in Her foundation,[48]
giving Her pleasure, squeezing out His strength.

Torment and trouble are ended.
Now there are joyous faces and spirits and souls.[49]

He gives Her great joy in twofold measure.
Light shines upon Her and streams of blessing.

Bridesmen, go forth and prepare the Bride's adornments,
food of various kinds all manner of fish.

To beget souls and new spirits
on the thirty-two paths and three branches.[50]

She has seventy crowns and the supernal King,
that all may be crowned in the Holy of Holies.

All the worlds are engraved and concealed within Her,
but all shine forth from the "Ancient of Days."

May it be His will that He dwell among His people,
who take joy for His sake with sweets and honey.

In the south I set the hidden candelabrum,
I make room in the north for the table with the loaves.

With wine in beakers and boughs of myrtle
to fortify the Betrothed, to strengthen the weak.

We plait them wreaths of precious words
for the crowning of the seventy in fifty gates.

Let *shekhinah* be adorned by six Sabbath loaves
connected on every side with the Heavenly Sanctuary.[51]

Weakened and cast out, the impure powers,
the menacing demons are now in fetters.[52]

The *Book of Visions*[53] by R. Hayyim Vital

Part One: Events in My Life

These are the things that occurred to me since the day of my birth, which was the first day of *Heshvan* in the year 5303 after creation [1542 CE].

1. When my father and teacher, of blessed memory, was living outside the land of Israel, before he migrated there, a great scholar, whose name was R. Hayyim Ashkenazi, was a guest in his home. He said to him: "Know that in the future you will travel to the land of Israel to live there, and a son will be born to you there. Call him Hayyim after me. He will be a great scholar, and there will be none like him in his generation."

3. In the year 5317 [1557], R. Yosef Karo, of blessed memory, commanded my teacher, R. Moshe Alshekh, in the name of the angelic *maggid*, who had told him that he should be very careful to teach me to the best of his ability, because in the future, I will be the successor of R. Yosef Karo...

6. In the year 5330 [1570] there was a wise woman who foretold the future and was also expert in oil-drop divination. She was called Soniadora.[54] I asked her to cast a spell over the oil as was customary, concerning my comprehension of kabbalistic wisdom. She did not know what to answer me until she assumed a "spirit of jealousy" (Num 5:30), and strengthened her incantations. She stood up on her legs, kissed my feet, and said: "Forgive me that I did not recognize the greatness of your Soul—the importance of your Soul is not that of the sages of this generation, but that of the generation of the early *Tannaim*, according to what I saw in this oil. In response to your question, I was shown in the oil the following, written in square letters: "Concerning this man who asks, the Talmudic Sages, of blessed memory, gave an analogy through the parable mentioned in *Shir ha-Shirim Rabbah* concerning King Solomon, of blessed memory: "Very sweet waters bubble forth from a very deep well. Nobody knows how to draw the waters up until an intelligent person comes and ties together several ropes and descends to drink."[55] You have a desire and thirst to know a discipline called Kabbalah and you are asking about it; know that you will comprehend, as in the parable about King Solomon mentioned above, that which none of the scholars who preceded you were able to comprehend. A great sage will come this year to Safed from the south, e.g., from Egypt, and he will teach you this wisdom." So it was, for in that year [1571] my teacher, of blessed memory, came from Egypt....

Part Two: My Dreams

5. 5326 [1566]. Friday night, the eighth of *Tevet*. I recited the *kiddush* and sat down at the table to eat. I was shedding copious tears and was depressed and melancholy because the previous tenth of *Heshvan* I had married my wife…Hannah, and I had been bound with witchcraft.[56] I said to God, Blessed be He: "…How is it possible for such a great tragedy to befall me—in particular, since it relates to the sin of nocturnal emissions, from which I guard myself?" I also cried over the two years that I neglected the study of Torah, which I wrote about in the section concerning my Soul. My anguish was so great that I did not eat anything. I lay on my bed crying, face down, until I dozed off from the many tears and I had a wondrous dream.[57]

I saw myself sitting in the house of Rabbi Shem Tov ha-Levi, reciting the *minhah* prayers, which is called a time of grace on the Sabbath. After the prayers, an old man stood before me who looked like my neighbor Rabbi Hayyim ha-Levi Ashkenazi. He called me by my name and said to me: Rabbi Hayyim, do you want to go out to the fields now with me to accompany the Sabbath Queen as she departs, as you are accustomed to do when she arrives,[58] and I will show you wondrous things there? I said to him, "I am here." We went out to the wall of the hold tower which is on the western side of Safed, opposite the *khan*, a place where there had previously been a gateway in the wall.

I looked and saw a very tall mountain, the top of which was in the heavens. Come up with me and I will tell you why I was sent to you. In the blink of an eye I saw him ascend to the top of the mountain and I remained at the bottom, unable to ascend, because it was perpendicular, like a wall, and not sloping as other mountains. I said to him: I am amazed. I am a young man and cannot ascend at all and you are old, yet you ascended it in the blink of an eye. He said to me: Hayyim, you do not know that every day I ascend and descend this mountain a thousand times to fulfill the missions of God. How can you be amazed at me? When I saw that he had earlier called me Rabbi Hayyim and now called me Hayyim and not Rabbi Hayyim, and also when I heard his terrifying words, I knew that he was certainly [the prophet] Elijah, of blessed memory, of the tribe of Levi. I broke down and began to cry from great fear. I then tearfully pleaded with him and said to him: "Have regard for my life" (2 Kgs 1:14) and bring me up to you. He said to me: Do not fear, this is why I was sent to you. He grasped my arms and brought me up to the top of the mountain with him, in the blink of an eye. I looked and saw a ladder, the bottom of which was standing on the top of the mountain and its top reached the heavens (cf. Gen 28:12). The ladder only had three rungs and the distance between each rung was approximately the height of a man. He said to me: I have been given permission to accompany you only until here. From here and further, see what you can do. He disappeared and I cried with great anguish.

A distinguished woman, beautiful as the sun, approached the top of the ladder. I thought in my heart that it was my mother. She said: My son, Hayyim, why are you crying? I have heard your tears and have come to help you. She stretched out her right hand and raised me to the top of the ladder. I saw there a large round window and a large flame coming out of it, back and forth, like a bolt of lightning and it burned everything found there (cf. Ez 1:14). I knew in my soul that it was the flame of the whirling sword that is at the entrance to the Garden of Eden (Gen 3:24). I called to the woman with great grief and said to her: My mother, my mother, help me that the sword should not burn me. [She said:] Nobody can help you with this flame; you are on your own! But I will advise you on what to do: Put your hand on your head and you will find there cotton-wool, white as snow. Take some and put it in the flaming window and it will close.[59] Pass by quickly.

In my humble opinion, the cotton, which had been changed to white, was the black hairs of my head—which are judgment—through certain merits in the secret of "And the hair of His head was like clean wool" (Dan 7:9). I did so and passed by quickly. In a moment the flame again shot out as before. Then the woman disappeared.

Elijah again appeared as earlier, grasped my right hand, and said to me: "Come with me to the place where I had originally been sent to bring you." He brought me to an immensely large courtyard with large rivers flowing through it to water the garden. On both banks of the rivers were innumerable beautifully full and ripe fruit trees. The majority were apple trees, smelling like myrrh and aloe. The trees were very tall and the branches bent downward almost touching the ground. Their ends looked like a *sukkah*. There were innumerable birds in the garden, which looked like white geese, traversing the length and breadth of the garden, reciting *mishnahs* of tractate Shabbat. It was then the night of the Sabbath, at the beginning of the dream. In the course of their wandering they would recite a *mishnah* or a chapter, raise their necks and eat apples from the trees, and afterwards drink from the rivers. This was their constant activity. It had been made known to me that these were the souls of *tsaddikim*, Masters of the *Mishnah*.[60] However, I did not know why they had the form of geese and birds and not the form of people. He led me further into the center of the garden until I saw a large and tall attic, as if it was on top of a great height, but there was no house under it. Its height above the garden was about a man's height. Its door was in the west and there was a ladder of three stone steps from the ground to the door of the attic. Elijah, of blessed memory, disappeared. I ascended the ladder alone and entered the door of the attic. I saw God, Blessed be He, sitting on a chair in the middle of the southern wall. He looked like the Ancient of Days, with a beard white as snow, in infinite splendor. *Tsaddikim* sat before Him on the ground, on beautiful carpets and couches, learning Torah from Him. I knew in my Soul that they were the *tsaddikim* called *benei aliyah*.[61] They have human features, continually see the Divine Presence and learn Torah directly from Him. This was not the level of Masters of the *Mishnah*. They had the form of birds and geese, because about them it is said: "He who sees a goose in his dreams should hope for wisdom" (b. Berakhot 57a). They stand in the courtyard and in the garden, but do not see the Divine Presence regularly, like the inhabitants of the attic, and do not learn Torah from Him.

When I entered and saw his face, I became confused and was seized with fear. I fell to the ground on my face before his feet and could not summon any strength. He stretched out his hand and grasped my right hand and said to me: "Hayyim my son, stand up, why did you fall on your face? Do not be afraid." I said to Him: "Lord, I could not summon any strength and my beauty turned into corruption out of my great fear and I have no strength to stand." He said to me: "Strengthen and fortify yourself, stand up and sit at my right in this empty place, near me." I said to Him: "How can I sit at your right in this place, for it has been prepared for Rabbi Joseph Karo?" He said to me: "I thought so at first, but afterwards I gave him another place and this has been prepared for you." I said to Him that this was the place of the prophet Samuel, of blessed memory. He said to me: "True, this is his place, but when the Temple was destroyed, he took upon himself not to sit in this place until the Temple is rebuilt in the future. Since then, he went to Jerusalem, to the destroyed Temple, and stands there constantly to mourn it until the time that it will be rebuilt. Therefore, his place remains empty, and I have given you permission to sit there." Then I sat at His right, literally next to Him, on the couch, like the other *tsaddikim* who were there.

He said to me: "Do you like this place?" I said to Him: "Who can praise the greatness of this attic? Indeed, explain to me: Why are the Masters of the *Mishnah* different from these inhabitants of the attic, that there should be such a great difference between them as I have seen with my own eyes? Have you forgotten what the Sages said, that in the future God will give them wings and they will roam over the waters?[62] They said this about this sect called Masters of the *Mishnah*, who have the image of birds with wings and they roam over the waters which are the rivers of the Garden of Eden, as you saw with your own eyes. Then I said to Him: Lord, I remember what is written in the introduction to *Tikkunei Zohar* (1b) concerning the verse, 'If you chance [upon a bird's nest...and] the mother is sitting over the fledglings...take only the young' (Deut 22:6)—the fledglings are the Masters of the *Mishnah*, the young are the Kabbalists. They are the elite, they have the image of children."

I continued and said to Him: "Lord, 'If my soul is worthy in your eyes' (2 Kgs 1:13, 14), leave me here and do not return me to the mundane world, 'for it is clear to you that my intent is to do your will and I fear lest my passions cause me to sin'[63] and I will forfeit this holy place." He said to me: "You are still a young man and you still have time to occupy yourself with my Torah and commandments. You need to return to complete your Soul and at the end of your days you will return to this place. If you fear to return to the mundane world, give me your right hand and swear that you will not put aside the Torah for any other task and I will also swear to you that if you do so, this place will not be given to anyone else under any circumstances. This will be your place, at my right, forever." I extended my hand and swore to fulfill all the above and He too swore to fulfill His words. He said to me: Go in peace and do not forget all these things. I then descended from there alone and found myself in the mundane world, in the midst of the dream, and I did not see any of the things that I had seen when I first ascended.

16. Three days after my teacher's death, I saw him in a dream and asked him why he had died so hastily. He told me: Because I had not found even one who was complete, as I desired.[64] I said to him: If so, Heaven forbid, I despair of everything you promised me and of all the good that you told me will come into the world through me. He told me: Do not despair; when the time comes I will come and reveal to you what to do. And I awoke.

From then on, he revealed himself to me most nights to console me, that I should not despair. This continued for twenty years after his death. For the next ten years he only came to me once a month. From then on he came once every three months. All the dreams I had of him were always in one form. He taught me Torah and consoled me that I should not despair. "For there is yet a prophecy for a set term…" (Hab 2:3), and all will be fulfilled, praise God.

17. 5333 [1572]. *Rosh Hodesh Heshvan*. Three months after my teacher's, of blessed memory, death, I saw R. Moshe Cordovero in the doorway of the Torah Study Society in Safed. I adjured him that he should tell me the truth about how Kabbalah is studied in the world of souls. Was it according to his method or according to the method of my teacher, of blessed memory? He told me: Both methods are true. Indeed, my method is the method of the plain meaning for the beginners in this wisdom and the method of your teaching is the esoteric and primary. Even I, in Heaven, only study according to your teacher's method.[65] I said to him: if so, why did he leave the world? He said to me: Because he did not find even a single *tsaddik* in this generation who was complete, as he desired. Had he found him, he would not have died.

Part Three: The Dreams of Others

[32] (31). On that night, R. Caleb dreamed that we were studying in the Yeshiva and my teacher, of blessed memory, the Ashkenazi, came there and said to us: "I want to teach you the meaning of 'a *halakhah* from Moses on Sinai,' ordinary *halakhah*, deduction, and tradition. He explained wondrous things. And he awoke.

He returned to sleep and saw how we were in a synagogue studying Torah and there were more than 200 oil lamps burning, but their light was very dark. My teacher, of blessed memory, returned and entered in great haste. R. Caleb said, "I do not know why these lamps are so dark." My teacher said, "I will repair their light." He stood up and repaired one large candelabra that was there, close to me. Then it was very bright. My teacher said, "I do not need to repair all of the lights that are here; since I repaired this large candelabra the other lights will be illumined by themselves.[66] So it was, as he had spoken.

Part Four: Things My Teacher Told Me About My Soul

These are the things that my teacher told me which relate to me and the source of my Soul.

1. On *Rosh Hodesh Adar* in the year 5381 [1571], he told me that he began to attain his comprehension when he was in Egypt. There, he was told to come to the city of Safed because I, Hayyim, was living there, in order to teach me. He told me that he came to live in Safed, may it be rebuilt and reestablished speedily, only for me and for no other. Not only that, but the primary reason for his transmigration this time was only for my sake, to complete me. He did not come for his own needs, because he had no need to come.

He also told me that he was not required to teach any person other than myself and when I will have learned there will be no reason for him to remain in this world. He also told me that the essence of my Soul was on a higher plane than numerous very exalted angels and I would be able to ascend with my Soul, by means of my deeds, higher than the firmament of *Aravot*.[67]

2. I asked him to inform me about my Soul, but he did not want to reveal all the details. Indeed, he told me the following in general terms.

Previously I was R. Vidal of Tolosa, author of *Sefer Maggid Mishneh*, and his name was the same as mine is now.[68] Afterwards, I transmigrated into a man named R. Joshua Soriano. He was wealthy, long-lived, charitable, and frequented the synagogue morning and evening. Afterwards, I transmigrated into a boy whose name was Avraham, a thirteen-year-old who died in his fourteenth year. Finally,

I have come to this transmigration at this time and my name is Hayyim as was the name of the first Don Vidal, the author of the *Maggid Mishneh*. He told me that should I need to transmigrate again, the reason for this would be that in one of my earlier transmigrations I did not believe very much in the wisdom of the *Zohar*. From his words I understood that this was during the transmigration when I was the [author of the] *Maggid Mishneh*, but he did not want to reveal the matter.

He told me that the primary thing that I needed to repair in this transmigration was to occupy myself with the wisdom of the *Zohar*.

He told me that when I was in the transmigration of the [author of the] *Maggid Mishneh*, I was a profound student of philosophy. Therefore, I have no desire to engage in the study of philosophy at present. He also told me that all these transmigrations are only from the aspect of my Animus (*nefesh*), but the aspects of Spirit (*ruah*) and Soul (*neshamah*) have different concerns from other transmigrations.[69]

11. He asked my Soul about my comprehension and it told him that I should fast for forty consecutive days, in sackcloth and ashes, and then I should fast the first Monday, Thursday, and Monday of each month for two and one-half years and then I will attain complete comprehension, without any admixture of the evil inclination, as occurs to others. Another day he again asked and was told: I should spend a whole month in sackcloth, ashes, and fasting and I should behave humbly and not mock any person. He told me that the essence of my comprehension depends on these two things in particular, humility and refraining from mockery....

15. He also commanded me not to cease performing the Unifications which he transmitted to me. If I should go to prostrate myself on the graves of *tsaddikim*, I should do so on the eve of *Rosh Hodesh* or on the fifteenth of the month, because there is greater [spiritual] readiness on those days. I should not go on Sabbaths, festivals, or on *Rosh Hodesh*, because on those days their Souls ascend to Heaven and cannot be communed with on the grave. Once he sent me to the graves of the *tsaddikim* on the intermediate days of a festival to pray there, but I did not prostrate myself....

17. Once I went with my teacher, of blessed memory, to the place where Rabbi Shim'on bar Yohai and his colleagues gathered when they composed the *Idra Rabba*.[70] There, on the east side of the road, is a

boulder with two large fissures in it. Rabbi Shim'on bar Yohai sat in the fissure on the northern side during the Great Assembly. Rabbi Abba sat in the fissure that is on the southern side. Rabbi Ele'azar sat next to a tree that is opposite the fissures and to the west of them. My teacher sat in the northern fissure, in Rabbi Shim'on bar Yohai's place, and I sat in the southern fissure, in Rabbi Abba's place, without knowing it. Afterwards, my teacher explained this matter to me. I did not know that one of the participants was from the source of my Soul. It was Rabbi Abba and therefore I sat in his place without knowing it. I am uncertain if it was not the reverse of what was mentioned with regard to our sitting in the above-mentioned two fissures.[71]

37. He explained to me the concept of the sources of the Souls: Know that all Souls are derived from Adam, since he incorporates all five sources of Souls, which are: *arikh* [*anpin*], *abba*, *imma*, *ze'ir* [*anpin*], and *nukvah*. The 248 organs and 365 blood vessels which are in a person are the 613 sources.[72] That is, each of the 248 organs and each of the 365 vessels has within it one *partsuf* in each of the 613 organs and vessels and are called one source. Each organ consists of flesh, vessels, and bones, as the Talmudic sages said, concerning ritual impurity and the limb of a living animal (m. Ohalot 1:8). However, these vessels are not counted in the 365 vessels, which are independent vessels, separate from the 248 organs. The vessels which are with the organs are the small channels which are spread through the flesh of the organ and are not counted in the 365 vessels. We find that the 613 sources are in Adam and each source contains 613 sparks of Souls. Each of the sparks is called a Soul. All of this is part of the externality of the Animus, as will be explained below. This is the essential truth of the matter. Indeed, through the sins and defects of the lower elements [people], the two above-mentioned aspects separate and divide into a number of parts. Explanation: The 613 great sources are able to divide into 600,000 small sources.[73] Similarly, the 613 great sparks are able to divide into 600,000 small sparks....

38. ...As a result of Adam's sin, the sparks from the rest of Adam's organs were mixed up with the *kelippot* of evil from the sources of Cain and Abel and in the course of the transmigrations, they are revealed and each will return to its original source. Now, I will explain the source of Cain alone, in whom inheres the spark of my Animus, of me, Hayyim.[74] The source of Cain is the joint of the left shoulder

where the arm joins the body and it has flesh, sinews, and bones. As is already known, it is not called an organ (*ever*), unless it has flesh, sinews, and bone.... These three components of the organ are divided into 600,000 small sparks and every organ of this shoulder is one complete *partsuf*. Indeed, the source of the spark of my Animus is the lower left "heel" which is in this *partsuf*, which is the left shoulder of Adam....

40. Know that a person does not have to repair all the damages that are in his whole source, as in the following analogy: Whoever is from the left shoulder of Adam, which is called the source of Cain, is from a particular organ which is in this *partsuf*, like the "heel" mentioned above. No single spark is required to complete and repair all the damage which his found in the whole *partsuf*, but only in the "heel" itself. We find that all the sparks which are from the left "heel" of this *partsuf* of the left shoulder of Adam are all guarantors for one another to repair them all, each one for all of them and all for one of them. When the repair of this "heel" will be completed there will be no need for this "heel" to transmigrate, even if the rest of the shoulder will not yet be repaired....

46. ...There is a difference and distinction between transmigration and impregnation. Transmigration includes those who are transmigrated and come together with the person from the time of birth and do not separate from him at all until the day of his death. They are made into one Animus and suffer the pains and tribulations of that body. However, impregnation is divided into two aspects: The first is where it comes for the needs of the one who is being impregnated, as will be explained in its place, with God's help. The second is one that comes for the needs of the person [who is the recipient of the impregnation]. When he comes for his own needs, then he does not come until the person is thirteen years and a day,[75] since before this time the deeds of a person are not accountable as he is not yet obligated in the commandments and the whole purpose of his coming is to effect a repair for himself. Therefore, he does not come until this person is thirteen years and a day.

Then he enters and disseminates throughout the body of this person, in the image of his Animus, and suffers with it the pains and tribulations of this body, like the person's Animus. It resides there in this way for its allotted span of time until it has completed and repaired what it needed. Then it leaves and returns to its supernal place. However, when it comes for the needs of the person, to assist and aid him, then it also comes after the age of thirteen years, but it comes of its own volition and it is not forced to suffer the anguish of the person and his body and does not feel the body's pains and tribulations. If it finds satisfaction in this person it resides with him and if not, it leaves and says, "Move away from the tents of these wicked men" (Num 16:26)....

50. Know that if two Souls from one source are found in the same generation, whether in two brothers or two friends, they will be natural enemies and accuse each other, since one will want to grasp and suckle more than the other and they will be naturally and unconsciously jealous of each other. Indeed, if they will comprehend that they are from one source, then they will certainly not accuse each other. Also know that this is only during their lifetime. However, the Souls of the deceased *tsaddikim* very much desire to complete the Souls of those who come from their source who are still alive, since there is no reason for them to be envious and say that they want to comprehend more than the other one, "For there is no action or wisdom in She'ol where you are going" (Eccl 9:10). On the contrary, they have great benefit from the deeds of the living....

The *Beginning of Wisdom* by R. Eliyahu de Vidas

The Gate of Repentance

INTRODUCTION

A person who desires to achieve perfect repentance must begin by acquiring knowledge of the fear and love of God, of which there are two aspects. First, when an individual recognizes that the Creator, may He be blessed, is the Master who created all humankind, he will learn to appreciate God's greatness. He will realize that everything which the Holy One, blessed be He, created was for the sake of His glory only, and that all living things are subject to His will. No person may go beyond the parameters within which the Creator of all things has placed him, as exemplified in the case of the sea, concerning which it is said, "Thus far shall you come, but no further" (Job 38:11). And thus, if a person strays beyond the boundaries of the Torah, it is proper for him to return to the place to which he belongs as the Creator has enjoined him, and not disobey His word. The second aspect concerns the blemish which extends throughout all the upper regions, whether it be injury incurred by one's body, vital-soul, spirit, or super-soul.[76] This is the most important reason that a person should practice repentance and be completely remorseful; that is, when he clearly realizes the harm caused by his deeds, in addition to considering the punishment which he will receive in this world as well as in the next. Sin causes the body to be cut off from this world and the soul from the world to come....

CHAPTER ONE

3. It is appropriate for a person to arouse himself in repentance when he considers that *shekhinah* is exiled on his account, as it is written, "And for your transgressions was your mother put away" (Isa 50:1). The return of *shekhinah* from exile is dependent upon our repentance. Ought not each and every person arouse himself to repent in order to lighten Her yoke of exile and to shed light on the ways in which She is blemished, how we injure Her and prolong the exile, as we explain in the "Gate of Fear"? This matter is taken up in the *Tikkunim* (22a), where you will learn how important it is that we awaken repentance so as to love *shekhinah* and extricate Her from exile. This should not be done for the sake of receiving reward....

The Gate of Holiness

CHAPTER ONE

Holiness is the root underlying observance of the commandments; because of this it is mentioned with such frequency in the Torah. For when an individual acts in a holy manner and detaches himself from the alluring things of this world, he will earnestly seek to fulfill the will of his Maker. He will bind himself to God's love, may He be blessed, so as to carry out His precepts with strong passion and love. For what benefit does this world and all its good things hold for a person, inasmuch as they are worthless vanities, as will be explained with the help of God? Thus, the subject of holiness is mentioned so often in the Torah on account of the enormous benefit which the soul derives from it.

...At first we are sanctified through God, and draw down holiness upon us from Him in order that we may sanctify ourselves through fulfillment of the commandments. Afterwards, He is made holy through us by means of the arousal from below which ascends heavenward as a consequence of our righteous deeds. The reason for this is that everything requires arousal from below, as Scripture says: "...but there went up a mist from the earth, and watered the whole face of the ground" (Gen 1:6)....

There are two dimensions to the general principle of holiness. The first is abstinence from material things and the establishment of a boundary for oneself beyond which one should not stray. The word "sanctity" signifies abstinence, as in: "Set bounds about the mount, and sanctify it" (Ex 19:23). This is the meaning of the words, "Depart from evil..." (Ps 34:15), an expression which alludes to the observance of the *negative* commandments.

The second dimension consists in drawing down the light of holiness upon us so that we can clothe ourselves in it. This corresponds to the rest of the aforementioned verse, "and do good." Through the *positive* commandments we invest ourselves with sanctity; this is the esoteric meaning of the "divine garment."[77] For fulfillment of the positive commandments becomes a garment of light for the soul, the same garment in which the soul is clothed at a subsequent time in the lower Paradise. Thus, as part of those blessings which accompany the performance of commandment we recite the phrase, "Who has sanctified us by His commandments." For through the fulfillment of the precepts one sanctifies the soul and clothes it in a new light. Likewise, in connection with the *kedushah* ("Sanctification") prayer which we recite each day: "Holy, holy, holy...," R. Shim'on bar Yohai, may he rest in peace, commented that its purpose is to enable each person to draw down upon himself holiness from on high (*Zohar* 3:93a).

CHAPTER SEVEN

...One must accustom himself to rising every night at midnight and studying Torah until dawn. How many marvelous things occur by virtue of rising at midnight for the purpose of studying Torah? Among these is the subjugation of the evil shells, a topic which is treated in the *Zohar* (1:242a–b).[78]

We have already mentioned above that the confusion of mind which a person may experience while engaged in praying or in studying Torah is on account of his sins, insofar as he renders himself unqualified for unifying God. Sin functions as an evil accuser which comes between a person and God; but when an individual accustoms himself to rise in the middle of the night in order to study Torah, he throws off the Evil One and atones for his sins. Through such means he purifies his thoughts, and his efforts to unify God are not hampered. The reason for this is that night normally nourishes the forces of strict judgment. The night is transformed from darkness into light, from the quality of judgment to the quality of compassion, however, by virtue of the study of Torah. And since the night becomes "sweetened," so too are all those who are bound up with it.[79]...

The pattern for the midnight vigil is as follows (*Zohar* 3:178a): Before lying down [in the early evening to sleep], one should examine his deeds for that day and commit them to writing so that he does not forget them. This is so as to fulfill the verse: "and my sin is always before me" (Ps 51:5). Thus, let a person confess his sins. Additional details are provided with respect to the matter of confession in the portion *Tsav* of the *Zohar* (3:33a). It is also exceedingly beneficial to weep on account of one's sins, for when one's soul ascends because of his tears, it assuredly does so in a state of holiness. For all the heavenly gates are locked except the gates of tears (b. Berakhot 32b)....

One who wishes to sanctify himself when he arises at midnight ought to feel the distress of *shekhinah*, weep and mourn over the destruction of the Sanctuary; he should weep on account of God's desecrated name, as well as on account of his sins, which prolong the exile of *shekhinah*...After all this, he should rise to study Torah, clothe himself, and ready himself to call out to God. When he rises he should study Oral Torah or Mishnah as well as the Aramaic version of the verse, "Arise, cry out in the night..." (Lam 2:19). And it is especially good if one stands during this time to the extent possible in order to ensure that he avoids falling asleep. This is what King David did, as Scripture says, "At midnight I will stand up to praise You" (Ps 119:62), as explained in the *Zohar* (1:82b).

The Gate of Humility

CHAPTER ONE

... Now the attributes of submissiveness and humility also characterize the Creator, blessed be He. Even though God is exalted above all things, and higher in majesty than all else, as it is written, "The Lord reigns; he is clothed in majesty" (Ps 93:1), He is nevertheless humble, as King David, may he rest in peace, said, "And Your condescension has made me great" (Ps 18:36)...It is a general principle that the quality of humility may be found at every stage of divine emanation; at each stage it manifests itself in a particular way. Refer to the *Tikkunim* (5b), where you will see that *shekhinah* is associated with the quality of humility. The quality of humility is associated even with the sefirah *keter*,[80] for the attribute of modesty enables a person to act with forbearance and to show mercy and the like, these being the thirteen attributes of God which we recite, "Y-H-V-H, Y-H-V-H, God, merciful and gracious, long-suffering..." (Ex 34:6–7).[81]...

Behold, every place in which you find a manifestation of God's greatness, even in the supernal world above, which is the site of His glorious majesty, there you will discover humility (b. Megillah 31a). Therefore, an individual must imitate his creator so as to behave with forbearance towards others, as well as with the other qualities which are associated with the Holy One, blessed be He, as indicated in His thirteen attributes of mercy. Just as God is gracious, so you too must be gracious; just as God is merciful, so you too must be merciful; and so on with the other qualities of spirit.

CHAPTER TWO

Should an individual act in a conceited manner on account of his own knowledge, let him reflect upon the wisdom of the ancient Sages; by doing so he will realize that the totality of our knowledge is tantamount to outer shells and is insignificant when compared to the knowledge which they possessed.... Should a man grow arrogant on account of his wealth, let him concern himself with the financial well-being of his friend, or worry about whether he is fulfilling his obligations with regard to what God obliges us to give the poor....

Vanity is among those things which drive a person from this world as well as from the world to come.... It seems to me that this is a case of measure of measure; just as such an individual drives *shekhinah* from his house, so those in the world above who are responsible for his soul will force him out of the circle of the Holy One, blessed be He. For *shekhinah* does not reside except in a heart which his contrite. This is what is taught in the *Tikkunim*, namely, that a person must prepare a lovely dwelling place in his heart for *shekhinah*. This means that an individual has to act humbly and avoid losing his temper. For when he behaves in an arrogant manner, *shekhinah* takes flight and a handmaiden rules in her mistress' place. She will not abide with an individual who is not pleasing to the Holy One, blessed be He, and She will not glorify his soul in the world to come. Among those things for which the redemption is delayed is arrogant behavior, as our Sages, of blessed memory, taught: "The Son of David will not come until there are no conceited men in Israel" (b. Sanhedrin 98a).

The Gate of Fear

CHAPTER FOUR

This chapter will elucidate various dimensions of the fear of sin. First, a person must be fearful lest he fall prey to any sin whatsoever, even unintentionally. The reason for this is that the divine soul is delicate and pure, deriving from an exalted place.[82] Anything which injures an individual, even inadvertently, harms his soul.... If an individual is virtuous in his actions, he cleaves to the realm of goodness—which corresponds to the name Y-H-V-H, the Tree of Life, the side of mercy and compassion.[83] That is the meaning of, "Y-H-V-H is good to all, His tender mercies are over all His works" (Ps 145:9). Thus, the numerical value of the name Y-H-V-H equals that of the word *tov* ("good," 17) in "small" numbers.[84] And if an individual does not act virtuously, he cleaves to the realm of evil, the Tree of Death, the exterior husks. After a person's death, his soul cleaves to one realm or another in accordance with his actions of the world. For a man is composed of both good and evil, that is, the good inclination and the evil inclination. If he subdues his evil inclination, he subjugates the forces of strictness and evil, and enables goodness to descend upon him. An individual must strengthen the good inclination so that it prevails over the evil inclination. And if, heaven forbid, he does the reverse, he injures the supernal roots and prevents blessing and divine abundance from flowing into this world. Therefore, he must always stand in awe of heaven lest he injure himself, that is, his soul, depriving it of its supernal light.

The husk, deriving from the realm of evil, is like the shell of a nut. The good element—which is concealed—is the kernel of the nut. Therefore, in order to achieve the fear of God—which is the good that is concealed—one must break and destroy one's evil obstinacy and distance himself from this quality to such a degree that he will be loathe to draw near to it again. Just as one must crack the shell of the nut in order to consume the wholesome kernel, and just as the nut possesses three layers of shells, so must one distance himself from three husks. The first of these is pride, for this is the root of all evil qualities. Second, corresponding to the nut's hard shell, is a man's stubbornness. The third is an angry person's fury and harsh words which make him seethe with the fire of the evil impulse and lead him to sin. When a man separates himself from the pleasure of this world, all of which derive from the husks, the serpent's skin, and the evil inclination, this realm is subdued. The same holds true when he is careful to avoid transgressing the Torah's negative commandments. For anyone who violates the negative commandments enables the evil serpent to penetrate the realm of holiness.

The Gate of Love

CHAPTER FOUR

"Cleaving" to God consists in a person's attaching himself with his soul to *shekhinah* and concentrating all his attention upon Her unifications, as well as upon the separation from Her of all the evil shells. Similarly, a person ought to remove from his mind all impure thoughts, as R. Shim'on bar Yohai, may he rest in peace, explained. For at the moment of unification he must contemplatively unite *shekhinah* without allowing any extraneous thoughts to distract him.[85]

This is what our Sages, of blessed memory, meant when they taught: "One may not drink out of one goblet and think of another" (b. Nedarim 20b). This is also what is known as a child born of "a woman mistaken for another" (b. Nedarim 20b).[86] A person must concentrate exclusively on *shekhinah* and recognize that his impure thoughts are distractions from without which he can separate him from Her, God forbid. Instead, one should cleave to *shekhinah* in the proper manner, and divest Her of all evil.

As in the case of cleaving to God, there are two aspects to one's "longing" for Him. First, a person should cleave to *shekhinah* with his soul by means of each and every commandment that he performs; he must carry them out with longing, heartfelt enthusiasm, and very great love. This is what is intended by the quality of "desire of the heart" of which the *Zohar* frequently speaks. It is not possible to attain such desire of the heart—which is what this longing is—unless a person initially sets his mind on God, may He be blessed, and upon the love which he feels for Him. This longing derives from the realm of love. The nature of longing is discussed by R. Shim'on bar Yohai in *Zohar* 2:198b. He also comments (2:128a–b) that the means by which an individual draws upon himself *shekhinah* is primarily the desire of the heart. We find there that the evil powers rest upon a man "for free," provoking him to act foolishly so that they might abide in him.... Therefore, a person needs to gain control over his evil inclination and not be deflected from his goal by worldly considerations. Instead, his soul should continuously yearn for *shekhinah* whose name is "heart." That is what is meant by "desire of the heart."...

In reality, a man would not delay making love to his wife when he feels passion for her, even if he were given all the money in the world. In a similar manner, it is proper that he feels passionate about carrying out the commandments since through their performance, he makes love to the King's Daughter, that is, *shekhinah*, the daughter of Jacob; for every wife is her husband's daughter. It is not proper to postpone such lovemaking; rather, he must perform the commandments unhesitatingly and with intense zeal. In this way, he will cleave to the "upper life" and his soul will be illuminated by the upper light which shines upon a person when he performs as precept.

Just as "desire" may be found in connection with the performance of the commandments, so too when it comes to the study of Torah.

Study will strengthen his soul's desire for God, causing all physical sensations to fade away. His soul will cleave to God in the source of the intensive study of Torah until he feels absolutely no worldly sensation. For just as an individual who longs for the one whom he loves eliminates all other thought from his mind because of his preoccupation with his lover, and a fire of love burns in his heart even while he eats, drinks and sleeps, so should a person's love for God be likewise. We learn this from a story told by R. Yitshak of Akko.[87] Among the stories having to do with ascetics which this sage reported, he wrote that a person who has never experienced longing for a woman is like a donkey—even worse. The reason for this is that as a result of the feeling of longing for a woman, one learns to cultivate longing for God. We can learn from this that the man who loves the Torah with such great passion that he thinks of no worldly matters whatsoever, either by day or by night, will assuredly attain a most wonderful grade of soul. He will have no need for mortification of the body or for fasts, for cleaving to God depends on nothing but the longing for and loving of the Torah. He should love the Torah with as a great a passion as he loves his wife. One also expresses this love for God by rising regularly at midnight out of great desire.

CHAPTERS FIVE AND SIX

There are numerous reasons why a person is obligated to love God, may He be blessed. Firstly, he must love God on account of the soul which He created within him, and which is a divine portion from on high. He must also love God, may He be blessed, inasmuch as He desires that a person cleave to Him.... A student of Torah who is separated from his wife during the six days of the week while he is studying Torah is bound to the supernal union and *shekhinah* remains attached to him.[88] Upon learning this from the words of R. Shim'on bar Yohai it is proper for an individual to kindle his heart to love *shekhinah* as he loves his wife. And he should prepare a lovely dwelling place in his heart for *shekhinah* in order that She may be able to find somewhere to rest; for She does not abide in a place which is not pure....

A person must also reflect upon God's providential concern for Israel as demonstrated by the sharing of His knowledge with those who are worthy of it.... In Safed, located in the Upper Galilee, there have recently appeared sages for whom it was appropriate to recite this blessing. They used to be capable of practicing the science of physiognomy and were able to inform a man concerning all that they had done—whether it was good or evil.[89] To be sure, these individuals did not merit this wonderful wisdom [which is akin to possessing the Holy Spirit] except on account of their virtuous deeds and saintly behavior.

Another kind of knowledge of this same sort is practical Kabbalah, that is the formation of God's holy names which can be permutated in a number of different forms, such as the "fifty-two," "forty-two," and "seventy-two" letter names of God. And even though the truth is that it is not appropriate for every individual to practice the permutation of holy names—for who is worthy to use the King's scepter other than one who is close to the King—nevertheless, we know with absolute certainty that a person who knows how to practice this science and is qualified to do so can bring about wondrous things, as I have personally witnessed and heard from one who has done so.[90]...

CHAPTER TEN

We wish to explain in this chapter that all the stringent practices which an individual is obligated to perform so as to restore *shekhinah* have to be carried out with joy, as it is said, "Because you would not serve Y-H-V-H your God in joy and gladness over the abundance of everything, therefore shall you serve your enemy" (Deut 28:47). In connection with this verse, see the *Zohar* (1:116a–b). The meaning of this is that a person ought to derive greater pleasure from the joy of serving God and fulfilling His commandments than from all the money in the world, as it says concerning the Torah, "And all things desirable are not to be compared with her" (Prov 8:11). Likewise, no joy in the world may be compared with that of the commandments....

A person who desires to gladden his soul ought to seclude himself for a portion of the day for the purpose of meditating upon the splendor of the letters Y-H-V-H.... For our soul issues forth from the name Y-H-V-H, as it is said, "You are the children of Y-H-V-H your God" (Deut 14:1). Therefore, when an individual meditates upon this name his soul lights up and shines wondrously. The soul becomes filled with happiness, and by virtue of the power of this illumination, it is invested with the strength with which to emit sparks. This joy extends even to the body, as it says, "My flesh dwells in safety" (Ps 16:90, so that deceit is unable to govern it. Such is the status accorded the righteous who cleave to the name of God. For even in death the righteous are called "living." By virtue of their cleaving to the name Y-H-V-H—the wellspring of all life—they are invested with a degree of vitality.

...A person cleaves to God when he recites the "Verses of Praise" out loud with appropriate concentration.[91] In the same way, he should accustom himself to recite verses from the Psalms each day in a loud voice and with proper concentration while in the synagogue. How much better it is if he concentrates upon them according to their mystical meanings, by means of some of the divine epithets commonly found in the *Zohar*. For as a consequence of one's love for the King, a person should praise Him and sing before Him in the synagogue, just as it is the custom to sing before a king of flesh and blood. By [our] singing His praise, the King is glorified.... [It is true that] Our Sages, of blessed memory, taught that singing is forbidden.[92] This applies, however, to songs having to do with love between friends and those which praise physical beauty. But a Jew should not desist from singing songs of praise for God, or those that speak of God's compassion. Indeed, it is a custom among all Israel to sing at weddings or at festive banquets in a melodic and joyous way. We have never seen anyone oppose this....

PART TWO: LURIANIC KABBALAH AND ITS INTERPRETERS IN THE SEVENTEENTH CENTURY

Introduction

The spread of the new kabbalistic systems of Safed ushered in a new era of Jewish mysticism.[93] Moshe Cordovero's magnum opus *Pardes Rimonim* was published within a few decades of the author's death. His works were relatively popular, and later mystics like Rabbi Menahem 'Azariah da Fano (1548–1620) and Rabbi Avraham Azulai

(1570–1643) further spread Cordovero's teachings through their own writings.[94] In contrast, Yitshak Luria wrote very little, and his teachings could only become more widely known through his disciples' transcriptions. Hayyim Vital actively fought to keep his versions of his master's teachings out of circulation and suppress other traditions, but manuscripts of Lurianic Kabbalah, referred to collectively as the "writings of the holy ARI," began to disperse throughout the Mediterranean and Europe despite his best attempts.[95] Some seventeenth-century Kabbalists added to this growing literature by composing their own creative and original interpretations of Lurianic Kabbalah.[96] Other scholars took it upon themselves to compare, and often harmonize, the Lurianic teachings with earlier mystical traditions.

Perhaps the greatest of these efforts at synthesis in terms of both size and impact was the *Shenei Luhot ha-Brit* (*The Two Tablets of the Covenant*) by Rabbi Yeshaya Horowitz (c. 1570–1626).[97] The *SheLaH*, the acronym by which this work was popularly known, was an important conduit through which the Kabbalah of Safed came to Europe. Horowitz was born in Prague into an established rabbinic family. He was first exposed to Kabbalah in the 1580s, but his mystical writings from the 1590s reveal that he was not yet acquainted with the Lurianic system. Horowitz's first encounter with Luria's teachings came in the early 1600s, most likely through digests such as Poyetto's summary of *Reshit Hokhmah*, translated above.

Yeshaya Horowitz moved to Jerusalem in 1621 after serving as rabbi in several prominent European communities. He had been deeply influenced by the Kabbalah of Cordovero, yet, by the time of his immigration, he seems to have turned to the theosophy of Luria.[98] Horowitz's decision to immigrate to the land of Israel may have been fueled by his desire to study Lurianic Kabbalah, which was only available in Europe through a very limited selection of manuscripts and books. Once in Israel he opted to settle in Jerusalem instead of Safed, since, by the seventeenth century, this northern city was no longer the kabbalistic epicenter. There in Jerusalem Horowitz immersed himself in the study of Jewish mysticism as never before.

Horowitz began the *SheLaH* while still in Europe, and the work was originally intended as a spiritual and ethical will for his children. However, the book expanded far beyond these modest confines and grew into a voluminous commentary on the Torah and highly unsystematic treatment of major issues in Jewish thought. From this work it is clear that Horowitz saw no tension between the exoteric and esoteric elements of Judaism; he freely deploys legal, philosophical, and kabbalistic sources in his anthological work. The *SheLaH* enjoyed a vast European readership, thereby exposing continental Jewry to the intricacies of Safed Kabbalah. As with Eliyahu de Vidas' *Reshit Hokhmah*, there was also a popular condensation of the *SheLaH*.[99] The excerpts below are taken from the book's introduction *Toledot Adam* (*Generations of Adam*), a lengthy preface that is a treatise of its own. This introduction is divided into some twenty "houses" or "gates" (chapters) that succinctly articulate the themes found in the body of the work.

The popularization of Kabbalah in the seventeenth century opened the gates of mysticism in an unprecedented manner, but it also paved the way for the Sabbatean disaster. This messianic movement was one of the greatest mystical revivals and disappointments of Jewish history.[100] It began with Shabbatai Tsevi, born in 1626 in the prosperous economic hub of Izmir (present-day Turkey). He grew up in this Ottoman city surrounded by a community descended from Spanish exiles who had once converted to Christianity and only later reclaimed their Jewish faith. He proved an adept student, given to periods of intense piety and asceticism, but these were increasingly coupled with severe mood swings and eventually flagrant transgression of normative boundaries of Jewish law. In 1648, still in his early twenties, Shabbatai Tsevi declared himself the Messiah.[101] He was excommunicated, exiled, and forced into a peripatetic existence for the next decade, during which he was married several times.

The turning point in his career came in 1665 when Shabbatai Tsevi met the young and spiritually talented Rabbi Natan Ashkenazi of Gaza (c. 1643/4–80). Rabbi Natan came from a rabbinic family, and had already made a name as an accomplished scholar and mystic in his twenties.[102] He was primarily a student of Lurianic Kabbalah, but Rabbi Natan was influenced by the teachings of Avraham Abulafia and Sufi spiritual practices. Among Natan of Gaza's talents was the ability to divine people's sins and give them the correct spiritual remedy (*tikkun*).[103] It is likely that Shabbatai Tsevi traveled to him for this purpose. In early 1665, Rabbi Natan experienced a prophetic vision that identified Shabbatai Tsevi as the Messiah, which was confirmed by a *Maggid* that possessed him on Shavu'ot the same year.[104]

Natan of Gaza thus became Shabbatai Tsevi's prophet, and though he never performed miracles or wonders, Rabbi Natan's literary propaganda catalyzed his master's messianic claims into a mass movement. His endorsement sparked a veritable deluge of prophets among the lay people and rabbinic figures alike, many of whom were female.[105] Perhaps even more than Rabbi Natan's own complicated arguments based on creative rereadings of Lurianic Kabbalah, these popular prophets were instrumental in convincing large numbers of people that Sabbatai Tsevi was indeed the Messiah.[106]

With multitudes of visionaries publicly championing his cause, and with the support of a large percentage of Turkish Jewry, in late 1665 Shabbatai Tsevi set out to usurp the crown from the sultan. His audacity was swiftly rewarded with imprisonment in 1666, and later that year he converted to Islam, most likely after having been threatened with death by the sultan. For many believers this was the end of the road. However, the messianic fever did not end here, and some of Sabbatai Tsevi's faithful reinterpreted his apostasy as an integral step of the redemptive process.[107] He was exiled to Dulcigno in 1673, where he died three years later. Shabbatai Tsevi's death was surely an even greater blow to his messianic candidacy than his conversion, but some believers maintained the faith and claimed that he had simply escaped to a faraway land and would imminently return. Others contended that while Shabbatai Tsevi had been the Messiah of the Davidic line, another messiah from the house of Jacob would now arise to complete the process of redemption. The *converso* Avraham Michael Cardozo claimed to be just such a figure, and we shall turn to his writings shortly.

Shabbatai Tsevi and his prophet Natan of Gaza were extremely controversial figures, during their lifetimes as well as after their deaths. Their acute messianic message and Shabbatai Tsevi's "strange actions"—erratic, violent, and often antinomian behavior—flaunted the norms of rabbinic Judaism and garnered significant opposition. The European sage Rabbi Ya'akov Sasportas (1610–98) had a reputation for being a trenchant guardian of tradition, and he viciously sought to undercut the budding heresy by denying Rabbi Natan's claims to prophecy and accusing the Sabbateans of drawing upon

Christian dogmas.[108] In the eighteenth century, Rabbi Ya'akov Emden of Amsterdam (1697–1776) became the movement's most vociferous critic, and, as a part of his crusade, he took up the task of identifying rabbis who were hidden Sabbateans. His most famous battle was waged against the reputable Rabbi Yonatan Eybeschuetz of Prague, and the prolonged controversy between these two eminent leaders bitterly divided the European rabbinate.[109]

Why was Shabbatai Tsevi so successful? In part it was his dynamic charisma, which galvanized those around him despite his penchant for outlandish and even ghoulish theatrics. The spread of popular forms of Lurianic mysticism throughout Europe and the Ottoman Empire had primed these communities for a messianic movement that employed the symbolic language of the Kabbalah. Yet, something more than this must have been in the air, for the masses supported Shabbatai Tsevi without reading the recondite kabbalistic texts of Sabbatean theology. The sixteenth and seventeenth centuries were a period of acute messianic expectation in both Christian and Islamic lands. The obvious similarities between the epidemic of Sabbatean prophets and other European spiritualist movements (such as the Quakers) were clear even to contemporary observers.[110] The quest for knowledge at the heart of the scientific renaissance also had important, if subtle, messianic undertones.[111] This period was the very cusp of modernity, and society was undergoing a profound transformation into a new, mercantile system.[112] Finally, we should avoid the gross oversimplification of reducing this movement to its leader's bizarre antinomianism. Sabbateanism was first and foremost an attempt at profound theological and religious renewal, and its success in capturing the hearts of so many should be seen in this light.[113]

If Natan of Gaza was the most iconic theologian and prophet of the Sabbatean movement, Avraham Miguel Cardozo (1626–1706) follows shortly on his heels in terms of both importance and creativity. He was a Spanish-born *converso* who studied Catholic theology extensively before fleeing to Italy in 1648, where he reconnected with the Jewish community and began to occupy himself with a wide variety of Jewish texts. The origins of Cardozo's knowledge of Kabbalah are obscure: according to some autobiographical accounts, he studied with prominent Kabbalists during a sojourn in Egypt, whereas, in others, he claims to have been entirely self-taught. However he did so,

Cardozo's writings show that he had become well-versed in the *Zohar*, the later medieval mystics such as Rabbi Menahem Reccanati and Rabbi Me'ir ibn Gabbai, and the writings of the Safed Kabbalists.

Cardozo had visions heralding the imminent arrival of the Messiah in the late 1640s, which intensified in the early 1660s. In 1666 he experienced several electrifying prophecies confirming that Shabbatai Tsevi was indeed the Messiah. Cardozo does not seem to have been part of the movement during its height, and was never a member of the inner circle of Sabbatean mystics. Yet, Cardozo was one of the most brilliant expositors of Sabbatean theology, and he claimed that he too would have a messianic role after Shabbatai Tsevi's death. Cardozo argued that, like himself, the Messiah must be a *converso* who had descended to the depths of another religion and only then could bring about the redemption. Shabbatai Tsevi had begun this process, but Cardozo's efforts were needed to bring it to full fruition.

Cardozo's mystical and autobiographical writings are at once erudite and eclectic. He argued tirelessly and publicly that Shabbatai Tsevi was truly the Messiah, a fact that remained true after the leader's death. Like other Sabbateans, he gave numerous formulae and rituals (*tikkunim*) meant to repair the shattered cosmos and usher in the Messianic era in which Shabbatai Tsevi was to become the king. Despite his obvious rancor for Christianity, he was influenced by the elements of Christian theology imbibed in his youth. His quick adoption of and unique way of formulating the *sefirot*, especially the Lurianic *partsufim*, may reflect the Christian Trinity. Yet, his endorsement of the Kabbalist belief that the Godhead is composed of different elements was only partial, and Cardozo believed in a deeper theological truth as well—the ultimate God and the only One worthy of true worship is neither the God of the Kabbalists nor that of rabbinic tradition, but rather the unmovable First Cause. Lurianic Kabbalah gave the Jewish people an important language for speaking about God's lower manifestations, but even this exalted system falls short of illustrating God's true nature. The purely transcendent and abstract First Cause cannot be described with any anthropomorphic terms whatsoever.

Sabbateanism did not end with the death of Shabbatai Tsevi or his first generation of mystical prophets. Crypto-sabbateans, both isolated individuals and entire sects, continued to operate for hundreds of years throughout the Ottoman Empire and Europe. A group of Shabbatai Tsevi's followers converted to Islam in the 1680s and were subsequently known as the Donmeh ("converts"). Despite their external change in religious praxis, they were endogamous and maintained an inner, Sabbatean Jewish identity well into the twentieth century.[114] In eighteenth-century Poland, the wild anarchist Jacob Frank (1726–91) founded a new type of Sabbatean circle.[115] Frank rejected all rabbinic law and authority, claiming only to follow the teachings of the *Zohar*. He eventually converted to Catholicism along with many of his followers. Sabbateanism and its various later iterations did not entirely blacken the name of Lurianic Kabbalah, but these mystical heresies forever changed the way that Jewish mysticism was approached.

Further Reading

Goldish, Matt. *The Sabbatean Prophets*. Cambridge, MA: Harvard University Press, 2004.

Newman, Eugene. *Life and Teachings of Isaiah Horowitz*. London: E. Newman, 1972.

Rapoport-Albert, Ada. *Women and the Messianic Heresy of Sabbatai Zevi 1666–1816*. Translated by Deborah Greniman. Oxford and Portland, OR: The Littman Library of Jewish Civilization, 2011.

Scholem, Gershom. *Sabbatai Sevi: The Mystical Messiah*. Translated by R. J. Zwi Werblowsky. Princeton: Princeton University Press, 1975.

The Generations of Adam

The House of Y-H-V-H [I]

All interpreters of our Torah, whether Kabbalists, explicators of the simple meaning, or philosophical commentators on our holy Torah, unanimously agree that Y-H-V-H is the proper Divine Name and the root for all the names. They are emanated from It and It contains them all....

There are ten Divine Names written in the Torah which it is forbidden to erase: *EHYeH*, *Yah*, Y-H-V-H with the vocalization of

Elohim, El, Elohim, Y-H-V-H with the vocalization of *Tseva'ot*, Y-H-V-H *Tseva'ot, Elohim Tseva'ot, Shadday, Adonay*. And these ten Divine Names are the emanation of ten *sefirot*: *keter*, *hokhmah*, *binah*, and so on. The *sefirot* are the Divine Names and the Divine Names are the *sefirot*. For the *ruhaniyut*[116] of the *sefirot* breathes and shines over the Divine Names through the intention of the one who writes them or who utters them in holiness and purity. Just as the Temple is a chamber and resting place for *shekhinah*, since the divine light is concentrated between the two boards of the ark [of the covenant],[117] so these ten Divine Names are the chambers for the *ruhaniyut* of the *sefirot*, which are alluded to in the Name Y-H-V-H. For *yod* alludes to *hokhmah* and the tip [of the *yod*] alludes to *keter*. The first *heh* alludes to *binah*, *vav* alludes to *tif'eret* with the six extremities.[118] The final *heh* alludes to *malkhut*....

The Kabbalists, especially in *Sefer ha-Pardes*, have already discussed at length the linkage of the worlds. For the upper and the lower cleave together. The upper bestows upon the lower, and the lower is a shadow of the upper. What is in one is in the other—even if the one below is material and the one above spiritual. It is always a case of one being parallel to the other. The entire *Ma'aseh Bereshit*[119] speaks of [matters in] the lower worlds and alludes to the higher worlds. For He, blessed be He, brought all the worlds into existence and all the worlds depend on His great light. Although the light is revealed in a much more refined way in a certain world than in another, this is due to the process of extension. However, everything is from His great light. I will give you an example. The light of the sun casts its light on the moon. Afterward the moon shines in the atmosphere of the world. From there, the light proceeds from the atmosphere of the world into a single room. The light progressively becomes coarsened because of the process of extension, but it is all one light. So it is with the extension of the worlds, *Atsilut* ("emanation"), *Beri'ah* ("creation"), *Yetsirah* ("formation"), *'Assiyah* ("action").

The secret of the world of *Atsilut* is that it is like a flame attached to a coal. It is not something separate from it. For [the source of] the flame is in the coal and in hovering over the coal, the flame is revealed and it is tightly bound to it. Similarly, [the world of] emanation (*Atsilut*) consists of rays of light from the coal, which were concealed [within it] in perfect unity. The light of emanation consists of supernal lights, beyond comprehension. These lights were revealed in the secret of the verses, "and God said let there be light, and there was light" (Gen 1:3) [and] "and the spirit of God hovered [above the water]" (Gen 1:2). The secret alluded to by the hovering is the arising of the will to contract his light so that it *could* emanate. This involves no change in either the emanatory or the emanation, according to the secret meaning of "and there was light," which our sages, of blessed memory, said means that there already was light. Only, [the light] was completely concealed in its root and supernal source, as was said above. That is the secret of his divinity. For the *Ein Sof* is a soul to the soul of the *sefirot*. They are the souls of everything that would later be brought into existence. And the Cause of Causes is a soul to them, according to the secret of emanated divine essence. Afterward, the world of *Atsilut* was extended by means of *Malkhut*, through the contraction of its light, and the world [of *Beri'ah*] came into existence. The world of *Atsilut* is a soul to the world of *Beri'ah*, just as *Ein Sof* is a soul to the world of *Atsilut*. Afterward, the world of *Beri'ah* was extended through the contraction of its light and the world of *Yetsirah* came onto existence. The world of *Beri'ah* is a soul to the world of *Yetsirah*. Afterward the world of *Yetsirah* was extended through the contraction of its light and the world of *'Assiyah* came into existence....

The House of Israel [I]

The soul of a human being derives from the extension of the Name Y-H-V-H. Even the appearance of one's body is inscribed and indicated by the Name Y-H-V-H. Thus one may explain the divine image (*tselem*) and likeness (*demut*) in which the human being was created and fashioned. This matter requires an extensive explanation. As a result, a person's heart will be aroused to "turn from evil and do good" (Ps 34:15, 37:27) and to sanctify himself....

The will and simple desire arose in the Unique Lord, Root of Roots, *Ein Sof*, to manifest a holy emanation from His concealed light, which would testify to the necessity of His absolute and concealed existence. Similarly, the will arose to create one perfected and complete creature, fashioned in the divine image and likeness, according to the pattern of the sacred, supernal sanctuary, the divine emanation which is called Supernal Person, as we shall explain.

Concerning this creature, it was said, "Let us make a human being in our image" (Gen 1:26).... The Name Y-H-V-H is alluded to in the structure of a human being, from top to bottom and from bottom to top. How so? The head is like a *yod*. The torso is like a *vav*. The ten fingers, five on each hand, are the two *hehs*. Also, ten toes, five on each foot, are the two *hehs*. The length of the penis is a *vav*. Its tip is a *yod*. In the beginning of *Pardes* [*Rimmonim*], it is written that toes are like shadows to the fingers. This alludes to the world of *Beri'ah* (Creation), which is a shadow to the world of *Atsilut* (Emanation).... There is also an allusion to Y-H-V-H in the ten fingers of the hands, which are the number of the ten *sefirot*....

I have more to say concerning the spiritual body that acts as an intermediary between the soul and the body. For the form, if one might say so, is similar to the One who fashioned it. For the Kabbalists have already said, by way of example, that *Ein Sof* is a soul to the souls. For we call the divine emanations souls for all that exists, and *Ein Sof* is a soul for those souls. For, in comparison to Him, those souls are like a body to a soul. The divine emanation is called the Great Adam, as it is written, "And on the [likeness of the] Throne, the likeness of [the appearance of] a human being" (Ez 1:26)...And the human being, who is called the Small Adam, was created in the image and likeness. The soul in the body is, *mutatis mutandis*, like *Ein Sof* in regard to the divine emanation. As we explained above, there is a concealed aspect between the essence of *Ein Sof* and the unity of the divine emanation.

The Faithful House [II]

Know that the holy letters and holy words are entirely spiritual in their root. The Kabbalists said that the letters are from *binah*, the vowel points from *hokhmah*, and their cantillation signs are from *keter*....

When a person approaches the study of Torah, he must have in mind that what he is learning are words of God, whose essential inner aspect is concealed from him. In this way, all the Torah that emerges from his mouth "will be more pleasing before Holy One, blessed be He, than oxen" (cf. Ps 69:32), even if he understands nothing in it but the basic story. And there is no need to say that even someone who does not understand at all [what he is learning in the Torah], because he is not proficient in the meaning of the language, but is merely occupied in reading [aloud], also has a good reward for his effort. Concerning these and similar cases, it is written, "and he studies his Torah day and night" (Ps 1:2). The [rabbis] taught, the verse does not say "he studies Torah" but "he studies his Torah," meaning according to the measure of knowledge (cf. b. 'Avodah Zarah 19a). For even a person who does not know how to combine the word will also receive a reward if he concerns himself with it day and night. His labor is before him, as long as he constantly progresses....

The letters have *ruhaniyut*, both because of their image and their number. The image of the letters and what they allude to is explained in *Sefer ha-Temunah* and in *Pardes, Gate of the Letters*. [After learning these sources], you will know that most of all, when the holy letters are combined and words are made from them, the *ruhaniyut* of this word is a great matter above. And just as the vocalized forms of Y-H-V-H and the Divine Names are the secret of divine emanation, except that the Divine Names are an extension of the vocalized forms of Y-H-V-H, so the epithets are an extension of the divine names and there are epithets to the epithets. Similar are all the words of our Holy Language. All the words are above. Everything that exists below in corporeality is a manifestation and extension of *shefa'* from above that was extended level after level, through thousands upon thousands of stages, until it took on a material form in this material world.

Now the name for a certain thing is really the name for what is above in its root. For the root is where these letters are joined together, except that every stage of the chain of manifestation is called by this name, as a metaphor for its root. Therefore our language is called a Holy Language because all of the names and words exist above in their root, in the supernal place of holiness. Later, when something descends and is extended from this holy place, this manifestation is called by that [supernal] name, as a metaphor. As the author of *Pardes* wrote, the "handles" of a vessel are metaphors for human hands. Similarly, [one speaks of] the foot of the throne. Thus I say that this *ruhaniyut*, the power of the human hand, which is called "hand," is not properly so called, but is metaphorical. The same applies to "eye," which refers to the eye's power of sight, and "ear," which refers to the ear's power of hearing. All the names are metaphorical, for a hand for a hand, an eye for an eye, a foot for a foot, and all of the rest (Ex 21:24)....

This is the wisdom that Adam used when he indicated the names by which everything would be known. Thus it was said that his level in this [wisdom] was greater than the ministering angels. For through the Holy Spirit that [rested] upon him, he built letters and words connected to the inner speech,[120] so that those names would indicate the root of that particular thing. It is practically said that through knowing the things below, he knew the secret of the supernal Chariots. For every creature below has a root above. For otherwise, how could the parts of this world be interconnected if there is no root above for the elements? If the creatures have no root above, how can *shefa'* and providence reach them from the Lord of all? This was a wondrous wisdom. For he grasped the source and root of everything and called it by that name, which is its name indeed.

The House of Wisdom [II]

It has been explained that the Torah, in its root, is entirely Names of God, blessed be He, according to the secret of the Holy Language that we explained above. It has been extended [from its root] in stage after stage until it took on material form. It is similar in regard to the actions of the commandments which a person does. Through them, he lives the life of the souls, the 600,000 souls of Israel, from the 600,000 letters of the Torah. For there is one judgment for the Torah and the person who fulfills it. For the Torah has taken on a material form, and in ascending the stages, one after another, the words [begin] to shine. The same is true for Adam. Had he not sinned, his matter would only have been spiritual[121] and "the earth [would be] filled with knowledge [of Y-H-V-H]" (Isa 11:9), even the earthiness that is in him.[122] Now, no part of his body remains that knows except the heart.... If Adam had not sinned, he would have remained in the Garden of Eden, "to work it and guard it" (Gen 2:15). Our rabbis explained this as alluding to the positive and negative commandments (*Zohar* 1:27a). He would have fulfilled the commandments in a different way which is more spiritual,[123] as is written in the *Pardes*, *Gate of the Soul*.

A human being and the Torah are comparable. (This is indicated by "This is the Torah of Man"; 2 Sam 7:19). 248 limbs and 365 sinews correspond to the 613 commandments. Six hundred thousand souls correspond to 600,000 letters of the Torah. The aspect of "to work it and guard it" has become corporeal. Nevertheless, they emerge from the source of holiness and [the two levels] correspond. For the reward of [fulfilling] a corporeal commandment is the spirituality of that commandment. This is the meaning of the saying of the rabbis, "If a person sanctifies himself a little below, he is sanctified a lot from above" (b. Yoma 39a)....

From this the matter of revealed and concealed in the entire Torah can be explained. The world thinks that the concealed is something separate from the revealed. This is not so. Only the concealed has coarsened and taken on material form, which reveals it. It is like the verse, "apple of gold in settings of silver, each matter according to its manner" (Prov 25:11). In other words, just as silver is similar to gold, but is a lower level than it, so is the revealed in comparison to the concealed...

[The Torah is compared to] "golden apples in settings of silver." Thus one finds in the Torah secrets and allusions, which the scholars have designated *PaRDeS*,[124] which is an acronym for [the four levels of scriptural interpretation], *peshat* (plain meaning), *remez* (allusion), *derash* (homiletical meaning), and *sod* (mystical meaning). *Sod* is the hidden light, which is presently concealed from us due to the departure of the light of the garments of light. It is the essence of the Holy Language. *Remez* refers to the actions of fulfilling the material commandments, because it is their name, as I explained.[125] The oral Torah is alluded to in the written Torah, for example, "every time [it says] from where do we [know this], it means from what [verse] are these matters [derived]." There is nothing that is not clearly alluded to in the Torah, except that the intellect has darkened from what it should have been....

Therefore, the Torah requires explanation and commentary, namely the Talmud. For otherwise, it would have been self-explanatory, as we see in another age, the age of the earliest authorities. They possess a clear intellect and thus understood a deep matter without commentary. Later, they did not understand without a commentary. And then there were commentaries on the commentaries, as a result of the darkening of the intellect. Therefore, if Adam had not sinned and had [retained] a clear intellect, he would have understood the written Torah. From this understanding, he would have known everything and there would have been no need for an oral Torah. But since he sinned, the light departed, and he brought death to the world.

The House of Wisdom [III]

The meaning of [the blessing], "who gives the Torah," is as follows. In truth, God has already given the Torah. However, He continues to give it and will not cease [doing so]. This requires a broad explanation. The verse says, "Y-H-V-H said these words to your entire community on the mountain, from the midst of the fire, the cloud and the darkness, [in] a great voice, *ve-lo yasaf*" (Deut 5:19). RaSHI explained, "We translate *ve-lo yasaf* 'and it did not cease,' because His voice is strong and continues forever. Another possibility is that '*ve-lo yasaf* means that 'He did not add to' what appeared in that display." There is a secret concealed here and both of the interpretations are entirely true. When "*lo yasaf*" is understood as "He did not add to," it indicates that the commandments of the rabbis, with their stringencies and precautionary measures, were not yet commanded from the mouth of the Almighty. And the meaning of "it did not cease" is that [God's commandments] did not cease with what was explicitly stated by that voice, for [the rabbinic commandments] were contained in that voice, potentially. However, the proper time had not arrived for each to emerge from potential to actuality. For this requires the arousal below, depending on their being, quality, and the level of their souls, in each and every generation. Then the Sages went on to arouse additional supernal power, and it was actualized in their time and knowledge. This is not to say, God forbid, that the sages introduced anything from their own minds. Rather, they focused on the supernal mind (*da'at 'elyon*) and their souls which had stood on Mount Sinai. For all of the souls received [the Torah] there. So, on the basis of their souls and [the merits of] their generation, it was fitting [for them to bring into actuality what was concealed in God's voice]. [Thus their commandments] are from the mouth of the Almighty. There is an allusion to this: *mi-de-rabbanan* (commandments of the rabbis) has the same numerical value [346] as *mi-pi Gevurah* (from the mouth of the Almighty)....

This is related to the saying, "The Holy One, blessed be He, says Torah from the mouth of all of the rabbis" (b. Hagigah 15b). Some use [this saying] to explain the meaning of our request [in the Sabbath prayer], "Grant us a portion in Your Torah." In other words, let our portion be in the Torah that the Holy One, blessed be He, teaches. May we merit that the teaching be said in our name. The meaning is that the Sages say new things or [they emerge] from their argumentations. However, it is all from the power of the voice that was mentioned, and the time has arrived for them to bring it from potential into actuality through their mediation. Surely, "our Lord is great and full of power, there is no limit to His understanding" (Ps 147:5). For this power did not cease [at Sinai]. It is limitless and infinite in regard to the innovation and source of souls in every generation and in regard to the power of the people below who arouse the supernal power. Therefore, the Holy One, blessed be He, gave the Torah and He [continues to] give the Torah at every moment. The flowing source does not cease. What He [continues to] give was contained in the potential of what He gave [at Sinai].

The House of David [I]

Now I will explain the matter. Know that the Holy One, blessed be He, created the world for the ultimate purpose of the human being. God made man upright in order to be entirely good and light. In this sense, if Adam had not aroused evil and had been completely good, everyone would agree that it was good for him to have been created. The disagreement concerning whether it would have been better for him not to have been created or to have been created, arises after Adam misused his free will and the intention of creation was annulled.

I will advance another principle concerning the damage caused by Adam. The world has not yet realized the intention of creation, as long as the damage has not been rectified.[126] You have to know that when the human being will be rectified, the garments of skin (*'or*) that are now blindness and darkness and not light will become light (*or*) again. And they will be more light than they were before he sinned. This is the meaning of "light is superior to darkness" (Eccl 2:13). For light has a superiority over the power of darkness.... When he [Adam] was in garments of light and entirely good, he still contained a potential arousal of the *kelippah* in concealment. But now, in causing it to emerge [from concealment], it truly becomes an evil *kelippah*. It is Satan, the evil urge. But when someone overcomes, subdues, and annuls it completely, it swiftly departs. [Then] the good of the soul is a clear and pure goodness without any residue.

This is the "whole person" who conquers his evil urge and overcomes it.[127] It is said, "who conquers [it]" and not "who kills [it]" (m. Avot 4:1). This indicates that he does not kill it but holds it in submission, so that it will be good, the opposite of what it was. This is a great matter. For he overcomes [his evil urge] and purifies it, until an evil angel is transformed to good.

Take, for example, evil attributes, such as jealousy, lust, and hate, and so on. He does not eliminate them but gains control over them, in order to purify them. That is, jealousy is transformed to the rivalry of scholars, lust becomes concealed passion [for God], and hate becomes the hatred of the wicked, as David wrote, "I hate them with perfect hatred" (Ps 139:22). There are a thousand matters like these.

This is the meaning of "very good" (Gen 1:31). As the rabbis explained, "'Good' refers to the good urge, 'very' refers to the evil urge" (*Bereshit Rabbah* 9:7). For then evil is the cause of great good. For evil is not merely eliminated but transformed to good. This will occur in the future, after the purification through destructions and sorrows that will be endured. Repentance will be aroused and the *kelippot* will rest.

The House of Choosing

Now listen to me and stir your souls. God's knowing is His will, and His will is His knowing. For the will involves what one desires to do and is the root of the entire chain of emanation, from great to small. There is nothing other than it. For "all that Y-H-V-H desires to do, He does" (cf. Ps 135:6). This is in itself the knowing, through knowing the essence of His will. He is the will and He is the knowing. He knows everything from the essence of His will. I already wrote at length above that the will contains opposites. All ways are within it. The choice is granted to human beings to arouse whatever power they wish. God created Adam upright and commanded him not to arouse the power of evil. But as a result of his sin, he came to know good and evil. As a result, darkness and punishment were drawn [from the will]. These are not merely arbitrary (*heskemii*). Rather, the reward of a commandment is the root of the commandment, above in its root. And the reward of a transgression is a transgression. All of this is rooted in the will, because the will contains all things and their opposites. Similarly, the Torah, which is drawn from this will, contains forty-nine aspects of impurity and forty-nine aspects of purity, forbidden and permitted, guilty and innocent. And "both of these are words of the Living God" (b. 'Eruvin 13b). For all are contained in the power of the "great voice that does not cease" (Deut 5:19). According to the arousal below, so is the inclination to bring to realization. No matter what it is, nothing is separate, God forbid. Each is an actualization of one of the ways [contained in the will]....

The reason that a person has the power to arouse above, according to his choice and will, is because he is made in the holy likeness and image. He also contains the "other side." Therefore, the key of the sources is in his hand and the advice for him is, "therefore, choose life" (Deut 30:19). For the divine will is more pleased with goodness. For [it is the nature] of the truly good will to do good to others. For its good impulse was to bring goodness into existence so that it could be received. Even evil was not essentially created so that evil would exist, but in order to be transformed to good, as I discussed at length above....

The Great Gate

Know my sons, may their Rock protect them, that this matter of the keys that are entrusted to human hands has remained a secret concealed by the true Kabbalists who enter into the counsel of God. It has been passed on from Kabbalist to Kabbalist, going back to Moses on Sinai. For both the external and internal keys truly have been given over to human beings. Thus a person does not only worship in order to open [the sources which supply his needs], but the essence of worship is required above (*tsorekh gavoha*), in order to unite the Great Name with its powers, until *Ein Sof*. This is accomplished through learning Torah and fulfilling the commandments. Their root is the divine emanation that has been manifested for the human being who is in the supernal image and likeness. By means of fulfilling the Torah and commandments, he arouses supernal power and, so to speak, strengthens it. For I have already alluded above in many places that the basis of the emanation of the structure is *Tif'eret* and *Malkhut*. They are the roots of the worlds and the secret of "turn from evil and do good," (Ps 34:15) in other words, the negative and positive commandments. Thus, since "first in thought, last in deed," through performing a good deed below, force is added to the power above, so to speak, and great love, friendship, and bonding [is increased] between the two lovers, mentioned above. The faces of those two cherubs were turned toward each other, "like a male and female embracing" (1 Kgs 7:36).[128]...

The Writings of Avraham Miguel Cardozo

Epistle to the Judges of Izmir [1669]

[PART TWO: THE TESTIMONY][129]

I shall now tell your worships the Absolute truth. But I must first provide a preface.... Keep in mind, as well, that I am far distant from both Gaza and Izmir. I could not possibly have conspired with Nathan Benjamin for the two of us to announce in unison that Shabbatai Tsevi is the Messiah. What, moreover, can be supposed to motivate my yearning for the Redeemer's advent? Certainly not my being in exile, for I experience no exile.[130] It cannot be the need to struggle for a living, for I am at ease. Nor can it be the wish for time to study Torah, for I have both time and preparation. I am indeed among those who long for our salvation. But this is not for the sake of any material gratification. No: it is because I seek to fulfill the injunction that we must look with eagerness toward our salvation (b. Shabbat 31a). It will be wholly evident from this that my purpose is not, God forbid, to seduce the Jewish people into false worship and that anyone who suspects me of this crime is a devilish villain. What can I possibly gain by revealing these matters?...

In the year 5409 [1648–49] I was studying Torah in Venice. That was where I began my studies at the age of twenty-two, having left Spain when I was twenty-one. I had a dream that the messiah had appeared and that the people of Venice did not believe in him. But God gave me strength, and I seated him on my shoulders and proclaimed through the marketplaces, "This is the true Messiah!"...After the year 5423 [1662–63] had begun, moreover, I saw in a dream the following words written out: "The Redeemer will come in the year 5425" [1664–65]....

A great and mysterious event befell me another night. My head was filled with ideas as I lay in bed,[131] yet I was not dreaming but was fully awake. The next morning I told the people of my household that a baby boy was going to be born to me, and that he would prove to be a lamp for the Messiah. But they should not rejoice over him till ten days had passed, I told them, for before the tenth day he would suddenly die. And so it happened! The boy was born, and on the day of his birth this town received the good news that the Messiah had been revealed. He then died suddenly on the eighth day, before he could be circumcised. This is all true as the Torah of Moses.

Subsequently, in the month of Shevat 5426 [January 7–February 5, 1666], during the predawn hours, a light appeared in my house to an old lady. For thirty-one years now the woman has been ill with the disease called *paralyza*, such that her left arm is emaciated like a dead limb and she cannot move it at all. The disease recurred nine years ago, with the effect that the bone of her upper leg became dislocated, the tendons contracted, and the entire leg was left as immobile as the arm.

When she saw the bright light, she assumed the sun had risen. She then went back to sleep and woke to find the whole house dark. She became alarmed. "Master of the universe!" she said. "Is it not enough that I am like a dead woman? Must I go blind as well?" (For she thought she had suddenly lost her vision.) But then the lunatic [the Muslim muezzin, that is][132] sounded his customary call [to prayer], and she was relieved, for she knew it must still be night. When she told us her story the next morning, we laughed at her. Over the next fifteen days, the lights appeared to her three or four times more. But I still did not take her seriously.

One night I was given the premonition that a star, big as the full moon, was going to appear in the sky. The lady told me the next morning that, in the predawn hours, she had seen a star like the sun and the moon, which had illuminated the entire house. It was then that I realized that what she had been saying was absolutely true. I thereupon begged God for an explanation of these events, and He heard my prayer.

I was given yet another premonition of the star's appearance during the month of Adar [March 8–April 5, 1666], and a third time, with greater clarity, on the night of the Great Sabbath [April 16].[133] And on Saturday, the twenty-fifth day of the 'Omer of the year 5425 [May 15, 1666], the star appeared in the eastern sky half an hour past sunrise, to the right of the sun. It was the size of the moon; people saw it shining with a clear, brilliant light. God covered the sun with a thick cloud, so that the witnesses would be able to gaze at that star as it rose along with the sun. They watched it for about half an hour, till the sun had risen further and left the cloud behind. The witnesses' vision then began to suffer, and the star gradually faded from their view.

I myself did not see it. I had contracted an eye disease and had not yet gotten out of bed. But I could hear the sounds of great amazement from those who did see it from the upper story of my house.... Why this sign was granted me cannot be explained. Inasmuch as I did not see it, I prayed God to tell me if it was indeed the star of which I had had the premonition. Now, the old lady was by the courtyard entrance late that Tuesday afternoon, and she began yelling that she had just seen for the fourth time a star as big as the sun, which had all but blinded her by its sheer brilliance. Wednesday I kept on praying, and it was seen yet again in the late afternoon, in the middle of the courtyard.

In the month of Shevat [January 7–February 5, 1666], and in First Adar [February 6–March 7], I dreamed that I saw seven *Tannaim* sitting studying the Torah, Rabbi Shim'on ben Yohai and Rabbi Hiyya the Great among them. In my presence, the Patriarch ordered them to summon a certain man. I heard the Patriarch say to the seven Tannaim, "Give honor to the king." They all stood up, and the Patriarch gave a loud shout, "Bring a throne for the king; bring a throne for the king!" And the man said, "No need; sit down; sit down and busy yourselves with a profound *halakhah*."

I woke up then, and immediately the dream came back to me. The ceiling of the room opened, and I saw the Lord sitting on a throne high and exalted. I had previously been composing an original hymn about *shekhinah*'s having gone back up to Her proper place,[134] and now God said to me that "I have received this hymn." He assured me, moreover, that "salvation is not at hand, so give the Jewish people message of great consolation and honor." That morning the old lady had told me that she had been shown, within the light that had appeared to her, a throne white as snow. So I said, "May it be Your will, Lord my God, that I be shown who is going to sit on this throne," whereupon a cloud appeared and covered the throne. I thus began to be entirely convinced that the old lady had been speaking the truth.

On one occasion afterward, I spent the entire night begging and pleading with God to grant me a trustworthy token by healing the old lady. When I got up in the morning, the token and the wonder turned out to be in the healing of my own eyes.

Your Worships must know that, a year and a half earlier, I had contracted (for my sins) a grave eye disease called *cataratas*: [cataracts]. I had tried every cure known to man, but to no avail. My blindness actually grew progressively worse, till I had despaired of my vision. Now I praised and thanked God for the grace He had shown me. Yet I nevertheless resumed my prayers and my pleas. This, I said, was an inner sign that people would never believe if I told them about it. But if God would only do me the very great favor of restoring the old lady's arm and leg to their former condition, then the people would surely become firm believers upon seeing the great miracle, would surely turn themselves to repentance and good deeds!

Sure enough: a light was revealed to her shortly before dawn. Her arm relaxed. Her big toe stretched itself out, and the bone of her upper leg went back into its socket. Her mouth and her left eye were healed; her right eye did indeed wobble a bit, but not as badly as before. Her left shoulder went back up to its proper place, and the arm came away from her body. Her leg extended itself, though not such that she could stand on it. This was because God did not wish to publicize the sign, but only granted it to me so that I might believe in the mission He had given me.

The lady remains well to this day. After three days, alas, my own illness began to come back, and my cure did not last. Perhaps this was because I had asked for the second sign.

I asked God's favor on yet another occasion. I was suffering greatly, in intense and enduring pain. I asked that He allay my doubts by letting me have an answer to the question that I would formulate in my mind. I thought upon the kingship and wondered to whom it would belong—and hardly had I finished when a heavenly voice proclaimed: "It is Shabbatai Tsevi who is destined to reign."...

I call heaven and earth to witness that, on one single day, I saw two or three extraordinary signs and tokens, each of them indispensible. Oh, I could go on like this endlessly! But I have written only the tiniest fraction. And through all these experiences I have come to know that the true messiah is Shabbatai Tsevi, for whom I am obliged to sacrifice my life.

This Is My God and I Will Praise Him [1685/6]

CHAPTER XVI: THAT THE BLESSED HOLY ONE, GOD OF ISRAEL, IS THE SPIRIT OF THE *SEFIROT*; THAT HE IS NOT THE FIRST CAUSE

The rabbis say in the Talmud (*Berakhot*) that God prays; that He enwraps Himself in a fringed garment; that He wears phylacteries; and that He studies Torah.[135] They relate how the serpent told Eve that God ate from the Tree, and thus created the world.[136] [He therefore requires something outside Himself, in order to be Creator.] They write, in their story of how the moon's stature came to be diminished, that God told the Jews to "bring a sin-offering on My behalf, to atone for My having diminished the moon."[137] [He therefore requires human cooperation, in His own "Mending."] And there are many more passages of this sort.

These same rabbis declare, unanimously, that God is possessor of the attributes. He is too lofty, too much concealed, to have any name beyond those of His attributes, and in accord with the actions He performs. Yet He prays, and these passages were therefore spoken of Him—passages from which it is clear that He cannot be the First Cause. Anyone who dares attack Him, on the basis of these passages, will pay for it dearly![138]

We read in the *Yalkut* that, when God says, "Let Us make humanity in Our image, after Our likeness" (Gen 1:26), He means: "Not male without female, nor female without male, but rather like Us."[139] The commentators explain [this combination of male and female in the Deity] as referring to the Blessed Holy One and His *shekhinah*. Now, it was the Creator who said, "Let Us make humanity." He therefore cannot be the First Cause, who has neither image nor likeness, who is neither male nor female. (*Shekhinah*, I have already demonstrated, is a divinity in the full sense of the word.) How is it even conceivable that this is the First Cause?

The twenty-second of the *Tikkunei Zohar* (65a) introduces the Divinity in all its aspects. The *sefirot* are there declared the "body," while the Blessed Holy One is the "spirit" shining within that body. Inside it all shines that concealed entity that binds it all into one, yet concerning which there is not the smallest hint—the First Cause, in other words. The passage thus states explicitly that the Blessed Holy One is a Spirit within the *se*firot. He is not the *sefirot* themselves. Nor, on the other hand, is He the First Cause.

From the treatise on the "Secrets of the Letters" (in *Zohar Hadash* 4b), we learn that the *sefirot* are the sacred names used for the Blessed Holy One. They are pure, lofty Intelligences, whose essential being cannot be known even to a prophet. Yet they function as His body, and He is called the "inner spirit" within them, which human knowledge has no capacity to attain. All the more unattainable is the mystery of the Infinite. The *Zohar* on the Torah portion *Va-Yera* (1:103a–b, commenting on the verse "Her husband is known by means of the 'gates'" (Prov 31:23)) says much the same.[140]...

These passages, and a thousand more like them, speak plainly and leave no room for doubt. They declare that the Blessed Holy One, God of Israel, Creator of the world, is not the First Cause. Rather, He is a certain entity, in His essence unfathomable, who developed out of the First Cause by a process of emanation—or, perhaps, evolved by some more august process that we call "emanation" because the Hebrew language has no proper word for it. He is not any one *sefirah*, but a Spirit to all the *sefirot*, embodied within them. Making use of the *sefirot*, and drawing upon the power of the Infinite [First Cause], He created and administers everything that exists. In the *sefirah yesod*, He appeared to the patriarchs. In *tif'eret*, He appeared to Moses and revealed the Torah. All of this was and is accomplished through *shekhinah*.

It will now be evident that the ancient philosophers and pagans spoke the truth. So did the Jews: the Tannaim and the Amoraim, the *Zohar* and *Tikkunei Zohar*, the books Yetsirah and Bahir and *Berit Menuhah*.[141] All agreed that the Blessed Holy One, God of Israel, is not the First Cause, but rather an emanated being. He is not a *sefirah* or an attribute, but rather the maker of the attributes and the Spirit of them all. It is He whom we worship, He, and not His attributes, whom we invoke....

The Blessed Holy One, furthermore, has no name, other than in accord with His actions or in accord with the attribute through which He manifests Himself. He prays to the First Cause, which is within Himself, the purpose being to benefit His children and to accomplish His own unification with *shekhinah*....

It is certain, likewise, that the [modern] philosophers, the [Jewish] scholars of the past, and the Muslims as well, have no true God, inasmuch as the Creator and the First Cause are not identical. The Christian religion is false, down to every last detail. The Kabbalists, too, are wrong. The First Cause, even as embodied within the *sefirot*, is something other than the Blessed Holy One, God of Israel, and It did not Itself create the world by using the *sefirot*.

Finally, it can now be grasped how it is that *shekhinah* is a true divinity, along with the Blessed Holy One. He and She are two aspects—certainly not two gods—but one single and unified Deity.[142]...

Nowhere do we find, among all the *sefirot* and spirits of the Lurianic hierarchies, any one entity precisely identical with that being whom we call Blessed Holy One: the world's Creator, Israel's God. From Rabbi Simeon ben Yohai's time down to Luria's own, no one had ever discussed the subject of the emanations in terms of "body" and "spirit" as Luria did, in precise detail as well as general principle. Yet never did he speak of this one Spirit whose existence we have now discovered, and whose divinity we now proclaim. Yet how might it have been possible for anyone to have discovered the identity of the God of Israel, if Luria's scholarship had not paved the way? From the end of the Amoraic period onward, it would seem, generation after generation of Jewish thinkers have investigated the Kabbalah, each scholar adding his fresh discoveries to those of his predecessors. Little by little, bit by bit, piece by piece, they built up our understanding of Divinity. In holiness, in purity, with the most tireless effort, they laid the foundations for the achievement that is at last within our grasp: comprehension of God's identity and of *shekhinah*'s divinity, which we had forgotten in our exile.

Surely our predecessors, ancient and modern, deserve to be credited as though they themselves had made this discovery! It was through their labors and by dint of their efforts that God's faith has now come to be understood, and that it has begun to be communicated to the wider public, thereby effecting the Redemption of the Jewish people. Unless we know the mystery of Divinity, which our ancestors first denied and then forgot, we will have no possibility of leaving our exile. All of us moderns—Jews, Muslims, philosophers, Christians—believe in the First Cause. We worship the First Cause; we give It our blessings. But it was through God and *shekhinah* that the First Cause created us and gave us the Torah, and, accordingly, it is only by invoking Him that we may find salvation. It will thus be seen how thoroughly necessary it is for us to know God, to worship Him, and to bless Him truly and rightly.

Israel, Holiness to the Lord [1682–1686]

You must know, now, that when the Temple was destroyed the light of the [higher] *sefirah hokhmah* was withdrawn from the *sefirah tif'eret*.[143] The light of "Adam of the World of Emanation," too, was reduced. The *sefirot* of the Irascible One and His Female were thus left in the state of being "disfigured in appearance from that of a man, in form [from that of humanity," Isa 52:14]; the reference being to *tif'eret* and *malkhut*. The Blessed Holy One,...[which is] the rational soul of the Irascible One, had withdrawn Itself into the heights, leaving the Irascible One diminished, and as though He were asleep. (This is the secret meaning of the verse, "Wake up! why do You sleep, O Lord?" (Ps 44:24).)...

In the exile, the river that goes forth from Eden has been reduced to a trickle. The "Five Persons" of the World of Emanation are left as beached stones, at least as far as the outer aspects of the *sefirot* are concerned.[144] In their interiors, to be sure, there is still living water. This is the hidden meaning of the passage, "You shall speak to the rock and it will yield its water" (Num 20:8). The *sefirot*, after all, are the moist Stones from which the waters emerge.[145]

Yet nowadays, thanks to our transgressions, the demonic Stones have nourished themselves from the divine effluence. They must be separated from this river and distanced from it as far as they possibly can be. Therefore: You must first take five stones from the river bank, corresponding to the five demonic Persons: Patient One (*arikh anpin*), *hokhmah*, *binah*, Irascible One (*ze'ir anpin*), and *malkhut*. Stand you at the river's edge, and, in one single action, hurl three stones—which you must take from a higher spot, farther removed from the river—into a distant place, where the river cannot water them any more.

Then set the remaining two stones, corresponding to the demonic Irascible One and His Female, at a greater distance from one another. Throw the one with all your strength to the other side of the river. Throw the other...in the place where you stand, far away, so that the two stones are separated by the river. Before taking up the stones, recite the passage from "A river goes forth from Eden" up to the word "Euphrates" (Gen 2:10–14)....

"He has put an end (*kets*) to darkness. He is the Searcher-out, on behalf of every Extremity, of the Stone of darkness and the shadow of death" (Job 28:31). "Darkness" is a term for the demonic forces. The Infinite One has set a boundary to this darkness, and an "end" to its dominion and to its nourishing itself from the river. This "end" has come about through Cardozo and Tsevi, who are *kof-tsadde* [*kof*, the initial letter of "Cardozo," and *tsadde*, the initial letter of "Tsevi"], *kets*, "end."

When shall the end come for the dominion of darkness? When the Infinite One hands Cardozo and Tsevi over to that darkness! He has put Messiah ben David outside the Torah's light, and now has buried him. He has put Messiah ben Ephraim in the darkness of the failed Redemption and has subjected him to endless trials.... Our entire purpose now is to destroy the structure of impure *binah*, *tif'eret*, and *malkhut*, which are "darkness and the shadow of death," Sama'el and the Snake....

The prayers of the saints in heaven are indeed of assistance to the living. But it is performance of the commandments—and study and good deeds, and prayers uttered with the proper intentions—that brings about "Mending" and effluence in the supernal realms. The souls of the saints have no way to effect this, except by joining and attaching themselves to people who are currently alive on earth. This is the reason why spirit-guides are so active nowadays. You must understand it well.

CHAPTER 4

Hasidic Spirituality

Introduction

The disastrous collapse of the Sabbatean movement left many Jews suspicious of mystical religion and its misuses. In Central Europe, bans were issued against the dissemination of Kabbalah in an attempt to restrict its knowledge to small circles of elites. But in Eastern Europe, a region whose culture had long been infused with mystical pietism and magical practices, the roots of popular kabbalistic ideas and rituals were deeply entrenched.[1] In the late seventeenth and eighteenth centuries, numerous *kloyzen* (elite "study-houses") were established where scholars might study mystical texts in a sequestered environment, but Kabbalah remained an integral part of folk religion.[2] One particularly common expression of the popular mystical dimension of Eastern European Jewish culture were the professional *ba'alei shem*, "masters of the Name." These individuals were faith healers or shamans, and many boasted of clairvoyance in addition to expertise in practical Kabbalah. *Ba'alei shem* wrote amulets based on divine names, proffered incantations to cure the sick, and performed similar pseudo-magical feats. A great figure in the history of European Jewish mysticism was to come from among these folk healers, one who distinguished himself as a spiritual teacher of great profundity and not simply a magician.

The revivalist movement known as Hasidism grew out of the teachings of Rabbi Yisra'el ben Eli'ezer of Miedzhybozh (Ukr. Medzhibizh, d. 1760), known as the Ba'al Shem Tov ("Master of the Good Name").[3] This enigmatic and creative mystic lived in Podolia (modern Ukraine) near the Carpathian Mountains. We know very little about his life that does not come from internal Hasidic sources, but legends tell of his humble beginnings, followed by a period of prolonged solitude and mystical study with heavenly teachers. In the 1730s he "revealed" himself and began to spread a new approach to religious life that foregrounded the values of joy and ecstatic prayer.[4] As we have seen, since the German Pietists of the twelfth century, Jewish mystics have often tended toward asceticism and even self-mortification, but the Ba'al Shem Tov (or BeSHT) was wary of the dangers of religious guilt and the psychological and physical damage wrought by penitential practices taken to the extreme. The BeSHT's teachings had an important mystical dimension as well. *Devekut*, or the radical experience of God's immanent presence, is the very heart of his spiritual path.[5] The BeSHT emphasized that one must be ever mindful of the divine vitality in all aspects of existence, often described as sparks of holiness trapped within the corporeal world.[6] Freeing these sparks is one of the ultimate goals of religious service, and it means that one may serve God through ordinary physical deeds, such as eating, drinking, and dancing, as well as by performing the commandments.[7]

The BeSHT's writings are quite scant. We have only a few letters to his family and students, including a fascinating epistle to his brother-in-law describing a mystical ascent he experienced on the holiday of Rosh Hashanah in 1747.[8] The vast majority of his teachings were transmitted orally and later written down in the books of his disciple Rabbi Ya'akov Yosef of Polnoye (Pol. Połonne, d. 1783) and his grandson Rabbi Moshe Hayyim Efrayim of Sudylkov (Pol. Sudylków, d. 1800). These two important repositories are complemented by hundreds of quotations scattered throughout Hasidic works early and late.[9] That he wrote very little is unsurprising, for the BeSHT was not a systematic philosopher or a technical Kabbalist. Furthermore, though he was a *ba'al shem*, his teachings and the legends surrounding him contain relatively few examples of the typical legerdemain common in that profession. His remarkable effectiveness as a spiritual educator came from inspiring others with his personal charisma and giving short, but illuminating, new interpretations of familiar old texts.

There is no evidence that the BeSHT saw himself as establishing a new religious movement, though later Hasidic schools unanimously consider him to be the founder of their spiritual path. Nor do his teachings have an acute messianic element.[10] His teachings revitalized Jewish observance from within the existing religious framework, and it was only in the decades after his death that the social movement known as Hasidism began to crystallize. In particular, the next phase of this emerging spiritual ethos was shaped by the religious personality and leadership of one of the BeSHT's foremost disciples: Rabbi Dov Baer, the famed *Maggid* ("preacher") of Mezritch (Pol. Miedzyrzecz; d. 1772). Rabbi Dov Baer was a Talmudic scholar and ascetic Kabbalist long before he met the BeSHT. His sermons rarely quote the BeSHT by name, suggesting that the Maggid absorbed a set of values and an approach to the spiritual life from his master, but not necessarily a large volume of specific teachings. The Maggid remained an introspective and contemplative mystic even after meeting the BeSHT, but Rabbi Dov Baer's teachings reflect the fiery ecstasy and positive view of the physical world he learned from his master. Later Hasidic thought has preserved the voices of the BeSHT and the Maggid, and its spiritual path allows for both introverted (contemplative) and extroverted (ecstatic) mystical types.[11]

The Maggid attracted a substantial number of followers to his study hall, many of whom were brilliant scholars from the most illustrious families in Eastern Europe. These disciples became the next generation of leaders after the Maggid's death in 1772. This chorus of voices around the Maggid's table was polychromatic indeed, for rarely do all of these Hasidic masters speak with a single voice on any given issue.[12] Yet despite their differences, the leaders of the movement were united by a shared cluster of theological beliefs regarding the devotional life. These include: worshiping God with joy; striving for *devekut* in prayer and study; cultivating *da'at*, or an awareness of God's immanence; recognizing that the initial *tsimtsum*, the withdrawal of the Divine from the physical world, is but an illusion; raising up sparks of holiness by serving God in ordinary deeds; and reorienting all of one's *middot*, or emotional, intellectual, and ethical character traits, toward God.[13]

Hasidism offered a new type of religious leadership that brought together older models such as priest, sage, and prophet.[14] The traditional Eastern European *rav* ("rabbi") was hired by a community and granted the authority to decide issues of ritual law, and to a lesser degree, monetary disputes. By contrast, the Hasidic *rebbe* was a charismatic and inspiring figure. While some were extremely learned in traditional rabbinic law, this acumen did not define the *rebbe*'s role.

Hasidic leaders were also referred to as *tsaddikim* (sing. *tsaddik*), righteous persons of tremendous spiritual power graced with a special ability to bring divine blessing (*shefa'*) into the world, intercede on high on behalf of the Jewish people, and even perform miracles. Some used the amulets and magical formulae like the *ba'al shem*, but early *tsaddikim* often accomplished their goals by means of their impassioned prayer and faith alone.

Many *rebbes*, though not all, were mystics who cultivated rich inner spiritual lives. Yet this was not an attempt to escape from the physical world or their obligations as religious leaders. Hasidic teachings repeatedly underscore that a *tsaddik*'s experience of divine unity compels him to return to his flock in order to bestow them with blessing and inspire them to attain greater mystical heights.[15] This commitment to the community is paramount, since one of the more glaring criticisms of the traditional rabbinate found in early Hasidic literature is their aloof and dispassionate stance vis-à-vis the people. Thus the *rebbe* is not a *rav*, a *ba'al shem*, or the head of a small devotional circle like the leaders of the Safed revival; the Hasidic *tsaddik* is a mystical type of its own.

The Maggid's disciples moved across Eastern Europe and spread the new religious ethos of Hasidism.[16] However, their ideas disturbed some members of the rabbinic establishment, especially the intellectual elites to the north in Lithuania. Some of these scholars were dedicated Kabbalists themselves,[17] but they were particularly horrified by the Hasidic masters' elevation of mystical prayer filled with ecstatic yells and boisterous movements above the traditional ideal of constant Torah study. They were similarly incensed by the way the Hasidim changed the liturgy, formed their own prayer quorums, slaughtered their own meat, and showed disrespect for the rabbinic hierarchy. The Hasidim's "strange acts" reminded the Lithuanian scholars of Sabbatean heresy. The opponents (*mitnaggedim*) of Hasidism issued a series of excommunications and harshly polemical treatises condemning the new sect. The first of these bans was proclaimed in 1772, and it bore the approval of the *Ga'on* ("genius") Rabbi Elijah ben Solomon of Vilna (1720–97). This intellectual giant occupied no official rabbinic post, but wielded enormous authority in Lithuanian Jewry by dint of his tremendous erudition.[18] This controversy continued for the next several decades, only beginning to cool as both sides became less wary of the other: the Hasidim became less extreme, particularly in their bizarre conduct and relaxed attitude toward Torah study, and the *mitnaggedim* recognized that the Hasidim had not deviated from the core of Jewish religious norms.[19]

The theology of Hasidism was inspired by earlier Jewish mystical traditions. Gershom Scholem suggested that Hasidism was a direct reaction to the Sabbatean movement, and that its primary inspiration lay in Lurianic Kabbalah.[20] Moshe Idel and others have since shown that despite their temporal proximity and shared mystical heritage, Hasidism represents far more than a backlash or sublimation of Sabbateanism. Hasidic thought draws richly upon *Hekhalot* literature, Ashkenazi Pietism, the *Zohar* and works of other Spanish Kabbalists, and the teachings of both Cordovero and Luria as well as their later synthesizers and interpreters.[21] A properly annotated Hasidic text may be seen to melt away into a multitude of footnotes to earlier material. However, the unique spiritual world of Hasidism is found precisely in its creative synthesis of these traditional sources, offering them in a simplified, and thus accessible, reformulation. The Hasidic masters used the symbolic language of Kabbalah in order to describe a vast range of psychological processes and interior mystical experiences. For example, instead of emphasizing that prayer requires the precise *kavvanot*, defined permutations of divine names, Hasidism stressed the need for *kavvanah*, enthusiasm and absolute focus.[22] The *sefirot* remained a model for understanding the Godhead and the emanated cosmos, but their role as the emotional and intellectual structure of the human psyche was far more important to the Hasidic masters. While some Hasidic leaders were quite learned in traditional Kabbalah, their teachings generally employ the terminology of Kabbalah to articulate Hasidic values in ways that offered direct relevance to the spiritual lives of their disciples.

The library of Hasidic texts is composed of many different genres. Most well-known is the Hasidic homily, sermons delivered on the weekly Torah reading. These were originally given in Yiddish, and only later translated into Hebrew and written down. Hasidism was first and foremost an oral movement, and listening to the *rebbe* deliver words of Torah on the Sabbath was an electrifying event likened to the revelation at Sinai. Written texts served an important role in disseminating Hasidic thought, but they never replaced (or surpassed) the power of hearing the sermon directly from the *rebbe* himself. Early Hasidic teachings circulated first as manuscripts and then as printed books; the first collection of Hasidic homilies was not published until 1780, some two decades after the BeSHT's death.[23] Yet the homiletical literature represents just one aspect of Hasidic thought. Hasidic *hanhagot* (rules for personal conduct) show a more concrete spirituality grounded in daily practice.[24] Like those of the Safed fellowships, Hasidic *hanhagot* formulate theology as practical teachings intended to imbue religious life with deeper mystical significance.

The tales of Hasidism also reveal an important aspect of this religious movement. Stories about the *tsaddikim* were a crucial method of transmitting Hasidic teachings and values.[25] The first of these tales were published in *Shivei ha-BeSHT* (1815), a legendary biography of the Ba'al Shem Tov.[26] In the later nineteenth and early twentieth centuries, hundreds of booklets of such tales were published, making them an important and much-beloved aspect of the Hasidic legacy.[27] These stories inspired philosophers and writers such as Martin Buber, I. L. Peretz, and S. Y. Agnon.[28] But Rabbi Nahman of Bratslav (1772–1811), a controversial Hasidic leader and great-grandson of the BeSHT, told stories of a very different sort.[29] Over the last four years of his life, he related a series of imaginative tales that display an exceptional degree of literary creativity and freedom. These stories incorporate motifs and characters common to multicultural folklore throughout Eastern Europe, such as princesses, kings, giants, dwarves, and witches. The tales are richly symbolic, and their structure and language often reflect layers of kabbalistic significance hidden just beneath the surface.[30]

After the death of the Maggid's disciples in the early decades of the nineteenth century, Hasidism underwent a profound transformation from religious revival to a socially and theologically conservative movement.[31] The Hasidim, who now dominated the former Polish Commonwealth (Galicia and Western Russia), joined forces with their old opponents the *mitnaggedim* to combat the new ideas of the Enlightenment making inroads from the West.[32] Kabbalah now played a minor role for most Lithuanian scholars,[33] but the two groups became political allies as ultra-orthodoxy closed ranks against the modernization. Dynastic succession of Hasidic leadership had become the norm in most areas, and the office of *tsaddik* was passed down directly from father to son.[34] This brought the movement stability, but greatly weakened the dynamism of its leadership. Hasidism had also become increasingly involved in politics and was plagued with fights between *rebbes* over geography and economics. Some Hasidic leaders were aware of this decline, and starting with Rabbi Nahman of Bratslav in early 1800s, a series of *rebbes* attempted to reinvigorate Hasidism with a renewed sense of creativity and spiritual vitality. Indeed, the Hasidic world produced a few great luminaries in the mid to late nineteenth century, including Rabbi Kalonymous Kalman Epstein of Cracow (the "*Ma'or va-Shamesh*," 1754–1823), Rabbi Menahem Mendel of Kotsk (1787–1859), Rabbi Mordecai Yosef of Izhbitz (1800–54),[35] Rabbi Tsadok ha-Kohen of Lublin (1823–1900),[36] and Rabbi Yehudah Aryeh Leib of Ger (the "*Sefat Emet*," 1847–1905).[37] Hasidism remained a dominant religious and political force in Eastern Europe up until the destruction of European Jewry in the fires of the Holocaust.[38]

Further Reading

Ben-Amos, Dan and Jerome R. Mintz, trans. *In Praise of the Baal Shem Tov*. Bloomington: Indiana University Press, 1970.

Green, Arthur. *Speaking Torah: Spiritual Teachings from Around the Maggid's Table*, 2 vols. With Ebn Leader, Ariel Evan Mayse, and Or N. Rose. Woodstock, VT: Jewish Lights, 2013.

———. *Tormented Master: The Life and Spiritual Quest of Rabbi Nahman of Bratslav*. Woodstock, VT: Jewish Lights, 1992.

Hundert, Gershon David, ed. *Essential Papers On Hasidism: Origins to Present*. New York: New York University Press, 1991.

Idel, Moshe. *Hasidism: Between Ecstasy and Magic*. Albany: State University of New York Press, 1995.

Rapoport-Albert, Ada, ed. *Hasidism Reappraised*. London and Portland, OR: Valentine Mitchell & Co. Ltd., 1997.

Upright Practices by R. Menahem Nahum of Chernobyl

Editor's introduction: Rabbi Menahem Nahum of Chernobyl (c. 1730–97), a student of both the BeSHT and the Maggid, founded a prominent Hasidic dynasty in what is now Ukraine. His teachings combine the simple, holistic spiritual approach of the BeSHT with the more contemplative elements of the Maggid's theology. Rabbi Menahem Nahum's homilies were collected and printed shortly after his death as *Me'or 'Eynayim* (*Light of the Eyes*), one of the true classics of early Hasidic literature. The following translations come from his teachings on the Book of Genesis. Included as well is a set of *hanhagot* called *Upright Practices* (*Hanhagot Yesharot*, 1796), rules for personal conduct, which demonstrate how his theology finds expression in religious praxis.

Upright Practices

I

1. "The beginning of wisdom is the fear of the Lord" (Ps 111:10); keep this ever before you. Believe with full faith that the Creator, blessed be He, the King of kings whose glory fills all the earth, stands before you in each moment and sees all your deeds, both those that are public and those hidden in the depths of your heart. This should lead you to a constant sense of shame, of which Scripture says: "So that His fear be on your faces and you will not Sin" (Exod 20:20). On this verse the sages asked: "How is the fear of God present on a person's face?" And they answered: "In shame" (b. Yevamot 20a).[39]

2. Purify your mind and thought from thinking too many different thoughts. You have only to think about one thing: serving God in joy. The word *Be-SiMHaH* ("in joy") has the same letters as *MaHaShaBah* ("thought"); all thoughts that come to you should be included in this single one. Of this Scripture speaks in "Many are the thoughts in a

person's mind, but it is the counsel of the Lord that will stand" (Prov 19:21). Understand this.

3. Our rabbis say: "Sanctify yourself within the realm of that which is permitted" (b. Yevamot 20a).[40] In the moment of sexual union turn your thought to the sake of heaven. Recite the prayer of the RaMBaN as it is printed in *Sha'arei Tsiyon* (*The Gates of Zion*). [Before the sex act] say: "For the sake of the union of the Holy One, blessed be He, with His *shekhinah*...." See further what is written in the *Shulhan 'Arukh, Orah Hayyim,* section two hundred forty, concerning holiness before the act of union. Remember how careful the sages sought to be concerning this holiness.[41]

4. Give as much in alms as you are able, as Scripture says "You establish me in righteousness" (i.e., almsgiving; Isa 54:14). How good and pleasant it is to have a box for alms and to place three coins in it (or at least one) before each prayer. Before eating too you should set aside a coin.

5. Fast one day in each week. Be alone with your Maker on that day and confess explicitly all your sins against Him, even those of your youth. Be ashamed and ask forgiveness; cry, for "all the gates are locked except that of tears" (b. Berakhot 32b). Then turn back to rejoicing over the fact that you have attained full repentance.

6. Keep away from depression to the utmost degree. Thus you will be saved from several sins, especially those of anger and pride. Be intelligent and judicious in the matter of worry over your sins.[42] Depart from them with a whole heart, ask God for forgiveness, and then serve him wholeheartedly. Have complete faith [in the effectiveness of your repentance], following the rabbis' teaching: "If a man betrothe a woman on the condition that he be a righteous person, that woman is considered betrothed, even if he had been completely wicked. He might have had a thought of repentance" (b. Kiddushin 49b).[43]

7. Fulfill the teaching of the *Sayings of the Fathers* that taught: "Be of very very humble spirit before every person" (m. Avot 4:1). When you see a wicked person, say in your heart "Even he is greater than I." "The more the knowledge, the greater the pain" (Eccl 1:18).

8. Pray and study with fear and love.[44] Know that the letters [of the text before you] are called heaven and earth, and that all the

worlds and all creatures great and small are given life by His word. "This is the whole of man" (Eccl 12:13). Understand this.

9. Keep yourself from being cross toward your household in any matter. Let your speech be pleasant, for "the words of the wise are heard when pleasant" (Eccl 9:17).[45]

10. Cleave to the wise and to their disciples; learn always from their deeds. Keep away from people who do not have good qualities of character. This is the main thing: good qualities.[46]

11. Study books of moral teaching each day, something on the order of the *Reshit Hokhmah*. That work is filled to overflowing with wisdom, fear of God, and praiseworthy qualities.[47]

12. Keep away from having your head turned; accept not a drop of human praise. Praise that you receive from people is to be considered a great liability. Those who speak ill of you are in fact doing you a great favor. Your intent should be only for the sake of His great name, to do that which is pleasing to Him.

13. Accept whatever portion the Lord gives you in love, whether it be for good or for ill and suffering. Thus did our rabbis teach on "with all your might" (Deut 6:5)—thank God for every portion that He gives you, whether good or ill (m. Berakhot 9:5).[48] "Evil does not come from the mouth of the most high" (Lam 3:38), but only good. Compare this to those bitter medicines that are needed to heal the body. The same are needed for healing the soul.[49]

14. If you find yourself unable to study or pray with fear and love, continue in any case to study and pray to God with complete faith. This is what the rabbis have taught: "A person should ever involve himself with Torah and the commandments, even if not for their own sake."[50] "Not for their own sake" means that even if he has no fear or love, he should keep doing them for the sake of heaven. They also said: "From doing not for their own sake he will reach the stage of doing for their own sake," that is, he will attain to fear and love. Of this the prophet speaks when he says, "'Are not My words like fire?' says the Lord" (Jer 23:29).[51]

15. Do many acts of loving-kindness: dowering poor brides, visiting the sick, and all the other things of which the sages spoke. This is one of three things that stand at the very pinnacle of the world order.[52] Praise no one and speak ill of no one. The Ba'al Shem Tov has already said it: "If you want to praise anyone, praise God, if you want to speak

ill of anyone, speak ill of yourself" and know your lowly state.[53] If you possess some good quality, it belongs not to you but to God. Thus Scripture says: "Let not the wise man praise himself for his wisdom, nor the rich man for his wealth" (Jer 9:22). All this was given you by God. Your bad qualities—those are indeed your own.

16. Remember God always: "I place Y-H-V-H ever before me" (Ps 16:8). If you fail to do so even for a moment it is considered a sin. Thus the Ba'al Shem Tov taught on "Blessed is the man for whom God does not think of a sin" (Ps 32:2).[54] "Does the Lord give up on sins?" he asked. Rather interpret this way: When a person does not think of God—when God is out of his thoughts—that is sin. Consider this to be a very grave sin: Thus you will take care and not forget Him. In such a case, "blessed is the man."

17. Each day study from the Torah, Prophets, and Writings, from the Mishnah and the Gemara, each in accord with his abilities.[55] Do it all for the sake of His great name, and for no other purpose. "Then you will walk surely on your way."

18. Take care, insofar as possible, not to speak before prayer [in the morning]. Do so only for very great need. Consider your deeds before you pray, and repent of them. Humble your heart by considering your own smallness and lowliness. Thus will you prepare all the rungs of your soul to receive some bit of the fear of heaven as you stand before Him. Of this Scripture says: "Prepare to meet your God, O Israel" (Amos 4:12).

II

Know first that God exists. He was first, and He created all things, both above and below. His creations are without end! All began with a single point—the point of supernal wisdom, *hokhmah*. The power of the Creator is present in all of His creations; the wisdom of God fills and takes on the garb of every thing that is. Of this Scripture speaks in saying: "Wisdom gives life to those who possess it" (Eccl 7:12).

Believe with a whole and strong faith that the Creator is one, single, and united.[56] He is the first of all causes and origins, utterly endless, blessed is He and blessed is His name. He created many worlds, higher and lower, without limit and without end. Of these Scripture says: "Worlds without number" (Song 6:8; *'alamot/'olamot*).

Believe with a whole and strong faith that He both fills all the worlds and surrounds them,[57] that He is both within and beyond them all. He created the lower world for the sake of the Torah and Israel, that His blessed divine Self might be revealed. There is no King without His people Israel. Believe with a whole and strong faith that "the whole earth is full of His glory" (Isa 6:3) and that "there is no place devoid of Him."[58] His blessed glory inhabits all that is. This glory serves as a garment, as the sages taught: "Rabbi Yohanan called his garment 'glory'" (b. Shabbat 113a). His divine Self wears all things as one wears a cloak, as Scripture teaches: "You give life to them all" (Neh 9:6). This applies even to the forces of evil, in accord with the secret of "His kingdom rules over all" (Ps 103:19). All life is sustained by the flow that issues forth from Him. Were the life-flow to cease, even for a moment, the thing sustained would become but an empty breath, as though it had never been.

Believe with a whole faith that the slightest motion of your little finger can move great spiritual worlds above, as the Ba'al Shem Tov has taught.[59]

Believe with whole faith that man contains all the worlds within him, as the ARI, the holy *Zohar*, and various Midrashim have taught. This being the case, God must be proclaimed King through every single deed we do, through study and prayer as well as fulfilling the commandments [for thus is His kingdom proclaimed] over all our limbs. Even ordinary conversation must be made holy. God's sight should be brought into our daily words and thoughts. With every word and with each thought we must cleave again to their root in God, since it is only by His power that we think or speak.[60] When you have full faith in this, you will come to realize that all the events of your life have come about through God. Whether or not they have turned out as you wanted, you will consider them all to be for the good, since "evil does not come from the mouth of the most high" (Lam 3:38), but only good. Of this I have spoken earlier. Within every bad thing there dwells His power of good, that which gives it life. This can be seen only by the one whose eyes are properly directed; otherwise the veils of sin tend to intervene and blind the human eye. To purify your sight, do not look beyond your own four ells; these will be the four letters of the name Y-H-V-H, that which calls all being to be. Mend all your bad qualities by means of goodness; subsume the left within the right, as the holy *Zohar* has taught (3:178a). [Cultivate] all those qualities of which the pious authors speak. Then the good will gain in strength and lift itself out of the evil in which it had been enshrouded. Once evil is left on its own it will vanish altogether, and then our righteous messiah will arrive—speedily and in our day! Amen. *Selah.*

You must believe all of the above with a whole faith, and at every single moment be prepared to give your life for it. Do not let your mind wander off amid passing vanities. Cleave rather to the praise of God, and join together His three names: Eheyeh, Y-H-V-H, and Adonay.[61] Human thought is derived from the World of Thought, identical to the name Eheyeh. Everything is purified by means of this thought. Within all things are contained [sacred] letters in a broken state; through this binding of the mind to its source in the Thought of God you raise them up.

This too is the meaning of the *mikveh*.[62] It similarly is drawn from the *mikveh* above, the name Eheyeh, the world of *binah*. It is there that the forces of evil are transformed or "sweetened." These forces were made by the sins of man; as you enter the *mikveh* and repent thoroughly of them, departing from your sins with a whole heart, the one who confesses and leaves them will find mercy. Surely then you will be forgiven.

The human being represents the name Adonay, also called *shekhinah* or indwelling, for it dwells within the lower world. Thus a person's thought, when turned to good and aimed toward repentance, contains within it the unification of all three names, Eheyeh, Y-H-V-H, Adonay.[63] By concentrating on this you will be able to draw unto yourself sublime holiness and great purity....

By holding fast to the praise of God, by singing the hymns of Israel's sweet singer,[64] you will be able to destroy the accusing and evil forces. Indeed King David prayed that his songs would be sung in the synagogues and houses of study. By them we can restore the crown to its former place, and the lily will awaken.[65]

Be among those who take stock of themselves each night before they lie down. Give an account of your sins and repent of them. Even a thought of repentance will suffice. Since *teshuvah* was one of the seven things that preceded the world into existence,[66] time does not apply to it, and thus a thought alone will do to "sweeten" all. In this way you can send forth your soul (all three of its levels) to rise upward to the place of contemplation.

Rise up from sleep at midnight, for that is a time when God's desire is especially to be found. Serve Him in the midst of night and perform the midnight vigil. As that vigil is joined to your morning prayer, you will be unified and will attach yourself to that which is above; then you will be able to bring forth whatever it is that you seek from God. Midnight prayer and service is a great thing; it is this that brings about peace above. If not for this, God forbid, those who are joined together[67] would be separated.

Take special care when reciting the *Shema'* to pronounce each word. See that you are not distracted, at least not during the *Shema'*, but recite it in fear and love. Each letter you recite in this way will help to bring life to your limbs.[68]

See too that you honor the Sabbath as fully as you are able within your means. Do so with food and drink and in other ways as well. The letters of *SHaBat* are those of *TaSheB*, to indicate that "he who keeps the Sabbath, even if he is as idolatrous as was the generation of Enosh, will be forgiven."[69]

Here is a basic principle: The root of all things is in almsgiving. By this deed you uplift the sparks from their broken state, and in this way you uplift your own soul as well. The letters of *TSeDaKaH* ("almsgiving") contain the letters of *TSeDeK* ("righteousness"). In acting as a *TSaDiK* you are a holy spark of the cosmic *TSaDiK*; [by your righteous act you partake in that *tsaddik*'s uplifting of *tsedek-shekhinah*] from poverty and exile. Enough said.[70] Here is the rule: By any holy deed or by any life-sustaining alms that you offer to the poor, you uplift a holy spark that lay amid the evil forces, and thus you come to holiness. No "act of holiness" can take place, however, in the presence of fewer than ten, and those ten are in turn a hundred. In this way is *TSeDaKah* formed, and thus is a soul uplifted from its broken state.[71]

This too is a basic principle: See that you bring your own negative qualities to submission. Hold fast to good qualities. In this way too you will cause sparks to rise from their broken state. This is why a person must recite a hundred blessings each day. The meaning of this is as follows: "Blessings" refer to the pond above (*BeRaKHaH/BeReKHaH*) and the streams that flow forth from it. You have to bring about the flow of these hundred blessings upon you, these hundred that also represent the ten good qualities. Overcome your own bad qualities and cleave to Him, bless His name, and in every way bring down the flow of His bounty upon you.

When you stand up to pray, decide first that you will attach yourself only to pure and virtuous thoughts, rejecting this lowly world down to the very last degree. Thus you may bring yourself to the most sublime joy of spirit, becoming joined to Him in a wondrous way. In this you attain to *malkhut*, the "I" of God.[72] Thence you may bind yourself further and enter into a state of union, until you reach the Nothing, the World of Contemplation, that which is referred to as "Who?". Of this the sages say "Know before whom you stand" (b. Berakhot 28b)—you stand before the "Who?".[73] Unification means that you do not separate mind from words, especially during the *'amidah*, when the true union and coupling takes place.[74] In this way that union may come to be revealed in the lower world as well. Amen. May this be His will.

When you awake at midnight, as we have suggested above, be sure that your very first thought is that of attachment to God. How great is the Creator! He has just restored your soul to you! As you glorify Him, ask yourself for what purpose He has sent that soul back to you.[75] Realize that it is for the sake of His service, that you serve Him with soul through Torah, worship and the commandments. As you begin to pray, accept the fact that you worship Him even though your soul may pass out of you in prayer.[76] Keep your thought fastened on your blessed Creator throughout the day.

Do the same with your emotions:[77] Should something like improper *love* or this-worldly pleasure be aroused in you, know that it stems from a spark of divine *hesed*. You have caused that spark to fall into the hands of evil; it alone gives life to those evil forces. It is within your power to uplift those holy sparks, to separate the proper food from that which is to be cast aside, to find the hidden good The Creator has made it that we might have a choice: "See that I place before you life and death, good and evil. Choose life..." (Deut 30:19). Treat all other emotions and human qualities in the same manner: improper desire for glory, for praise, improper attachments and loyalties.

Fear no one but God. Scripture's words "The fear of the Lord is His treasure" (Isa 33:6) are to be understood thus: [Our] awe before

His greatness is God's own treasure. There are various types of fear, to be sure, but [the true treasure is] that sense of awe before His greatness, fear of the Lord because He is Master and Ruler, indeed the very source[78] of all the worlds. Such awe will lead you to serve Him with all your strength and intensity. No longer will you be pulled away by the attractions of this lowly and despicable world. Day by day you will grow in the strength of His service. You will do this not for fear of death, of punishment, or of hell: all of these are nought in the face of your true fear of the Creator.

Further: Do not *glorify* yourself, however great your learning or your good deeds, your wealth or your fine qualities. Glory belongs only to God.

So too all the rest. Do not *triumph* over any person. Grant triumph only to Him, His alone is the only true victory. Yours is rather to triumph over your evil urge, that which leads you away from the good and into the path of evil.

Further: If people should come to *praise* you, do not let it lead you to self-importance. Rather give praise constantly to God, to Him who created you out of nothing and brought you into being. It is He who sustains you from your mother's womb unto the very day of your death. Were the Creator's concern to depart from you for but a moment, you would not survive that moment in the world.

Further: with regard to *attachment*.[79] Attach your thought always to the Creator; do not turn it away even for a moment to think of the vanities of this world. As soon as you turn your thought elsewhere you are considered as an idolator, as Scripture says: "You will turn aside and worship other gods" (Deut 11:16).

Further: with regard to *kingship*. Proclaim God King over all your limbs; "Let there be in you no other god" (Ps 81:10). On this verse the sages ask, "Who is the 'other god' that dwells in the human heart?" Their answer: "The evil urge and his retinue are called by this name" (b. Shabbat 105b).

God has made everything in parallel form. As there are seven holy qualities, so are there seven evil ones parallel to them. It was so made in order to "grant reward to the righteous who sustain a world that was created by ten utterances," who triumph over the seven wicked qualities and cleave to God through their own qualities of goodness, breaking down the evil urge and those that support it. So too in order to "take leave of the wicked who destroy a world that was created through ten utterances" (m. Avot 5:1), who spend all their days in pursuit of their own desires, seeking out the pleasures of this lowly and despicable world. In doing so they deny the One, Single, and Unified God. In the end they will have to give account to the King of Kings, the Holy One, blessed be He, for every single one of their deeds.

Should someone whisper to you, however, that he is so thoroughly defiled by the stain of sin that there is no repentance for him—God forbid that this be the case! There is *nothing* that stands in the way of repentance, for repentance was one of those seven things that preceded the Creation itself. No force of judgment has a place there, and just a thought—a thought of complete repentance and resolve never to return to that folly—will suffice to gain forgiveness for all one's sins.[80] From that day forward, of course, you must cleave firmly to God and break down all your bad qualities. Of this the rabbis said: "Whoever gives up on his *middot* has all his sins forgiven" (b. Yoma 23a): Subjugate your evil qualities and rise above them. Join your mind to your body (for the upper three *sefirot* are like the seven lower ones), and rise above all these measured qualities to that place where there is no judgment at all.[81]

Raise everything to the level of *binah* and there it will all be "sweetened," as the *Zohar* says: Even though *binah* is the source of judgment-forces, it is only in their root that they can be transformed (*Zohar* 3:98b). Then are all your sins forgiven. Everything you have done up to that day, however, you will still have to weigh, all in accord with the pleasure you took in this world and its delights. The same will apply to all the other qualities. You must bring your self to sorrow over them, fasting regularly on Mondays and Thursdays, either those following Passover or those following Sukkot, during the weeks referred to as *shovevim tat*.[82] So too every eve of the new moon, considered to be a small Day of Atonement. Fasting on that day has to do with the wandering of the moon.[83] We have mentioned its meaning above. The *shehkinah* is in exile, as scripture says: "I am with him in sorrow" (Ps 91:15). You have to participate in *shekhinah*'s suffering.

Me'or 'Eynayim on Genesis (The Light of the Eyes) by R. Menahem Nahum of Chernobyl

Parashat Bereshit

In the beginning God created heaven and earth. The earth was formless and void, with darkness over the face of the deep. The spirit of God was hovering over the face of the water. God said: "Let there be light"; and there was light. "God saw that the light was good, and God separated the light from the darkness. God called the light day and darkness he called night. There was evening and there was morning, one day (Gen 1:1–5).

In the beginning. It was through the Torah, called "the beginning of His way" (Prov 8:22), that God created the world; all things were created by means of Torah. Since the power of the Creator remains in the creature, Torah is to be found in all things and throughout all the worlds.[84] So too in the case of man, as Scripture says: "This is the Torah, a man…" (Num 19:14), as will be explained. And since God and Torah are one, the life of God is present in all things. "You give life to them all" (Neh 9:6)—He reduced Himself, as it were, down to the lowest of rungs, until a part of God above was placed into the darkness of matter. The intent of this was that the lower rungs themselves be uplifted, so that there be "a greater light that comes from darkness" (Eccl 2:13).

This was the meaning of Joseph's descent into Egypt, the lowest of rungs, the narrow strait in the great sea (*MiTSRaYiM/MeTSaR YaM*). Through him joy was to be increased and the light brightened, for joy is greater when it has been lifted out of darkness. For that reason his name was Joseph, which means "he adds." This also is the meaning of "Jacob saw that there was produce (*shever*) in Egypt" (Gen 42:1). *Shever* may also mean "breakage"; the fallen fruit of supernal wisdom is Torah, that which has fallen from above and become "broken." Anything that has fallen from its original rung may be referred to in this way. "In Egypt" here refers to the narrow straits: He saw in the straits the fallen fruit of Torah, needing to be purified and uplifted. Thus he said "Go down there" (Gen. 42:2), in order to raise them up. He went down in order to restore them to their living root.

In this manner we should understand Joseph's death as well: This descent of the Torah down to the lowest rung may be considered a death; we speak of one who has gone down from his rung as of one who has died. [But then why does Scripture say] "And they embalmed him" (Gen. 50:26)? The Torah is called a Tree of Life, and "in the case of trees we are concerned with their bearing fruit" (*va-yaHaNeTu/ HaNaTaH*).[85] This means that even there, at the lowest of rungs, the Torah bore fruit. "And he was placed in a casket (*aron*)," for the rabbis have taught that "both whole and broken tablets were placed in the ark (*aron*)."[86] Even the fallen fruits are raised up and placed in the ark along with the whole tablets, the Torah itself.

Now let us return to the first matter. Since it is the Torah in all things that gives them life, it behooves us not to look at their corporeal nature, but rather at their inner selves. Scripture says: "The Wise man has eyes in his head" (Eccles 2:14), on which the *Zohar* asks: "Where else would a person's eyes be?" (*Zohar* 3:187a). This means rather that a wise person looks at the head of things; he always tries to seek out the source and origin of whatever he sees. This then is the meaning of *In the beginning God created*: Through the Torah heaven and earth came into being, both in general and in each particular detail. Thus have our rabbis explained the fact that "heaven" and "earth" in this verse are both preceded by the particle *et*, to refer to all that would later be born of them.[87]

The earth was formless and void. This refers to those who are sunk into earthly concerns; they indeed are "formless and void" for they do not look to the flow of life. And earthly objects taken for themselves are truly void and without form. Now RaSHI has explained this verse to mean that a person is astonished (*tohe/tohu*) over the formlessness (*bohu*) that was there. He meant to say that one who is truly a person will be astonished at the fool, so busy with pursuits of matter, when in fact it is in him (*bo hu*), when the life of God is right there in his own self, and he fails to understand and keeps himself far off. But when a person looks in all things at the life that flows within them, he fulfills the verse: "I place Y-H-V-H ever before me" (Ps 16:8), for in all things he places before him the Being (H-V-Y-H) that causes all being to be.[88]

Our rabbis have said: "Whoever studies the Torah not for its own sake, better that the birth-fluids have turned around to destroy him" (b. Berakhot 17a). But elsewhere they claim that it is "always good for a person to study, even if not for its own sake, for improperly motivated study will lead to study for proper reasons" (b. Pesahim 50a). The contradiction may be understood if we ask whether there really exists a "not for its own sake" anywhere in the world, since all things receive their life through Torah. Who would give life to anything that was not ultimately "for the sake of," or derived from, the Torah? Study "not for its own sake" means study for some bad motive: to be glorified or exalted over others, for lust after money, or the like. These desires for glorification or money themselves are really forms of glory and desire in a broken state; their true roots are the glory of God and His desire. This person has taken those qualities for himself; when he understands that they are derived from the glory and love of God he will come to hold on to the root and origin of things. Then he is the "wise man with eyes in his head," of whom we have spoken. It is from his very self-centered thoughts of desire and glorification that he has returned to the root, and thus he has moved from "not for its own sake" to "for its own sake." This is why one should ever study Torah, even if for improper reasons, since the improper motive itself may lead one to do it "for its own sake." If this does not happen, however, and one continues to study only for the wrong reasons, then indeed better that he not have been born.

Now the Torah is called "light," but the fool who studies Torah not for its own sake walks in darkness, not kindling that light. He who sits in darkness needs to kindle the light. This is the meaning of *Darkness over the face of the deep*: He is so enmeshed in corporeality that he does not kindle the Torah's light. Thus study not for its own sake does indeed exist in the world, but Scripture says of it *The spirit of God was hovering over the face of the water*. Because of this one may return and bring oneself back to true life and to God. *God said: Let there be light.* When a person studies for its own sake, that is for the sake of God, his words kindle that light. At first light and darkness existed together in a confused state; the "light" here is Torah and the "darkness" is the improper motive. But afterwards *God separated the light from the darkness....*

Now man was created in an ordinary state of mind, with a "small" consciousness. But surely God's intent in creating man was that he serve Him. Why then did He create him without the proper mind for such service? This was for the very same reason we have stated: Wisdom is greater when it arises out of folly; the darkness longs to be included in the light. Thus the lesser state of mind is considered the "wife" of expanded mind, of whom Scripture says: "Your desire shall be for your husband" (Gen 3:16). It is the woman who first rouses desire in her bridegroom; thus a person is first in the lesser state. When his mind is expanded, however, the lesser state too is joined into that higher mind, and an act of coupling has taken place. This is the meaning of "As bridegroom rejoices over bride, so does God rejoice over you" (Isa 62:5), as will be explained elsewhere. Now it is impossible to come to the light of that higher state too suddenly; for that reason the lower state must precede it.... Each person must follow the order of Creation: darkness first and then light. This is the meaning of *God called the light day and the darkness He called night*. Just as there is not day without night, but rather *There was evening*, the lesser state of mind comes first, and afterwards *there was morning* (*BoKeR*), then comes the expanded state, by which a person can examine (*meBaKeR*) his deeds. *One day*: The two form a single unity....

The rabbis' other statement about Joseph, that "he came home to fulfill his [bodily] needs," is thus also not in conflict with that which has been said [that he came to do God's work of unification]. Here too there is merely a difference in form of expression: This one meant to say that even in the fulfillment of our bodily needs we may turn inward....

Parashat Noah

These are the generations of Noah. Noah was a righteous and whole-hearted man in his generations; Noah walked with God.... Now the earth was corrupt before God; the earth was filled with violence (Gen 6:9, 11).

The Torah is eternal and in every person. How [do these verses apply] in our time? The *tsaddik*, by means of his good deeds, brings joy to the Creator, as Scripture says: "You are my servant, Israel in whom I am glorified" (Isa 49:3). God is made proud before the heavenly hosts and says: "See my servant, how he worships Me in great desire and ecstasy!" That *tsaddik* causes God to bless all the worlds, including this lowly world and all its creatures, with goodness.

Now it is known that the word *hayah* ("was," as in *Noah was*) generally refers to a joyous event, while its other form, *va-yehi*, implies the opposite; we also know that the true "generations" or offspring of the righteous are their good deeds: *Noah*'s very name means "pleasant"—he brought about that which is pleasing both above and below. This *righteous and wholehearted man* was the source of joy to *his generation*, bringing them blessing and good. That is the service of the *tsaddik*—to bring that flow of goodness down into the world. *Noah walked with God*: The *tsaddik* also has to mitigate the forces of divine judgment. Since the "whisperer separates familiar friends" (Prov 16:28) and the cosmic *Aleph* is taken away from *shekhinah*, suffering and judgment forces abound. The *tsaddik* brings all of these to the Lord of Compassion and they are sweetened. This is the meaning of *with God*:[89] It is with the suffering and trouble in the world that Noah goes to serve the blessed Lord. He serves by means of that very fear and sorrow which the wicked bring into the world. All this he brings to the Lord of Love and has it sweetened. Indeed through the service of such a *tsaddik* God's own name is enhanced. "David made a name" (2 Sam 8:13).... *Now the earth was corrupt*: The earthliness and corporeality of man keep him from coming before God and cleaving to Him. The *tsaddik* breaks down these elements within himself. He "*corrupts*" or destroys the *earth* within him so that he may come *before the Lord*.

Parashat Lekh Lekha

...*And the souls which they had made in Haran* (Gen 12:5).

Onkelos translates this passage as: "The souls which they had brought to the service of Torah."

To understand this matter we must recall that all souls have some attachment to the Torah. One who studies Torah and fulfills its commandments properly, serving God in truth by means of that Torah, raises up such souls. But the fallen souls exist not only in Israel; various holy souls have been scattered among the nations as well. Abraham our Father fulfilled the entire Torah. This has been taught on "because Abraham...kept my charge, my commandments, my statutes and my laws" (Gen. 26:5), indicating that he observed even the laws of food preparation for the festivals (b. Yoma 28b).[90] Thus he raised up those souls among the nations that were related to Torah and drew them to their source. Because he attached himself to the root of those souls in Torah, they too were raised up along with the soul of Abraham himself. That is why they sought to be converted and joined to Abraham, so that he would point out a path for them. This is the meaning of "brought to the service of Torah": He returned those lost souls to their own root.

We must understand, however, why it was that God commanded Abraham to *Get yourself out of your land*... and *I will make you a great nation* (Gen 12:1). Nothing is impossible for the Creator. Could He not have made him a great nation right there in his own country?

God conducts the world by means of seven qualities. These are the seven-day cycle of the world, sometimes known as the cosmic days or the days of the construct.[91] They begin with *hesed*, of which Scripture says: "The world is built by *hesed*" (Ps 89:3). Just as the world is conducted by means of these seven "days," so must the individual servant of God, the microcosm in whom these are implanted in the form of love, fear, glory, and the rest, conduct his own life as well. Every person is given a choice, and he may turn these qualities any way he likes. Even though they flow from the highest place, as love is rooted in the world of supreme *hesed*, they may be used for good or for ill. In the state in which man receives them each contains a mixture of good and evil. Thus they are called the "fallen qualities."

This is what all our worship is about: to purify these qualities within us from their own evil and to raise them up to God by using them in the act of His service. This comes about by means of proper seeing: When a bad form of love or fear comes to a person, he must look into it and tremblingly say in his heart: "This love is fallen from the World of Love, from the love of the Creator, blessed be He. It is my task to raise it up. How then can I do the evil act, causing it to fall still further? And if I find my love-energy aroused by this wicked object, fallen material creature that it is, how much greater should my love be for God and His Torah, through which all being was created; He is the joy of all joys!" Similarly should one deal with all the other qualities as they arise; a person should be entirely too much in awe of God to use the King's own scepter in such a way as to arouse His anger, rebelling against His will as though He does not see. Rather, when some quality wells up in him, even if manifesting itself in a negative or external way, he should take this opportunity as an opening to bind himself to that same attribute as it exists above in God. Then he raises all that is fallen to its root. God has no greater joy than this.

Abraham our father, peace be upon him, held fast to that quality of love until he was called "Abraham My lover" (Isa 41:8). It is with *hesed*, love, that one must begin in the repair of one's personal qualities. God wanted Abraham to go down into the nations of the world where those qualities were in a very fallen state, especially to Egypt, in a place steeped in carnality, of which Scripture says: "Their issue is like that of horses" (Ezek 23:20). Abraham, the master of love, had to go and lower himself to their level in order to uplift the love that had fallen there. In order to raise any person, as we know, you have to lower yourself to his rung. That was why Abraham used to take in guests, share food and drink with them, and afterwards say to them: "It is not *my* food you have been eating" and so forth. It was through their attachment to things of this world, such as eating and drinking, that Abraham was able to bring himself to their level; as he ate and drank with them, he brought them under the wings of the *shekhinah*.

Thus we speak of bringing guests in, and for this reason the act of hospitality is said to be greater than that of greeting the *shekhinah*.[92] In this way a person binds fallen things to their root, fulfilling heaven's greatest joy. This is why it was after eating that he said: "It is not my food you have been eating." So it was when Abraham wanted to repair *hesed*, uplifting the bad forms of love from among those nations in whose midst there dwelt holy souls. Then too he had to lower himself to their level. Of this Scripture says: "There was a famine in the land and Abram went down into Egypt" (Gen 12:10). This was "a famine not for bread and a thirst not for water, but to hear the word of the Lord" (Amos 8:11). The qualities were very much fallen; Abraham first wanted to raise up his own quality, that of love, which was in a fallen state. Of this Scripture says: "A man who takes his sister—that is *hesed*" (Lev 20:17).[93] The point is that you must set your mind to know that even this love is a fallen fruit of the divine tree, the attribute of based above. As he sought to raise them up Scripture takes care to say: "Abram went down into Egypt"—an act of descent and humiliation, lowering himself to their rung so that he be related to them in order to raise them up. The verse goes on to say that Abram went "to dwell there" (*la-GUR sham*). The same term could be translated "to be fearful there" as in "Be frightened (*GURu*) before the sword" (Job 19:29). As one goes down to their level one has to do so with a certain trepidation, maintaining great fear of the Lord so as not to become like them in their failings, making sure that the journey downward is for the sake of rising up again....

That is why God commanded Abraham to go forth from his land so that He make his name great, to answer our question above. A person has to humble himself, becoming close to those he seeks to raise up, in order that the border of the holy be expanded and the love of God truly spread forth in the world as fallen love is returned to its root. One who does this is the more to be called a lover of God. This is the meaning of *I will make your name great*: by your going, by leaving your land and proclaiming God's love even in the fallen rungs, you become "Abraham My lover." By this you will be considered a greater lover than previously....

Now I shall tell you a great thing in connection with this matter. It sometimes happens that a person feels himself to be in a fallen state, overtaken by the negative side of his own inner qualities, especially by improper love in the form of sexual desire. This may even happen when the desired sexual act is a permitted one![94] Such a person should know that heaven desires to uplift him, using his own natural emotions in order to open his heart to the love of God, so that he may receive the Torah as a gift. Before he is raised, however, he must be lowered, just as our father Abraham went down into Egypt, lowering himself in order to uplift others, fearing God there in the place of which it says: "There is no fear of God in this place" (Gen 20:11). So it is in every person: When he falls to that place of bad love, he must stand where he is and fear the Lord, having the strength in his very arousal to defeat the evil urge, not to do its bidding or to fulfill his lust. He must use that arousal of love itself for the love of God! This may be done even if a person in fact has to fulfill his conjugal duty as stated in the Torah. Even then he may perform only for the sake of his Creator, fulfilling this commandment as he would those of *tsitsit* or *tefillin*, making no distinction at all between them, and not seeking to satisfy his lust. One who does this is elevated to a very high rung, raising up with him all the love that had fallen there and restoring it to the heights, to the world of Love itself.

That which we have said of Abraham, whose name was made great because he went down into Egypt is true of all people in all times. In this way one merits the giving of the Torah, just as Jacob went to Egypt "forced by the Word," in order that Israel deserve to receive the Torah. This too is in each person and at every time...

Parashat Va-Yera

In the Tractate Shabbat: "Rabbi Yehudah said in the name of Rav: 'The welcoming of guests is greater than greeting the *shekhinah*,' for Scripture says, '*Pass not away, I pray you, from your servant*' (Gen 18:3). Said Rabbi El'azar: 'Note that the ways of God are not those of man. Among people, a lesser person could not say to a greater one "Wait until I come to you," but Abraham was able to say that to God'" (b. Shabbat 127a).

We must understand this verse that says *Pass not away*. How could this be said with regard to the presence of God, since the whole earth is filled with His glory and there is no place devoid of Him? How then could one possibly say *Pass not away*, as though to assume that afterwards that place would not contain his glory? This is simply impossible. We must also understand how Rav's claim that making guests welcome is greater than greeting *shekhinah* can be proven from this passage. Might we not say that in the performing of that commandment one also evokes the presence of the *shekhinah*? Commandment, after all, is called *mitsvah* because it joins together (*tsavta*) the part of God that dwells within the person with the infinite God beyond. It may be, then, that the *mitsvah* is not really greater than greeting *shekhinah*, but rather that it too contains *shekhinah*, and in fulfilling it one has both [commandment and presence]. We also have to understand Rabbi El'azar's point here, that the lesser does not ask the greater one to wait, and yet Abraham did so.[95] Could we not say that there too, in the greeting of guests, there was a receiving of the *shekhinah*? This is especially so since the righteous are called "the face of the *shekhinah*" in the *Zohar*, as His presence dwells in them. When Abraham received the guests, that is, the angels who appeared to him in human form, surely that in itself was an act of greeting the *shekhinah*.

The truth is, however, that the real fulfilling of any commandment lies in the greeting of the *shekhinah*, in becoming attached to God or joined together. Thus the rabbis said: "The reward of a *mitsvah* is a *mitsvah*" (m. Avot 4:2), meaning that the commandment is rewarded by the nearness to God that the one who performs it feels, the joy of spirit that lies within the deed. This indeed is a "greeting of the *shekhinah*," and without it the commandment is empty and lifeless, the body-shell of a *mitsvah* without any soul. Only when it is done with the longing of the divine part within to be connected to its root, along with the divine part of all the rest of Israel, can it be called a *mitsvah*. In all service of God, whether in speech or in deed, both body and soul are needed to give it life. That is why the wicked are called dead within their own lifetime:[96] their deeds are without life.

This is what really happened to our father Abraham. He was engaged in discourse with God ("greeting the *shekhinah*"), as we learn from the verse *The Lord appeared to him*. When he saw the guests coming, he asked of God that there too, while he was to be engaged in welcoming the guests, *Pass not away, I pray you, from your servant*. There too may I remain attached to You, so that this not be an empty *mitsvah*. Be with me so that I may perform the *mitsvah* in such a state that it too be a "greeting of the *shekhinah*."

Now Rav's point that the welcoming of guests is greater than greeting the *shekhinah* is proved by Abraham's action. Were this not the case, Abraham would hardly have left off a conversation with God to go do something of less certain value. This is especially true since "they appeared to him as Arab nomads";[97] they did not have a divine appearance. The *mitsvah* itself was very great even if it were not a "greeting of the *shekhinah*." Abraham decided to fulfill this commandment with absolute wholeness. Therefore he said: *Do not pass away, I pray you, from your servant*.

Now we also understand the point being made by Rabbi El'azar. Indeed among people the lesser person cannot ask the greater to wait for him while he attends to some other matter. The greater one will not be present in that other place; if he is here he cannot be there! But of God it is said: "The whole earth is filled with His glory!" He asks that God not depart from him; "there too may I not be cut off from my attachment to You." He could say this only because wherever one goes he does not go away from God. He is there as He is here; Abraham only asked that he not be cut off from Him.[98] Understand this.

Parashat Va-Yetse

Jacob left Be'er-Sheva and he went to Haran. He came upon a certain place and stopped there for the night, for the sun had set. He took some of the stones of that place and put them at his head, and he lay down in that place. He had a dream; a ladder set upon the ground, its top reaching to the heaven, and the angels of God were going up and down on it. And behold Y-H-V-H was beside him...(Gen. 28:10–13).

The Midrash (*Va-Yikra Rabbah* 29:2) says that Jacob foresaw the four kingdoms of the four exiles, Babylonia, Medea, Greece, and Edom [Rome]. He saw each of them rise and fall. God said to him: Why do you not come up the ladder? He replied: I am afraid lest I fall like all the others. God answered: Had you had faith in Me and come up, no nation or culture could ever have had power over you or your seed. Now that you have shown this lack of faith, these nations shall enslave your children. And yet despite this, never say that I am deserting them in their exile. "I will make an end of all the nations among which I have banished you, but I will not make an end of you" (Jer 46:28).

In understanding this, we must first remember that the source of Torah and the fount of wisdom from which we receive the revealed word is in the thought of God Himself; God's *hokhmah* and *binah* are the World of Thought. There the Torah exists in a completely hidden way, not revealed at all. In that place there exists neither speech nor language. In order to be revealed as word, the Torah must pass through *da'at*, that which is to bring it from the World of Thought into the World of Speech. *Da'at* includes both love and fear, both compassion and rigor. It is because Moses represents *da'at* that the Torah so frequently says: "The Lord spoke unto Moses saying, 'Speak unto the children of Israel.'"[99] We have shown this elsewhere as well: Moses brings the hidden Torah from the World of Thought to the children of Israel in the form of speech. By means of *da'at*, the revelatory power of speech has been joined to the source of secret wisdom. For this reason the *Zohar* tells us that "any word spoken by a person without fear and love does not fly upward."[100] As we have said, *da'at* contains both love and fear; only through it can the revealed word be joined to its sublime and hidden source, [even] without understanding.[101]

This is why a person who studies Torah or prays with both love and fear can attain proper awareness and create a channel in his mind and speech so that the eternal fount of wisdom may flow into him. The Torah that he speaks has become completely one with its source in *hokhmah* and *binah* above. Study marked by such love and fear truly shows the rung of *da'at*; its words go right up to their very root, and a great act of union takes place. Study without this content, of course, is not the same. Here the words are cut off from their root; there is no one to join the revealed word to its source in the wellsprings above. Not rising and being joined to its source, the verbal Torah that you study cannot receive the flow of fine oil that might otherwise come upon it.

Thus should you understand "Judgment forces are sweetened only in their root": this refers to *binah*, as we have said earlier: "I am *binah* and *gevurah* is mine," says Scripture (Prov 8:14).[102] The Torah is called *binah* and it claims the judgment forces as its own; they must all be brought back to Torah, out of which they first arose. It is there that they can be transformed. When such forces come on a person, he begins to become more aware, and love and fear enter into his sacred speech. He then takes hold of himself with this renewed awareness, and this *da'at* binds his words to the World of Thought, bringing about that unification. Then are his words uplifted and bound to their root. Since *da'at* is the joining of love and fear, compassion and judgment, the judgment forces that are now surrounded by compassion may rise up to that World of Thought, the place where there is no judgment at all. Only down below are compassion and judgment split off from one another; up above there is only the Torah of Compassion…simple mercy…thus by means of *da'at*: does one attain in utter unity to the World of Thought, the place where judgment and compassion are rejoined and transformed….

All this can happen only when you have truly accepted that those fallen powers contain the holy letters; whatever judgment forces come down on you, they contain fallen letters. That is why we speak about and deal with events that happen to us through language. The very letters through which we talk about the event are letters through which, in their fallen state, the event had taken place. In holding fast to the letters of Torah, through love and fear, the person is drawn by the force of those letters to the Torah's source. Then the fallen letters...are also returned to their root, to the good....

This then is *Jacob left Be'er-sheva'*: Jacob, as *da'at*, left the realm of hidden Torah, that source of wisdom which is called the well of living waters or Beer-sheva (for of wisdom Scripture says: "She has hewn out her seven pillars"—Prov 9:1). *Da'at* draws forth from this spring and brings it out into speech; only in this way is the uplifting and sweetening of the fallen letters made possible. Thus *he went to Haran*: mind has to go forth to that place of divine anger (*HaRoN*)...to bring those forces back up to their original wellsprings in the World of Thought. *He came upon a certain place*: The Hebrew verb used for "came upon" can also refer to prayer;[103] you begin to pray from the very place to which you have fallen. If your prayer is a mindful one, combining both love and fear with the letters of Torah, the letters of that judgment place will be joined to them as well. [This place had represented] the hiding of God's face, as in "I will keep My countenance hidden" and this is "for there is no God within me" (Deut 31:18). It is the damage wrought by sin that takes one away from God: But now that the forces of judgment and the fallen letters are raised up by the presence of mind and are joined to the good, he is able to *stop there for the night*, as in "He lies between my breasts" (Song 1:13—*va-yaLeN/yaLiN*). By repairing the damage and uplifting the judgments he indeed can cleave to God. Evil is there only because "there is no God within me"; once the presence of God has been restored, all is goodness and blessing. And so Jacob lay down there, as one who "lies between my breasts." This refers to the dwelling of God in the midst of the people Israel.

For the sun had set: We learn elsewhere that "the Lord God is the sun and a shield" (Ps 84:12). His divinity, despite a thousand differences, is like the sun, in that one cannot look into it except through a shield or visor. Thus can the brilliant light of *Ein Sof* not be perceived except in greatly reduced form. Now the sun has set before its time by a person's fall into the place of judgment; as he is redeemed from there, the brilliant sun begins to shine on him once again...All this because he took *Some of the stones of that place*: He took the letters (which the *Sefer Yetsirah* calls stones) from that very place, and he *put them at his head*, he raised them up to the source of the letters, the wellspring of Torah, the World of Thought. In this sense *va-yahalom*, he became well again (*HaLom/HaLiM*—Aram.); he healed the sickness of the judgment forces and brought them back into the good.

Now there was *A ladder set upon the ground*. Mind is such a ladder, reaching downward to the most revealed of levels, its *Top reaching to heaven*, to the place of true liberation, the World of Thought.[104] The *Angels of God*, these emissaries of divine judgment, *were going up and down on it*. RaSHI says that each would first go up and then descend. This means that by the true application of mind to prayer and study, performing them with the proper combination of love and fear, the very letters that had formed words of judgment against a person are rejoined to the good. Then the evil is separated and falls aside, as we have said. *And behold Y-H-V-H was beside him*: Here the name used (Y-H-V-H) is that which indicates compassion; the transforming of judgments arouses the flow of divine compassion from the source of life. Now we see that *He lay down in that place* should indeed be interpreted as did the mystics, referring to the twenty-two letters of the alphabet.[105] The letters of Creation were there too, but in a fallen state. By cleaving to the Torah with presence of mind, he able to uplift these letters also and to join them to the good. In the exile of Israel, some of those judging forces from above take on the form of nations that bring us suffering. Were Israel to have full faith in the power of mind, and apply it to Torah study with proper devotion, they would uplift and transform all such judgments into pure good. Each of those nations would then have only one cycle of ascendency, followed by immediate decline, for the good would have been lifted out from it. It is only because our faith is imperfect that the exile lasts so long. Even those who do pray and study, if their minds are not fully attuned and if not accompanied by love and fear, cannot form the ladders needed for the transformation of judgment forces. This can be done only by mind. The true meaning of exile, then, is that mind is in exile because it is not employed properly in the service of God. The lessening of faith brings about a diminishing of mind; faith, the seventh of the upper rungs,[106] is the gateway through which one must enter to get to *da'at* and all the rest. The *Sefer Yetsirah* tells us that God chooses to group all in sevens: seven lands, seven seas, and so forth. Now we understand why this is, for any ascent to the higher rungs must begin with the seventh, that is, with faith....

We are told that the nations are given this world, while Israel will have the world to come. We should not, however, take this teaching too literally. We have also learned that all the worlds, all creatures great and small, were created for the sake of Israel. Surely they were not created for one from whom this world would entirely be taken away! Understand the matter rather this way: "For by *yod he* has the Lord formed the worlds" (Isa 26:4).[107] The world to come was created by *yod*, while this world was formed by *he*.[108] This *he* that follows the *yod* is the second letter of the divine name, and these two letters are referred to in the *Zohar* as "two companions who are never separated" (*Zohar* 3:4a). They are joined together as one; there exists no separation between them at all. So it is with the two worlds created through them: They too must be one and inseparable. This world is that of matter, the corporeal, while the other is that of form, of the soul. Just as in the case of a human being, so long as body and soul are joined together he lives, but they part company when he dies, so it is with the two worlds. Israel must therefore conduct themselves in this world by the ways of the soul, that which truly belongs to the next, so that the two worlds never be quite separate from one another. By purifying their bodies and avoiding in this world both the bad and the excessive, they are ever able to convert matter into form. Thy must use only that of this world needed for the soul, that element of the next world that gives them life. If they were indeed to do so entirely, matter and form would be completely one; matter would be so purified that it too could be called form, its corporeal existence only secondary. Then the life-force from above, that life of the world-to-come, would flow through it as well. All this would come about through the unifying force of mind, of that *da'at Set upon the ground* but whose *top reaches heaven*. Mind could make it so that this world too could be considered a world of life. People then would not fear to look at the light from above, their corporeal selves being so purified and joined to the soul...

It is only Israel's lack of faith and mind, needed to bind this world to the world of the soul, that causes the world to fall constantly and to remain cut off from life. Then judgment comes to the world, and it is only for the few righteous ones in each generation who serve God with mind and with love and fear that the world is allowed to exist and does not fall utterly. It is they who turn God's justice back to mercy and bind the world to soul again. Thus Scripture says: "When evildoers rise up against me, my ears shall hear" (Ps 92:12): The evildoers are the result of judgments, and I raise them up to that place where there is no speech but only hearing, the World of Thought.[109] There they are transformed.

In messianic times (speedily and in our day, God willing!) there will be so much mind-awareness in the world that this world and its corporeal self will indeed be purified and matter will be joined to form, the two worlds united. Then evil, excess, and dross will all fall to the side, [eventually] to be purified. The nations that hold fast to them will also then fall, as life is removed entirely from that dross...But this world, precious to God and beloved by Him, has in truth been given to Israel, the people He has loved from among all peoples and cultures. All is one: Divinity above, Israel, Torah, the world-to-come, and this world. All bring forth the flow of His Godliness, this world in a more external way, but containing within it that inward self of the world-to-come. These must be joined into a total oneness, such that will allow body to be translated into soul, just as happens within a single human person. This task has been given to Israel, the people close to Him; no others have a part in it until the redeemer comes. Then matter will be so purified that the term "this world" will no longer apply at all; everything will be one and it will be called the world-to-come. Of this Scripture says: "On that day shall the Lord be one and His name one" (Zech 14:9).

Amen, Selah unto eternity. Blessed is the Lord forever. Amen. Amen.

Rabbi Nahman's Tales

Editor's introduction: The following selections come from two of Rabbi Nahman of Bratslav's best-known and most influential stories. They, like all of the tales in *Sippurei Ma'asiyot*, are creative literary works saturated with rich kabbalistic symbolism. Brief explanatory notes may be found after each of the translations, but the reader should first encounter and explore these stories without the veil of commentary. *The Lost Princess*, which appears below in its entirety, is the tale of a quest filled with longing and redemption in the style of a medieval romance. *The Seven Beggars* is the most famous of Rabbi Nahman's stories. This long and rather complicated work has many layers of stories and parables embedded within the narrative. The introduction and the first of the nested tales have been translated below.

The Lost Princess

Rav Nahman answered and said: On the way, I told a tale (of such power) that whoever heard it had thoughts of repentance. This is it.

Once there was a king. The king had six sons and one daughter. The daughter was extremely important to him and he cherished her and enjoyed her company very much. Once, on a certain day when he was with her, he became enraged at her and from his mouth slipped the sentence: "May the Not-Good take you away." That night she went to her room, and in the morning no one knew where she was. Her father, the king, grieved deeply and he sent here and there searching for her.

Then the viceroy, seeing that the king was deeply grieved, rose and requested that a servant, a horse, and money (for expenses) be given to him. And he set out to search for her. And he searched for her for a very long time until he found her.

(Now Rav Nahman tells how he searched for her until he found her.)

He traveled for a long time, here and there, in deserts and fields and forests. And he searched for her for a very long time. While traveling in the desert, he saw a path off to the side and reflected: "Since I have been traveling such a long time in the desert and cannot find her, I shall follow this path—maybe I will come to a settled place." And he traveled for a long time. At last he saw a castle with many soldiers posted around it. The castle was very beautiful and the soldiers were standing around it in perfect order. And he feared that the soldiers would not let him in, but he reflected: "I shall attempt it."

He left his horse and walked to the castle. They let him pass and did not hinder him at all. He walked from room to room without hindrance and came to a hall where he saw a king sitting with his crown, and many musicians playing instruments in his presence. And it was lovely and beautiful there. Neither the king nor any other person asked him anything. He saw delicacies and fine foods there, and he stopped to eat and went to lie down in a corner to observe what was going on there. He observed that the king ordered that they bring the queen and they went to bring her. When they brought in the queen, there was a great tumult and great joy and the musicians played and sang mightily. They placed a throne for her next to the king. And she was the lost princess! And the viceroy recognized her. After a time, the queen glanced about and saw someone lying in the corner and recognized the viceroy. She rose from the throne and went there and touched him.

She asked him: "Do you recognize me?"

He answered: "Yes. I recognize you. You are the princess who has been lost." And he asked: "How did you get here?"

She answered: "Because that sentence slipped from my father's mouth. And this place is the *Not-Good.*" He told her that her father was deeply grieved and that he had searched for her for many years. And he asked her: "How can I free you from here?"

She told him: "You cannot free me unless you choose a place and stay there for one whole year. During this entire year you must yearn for me, to free me from here. You will constantly yearn and search and hope to free me. And you will fast. On the last day of the year, you shall fast and not sleep from sunset to sunset."

And he went and did so. At the end of the year, on the last day, he fasted and did not sleep. He set out to go to the princess to free her. As he went, he saw a tree, and on it grew very fine apples. He craved them very much, and he went to eat from them. As soon as he ate from the apple, he fell over and sleep seized him. And he slept for a very long time. His servant shook him, but he did not wake up. After some time, he stirred from his sleep and asked the servant: "Where am I in the world?"

The servant told the viceroy the entire story: "You have been sleeping a very long time, several years, and I, in the meanwhile, have lived off the fruit." The viceroy grieved deeply and went to the castle and found the princess. And she wailed bitterly to him: "If you had only come on that day you would have freed me from here. Because of that one day, you have lost everything. It is true that not eating is very difficult, especially on the last day when the evil impulse waxes strong. And so, choose another place and stay there, too, for a whole year. On the last day you will be allowed to eat. Only do not sleep and do not drink wine so that you will not fall asleep, because the main thing is sleep."

He went and did so. On the last day he was walking back there and he saw a spring gushing forth and it looked red and smelled of wine. He asked the servant: "Do you see this spring? There should be water in it, but it looks reddish and smells of wine." And he went and tasted a bit from the spring. Immediately, he fell over and slept some seventy years. During this period many soldiers passed by with their baggage trains traveling behind them. And the servant hid from the soldiers. Afterwards, there passed a carriage and the princess was sitting in it. She stopped next to the viceroy and alighted and sat next to him and recognized him. She shook him vigorously, but he could not wake up. She began to wail about him, that all the labors performed and travails endured for so many years in order to free her were lost because of that one day when he could have freed her. She wept much about it: "It's a great pity both for him and for me, because I have been here such a long time and cannot get out." Afterwards she took the kerchief off her head and wrote on it with her tears and left it next to him. She rose and sat in her carriage and rode off.

Later, he woke up and asked the servant: "Where am I in the world?" The servant told him the whole story, that many soldiers had passed by and that the carriage had been there and the princess had wept and cried out: "It's a great pity for you and for me!" In the meanwhile, the viceroy glanced about and saw that the kerchief was lying next to him. And he asked: "Where did this come from?" And the servant answered that the princess had left it after having written on it with her tears. The viceroy took it and raised it to the sun. He began to see the letters and read what was written there, all her lament and cry, that she was no longer in the former castle, but that he should search for a golden mountain and pearly castle. "There you shall find me!"

He left the servant behind and went on alone to search for her. And he traveled for several years searching for her. He reasoned that surely there is no golden mountain and pearly castle in a settled place because he was expert in the map of the world. And so (he concluded): "I shall go to the deserts." He went to search for her in the deserts for many and many a year. At last he saw a man so huge that his size was not human and he was carrying a tree so huge that no such tree is found in any settled place.

That giant asked him: "Who are you?"

The viceroy answered: "I am human being."

The giant wondered and said: "I have been in the desert for a long time, but I have never seen a human being here."

The viceroy told him the whole story, and that he was searching for a golden mountain and a pearly castle. The giant said to him: "Surely it does not exist at all." He rebuffed him and told him that they had deluded his mind with nonsense, that it surely did not exist at all. And the viceroy began to weep bitterly and said: "It surely, definitely exists somewhere." The wild man rebuffed him again saying that they surely had deluded him with nonsense. And the viceroy said that it surely exists.

The wild man said to the viceroy: "In my opinion, this is nonsense. But since you insist, I, who am in charge of all the animals, will do you a favor and summon them all. Since they roam throughout the entire world, one of them might know about that mountain and castle." And he summoned them all, from the smallest to the biggest, all kinds of animals. He asked them, but they answered that they had not seen anything of the sort. So he said to the viceroy: "See! They have deluded you with nonsense. If you listen to me, you will go back, because you will surely not find it since it does not exist anywhere in the world."

But the viceroy insisted vigorously and said that it surely, definitely exists. The wild man said to the viceroy: "Here, in the desert, I have a brother who is in charge of all the fowl. Perhaps they know since they fly high in the air. Perhaps they have seen that mountain and castle. Go to him and tell him that I have sent you." And the viceroy went on for many and many a year in search of him. Finally he again found a man as huge as the former one and he, too, carried a huge tree. And this giant asked the viceroy the same question. The viceroy told him the whole story adding that his brother had sent him. And he, too, rebuffed him saying that it surely does not exist. The viceroy insisted that it does. The giant said to the viceroy: "I am in charge of all the birds. I shall summon them—perhaps they know." He summoned all the birds and asked them all, from the smallest to the biggest, and they answered that they knew nothing about that mountain and castle. The man said to him: "You see that it surely does not exist anywhere in the world. If you listen to me, go back." But the viceroy insisted and said that it surely does exist somewhere in the world. The giant said: "Further in the desert you will find my brother who is in charge of all the winds. They roam throughout the whole world—perhaps they know."

The viceroy traveled and searched for many and many a year, and finally found a man as huge as the former one and he, too, carried a huge tree. This giant asked the viceroy the same question, and the viceroy told him the whole story. This giant, too, rebuffed him, but the viceroy insisted again. Finally, the third giant said to the viceroy that he would do him a favor and summon all the winds to come and he would ask them. He summoned them, and all the winds came and he asked them all. None of them knew anything about that mountain and castle. The giant said to the viceroy: "Don't you see that they have told you nonsense?" And the viceroy began to weep loudly and said: "I know that it surely must exist."

At that moment he saw that another wind had arrived. And the giant in charge of the winds was very angry with it: "Why are you late? Didn't I order all the winds to come? Why didn't you come with them?"

The wind answered him: "I was detained because I had to transport a princess to a golden mountain and a pearly castle." And the viceroy was overjoyed to hear this.

The giant in charge asked the wind: "What is expensive there?"

The wind said: "Everything is very expensive there."

So the giant in charge of the winds told the viceroy: "Since you have been searching for her for such a long time and have performed so many labors, and money might now be an obstacle, I am giving you a purse, and whenever you put your hand in it you will draw money from it." And he ordered a wind to take him there. The storm wind came and carried him there and brought him up to the gate. The soldiers standing guard there would not let him enter the city, but he put his hand into the purse and took out the money and bribed them and entered the city. And it was a beautiful city. He went to a rich man and arranged for his board, knowing that he had to spend time there, because he had to employ intelligence and wisdom to free her.

(And how he freed her, Rav Nahman did not tell.)

And finally he did free her.

Editor's commentary: *The Lost Princess* may be understood as a tale about the redemption of *shekhinah*, based in part upon the Lurianic creation myth. The king represents God, his sons are the lower six *sefirot* from *hesed* to *yesod*, and the princess herself plays the role of *shekhinah*. In more personal terms, the king's daughter may also represent the human soul. Her kidnapping (or banishment) from the kingdom is *shevirat ha-kelim*, the moment of cosmic fracture that forces the divine Presence into exile. The viceroy on his quest to save *shekhinah* may be Rabbi Nahman himself, but he may also represent any mystical seeker who longs for her redemption. The desert and strange palace are the domains of the evil forces that have captured *shekhinah*. The viceroy's eating the apple and drinking from the fountain of wine recall the falls of Adam and Noah. The slumber accompanying his failure is thus the sleep of the prolonged exile. The ending is startling and purposefully unclear, but the princess has nonetheless been redeemed, underscoring the spiritual potential of tears and the power of longing.[110]

The Seven Beggars

I will tell you how our people were once joyous.

1

Once there was a king who had an only son. The king wanted to transfer the royal power to his son during his own lifetime. So he gave a grand ball. Now whenever the king gave a ball, it was surely a very joyous affair. But when he transferred the royal power to his son during his own lifetime, there was surely a great celebration. And at the ball were all the ministers, all the dukes, and all the nobles. And they were all very joyous at the ball. And the people, too, were greatly pleased that the king handed his royal power over to his son during his lifetime, because this was a great honor for the king, and indeed there was a great celebration. There were all sorts of things for the celebration—musical bands and comedians and the like—all things used for a celebration were present at the ball.

And when everybody had become very joyous, the king arose and said to his son: "Since I am a star-gazer, and I foresee that you, too, will at some time abdicate the royal power, see to it that you have no sadness when you abdicate. Only be joyous, for when you are joyous, I shall be joyous, too. Even if you are sad, I shall be joyous that you are no longer king, because you do not deserve to be king if you are the kind of person who cannot always maintain his joy even when he abdicates the royal power. Only when you are joyous, shall I be exceedingly joyous."

And the prince assumed the royal power vigorously. He created ministers, and dukes, and officials, and an army. The prince was a wise man, he loved wisdom dearly, and gathered around him many wise men. Whosoever came to him with some sort of wisdom was highly esteemed by him. He gave them great respect and wealth for their wisdom. He gave each one whatever he desired. If one desired money, he gave him money. If one desired honor, he gave him honor. Everything for wisdom. Since wisdom was so esteemed, everyone adopted wisdom and the whole kingdom engaged in the practice of wisdom. One practiced wisdom because he desired money, and another, because he desired honor and esteem. And because they all engaged in wisdom only, people in that country forgot military tactics. They were all engaged only in wisdom until the least wise man in this country would be considered the wisest man in another country, and the truly wise in this country were marvelously wise.

Because of this wisdom, the wise men of the land fell into heresy and they drew the prince into their heresy. But the common people did not fall into heresy since there was a great depth in the wise men's wisdom which escaped the common people and they were not harmed. Only the wise men and the prince became heretics. And since the prince had goodness in him because he had been born with goodness and had good qualities, he always remembered: "Where am I in the world and what am I doing?" And he would groan deeply and remember: "What is this? I should be carried away by such things? What's happening to me? Where am I in the world?" Yet, no sooner had he begun to use his reason than the heretical ideas were strengthened within him. And so it happened several times. He would remember where he was in the world and what he was doing and would groan and sigh, but suddenly he would again use his reason and his heretical tendencies would be strengthened as before.

2

And it came to pass that there was a mass flight from a certain country and everyone fled. And as they fled, they passed through a forest, and lost two children there, a male and a female. One family lost a male, and another lost a female. And they were still little children, four or five years old. The children had nothing to eat. They screamed and they cried because they had nothing to eat.

Meanwhile, there came a beggar who was going along with sacks in which he carried bread. The children began to badger him and cling to him. He gave them bread and they ate. He asked them: "Where do you come from?" They answered: "We don't know," because they were little children. He started to leave them, but they asked him to take them along with him. He said to them: "I do not want you to go along with me." Meanwhile they looked and noticed that the beggar was blind. And this was to them a marvel: "If he is blind, how does he know where to go?" (It was also a marvel that the children raised this question, because they were little children. But since they were clever children, this was a marvel to them.) And this blind beggar blessed them: "May you be as I am. May you be as old as I am." He left them more bread and went away.

The children understood that the Blessed One was watching over them and sent them a blind beggar to give them food. After a while the bread ran out and again they began to scream for food. Then night came, and they slept there. In the morning, they still had nothing to eat. They screamed and cried. In the meanwhile another beggar appeared who was deaf. They began to speak to him. He pointed with his hands and said to them: "I don't hear a thing." And this beggar also gave them bread and began to leave them. Again they wanted him to take them with him. He didn't want to, but he, too, blessed them: "You should be like I am." And he also left bread and went off. Then this bread also ran out, and again they began to scream.

Again a beggar appeared who stuttered. They started speaking with him, but he stuttered his words, so they couldn't understand what he said. He knew what they were saying but they didn't know what he was saying because he stuttered. The beggar also gave them bread and left them as before. He also blessed them, that they should be as he was, and he left.

After a while another beggar came, who had a twisted neck. The same thing happened as before. Then came a beggar who was a hunchback. Then a beggar without hands came. Then came a beggar without feet. Each one of them gave bread and blessed them, that they should be as he was, exactly as the previous beggars.

Then the bread ran out again. They started walking toward an inhabited place until they reached a path. And they walked along the path until they came to a village. The children went into a house. People pitied them and gave them bread. They went into another house and there they were also given bread. And so they went from door to door. They saw that it was good that people gave them bread. The children agreed that they would always be together. They made themselves large sacks and went from door to door and they used to go to all celebrations, to circumcisions and to weddings. They roamed through all kinds of towns and went from door to door. They also went to fairs and sat among the beggars on the benches with the beggar's plates, until the children became widely known among all the beggars, since everyone recognized them and knew them as the children who had been lost in the forest.

Once there was a large fair someplace in a large city. All the beggars went there and the children went there too. The beggars hit upon the idea to arrange a wedding match between the children. Immediately, as soon as a few of the beggars began to discuss the issue, it pleased them all and they arranged the match. Only how does one make a wedding for them? They decided that on a certain day, when there would be a feast for the king's birthday, all the beggars would gather there, and from the meat and bread which they begged there, they would make a wedding.

And so it was. All the beggars went to the birthday party and begged for bread and meat, and they also gleaned all the leftovers, meat and egg bread. And they went and dug a huge pit which could hold one hundred people, and they covered it with beams and earth and rubbish and they all went in, and there they made the wedding for the children. They raised the wedding canopy and were very, very joyous. The bride and groom were also very joyous. The bride and groom recalled the favors that the Blessed One had bestowed upon them when they were in the forest and they cried and longed: "How do we find the first beggar, the blind beggar, who brought us bread in the forest?"

3

Just as they were longing for the blind beggar, he called out: "I am here, I have come to be with you on your wedding day. I present you with a wedding gift: You should be as old as I. Previously, I offered you my blessing but today I bestow this upon you outright as a wedding gift: You should be as old as I am. Do you think that I am blind? Not at all. It is just that the entire world does not amount to an eye's wink (moment) for me." (He looked like a blind man because he did not look at the world at all, since the entire world did not amount to an eye's wink for him. Therefore seeing and looking at this world did not pertain to him.) "For I am very old and yet I am still young. I haven't even begun to live, yet I am very old. Not only do I say so, but I have an affidavit to that effect from the large eagle and I will tell you a tale:

"Once, people set sail upon the seas in many ships. A tempest arose and smashed the ships, but the people were saved. The people came to a tower. They climbed the tower and found all manner of food and drink and clothes and all the essentials. All the good things and pleasures of the world were there. They called upon each one to recite an old tale, one he remembered from his earliest recollection, that is, what he remembered from the inception of his memory.

"The old and the young were there. They honored the oldest among them by allowing him to be the first to recount. The oldest declared: 'What can I tell you? I can still remember when they cut the apple from the branch.' No one understood what he said, but there were wise men there who said: 'Surely that is a very old tale.'

"They invited the next to tell a tale. The second, who was not as old as the first, declared while asking: 'Is that such an old tale? I remember that tale, too, but I even remember when the lamp burned.' They declared: 'This tale is even older than the first tale.' They wondered how the younger could recall a tale that was older.

"They invited the third old man to tell a tale. He was younger still and declared: 'I even recall the forming of the fruit, that is, when the first fruit began to form.' They declared: 'This is an older tale still.'

"The fourth old man, younger yet, declared, 'I even remember when they brought the seed for the planting of the fruit.'

"The fifth, younger yet, declared: 'I can even remember the wise men who invented the seed.'

"The sixth one, younger yet, declared: 'I remember the taste of the fruit before the taste entered the fruit.'

"The seventh one declared: 'I even remember the smell of the fruit before it entered the fruit.'

"The eighth one declared: 'I even remember the appearance of the fruit before it was on the fruit.'

"And I (the blind beggar) was at that time only a child. I was also there and declared: 'I remember all of these tales and I remember nothingness.' They all declared: 'That is a very much older tale, older than all the others.' It was a great marvel for them that the child remembered more than all of them.

"In the meanwhile a large eagle arrived and he knocked on the tower and said to them: 'Stop being paupers. Return to your treasures. Use your treasures.' And he told them to leave the tower in the order of their age, the oldest leaving first. He took them all out of the tower. He first took out the child, since truthfully he was the oldest of all. And so he took out the youngest ones first, and the oldest he took out last. For the younger one was older, and the oldest among them was the youngest of them all.

"And the great eagle declared to them as follows:

"'I will interpret all the tales that were told. He who told that he remembered how the apple was cut from the branch implied that he still remembers when they cut his umbilical cord, that is what occurred as soon as he was born, when they cut his umbilical cord. This, too, he still remembers.

"'And the second who said that he still remembers when the lamp burned implies that he still remembers when he was an embryo because that is the time when a candle burns over the head. (Thus it is written in the Gemara (b. Niddah 30b), that when a child is in the mother's womb a lamp burns over his head.)

"'And he who said he still remembers when the fruit began to form, still remembers when his body began to form, that is, when the child was created.

"'And he who still remembers when they brought the seed to plant the fruit denotes that he remembers how the semen was drawn out during copulation.

"'And he who still remembers the wise man who invented the

seed implies that he still remembers when the semen was still in the brain.

"'And he who remembers the taste, that is the lower spirit; and the smells, that is the soul; and the appearance, that is the higher spirit. And the child who said he remembers nothingness, he is greater than all since he still remembers what existed before the lower spirit, the soul, and the higher spirit and so he said that he still remembers when there was nothing, and what happened there. He is higher than all.'

"And the great eagle said to them: 'Return to your ships. Those are your bodies which were broken. They will be rebuilt. Now, return to them.' And he blessed them.

"And to me (the blind beggar who was a child at that time and who is telling these stories) the great eagle said: 'You come with me, because you are just like me in that you are extremely old and yet very young. And you have not yet even begun to live, though you are very old. And I am the same since I am extremely old and still young.'

Accordingly, I have an affidavit from the great eagle that I have lived a long life. And now I give you my long life as a wedding gift." And there was great happiness and delight…

Editor's commentary: As in Rabbi Nahman's other tales, the king represents God. However, this ruler chooses to withdraw his power from the kingdom and transfer his authority to the prince, perhaps the *rebbe* or *tsaddik*. This may reflect the kabbalistic idea that Creation could only be accomplished through withdrawal of the divine light (*tsimtsum*). At first there is great joy, as per the king's command. But the people are slowly seduced by wisdom, revealing the dangerous allure of knowledge and its close relationship to heresy; this is the recurrent theme in Rabbi Nahman's teachings. The ensuing madness may be what causes the exodus in which the children are abandoned. The beggars who take care of the youngsters and arrange for their wedding are hidden righteous individuals, and the particular blemish of each one actually proves to be an asset. The message of these characters and their parables is clear: the deepest truth of world lies beneath what we see.

In the blind beggar's story, the great eagle represents God, the ships are the human body shattered by death, and the survivors in the tower are the souls in an intermediate world before the afterlife truly begins.[111] Each of the souls recalls its earliest memory, which progress from the cutting of the umbilical cord to the one who remembers having been incorporated in the divine Nothing. It is no accident that the youngest of the souls indeed possesses the oldest memory, mirroring the reversal of a blind beggar who can see better than all. Like the conclusion of *The Lost Princess*, the conclusion of this tale is ambiguous. The seventh beggar, presumably the Messiah, never appears, and the ending of the story cannot be revealed until the time of the redemption.

The *Book of Secrets* of R. Yitshak Yehiel Safrin of Komarno

Editor's introduction: Rabbi Yitshak Yehiel Safrin of Komarno (1806–74) was a prolific author and an important Hasidic leader. This Kabbalist extraordinaire viewed himself as a transmigration of Yitshak Luria's soul, and his books of Jewish law and Scriptural commentaries are full of references to mystical concepts. Several of his works are devoted to unpacking the kabbalistic ideas he saw as undergirding the BeSHT's teachings. This reflects Safrin's belief that the BeSHT was essentially an expositor of Luria's thought. Rabbi Yitshak Yehiel's spiritual autobiography and dream journal *Megilat Setarim* (*Book of Secrets*) offers a rare window into the interior life of a Hasidic *tsaddik*. The first half of this work, entitled *Sefer ha-Hezyonot* (*Book of Visions*) was inspired by Hayyim Vital's book of the same name. The second half is a valuable collection of Hasidic stories that he heard from his teachers and family. Rabbi Yitshak Yehiel was the *rebbe* of a Hasidic dynasty that was particularly committed to mystical practices and rituals, which remained strong until the Second World War.[112]

Part One: *Book of Visions*

I will give my brethren a glimpse of God's ways...I will tell about the greatness of my Soul: Who and what I am and why I came into the world. However, I have not yet received permission to discuss where I was and from which place I am derived in the body of Adam....

On the third day after my circumcision, one of the disciples of our divine teacher, the BeSHT, was visiting the city of my birth, Sambor. Many townspeople and women with their children came to him. This is the accepted custom among the *tsaddikim* of our generation, to bless the holy people Israel, young and old, with the love of the Jewish Soul. My mother was among those who came, bringing me, so that the *tsaddik* should bless me. When he put his hand on my head, he cried out in a loud voice and said in Yiddish, "This small one has a great and awesome mind and a wondrous Soul." My mother was very frightened by his great outcry and he said to her, "Do not be afraid; this child will be a great light."

Between the ages of two to five years I attained wondrous visions and divine inspiration. I spoke prophetic words when a person would ask about divine matters, and literally gazed from one end of the world to the other.[113] My teacher and uncle, the awesome holy person, our teacher, Rabbi Tsevi of Zhidachov,[114] gave me two Rhenish coins every week so that I would tell him and respond to everything that he would ask of me. I clearly and precisely answered all the questions that he asked me and donated the money to charity.

The Soul of my teacher and uncle was from the same source as Rabbi Hayyim Vital, from the source close to the Soul of Rabbi Akiva.... My father, whose soul is in Paradise, was from the source of Maimonides. He was righteous, pious, and holy, and was also close to the source of Rabbi El'azar of Worms[115] and Rabbi Solomon ibn Adret.[116] Nonetheless, he did not completely attain the essence of kabbalistic wisdom. However, his heart was a fire burning for Torah and worship with self-sacrifice. He died with the Unification of self-sacrifice of Rabbi Akiva, one of the ten martyrs. A pillar of fire was seen over his grave on Friday afternoon that reached to the heart of heaven.[117]...

When I was seven, [a desire for] the wisdom of our divine teacher, Rabbi Yitshak Luria, burned in me like a torch. I studied his writings with awe, fear, and great enthusiasm. I asked my father about the difficult passages. I studied in want and poverty and I was worthy of several wondrous things and holy levels… At the age of sixteen I married my destined bride, who was from my aspect of the Spirit. There were several who opposed this match because the Spirit was not yet within me. However, as a result of my great penance and diligence in Torah study no stranger came between us. Afterwards, I [attained] several high and great levels of divine inspiration through diligence in Torah study and worship. In truth, I did not understand that this was not mine, since I was still far from the essence of worship.

Afterwards, I contemplated this and separated myself from all things of this world. This was in the year 5583 [1823], at the beginning of winter. I had a private room which was very cold and was not heated even once during the whole winter. It was my custom to sleep only two hours every day and the rest was spent [in the study of] Torah, Talmud and commentaries, *Zohar*, the writings of our teacher, Rabbi Yitshak Luria, and Rabbi Moshe Cordovero. As a result of all this, I fell into a state of great *katnut*[118] for more than three months, and I was faced with many difficult and evil *kelippot* that attempted to entice me to leave my study of Torah. Worst of all was the depression that descended on me. During this period my heart was strong as a stone and I did not eat anything during that period except for a little bread and water each day, and I had no pleasure from Torah study and prayer. The extreme cold and the *kelippot* were very powerful, and I was literally caught between two paths with free will to choose. The bitterness from these enticements that passed over me were literally worse than a thousand deaths.

Suddenly one day, after I overcame these enticements, while I sat studying tractate Yevamot for the sake of the Lord of the world and to adorn the *shekhinah*[119] with all my strength, a great and wondrous light descended on me which filled the whole house with the indwelling of the *shekhinah*.[120] This was the first time that I tasted a little of His light, may He be Blessed, without error or confusion and with wondrous pleasure. It is a light so pleasant that the mind cannot comprehend it. From then on, I entered into the worship of the Creator of the world with a wondrous infinite light and I was no longer overcome by enticements, as I had been previously. After this I again fell [spiritually] for a period of time and I understood that I needed to visit *tsad-*

dikim so that they would bring down His light, may He be Blessed, for me since I was already a clarified vessel....

5605 [1845]. On the twentieth day of the *'Omer*, I was in the city of Dukla.[121] I arrived on a dark and gloomy night and there was nobody to take me home, until a tanner came and took me to his house. I wanted to recite the evening prayers and count the *'Omer*, but I could not do it there. I went to the local *bet midrash* and prayed there. From this I understood the concept of the descent of the *shekhinah* and her pain in standing in the tanner's market.[122] I wept many tears before the Lord of all, because of the *shekhinah*'s anguish. I fainted from my own great anguish and dozed a little. I had a vision of a great light in the image of an adorned young woman, a glowing light, but I was not worthy to see her face. More cannot be written down. Her light was brighter than the noonday sun.

5606 [1846]. On the first day of Rosh Hashanah, I did several spiritual exercises on behalf of the community of Israel in Russia. I overcame their guardian angel and because of the severity of the decree against them, there occurred to me what occurred. On the second day, I did what I had to do and at night I saw the above-mentioned guardian angel with a drawn sword. He wanted to kill me if I did not leave him alone...I promised him that I would leave him alone. Afterwards, I saw the guardian angel of Edom and he assured me that he would not do anything bad as a result of the decree and I blessed him with the blessing of a king, and then awoke. Thus it was that all the decrees against the Jews of Edom were annulled....

5610 [1850]. The second of *Nisan*, Thursday night. It was the night of immersion in the *mikveh* and I studied Torah until midnight. I completed the study of the laws of Passover in the *Tur* and went to sleep. I had a dream and vision in the night. I saw our master Elimelekh of Lyzhansk[123] and he was very affectionate toward me. I was told that the place of our divine master, the BeSHT, was not far from that of the above-mentioned master. I quickly went to his dwelling, with great desire, to see the face of the holy master. I stood outside his house and was told that he was inside, in the midst of his prayers. Afterwards, the door opened and I was worthy to see the face of our master, the BeSHT, may his merit protect us. As a result of my great joy and fear I was not able to move from my spot. He walked over to me and greeted me with a joyful face and I had great pleasure.

His visage is engraved in my mind and is always before me. Perhaps I had been worthy to attain this because I had given charity that day, as is right and proper.

Part Two: The Deeds of the Lord

Now I will write about the deeds of the Lord, for the deeds done by the *tsaddikim* of our times are great.

My teacher and father-in-law, R. Avraham Mordecai of Pinczow, told me (I can testify that he would not change the story for everything in the world) that a righteous old man told him: My son, I once went to the *mikveh* at night with our teacher, the BeSHT. He tarried in the *mikveh* for a long time. I said to him: Master, the candle is almost extinguished! He responded in Yiddish: "Fool, take an icicle and light it. 'He who told the oil to burn will tell the icicle to burn' (b. Ta'anit 25a)." This means in Hebrew: "Fool, take the icicle from the roof during the winter and light it." The old man said that it burned until he accompanied the divine master to his house. When he arrived at the house, where there were lit candles, only a little water was left in his hand, which had melted from the heat of the flame. I heard this from my teacher and father-in-law. Believe me, my brothers, this and all the stories are true as the Lord your God is true....

My teacher and father-in-law told me, during his travels of more than two years to serve *tsaddikim*, he was also with the grandson of the divine teacher, the BeSHT, the author of *Degel Mahaneh Ephraim*.[124] Once he said to him: Come and I will tell you a wise thing that my grandfather did. In the city of Medzibozh there was a wealthy man who opposed my grandfather, the BeSHT, like the simpletons, sons of fools, who oppose the *tsaddikim*. Once, on the first night of Passover, an evil thing happened to him, Heaven forbid. The gentiles took a corpse and put it in the courtyard of the wealthy man, in order to falsely accuse him of having killed him for the Passover, as was the way of the evil gentiles in earlier times (and also in our time). It was the habit of these evildoers to leave guards after they left [the corpse], to ensure that nobody from the house left with a bundle on their shoulders. Afterwards, they would attack the inhabitants of the house and the other Jews, killing and robbing them, without fear of punishment (may God see the suffering of Israel and have mercy). When the wife of the wealthy man went out into the courtyard and found the corpse, she fainted from great fear and anguish. She was revived with great effort. Crying, screaming, and hitting her forehead, she told her husband about the nefarious evildoers and their leaving a corpse in their courtyard. They would certainly return soon to torment them mercilessly and kill them for no reason, as was their way. Out of great fear and anguish, she told her husband to go to the *tsaddik* and he would save them. He said to her: How can I go, I am his opponent? She responded: He is a *tsaddik* and will not bear a grudge. He went to our master, my grandfather, weeping greatly and told him the whole story, that he was in great danger. My grandfather said to me: Ephraim, my dear grandson, take the staff and go with this man to his house and say to the corpse, my grandfather sent me to you. You should immediately get up and come with me. I went with the man and spoke thus to the above-mentioned corpse. The corpse immediately got up and went with the bier in his hands to my grandfather, who lay him back on his bier. Afterwards, the plotters descended on the house of the wealthy man and they found nothing. Since our divine master was also famous among the gentiles as a wonder worker, they decided to also search my grandfather's house. My grandfather took the hat from my brother Baruch, may he live, who was then very young, and put it on the head of the corpse. He put the *Haggadah* in his hands and said to him: Mumble! He began to sway back and forth and read inarticulately, in a loud voice, from the *Haggadah*. When the plotters came, they searched the whole house but did not find the corpse. They did not recognize him, since he moved and made loud noises like the living. The gentiles went on their way. Afterwards, my grandfather sent for the rich man and told him: Take the corpse and bury it! He did so.

My teacher and father-in-law, of blessed memory, heard all this from the abovementioned *tsaddik*, the grandson of the BeSHT, of blessed memory, who was himself involved in the story. I heard the rest of the story from my teacher and father-in-law, who heard it from others. The following year, they gathered again to do a similar evil deed, to attack Israel with a blood libel. Among them was an anti-Semitic priest. When the *matsot* were being baked, the BeSHT went to the priest. Taking a walk with him, [the Besht] said to him: Why do you want to do this to a holy people, to shed blood like water for nothing, in a false and despicable accusation? Do you not know that I am in the world and I know all your secrets, those that you did and those that you want to do? You did not succeed last year when you left the corpse at the house of R. Lipa, the wealthy man. I resurrected him temporarily and you saw him sitting at my feet, at the edge of the bed, and did not recognize him. The priest then admitted to him that on his advice the corpse was thrown into the wealthy man's courtyard the previous year. In addition, he had already prepared a corpse to put into a Jewish house this coming Passover, in order to accuse them. The priest swore that he would never again do this to Israel. Afterwards, our divine teacher went to celebrate the festival of Passover with joy and gladness....

Once, our master was studying with his teacher, Ahijah the Shilonite, and they needed to ask a secret of the prince of the Torah. They made a mistake and brought down the prince of fire. As a result, a fire broke out in his house and burned the whole city.[125] Our divine master was afraid of accusations by the gentiles. He ran away and needed to cross the river Dniester. He put a piece of his belt on the river and crossed on it, not by means of a divine name, but through great faith. He believed and trusted in God that he would not drown, Heaven forbid.[126]

My teacher and father-in-law, the *tsaddik*, told me that when our divine master, the Holy of Holies, was secluded in the high mountains in communion with the Lord his God and studying with his well-known teacher, a group of thieves decided to kill him. They sat at a distance to observe his actions. They saw that when he quickly walked from mountain to mountain, the mountains quickly stuck to each other, as he went from mountain to mountain, so that he would not fall into the valleys between them, which were very abundant. A great fear fell upon them and they came before him and said: Man of God, if you wish, come with us to the Holy Land through a shortcut. The desire of our master for the Holy Land was very great (as has been told before) and he went with them. They came to a small and very dangerous crossing. He did not want to rely on a miracle and returned to his home, to connect his Soul with God.[127]

Once a singer came with musicians to sing for him. Our master understood through this all the sins that he had committed from the day of his birth until now. As a result, he thanked [the singer]. For even though our master saw from one end of the world to the other and

[knew] all the thoughts of a person from the day of his birth, nonetheless, "When he sees iniquity, does he not discern it?" (Job 11:11), until he sang before him and the Holy of Holies entered his ears....

Our master, Rabbi Yisra'el BeSHT, once asked our master, Rabbi Yitshak Luria, of blessed memory: Why did he speak of the secrets so openly and not in the path of worship? He answered him that if he had lived two more years everything would have been repaired.[128] He also told him how he spoke with the Messiah and with *Ra'aya Mehemna* [Moses][129] and their responses to him. He was an expert in the secrets of Creation and of the Chariot, in the whole Torah, in the speech of all living things and the heavenly angels. He was full of love and fear of God, good attributes, piety, humility, and love of Israel. The above-mentioned master said that all the attributes that were written about Rabbi Yitshak Luria, our master, the BeSHT, had them all and even more. In addition, that which was written about Rabbi Yitshak Luria was like a drop in the ocean compared to what he truly had. He also told him how every Sabbath eve, at the time of the afternoon service, myriads of Souls gathered around him. He repaired them all and raised them to their source....

I was told by reliable witnesses, truly righteous people, that in a certain place there was a rabbi. Once, a question was brought to him concerning a duck, on the eve of the Sabbath. He would have been able to declare it kosher because of poverty, in honor of the Sabbath, or excessive financial loss. He did not permit it because he was a strict decisor. Afterwards, when he died, the rabbi came before the Heavenly Tribunal and was acquitted, because he was completely righteous. In the midst of this, a certain duck came and complained that there was within it a Soul that had wandered for many years until the time for its repair had come in this duck. It is still wandering because he had declared it not kosher, for no reason. They decided that the righteous rabbi will have to wander. He went on in this way for several years until he was advised that he should go to our master, for he repairs all the (wandering) Souls. If he repairs the Soul, then there will no longer be any judgment against him. He did so and in a short time he ascended to his place....

He once said to his disciples on *Hoshanah Rabbah*: Prepare yourselves a teacher and rabbi, because I will die this year. His disciples said to him: Our master, the light of Israel, we have heard that there is one *tsaddik* in this land. Will we be able to affiliate with him? He answered them. When you travel to him, come to him when he is praying a certain prayer. Afterwards, examine him and ask him to give you some advice about how to remove haughtiness and arrogance. If he will tell you that he literally has no advice and will respond to you: God will help, for there is no advice for this—you will know that it is truthful, and he is a complete *tsaddik*. They traveled there and it happened as above. They asked him as above and he responded: Gentlemen, my dear and beloved ones, what can I tell you? There is no advice for this. There are those who can lower themselves to the ground, but their purest inner intent is arrogance and a wicked heart. There is also the opposite: One who behaves with haughtiness, but is brokenhearted. There is no counsel for this, but God's help, in His infinite mercy. They became attached to him in love, as our divine master had commanded, may his merit protect us, amen....

CHAPTER 5

Modern Mystics

Introduction

The late nineteenth and early twentieth century was a time of great social and intellectual change for the Jews of Eastern Europe. The authority of traditional religion was being challenged, and Judaism was now forced to compete with a multitude of new ideas. Vast numbers of Jews abandoned the observant lifestyle and became part of the modern world. The intellectuals among them gravitated toward the ideals of modern philosophy, secular humanism, and emerging scientific disciplines like psychology. For others, socialism provided an attractive solution to the gross economic inequality and class injustices of the Eastern European life. Still others, responding to rising anti-Semitism and the surge of European nationalism, believed that the Jewish future was to be found in Zionism; the only security was to leave Europe and establish a sovereign Jewish commonwealth, perhaps even in their ancestral homeland.[1]

In confronting these new ideas, many religious leaders sought to close the social and intellectual borders of their community, forbidding any and all changes to tradition. This stance successfully preserved their way of life, but it also caused profound ossification in the intellectual and spiritual dimensions of Judaism. But not all religious intellectuals felt this was the best path. Rabbi Abraham Isaac Kook (1865–1935) rejected the strict conservatism of many of his peers and called for a mystical rebirth of Jewish religious life that incorporated the best of modernity.[2] Hillel Zeitlin (1871–1942) returned to the tradition only after many years of immersion in philosophy, and he used the language and concepts of the Western intellectual tradition in articulating his vision of a new mystical renaissance. Both of these two great twentieth-century mystics, whose works are translated in the following pages, felt that philosophy and science need not be rejected out of hand. New ideas could be uplifted and reinterpreted, becoming an integral part of reviving Jewish observance and spirituality.

Rabbi Abraham Isaac Kook, reverently known as Rav Kook, emerged from the Lithuanian *yeshivah* world.[3] Born in Grieva (modern Latvia), the young Kook quickly distinguished himself as a brilliant scholar. He received his first European rabbinic position while in his early twenties, but immigrated to Israel in 1904 and served as the rabbi of the Jaffa area. Rav Kook was trapped in Europe when World War I broke out, and he returned to Palestine soon after its conclusion. He became the Chief Rabbi of Jerusalem in 1919 and Chief Ashkenazi Rabbi of the land of Israel in 1921. Rav Kook founded a *yeshivah* in Jerusalem, which was staunchly Zionist and had a far broader curriculum than other traditional Jewish academies. After his death in 1935, the school's administration and oversight were taken over by his disciples and family.

Rav Kook had full command of Jewish mystical literature, but did not see himself as a traditional Kabbalist. Though he rarely cites his sources explicitly, he drew freely upon *Sefer Yetsirah*, *Sefer ha-Bahir*, the *Zohar*, the Kabbalah of both Cordovero and Luria, the *SheLaH*, and early Hasidic works, combining them together in a uniquely creative and eclectic way. His dense but highly poetic writings are interwoven with biblical verses, kabbalistic symbols, and rabbinic allusions. His mystical works have very little of the complicated theology of earlier Kabbalah, but they reveal an intense yearning for an experience of the presence of God. Rav Kook's mysticism also had an important national element, and the love of the holy land of Israel was interwoven with his spiritual quest. In this he was influenced by the Zionist dream in the broadest sense. He saw his project as a rebirth of Jewish creativity, nourished by the deepest wellsprings of tradition, yet capable of taking place only in the sacred environment of a renewed Jewish life in *Erets Yisra'el*. Although that renewal of the Land was originally undertaken by secularized Jews, indeed by individuals who had rebelled against tradition and its authority, Rav Kook identified with them. He saw a "holy audacity" in their rebellious spirit, and found a spark of the sacred in their dedication to what he, if not they, understood as holy work.

Rav Kook's relative openness to the outside world, especially his tolerance of secular Zionism, earned him the fierce criticism of more traditionally minded religious figures. Yet his formative education and textual canon were strictly orthodox, and as a leader Rav Kook was very much a part of the rabbinic establishment. He endorsed the work of the Zionist pioneers, not because he approved of the values of the secular philosophy,[4] but because his nationalist reading of Kabbalah made room for them as an important part of the mystical rebirth of the people now at home in their land.[5] Rav Kook believed that Jewish theology had lost its way and was desperately in need of new life, and some important holy creativity might indeed be found in the ideas of modernity. In his own words, "the old will be renewed, and the new will be sanctified."[6]

Rav Kook was a prolific writer, and his works include a remarkable number of essays, poems, letters, and legal responsa. Yet the vast majority of his writings are simply short transcriptions of ideas as they came to him. He was unburdened by the notion that these spontaneous passages must all fit together into a single, comprehensive, and cohesive philosophical system. The language of Rav Kook's highly unsystematic writings is often cryptically poetic, leaving great room for interpretation. This is further complicated by the reality that his published works were heavily edited and censored by both family and disciples. Only recently have the highly revealing manuscripts of his personal diaries, from which the printed texts were culled, begun to emerge. In some cases the differences between the two versions are striking.[7]

Rav Kook's lasting influence on the spiritual culture and religious politics in the state of Israel has been enormous, though his legal writings have enjoyed somewhat less-enduring authority. The messianic ideology of the post-1967 Settler movement is deeply infused with his son Tsevi Yehudah's more radical reading of Rav Kook's mystical teachings about the spiritual qualities of the land of Israel. His *yeshivah* in Jersualem remains one of the important centers of the nationalist Religious Zionist community. The prominence of Rav Kook's personality and his mystical writings has had a major influence in Israel, imbuing the religious Zionist world (including its political organs) with a spiritual element that has a strong messianic tinge.[8]

Hillel Zeitlin was born into a Belorussian Hasidic family and raised in a traditional world steeped in contemplative mysticism.[9]

Early in his teens, he was overcome by a profound longing for the divine Presence, and Zeitlin enjoyed an extended period of overwhelming religious ecstasy. This rapture ended suddenly and left him stricken with debilitating feeling of distance from God. His subsequent spiritual quest led him away from traditional Jewish practice and toward the literature of the *haskalah* ("Enlightenment") and the Western intellectual tradition. With great fervor Zeitlin consumed the works of modern philosophers like Spinoza, Nietzsche, Schopenhauer, and William James. He also read extensively about Christianity and Buddhism. These new philosophical and religious ideas inspired and excited Zeitlin, but they also challenged his worldview, sometimes in uncomfortable ways. Particularly debilitating was his encounter with biblical criticism, which, by his own account, completely shattered Zeitlin's faith. He was attracted to a philosophy of pessimism, one that was to leave an imprint on many of his later writings.

Zeitlin moved to Warsaw in 1907, and there he re-immersed himself in the study of traditional Jewish thought.[10] He returned once more to the mystical texts of his youth, now reading them with the conceptual vocabulary developed during his study of Western philosophy. His own mystical writings may be described as a quest to develop an authentic and modern Jewish spiritual language. His mystically panentheistic understanding of the natural world, which is thoroughly suffused with the immanent divine Presence, draws on both the theologies of Spinoza (as well as the romantic poets) and the Hasidism of the Ba'al Shem Tov. Zeitlin's positive view of human creativity employs the philosophy of Nietzsche to articulate an idea found already at the heart of the *Zohar*. His short treatise *Yesodot ha-Hasidut* (*The Fundaments of Hasidism*, 1910) weaves together brief references to modern philosophy with a vast array of passages drawn from the classical works of Hasidic thought. Zeitlin's synthesis of these sources is creative and relatively well-organized, and this work, translated in part below, represents one of Zeitlin's most systematic attempts at articulating his own mystical theology, wrapped in a thick blanket of traditional quotations.[11]

Hillel Zeitlin envisioned a far-reaching revival of Jewish religion and culture grounded in the theologies of Kabbalah and Hasidism. However, this program was no naïve retreat into the idealized past, but rather an empowered renaissance of Jewish spiritual creativity.[12] He hoped to forge a new type of Hasidism that would fuse the spiritual vitality of the movement's early teachings with the noblest elements of modern philosophy. To this end Zeitlin undertook the project of translating the *Zohar* into Hebrew in the 1920s, with the hopes that the beauty of this sacred text would help nourish the spiritual revolution.[13] He dreamed of social reform as well, and addressing himself in particular to the youth, he called for Jews to leave the depraved capitalism of the city and move back to the land. Only there in the ideal pastoral setting could they build a new type of ethical Jewish society. As a part of this greater revolution, Zeitlin also hoped to form smaller, more elite groups of intensely committed spiritual individuals. These were to be modeled after the devotional fellowships of Safed and the close-knit Hasidic society. Zeitlin had various names for these communities, such as *Benei Heikhala* ("Children of the Palace") and Yavneh, but they seem to have remained only a dream. His spiritual manifesto for this imagined community, and the fifteen tenets by which the members were to conduct their lives, appear in translation below.

The years of World War I were extremely difficult ones for the Jews of Eastern Europe, and they were beset with persecution from all sides. Zeitlin believed the afflictions of this turbulent period were the travails immediately preceding the ultimate redemption. From this point on he began to speak with an increasingly prophetic and messianic tone, which reached a peak in the 1930s with his visions of the impending apocalypse.[14] Zeitlin was a true firebrand, and his later works are dominated by his painful awareness of Jewish suffering, and his outrage and bewilderment at God's apparent silence. These themes are particularly visible in his poetry and the vast number of articles he published in both the Yiddish and Hebrew presses. He had an ambivalent relationship to Zionism, seeing it as one way among many of delivering the Jews of Eastern Europe from their oppression.[15] His commitment to the movement was utilitarian and not bound to a mystical conception of the land of Israel. Unfortunately, Zeitlin lived to see his grim prophecy fulfilled. After the Nazis invaded Poland, he was incarcerated in the Warsaw Ghetto together with most of his family,[16] and in 1942 Zietlin died on a march to Treblinka. He was wearing his *tallit* and *tefillin*, and holding his beloved *Zohar* in his hand.[17]

Rav Kook and Hillel Zeitlin used the symbolic language and theology of Judaism's rich mystical tradition to engage with their increasingly complicated modern realities. Zeitlin and Rav Kook respected one another and were aware of each other's writings. They even met during Zeitlin's brief visit to Jerusalem for the opening of the Hebrew University in 1925.[18] Yet despite agreeing that Kabbalah and Hasidism held the keys to awakening modern spiritual life, their visions of that revival were quite different. For Rav Kook, this meant an embrace of the Zionist movement and its secular followers, in the hope of transforming and "uplifting them," amidst the complicated religious versus secular politics in interwar Palestine. For Zeitlin, the foremost issues facing Eastern European Jewry were its desperate economic plight, the cultural upheavals wrought by modernity, and the rise of racial anti-Semitism. He too envisioned a spiritual rebirth amid those dire outward circumstances. As the successful fruition of that dream grew less likely, he began to call for repentance with the rage and vehemence of a biblical prophet. Rav Kook's dream has been carried forward in different ways by intellectuals and religious leaders in Israel. Zeitlin's impassioned call for a new Hasidism remained unanswered until years after his murder, but his teachings were discovered once more during the revival of Jewish mysticism in America in the second half of the twentieth century.

Further Reading

Bar Sella, Shraga. *Between the Storm and the Quiet: The Life and Works of Hillel Zeitlin*. Tel Aviv: Hakibbutz Hameuchad, 1999 [Hebrew].

Ish-Shalom, Benjamin. *Rav Avraham Itzhak ha-Cohen Kook: Between Rationalism and Mysticism*. Translated by Ora Wiskind-Elper. Albany, NY: State University of New York Press, 1993.

Mirsky, Yehudah. *Rav Kook: Mystic in an Age of Revolution*. New Haven: Yale University Press, 2013.

From the Depth of the Well

The Writings of Rabbi Abraham Isaac Kook

Lights of Holiness

THE SUMMONS TO THE MYSTICAL

When an individual, and similarly a generation, has reached a state where its spiritual propensities are summoned to expression, then it will no longer satisfy its pressing thirst with any fragmentary knowledge unless this very knowledge leads to a content that is broad and free, that will engender great ecstasy in the root disposition of the soul, deriving from the source of its being. Thus the mystical elements of the world, the hidden meanings of the Torah, the secret knowledge about God, are called forth from each generation.

The stubbornness of seeking spiritual satisfaction in the outer aspect of things enfeebles one's powers, fragments the human spirit, and leads the stormy quest in a direction where it will find emptiness and disappointment. In disillusionment the quest will continue in another direction.

This is the mission of the strong, those for whom the light of God is the whole meaning of their lives. Even if they have been hurt by great disappointment, even if they have grown faint because of insufficient faith in themselves, even if they have become wearied by their battle against a great multitude that follows confidently its own opinion, let them not cease their beneficent labors, let them not allow their strength to give way. In their hands is the banner of the hidden meanings of the Torah, riches of knowledge, a comprehensible and inner-directed faith, abiding deliverance for the Jewish people and for man, for body and soul, for this world and for all worlds, for great and small, for old and young.

If we say something and turn speechless, if we commence an utterance and the concept is lost in silence, if we lack the strength to liberate the word, to find the expression, we will not, for this reason, become dismayed and retreat from our fixed goal. The difficulty of speech will not serve as a restraint on the stream of the lofty desire in which the word of God is revealed, which bids us speak, to gird the stumbling with strength, to proclaim peace to the adversaries of the world. "I will cause a new utterance to be heard in the land: Peace, peace to the far and near, said the Lord; and I will heal him" (Isa 57:19).

THE MYSTICAL DIMENSION THAT EMBRACES EVERYTHING

Philosophy embraces only a given part of the spiritual world. By nature it is detached from whatever is outside its sphere. By this itself it is fragmented in its being. The grace of perceiving how all feelings and tendencies, from the small to the large, are interdependent, how they act on each other, how separate worlds are organically related—this it cannot portray. For this reason it must always remain an aristocratic discipline, set apart for special individuals.

Greater than this is the mystical quest, which by its nature penetrates to the depths of all thought, all feelings, all tendencies, all aspirations, and all worlds, from beginning to end. It recognizes the inner unity of all existence, the physical and the spiritual, the great and the small, and for this reason there is, from its perspective, no bigness or smallness. Everything is important, and everything is invested with marked value. There is no lost gesture, there is no vain imagining.

Corresponding to this there is no limit to the possibility of ascending toward the heights. There is no wisdom or perception concerning which one may say that it is enough, and that it cannot be linked to a higher illumination, in comparison with which it seems in a state of dimness. Even the supernal crown,[19] which is a dazzling light, a pure light, is darkness in comparison with the Cause of causes, before whom all lights are turned into darkness.

Because of this advantage, mystical vision, in being able to embrace within itself all thoughts and all sparks of the spiritual, is alone fit to chart for us the way to go.

Therefore, the mystical dimension is the soul of religion, the soul of the Torah. From its substance derives all that is revealed, all that is circumscribed, all that can be conceived by logic, and all that can be carried out in actions. The far-reaching unity of the mystical dimension embraces all creatures, all conditions of thought and feeling, all forms of poetry and exposition, all expressions of life, all aspirations and hopes, all objectives and ideals, from the lowest depths to the loftiest heights. The source of life deriving from the highest realm of the divine, which only the light of prophecy, the clear illumination, the light seen by Adam [prior to his fall], the supernal lights can disclose, streams into and passes through all stirrings of thought, all movements of the spirit.

Only the mysterious mind of the Supreme One fixes the particular formations, what shall be regarded as first and what as last, which phenomenon shall obscure the unity because of its lowly state, and which is above it because of its greatness. "And before the One what can you count?" (*Sefer Yetsirah* 1:7).

THOSE DESTINED FOR THE MYSTICAL

Whoever feels within himself, after many trials, that his inner being can find peace only in pursuing the secret teachings of the Torah must know with certainty that it is for this that he was created. Let him not be troubled by any impediments in the world, whether physical or spiritual, from hastening after what is the essence of his life and his true perfection. He may assume that it is not only his own perfection and deliverance that hinges on the improvement of his character, but also the deliverance of the community and the perfection of the world.

Every soul that has reached fulfillment always perfects the general character of the world. All life is blessed through the truly enlightened ones, when they press on resolutely on their course, without being restrained by life's obstacles. To the extent that the soul is enhanced inwardly by attaining its full character does it become the sustaining basis for many souls and an influence for life and multitudes of blessing are channeled through it. But everything is dependent on the degree of the person's humility.

And let him not be confused by the question that always confronts those inclined to the inner life, that if he should devote himself to the pursuit of his hallowed sensibilities, when will he attend to his own needs, to the affairs of the world, and to the other branches of the Torah necessary for action, the analytical study of the Talmud, the performance of deeds of kindness, and the cultivation of the active forms of piety. It is only as he remains attached to his fructifying roots, to that dimension of the Torah which is singularly relevant for his soul, as he remains immersed in cultivating his inner disposition and yearns continually to devote himself to its perfection, will doors open to him, for all aspects of his needs, whether in the pursuits of practical life, or of peripheral spiritual pursuits. It is precisely one who pursues the Torah for its own sake who merits many things.

But if he should detach himself from his source, and stray to draw his water from other wells not substantively appropriate for him, he will wander from sea to sea, from one river to another to the end of the earth, but he will find no rest. A person who wanders away from his place is like a bird that strays from its nest.

A person should, therefore, always take courage in the Lord and trust in the God of his life, who fashioned his soul within him, with a singular disposition and with an inclination to a unique kind of holiness, through which alone he can find what he seeks.

Out of the depth of inner peace he will discover that the times of straying, too, physically and spiritually, have been prepared from the beginning for his benefit and for his perfection. There are times when one gains his sustenance from distant places. But he must not be disdainful of trouble and exertion. Though for the most part those who seek God are sated with delight and inner peace, the righteous are content to suffer injury for the sake of the Holy One, praised be He.

THE DOCTRINE OF EVOLUTION

The doctrine of evolution that is presently gaining acceptance in the world has a greater affinity with the secret teachings of the Kabbalah than all other philosophies.

Evolution, which proceeds on a course of improvement, offers us the basis of optimism in the world. How can we despair when we realize that everything evolves and improves? In probing the inner meaning of evolution toward an improved state, we find here an explanation of the divine concepts with absolute clarity. It is precisely the *Ein Sof* in action that manages to bring to realization the infinite potentiality.

Evolution sheds light on all the ways of God. All existence evolves and ascends, as this may be discerned in some of its parts. Its ascent is general as it is in particulars. It ascends toward the heights of the absolute good. Obviously the good and the comprehensive all go together. Existence is destined to reach a point when the whole will assimilate the good in all its constituted particulars. This is its general ascent: No particularity will remain outside, not a spark will be lost from the ensemble. All will share in the climactic culmination.

Toward this objective one needs to be sensitized spiritually to seek God on a higher plane. This is effected through a service of faith in God.

THE PERFECTION OF THE SPIRITUAL THROUGH THE MATERIAL

When spiritual decline sets in because of a deterioration in one's bodily state, it is necessary to deal with it on the basis of its cause: to mend one's bodily state, according to a definite regimen and with firm understanding. Through the mending of the bodily condition the spiritual damage will be repaired. In the course of life it often becomes apparent that spiritual deficiencies result from the breakdown in the proper order of the physical. The physical then asserts itself with full force, and it seems to many that it has risen as a destructive force against the spiritual order. In truth, however, it becomes clear in the light of developments that the thrust of the physical was directed to a general rehabilitation, which embraces all of the spiritual needs as well, in their purest form.

A FOURFOLD SONG

There is one who sings the song of his own life, and in himself he finds everything, his full spiritual satisfaction.

There is another who sings the song of his people. He leaves the circle of his own individual self, because he finds it without sufficient breadth, without an idealistic basis. He aspires toward the heights, and he attaches himself with a gentle love to the whole community of Israel. Together with her he sings her songs. He feels grieved in her afflictions and delights in her hopes. He contemplates noble and pure thoughts about her past and her future, and probes with love and wisdom her inner spiritual essence.

There is another who reaches toward more distant realms, and he goes beyond the boundary of Israel to sing the song of man. His spirit extends to the wider vistas of the majesty of man generally, and his noble essence. He aspires toward man's general goal and looks forward toward his higher perfection. From this source of life he draws the subjects of his meditation and study, his aspirations and his visions.

Then there is one who rises toward wider horizons, until he links himself with all existence, with all God's creatures, with all worlds, and he sings his song with all of them. It is of one such as this that tradition has said that whoever sings a portion of song each day is assured of having a share in the world to come.

And then there is one who rises with all these songs in one ensemble, and they all join their voices. Together they sing their songs with beauty, each one lends vitality and life to the other. They are sounds of joy and gladness, sounds of jubilation and celebration, sounds of ecstasy and holiness.

The song of the self, the song of the people, the song of man, the song of the world all merge in him at all times, in every hour. And this full comprehensiveness rises to become the song of holiness, the song of God, the song of Israel, in its full strength and beauty, in its full authenticity and greatness. The name "Israel" stands for *shir el*,[20] the song of God. It is a simple song, a twofold song, a threefold song and a fourfold song. It is the Song of Songs of Solomon, *shelomoh*, which means peace (*shalom*) or wholeness. It is the song of the King in whom is wholeness.

WITHDRAWAL AND SOCIABILITY

The person with a radiant soul must withdraw into privacy frequently. The constant company of other people, who are, for the most part, crude in comparison with him, even in their spirituality, dims the clear light of his higher soul. As a result his important work will diminish. He might have been able to benefit the people, his society, by frequent withdrawals, without terminating his relationship with them even then. He would have kept the needs of his generation before him, to pray for them, to delineate their virtues, the treasure of goodness that is in them. But they will suffer decline through his decline, through reducing his spiritual potency as a result of their distracting closeness to him.

It is very difficult to suffer the company of people, the encounter with persons who are totally immersed in a different world with which a person who is given to spiritually sensitive concerns, to lofty moral aspiration, has no contact. Nevertheless, it is this very sufferance that ennobles a person and elevates him. The spiritual influence that a person of higher stature exerts on the environment, which comes about through the constant encounter, purifies the environment. It lends the graces of holiness and freedom on all who come in contact with him.

And this nobility of a holy grace returns after a while with stronger force and acts on the person himself who exerted the influence, and he becomes sociable, abounding in spirituality and holiness. This is a higher attribute than the holiness in a state of withdrawal, which is the normal fate of the person to whom the higher spiritual concerns are the foundation of his life.

Essays

THE SAGE IS MORE IMPORTANT THAN THE PROPHET

As a rule poets know how to portray the nobler side of life, its beauty, its dynamism and vitality. They also know how to describe the evils of life and to protest against them vigorously. But it is outside the competence of the imaginative faculty to probe the particular conditions that preserve life and safeguard it from even the most minor defects that are due to generate very destructive consequences. This falls within the competence of a body of knowledge that deals with particulars. Here begins the work of physicians, economists, engineers, judges and all those who pursue practical wisdom.

This distinction has even wider application. Prophecy saw the great evil of idolatry in ancient Israel, and protested against it with all its might; it envisioned the majesty and delight associated with the belief in one God, and portrayed it in all its radiance. It saw the corruption in moral depravity, the oppression of the poor, murder, adultery and robbery, and it was infused with the spirit of God to offer help and to rectify these conditions through lofty and holy exhortations.

But the little lapses out of which was forged the gross body of sin—these remained hidden from the eye of every prophet and seer. Similarly it was not within the sphere of prophecy to grasp how the habituated performance and the study of commandments will, after a span of time, release their hidden inner graces, and a wholly divine influence will decisively vanquish the darkness of idolatry. Nor could it grasp how the slow negligence, which disparages the performance of the commandments, with their inferences and elaborations, will start a process of erosion, destroying the vessels in which is stored the exalted spirit, causing the human passions, the straying imagination, which abounds in beautiful shoots outside but in poisonous elements within, to become automatically ever more potent.

It is true that this perception was granted to the prophecy of Moses, of which God is quoted as saying that He revealed it to him "from mouth to mouth" (Num 12:8), the prophecy of undimmed clarity that discerned simultaneously the claims of general principles as well as of the exacting demands of the particulars. But there never arose another like Moses, as we are told, "There never arose another prophet like Moses whom the Lord knew face to face" (Deut 34:11). It was, therefore, necessary to assign the enunciation of general principles to the prophets and of the particulars to the sages; and, as the Talmud declares, "the sage is more important than the prophet" (b. Bava Batra 12a). And what prophecy with its impassioned and fiery exhortations could not accomplish in purging the Jewish people of idolatry and in uprooting the basic causes of the most degrading forms of oppression and violence, of murder, sexual perversity and bribery, was accomplished by the sages through the expanded development of the Torah, by raising many disciples and by the assiduous study of the particular laws and their derivative applications. "'The eternal paths lead to Him' (Hab 3:6);—the term of 'paths,' *halikhot,* may also be read as *halakhot*, and the text would then mean that the laws lead to Him" (b. Niddah 73a).

In the course of time the concern with the work of the sages predominated over the work of the prophets and the institution of prophecy ceased altogether; after some time the general principles declined, they were immanent in the particulars but were not readily apparent. At the end of the present epoch, when the light of prophecy will begin to have its revival, as we are promised, "I shall pour out My spirit on all flesh" (Joel 3:1), there will develop a reaction, a pronounced disdain for the particulars. This is alluded to in the Talmudic statement that at the dawn of the messianic age "the wisdom of the sages will become unsavory and those who live on the boundary [that is, the sages who define limits in the law] will turn from city to city without finding grace" (b. Sotah 49b).

This will continue until the radiance of prophecy will reemerge from its hiding and reveal itself not as an unripe fruit, but as the first fruits of all vitality and life, and prophecy itself will acknowledge the great efficacy in the work of the sages, and in righteous humility exclaim: "The sage is more important than the prophet." This transcending of one-sidedness will vindicate the vision of unity expressed by the psalmist: "mercy and truth have met, justice and peace have kissed, truth will rise out of the earth and mercy will show itself from heaven; the Lord will also bestow what is good and our earth will bring forth its bounty" (Ps 85:11). The soul of Moses will then reappear in the world.

THE SIGNIFICANCE OF THE REVIVAL

To be attached to God is the most natural aspiration of a person. What is throughout all existence in a state of dumbness and deafness, in a form of potentiality, is developed in man in a conceptual and experiential form. There can be no substitute in existence for the longing to be absolutely linked with the living God, with the infinite light. As we are under a compulsion to live, to be nourished, to grow, so are we under a compulsion to cleave to God. This cleaving to God, to which we are summoned with all our soul, must necessarily develop in us. It must grow in our feeling, it must become more clarified in our understanding. Under no circumstances can humanity and all existence dispense with the quest for divine cleaving, which is present within her, even if in a hidden form.

The primitive stage of humanity, the epoch of gross darkness, left in the world forms of life that impeded the full manifestation of the divine cleaving. It is impossible to assess the pain of the general world soul and the pain of the soul in every living creature and every person as a result of the spiritual oppression, the denial of its hidden good that was to offer so much light, so much joy, that can engender a life of breadth, of endurance, of higher vistas and strength. A person needs such a life; it is of the essence of his nature and existence. But human weakness intervened and fashioned dumb idols, gross, materialistic, vulgar, limited and defective divinities, and the light was shut out.

We can imagine the suffering of the great soul of the spiritual giant, the soul of Abraham, with all its aspirations, with its mighty longing for freedom and light, over the world's disgrace. How embittered it is on realizing the happiness, the light intended for all, for every living being, for every soul. Abraham heard the vast realm of the divine calling to existence: Be illumined; calling to every particular being: Fill yourself with happiness, greatness, loftiness, peace, good, strength, love and delight. But the wells have been shut, the "Philistines shut them and filled them with earth" (Gen 26:18). How this lion of a man breaks out of his confinement, how angrily he takes his staff in hand, breaks the idols and calls with a loud voice for the light, for one God, the God of the universe.

The Jewish people took this aspiration as the basis of its national existence, as conditioned by its historic destiny. Thus, out of free moral impulses—the universal moral system—were drawn the bases for the establishment of the faith of Israel, which is so vital to us and to the entire world. It is precisely when we imagine, invoke and focus on the name of the God of Israel that we give clarity to our inner visions, our profoundest experiences. Our peace of mind and our relaxation of soul, the conditioning of our lives in purity with firmness and holiness, are established through cleaving to God. Morality is not centered merely in good deeds on a societal level. Morality is primarily a refined, inner disposition within the soul to seek the good, the absolute good, to be good in oneness, to cleave to the good. This holy spirit can exist among us only within the context of an attachment to God, which is contributed to use by the faith of Israel, the practical and the ideational. Under this spiritual, this inner moral necessity, we must immerse ourselves in our people. From all its generations we have acquired the whole treasure of life, which is true life, the link to our existence, to the life of our soul of souls. In this state of purity we love the name of God, the divine light that abides in us, that abides in the whole people; we love the Torah and the commandments, the precepts of God and the laws He gave to Israel. And out of a strong sense of our own authenticity, the conviction is growing in us, the fruitful, lofty vision full of the substance of life, to broaden our philosophy, to disseminate our concept over the entire world....

Our strong commitment to assure the continuity of Judaism, with its ideas and pattern of behavior, together with its corporate self on its own land, stems from the widespread recognition by our people that we still have a long distance to travel in order to complete what we began. We began to say something of immense importance among ourselves and to the world, but we have not yet completed it. We are in the midst of our discourse, and we do not wish—and we are unable—to stop. Under no circumstances will we abandon our distinctive way of life nor our universal aspirations, which transcend every particular party, both of which are interrelated, just as we shall not abandon our hope to return and be rebuilt, and exist as a nation in our historic homeland, as in ancient days. We cannot abandon all these. Even though one does not discern readily the place of ideals in vitalizing the life of a people, it is they that give life to all life and when they recede the soul animating life recedes. If we stammer so much in speaking of our mission, the fault is not in the clarity of the concept or in its truth. Our truth is strong enough, but it is so rich and so overpowering that we are still unable to explain it in clear language, and for this reason we shall not retreat. We shall speak and explain as much as our power of speech permits us. In our inwardness we understand our ideas, and in the course of time our speech will also emerge from its hard exile in which it is confined, and we shall be able to speak, to explain in clear terms what we seek with our full being. But until that golden age we shall not cease from our practical and spiritual efforts. Only a people that has finished what it started can descend from the stage of history, when its vision has already been fully disclosed to the world. To begin and not to finish—this is not in accordance with the rhythm in existence.

The soul of the eternal people ponders its thoughts, it weaves into one fabric all its meditations, and again as in a flash there pass before it generations and epochs, from its earliest youthful dreams, from the blossoming of its springtime, to its latter years, the time of fruition that began after the long decline. They are all intertwined in the chain of its thoughts, its meditation and its actions. It muses itself as from sleep to renew its youth according to an old-new program, modest and weak, but held together with the mighty streams of the past flowing toward the future, to the accompaniment of ancient memories with residual strategies. Our work is like tiny growths of some mighty and majestic forest of Lebanon, which, after a holocaust of its beautiful cedar trees soaring toward the heights, has begun to renew its vitality and to bring forth tender, weak and impoverished plants, like pieces of foliage sprouting on a wall. But these are not pieces of foliage, they are mighty cedars at the beginning of their growth in a mighty forest.

Out of its inner depths the Jewish people will yet sound the same call that was issued by the rock from which it was hewn.[21] Out of its awareness of light and happiness, out of its profound compassion for every afflicted soul, for every confused creature, for the forms of national, social and moral life that proceed on paths full of entangling thorns, because of the absence of a source of light to reveal to them that yearning for which the soul of all existence cries out in its pain, it will sound the call: Seek me, search after me, and live. In dark paths some have fabricated imitations; with hearts full of hypocrisy and cowardice, they approach to portray the greatness of the King of kings, whose greatness and might they had heard about on the outside. Not so, the Jewish people; such service is inferior in its eyes, even though many individuals in its midst are drawn to it. Not so is the spirit of a mighty nation, an ancient people, a nation that seeks forcefully the light of God and the joy of life. It will release a fierce wind to destroy the imitation that invaded it from the other side of the boundary, and it will raise up against it an adversary in which the spirit of God will be embodied. With an ardent soul, full of life and enduring heroism, it will bestir itself and call out: Here is light, here is the voice of the living God calling to me from the depths of my being, here is the light of eternal freedom for all existence, that has come and shines from the light of God on Mount Zion, the place of the valley of vision, where the word of the living God has begun to be heard.

All the rebels of the world will yet hear, all the heretics of the world will understand, all who still have a spark of life will return, from the depths of the earth souls will ascend, the unfortunate ones will raise themselves from the bottom of the pit, "those lost in the land of Assyria and the forsaken ones in the land of Egypt will come and serve the Lord on the holy mountain in Jerusalem" (Isa 27:13). They will bow down and arise full of strength, they will be renewed, invigorated with light and strength, legions and legions of them, with firmness of heart they will arise and cry out: A people has arisen, has begun to be a nation, that will release a flow of divine life to all worlds, a mighty people that has made a way in the stormy sea, that has paved an eternal pathway for the vitality of life that is distilled by attachment to God. "The God of Israel gives strength and firmness to the people, praised be God" (Ps 68:36).

The Lights of Penitence

CHAPTER FOUR: PRIVATE PENITENCE AND PUBLIC PENITENCE—IN THE WORLD AND IN THE JEWISH PEOPLE

2. Through penitence all things are reunited with God; through the fact that penitence is operative in all worlds, all things are reunited and reattached to the realm of divine perfection. Through the thoughts of penitence, its conceptual implications and the feelings it engenders, the basic character of all our thinking, our imagination and our knowledge, our will and our feeling, is transformed and placed again within the context of the holy order of the divine.

11. In the deep recesses of life there is always stirring a new illumination of higher penitence, even as a new light radiates in all the worlds, with all their fullness, to renew them. According to the degree of the light, and the wisdom and the holiness it embodies, do human souls become filled with the treasures of new life. The highest expression of ethical culture and its programmatic implementation is the fruit grown as a result of this illumination. It thus turns out that the light of the whole world and its renewal in its diverse forms depend at all times on penitence. Certainly the light of the Messiah, the deliverance of Israel, the rebirth of the people and the restoration of its land, language and literature—all stem from the source of penitence, and all lead out of the depths to the heights of penitence.

CHAPTER FIVE: THE INEVITABILITY OF PENITENCE AND ITS EFFECTS IN MAN, IN THE WORLD, AND IN THE JEWISH PEOPLE

8. The future will disclose the remarkable power of penitence, and this revelation will prove of far greater interest to the world than all the wondrous phenomena that it is accustomed to behold in the vast areas of life and existence. The wonders of this new revelation will draw all hearts to it, exerting an influence on everyone. Then will the world rise to its true renewal and sin will come to an end. The spirit of impurity will be purged away, and all evil will vanish like smoke.

9. The people of Israel, because of their added spiritual sensitiv-

ity, will be the first with regard to penitence. They are the one sector of humanity in whom the special graces of penitence will become manifest. They experience a prodding to conform to the divine light radiant in the world, which is beyond sin and wrongdoing. Every deviation from this disposition damages the perfection that is characteristic of this people. In the end, the vigor of its life's rhythm will overcome the deviation, and they will attain full health, and they will assert it with great force. The light of penitence will be manifest first in Israel, and she will be the channel through which the life-giving force of the yearning for penitence will reach the whole world, to illuminate it and to raise its stature.

CHAPTER SIX: THE PREVALENCE AND INNER ACTION OF PENITENCE IN THE HIDDEN DEPTHS OF MAN, THE WORLD, AND THE JEWISH PEOPLE

1. Penitence emerges from the depths of being, from such great depths in which the individual stands not as a separate entity, but rather as a continuation of the vastness of universal existence. The desire for penitence is related to the universal will, to its highest source. From the moment the mighty stream for the universal will for life turns toward the good, many forces within the whole of existence are stirred to disclose the good and to bestow good to all. "Great is penitence for it brings healing to the world, and an individual who repeats is forgiven and the whole world is forgiven with him" (b. Yoma 86a). In the great channel in which the life-sustaining force flows, there is revealed the unitary source of all existence, and in the hovering life-serving spirit of penitence all things are renewed to a higher level of the good, the radiant and the pure.

Penitence is inspired by the yearning of all existence to be better, purer, more vigorous and on a higher plane than it is. Within this yearning is a hidden life-force for overcoming every factor that limits and weakens existence. The particular penitence of the individual and certainly of the group draws its strength from this source of life, which is always active with never-ending vigor.

2. Penitence is always present in the heart. At the very time of sin penitence is hidden in the soul, and it releases its impulses, which become manifest when remorse comes summoning to repent. Penitence

is present in the depths of existence because it was projected before the creation of the world, and before sin had occurred there had already been readied the repentance for it. Therefore, nothing is more certain than penitence, and in the end everything will be redressed and perfected. Certainly the people of Israel are bound to repent, to draw closer to their original goal to activate in life the nature of their soul, despite all the obstructions that impede the manifestation of this mighty force.

CHAPTER EIGHT: THE PANGS OF SIN, THE SUFFERING OF PENITENCE, AND THE HEALING OF ITS AFFLICTION

3. Every sin oppresses the heart because it disrupts the unity between the individual person and all existence. It can be healed through penitence, which is radiant with the light [of the higher influence] of the ideal embodied in universal existence. Thereby it becomes possible for the harmony with all existence to become once again manifest in him; when he repeats he finds healing. However, the basis of the anguish experienced is not merely the result of sin itself. It is rather due to the basic nature of sin and the nature of the life process that has become disoriented from the order of existence, which is resplendent with divine light radiant in all being in unity and high purpose. It is for this reason that those whose lives are basically evil and whose sins are rooted in their thoughts and aspirations and in the dispositions of their hearts become pessimists and see the whole world in such unduly dark colors. They are the ones who complain against the world and against life. They are the masters of the "melancholy spleen,"[22] whose mockery of existence is the laughter of a fool who does not realize that the Lord is good to all (Ps 145:9).

CHAPTER TEN: THE INTERDEPENDENCE OF PENITENCE AND THE TORAH IN THEIR GENERAL NATURE AND IN THEIR HIGHEST SIGNIFICANCE

1. Truly full penitence presupposes high vistas of contemplation, an ascent to the rarefied world that abounds in truth and holiness. One can achieve this only through the pursuit of the deeper levels of

Torah and divine wisdom concerning the mystical dimension of the world. This calls for physical purity and moral purity as aids, so that the clouds of lust shall not obscure the clarity of the mind. But prior to all these must come the study of the Torah, specifically the higher Torah for only this can break all the iron barriers that separate the individual and the community from their heavenly father.

8. This is certain, that one cannot succeed in the study of the mystical dimension of the Torah without penitence. In the study of those lofty subjects the will is joined with the understanding in one entity. When one comprehends the core of those subjects in congruence with the firmness of the will for the good, then one is spurred by a longing for it, and one projects many general and particular strategies as to how to reach it. But when sins form an obstruction, the will is damaged. Since the person cannot rise to the highest level of the will, and, being sunk in the filth of sin he cannot appreciate the importance of the will for the general and the particular good, knowledge cannot grow in him, and the channels for comprehending the secret teachings of the Torah are blocked. It is, therefore, important to strengthen oneself to do penance and to purify the will in order to attain a lucid understanding in the supernal subjects.

9. One cannot enter the spiritual world of mystical knowledge and gaze at the supernal light except through a preceding act of full penitence. When a person confronts the supernal illumination, there is at once revealed to him the splendor of absolute justice and beauty in the supernal holiness, and a fierce pressure is generated in him that he too shall be embraced by that splendor and beauty and that his life shall be rooted in them in all their manifestations. At once he assesses his actions and his morals and sees their defects. Then he experiences remorse and he repents out of genuine love. To the extent that he resolves to walk in the good path, in congruence with the light of the logic of equity—which becomes more ascendent with the illumination in the Torah, in which alone a Jew can find the deepest level of his responsibility—will he become rooted in the supernal world. Without any inner contradiction will his thoughts then become radiant, and the spiritual visions of the higher enlightenment that focuses on the mysteries of the world will rise before his eyes in their full radiance, in accordance with his previous state and preparedness, and in accordance with his true spiritual vitality and freedom.

The Moral Principles

LOVE

1. The heart must be filled with love for all.

2. The love of all creation comes first, then comes the love for all mankind, and then follows the love for the Jewish people, in which all other loves are included, since it is the destiny of the Jews to serve toward the perfection of all things. All these loves are to be expressed in practical action, by pursuing the welfare of those we are bidden to love, and to seek their advancement. But the highest of all loves is the love of God, which is love in its fullest maturing. This love is not intended for any derivative ends; when it fills the human heart, this itself spells man's greatest happiness.

3. One cannot but love God, and this sweet and necessary love must engender as a practical consequence an active love for everything in which we perceive the light of God. One cannot but love the Torah and the commandments, which are so intimately linked to the goodness of God. One cannot but love equity and righteousness, the benign order that engenders good for all, which is firmly linked to the reality of existence, and in which the heart envisions excellence, that, because of its majesty and beauty, we designate as the will of God. The divine will is manifest in it, but it is greater than all this, and distinct from all this, and it nourishes the soul of every living being with delight beyond anything to which thought could reach. And it is impossible not to be filled with love for every creature, for the flow of the light of God shines in everything, and everything discloses the pleasantness of the Lord. "The mercy of Y-H-V-H fills the earth" (Ps 33:5).

4. The flame of the holy fire of the love of God is always burning in the human heart. It is this that warms the human spirit and illumines life; the delights it yields are endless, there is no measure by which to assess it. And how cruel is man toward himself, that he allows himself to be sunk in the dark abyss of life, troubles himself with petty considerations, while he erases from his mind this that spells true life, that is the basis for all that gives meaning to life. It is for this reason that he does not share in it, and walks this world bound by the heavy burden of his material existence, without light to illumine his way. But all this is contrary to the nature of life; indeed it is contrary to the nature of all existence. The grace of God's love, a boon

from on high, is destined to break out from its confinements, and the holiness of life will hew a path toward this delight, so as to enable it to appear in its full splendor and might. "No eye has seen what God alone will do for those who wait for him" (Isa 64:3).

5. The love for people must be alive in heart and soul, a love for all people and a love for all nations, expressing itself in a desire for their spiritual and material advancement; hatred may direct itself only toward the evil and the filth in the world. One cannot reach the exalted position of being able to recite the verse from the morning prayer (1 Chr 16:8), "Praise the Lord, invoke His name, declare His works among the nations," without experiencing the deep, inner love stirring one to a solicitousness for all nations, to improve their material state, to promote their happiness. This disposition qualifies the Jewish people to experience the spirit of the Messiah.

Whenever in our classic tradition we encounter allusions to hatred, clearly the reference is to the phenomenon of evil, which has disrupted by force the unity of many nations at the present time, and certainly in ancient times when the world was in a much lower moral state. But we must realize that the life process, its inherent light and holiness, never leaves the divine image, with which each person and each nation has been endowed, each according to its level of qualification, and this nucleus of holiness will uplift all. It is because of this perspective on life that we are concerned for the fullest progress to prevail in the world, for the ascent of justice, merged with beauty and vitality, for the perfection of all creation, commencing with man, in all the particular groupings through which he functions. This is the essence that lies at the heart of the Jewish outlook, that, by the grace of God, we are now reviving on a practical and spiritual plane.

FAITH

5. Faith in God is the soil in which all values of life blossom. As the knowledge of cultivating the land brings riches to those who pursue it, while everyone once thought that the peasantry were on the lowest plane of the economy, so will the teachings associated with religious faith bring a great and enlightened happiness to the entire populace that is sincerely devoted to it, when they will be shown the riches stored in its treasure. What was once the possession of the spir-

itually affluent will be readied and made clear to everybody, after the passage of those epochs that, through their spiritual advances, have adapted the knowledge of religion that it might be manifested in all the splendor of its clarity.

6. In all cultures and in all religious philosophies we see only the expansion of the central point, the natural feeling of faith and of simple piety. In order to broaden its horizon, to develop the potency embodied in it, it is necessary to pursue all the peripheral studies, the practical and the speculative, the intellectual and the emotional. The success of those studies depends on the extent to which they are linked to this vital essence of the human soul, which radiates a mighty radiance of life, the Jewish soul especially. This is the holy element of faith in God, which is the basis of true piety, and which is inspired by an inner quest for life, pervaded by keen emotion, expressive of the most basic principles of life. The soul with all its impulses, with all its potencies, its lights and its inclinations, is rooted in it.

22. All the commandments are portrayals of faith, they derive from a depth of faith, and from what faith in the divine in its highest reaches implies for human behavior. Every commandment and its derivative particulars, as they are performed, deposit impressions in the inner life and in the world in which is spelled out the profound truth of faith in God. Every transgression and neglect of a commandment deposits in the inner life and in the world impressions that are completely contrary to what faith in God, in its fullest truth, requires. Whether this chain of causation is known or not, the effect takes place, and the strength of the divine dimension is enhanced with the keeping of the Torah, which derives ultimately from faith, and it diminishes with the voiding of the divine service or its neglect. The culture based on the Jewish people's inner quest for holiness spread the perception of this profound truth. The love for the Torah spreads in the world to the extent that the hidden meanings of the Torah are clarified in the world, and the holiness of a pure faith is strengthened. The holy logic that is above our worldly logic stirs the strings of the violin of the divine soul in man and in the world, and one's eyes can then see clearly the great truth of faith that spreads from the entire Torah, in its writings and its traditions, and even in Jewish customs that are also part of the Torah.

28. The fact that we conceive of religious faith in a distorted form, petty and dark, is responsible for atheism's rise to influence. This is

the reason that the providential pattern of building the world includes a place for atheism and its related notions. It is to stir to life the vitality of faith in every heart, so that religious faith might be brought to its highest level. By including the good that is embraced in the theoretical conceptions of atheism, religious faith reaches its fullest perfection. Then will all the damage atheism effects in the world be transmuted to good, and the domain damaged by atheism will become an area full of delight. "He shall make her wilderness like Eden and her desert like the garden of the Y-H-V-H" (Isa 51:3).

LINKING LIFE WITH GOD

1. The divine philosophy [the Kabbalah] teaches us the attributes of God, the divine *sefirot*, that we may know it is for us to link our lives with the attributes of the Holy One, praised be He.

2. We must study God's names, His attributes, the *sefirot*, so that we know it is incumbent on us to cleave to the attributes of God, that we have the capacity to cleave to them, and that we cannot cleave to God in His awesome transcendence. If this is not clear to us then we have no understanding of the concept of the divine attributes, of the basic meaning of the *sefirot*, and of the fundamental significance of the mysteries of the "chariot."[23]

3. Our ideals will always be advanced and they will bring to light each day and each moment new wellsprings of light and of a life of purity if we are convinced that there can be no morals and divine ideals in the world and in life, in the soul and in the spirit, unless there is a God, unless all existence is rooted in a source that transcends all existence.

5. One cannot avoid some semblance of idolatry unless one masters the concept that the cleaving to God called for in the verse "And you who cleave to the Lord your God" (Deut 4:4), refers to the attributes of the Holy One, praised be He. One cannot cleave to *shekhinah* Itself. We can cleave to His ways. As He is merciful and gracious, you be merciful and gracious; as He bestows kindness, so you bestow kindness.

BRINGING UP HOLY SPARKS

1. As there are holy sparks[24] in the food we eat, so are they in all human activities, and similarly so in everything we hear and read. At

times worldly pursuits from the most remote order of being become associated with the profound principles of the Torah; and everything serves a divine purpose, in the perspective of the holy.

3. The holy sparks imbedded in the food we eat rise together with the holy sparks that ascend from all movements, all speech, all actions and acquisitions. To the extent that there is good and uprightness in all expressions of life is there an ascent of the holy sparks in food and drink and in all things that yield keenly felt pleasures. What is naturally experienced in the soul in its relationship with all existence becomes the basis for perceiving the most profound wisdom concerning the nature of things, and serves as a free-flowing fountain and as a river that never ends its movement.

6. Eating in proper measure and in a holy disposition sanctifies the person and the world, and lends joy to life. Sadness induces overeating, and the act of eating takes on heaviness, and it expresses anger and despair. The holy sparks fall to a depth more dark than where they were before, and the soul is aggrieved. But a person can in the end turn everything to joy, and through the noble thoughts in the inwardness of his heart all forces that have any bearing on his life are elevated, and there is an enhancement of light. However, it is necessary to add to the dimension of the holy in the future, to eat in order to satisfy his hunger, and with ordered joy, without any timidity or sadness, thus raising the holy sparks directly, rather than in a roundabout way.

FREEDOM

The aspiration after freedom of thought has a good as well as a bad aspect, a dimension of the holy and a dimension of the profane. The good aspect is manifested when it is directed beyond the zone of the imagination and physical lusts. Then will thought proceed on its free course and bring happiness to the individual and to society. The bad aspect is manifested when the concept of free thought proceeds according to our natural impulses, in which temperament and imagination, lustful tendencies and all lower elements of our animal-like self are represented. Then free thought leads mankind to a frightful vulgarization, which is destructive of life's richness. It uproots the elements of beauty and eternity from the human soul in its individual as well as its social expression. "He who pleases God shall escape from it" (Eccl 7:27).[25]

FEAR OF GOD

1. The fear of God is the profoundest kind of wisdom. It is built on a world outlook that more than any other focuses on life in its most inward aspect. It offers the in-depth foundation for every branch of science and of Torah, whether in the realm of the sacred or the secular. Even the secular, when it seeks profundity in its basic position, must reach this conclusion, that without the fear of God science must necessarily hover over the external layer of concepts. In truth these do not constitute wisdom. The fear of God alone is wisdom.

5. The fear of God's punishment is to be differentiated from fear in the sense of awe before the grandeur of God and from the sensibility of love for Him, quantitatively as well as qualitatively. In the quantitative sense it is necessary to bring this concept to completion and to add the two missing elements [awe and love]. In the qualitative sense, however, it is necessary not only to bring it to completion but to enhance it and to perfect it and to develop new dimensions in the inner conception. The fear of God's punishment is like seeds planted in a garden, which are not eaten, but are planted in a small, narrow row where they will not reach their full fruition, but from where they will be plucked up and replanted in a large, spacious garden after they have grown to their first stage and are suitable to bear fruit. There they will reach their full fruition and become good food for people to enjoy.

18. In seeking comprehension in divine matters, it is good to be imbued with the fear of God on the level of awe before the divine majesty, to be inhibited from breaking into the realm of the eternal mysteries, not to depend in these matters on one's own understanding. But how much darkness comes into the world, and how many unfortunate ones are lost to Judaism and are grazing in alien fields from which there is no return, when this trait is carried to an excessive self-depreciation to a point of avoiding altogether the probing of the hidden teachings of the Torah, of avoiding all investigations in the subjects of religious faith, and an exaggerated fear of all scientific research. The spirit becomes soft like wax and is devoid of strength to

respond to challenge with knowledge and understanding, so that even those remote from our point of view might comprehend. All this was brought about by past abuses, and the present affliction has become necessary in order to mend them. In past generations there were times when we were alienated from God; "they denied the Lord, saying, 'Not He'" (Jer 5:12). The corrective reaction to this in our culture in the course of many generations was a simple and excessive fear of God. But in the end this itself will stimulate the corrective therapy.

TOLERANCE

When tolerance in the realm of ideas is inspired by a heart that is pure and free of every kind of evil, it is not likely to dim the feelings of holy enthusiasm that are part of the contents of a simple religious faith, the source of the happiness of all life. On the contrary, it will broaden and enhance the basis of the enthusiasm dedicated to God. Tolerance is equipped with a profound faith, reaching a point of recognizing that it is impossible for any soul to become altogether devoid of holy illumination, for the life of the living God is present in all life. Even in areas where we encounter destructive actions, where ideas take the form of negation, there must, nevertheless, remain hidden in the heart and in the depths of the soul a vital light of holiness. It is manifest in the noble qualities we encounter in many of the characteristics even among our barren elements, those afflicted with heresy and consumed with doubts. Out of this great and holy perception and faith is engendered tolerance, to encircle all with the thread of compassion. "I will gather together all of you, O Jacob" (Mic 2:12).

HUMILITY

4. Humility is associated with spiritual perfection. The more a person understands the world and life, their spiritual and material perfection, the many needs of humanity and of the individual person, the more he realizes his limitation of will to do good, and he becomes lowly in spirit, and is constantly elevated by his great desire to draw closer to the absolute good.

Letters

LETTER TO R. JUDAH LEIB SELTZER, 1913[26]

...We have abandoned the soul of the Torah. This is the great outcry that has been sounded mightily over many generations, from the days of the prophets, the teachers and the sages, the great spirits of the early and later generations.

Our most talented people concentrated for the most part on the practical aspects of the Torah, and even there only on specialized subjects. This they cultivated and made it the habituated subject of education. The emotional aspect, and more than this, the philosophical, and that which is beyond it and follows it automatically, the illumination of holiness, which bears within itself the mystery of the redemption—this they abandoned altogether. Anyone who challenges the shepherds of our people about this shameful neglect is regarded as mad and presumptuous. The earnest call of those who concern themselves with divine matters, the men of higher piety, the pure Kabbalists who attained to the mystical knowledge of God, the men of holy vision and mighty will, those who sought intimations of redemption—theirs was a voice calling in the wilderness. Thus far, after all our reproof, after heresy assaults us from the sides, with its despicable crudeness, apostasy ravages us like a pestilence, to seize from us thousands of souls each year, while in the camp that represents the cause of Torah and religious faith there is consternation and disorder, no clarity of purpose and no well-defined ideal. The dominant thought still is that we shall be able to heal our affliction with nostrums, nostrums that will not satisfy the soul, as long as we do not nourish it with that which is most essential to sustain its life.

Under no circumstances will a strategy prevail that runs counter to the voice of God, which calls to us from the souls of the highest saints, from ancient times to the present. We are summoned to a mighty penitence, a penitence stirred by love in all its dimensions. It is precisely when the crisis is great and the peril immense that we must choose the best of therapies. We must be radical. With compromise on the basis of a half, a third and a fourth we will accomplish nothing. Religious faith has declined, it continues to lose its vitality, because its ideological basis has been voided; no one studies it, no one seeks it. Orthodoxy in its present battle of negativism contents itself with illusions that are destroyed by life and reality, destroying those who entertain them together with them. We cannot find comfort in the fact that the element of our people that has yielded to heresy is even more vulnerable to destruction. The traditional statement that trouble shared by many people is half a consolation does not apply here; it is rather a double affliction. The invitation to look at the inadequacy of the thinkers among the nations will not lend us strength and life, when this is only an approach of negativism.

Why should we choose distant paths when the smooth road is open before us? There must be a rise of interest among us in the entire Torah with its spiritually, focused interpretations. Whoever is firm of heart, whoever wields a vigorous pen and whose soul is stirred by the spirit of God, is summoned to go forth into the battleground and cry out: Give us light. We would see a different picture, an altogether different picture in our generation if an appreciable part of our talented people, those who are knowledgeable in Torah and endowed with good sense, chose to toil in the vineyard of the Lord, in its inner dimension; to concern themselves with authenticating the concepts of religious faith and divine service, in clarifying the beliefs concerning divine matters, prophecy, the holy spirit, the redemption, the anticipation of deliverance, deliverance for our people and for the world, the perfection of the souls of individuals and of society, the evaluation of the spiritual state of past, future and present generations. A different courage would be engendered in the scattered flock of the Lord. A wondrous beauty would embrace the multitude of Torah scholars and higher illumination would emanate from them to our entire people and to the whole world. The recent tendencies in Jewish and world literature, which are steadily declining toward vulgarity, would experience a revival and liberation through us, through our profound thoughts, through our clear pronouncements that could become the life-giving principles for many nations, to bring them out of darkness toward the light. Evil and folly, the vanities of false beliefs, would be purged away, and we would be commencing the great heavenly work of clearing away the spirit of impurity from the land, and of launching the perfection of the world under the kingdom of the God of the universe.

This is what is expected of us, for this we were created. As long as we continue in our wandering, subject to slaughter like the deer because we fail to recognize our mission, small-minded people come to heal us with all sorts of ineffectual therapies, while the basic life-restoring medication is ignored. Some are moved by a lack of sensitivity and little faith, and others by pride and lack of knowledge, but again they think that the spread of Torah in its narrow and dry conception will serve as a general therapy for our afflictions. This has proven ineffectual in sustaining our position ever since various cultural forces and spiritual challenges have confronted us.

Your honor, my beloved, will not accuse me, and I hope that no one else will accuse me, of insufficient love for the practical aspect of the Torah, for the need of studying it diligently, with the fine points of textual and rational analysis, with acuteness and erudition. But matters have come to a point where the true meaning of the Torah, the higher level of the Torah, has been made void, where the deepest aspect of the soul has been crushed, where the capacity to think has been weakened, where our spiritual state and that of the world that is dependent on us has been brought to a state of fearful decline. If one should come and state that our help is to be found in the soul of the Torah, by enhancing the higher and true meaning of the Torah, the contrary-minded will come from all sides and bombard one with arguments: Are you advocating Kabbalah, moralistic writings, research, philosophy, homiletics, literature, poetry? All these are bankrupt, they have not delivered to us what they promised since the inception of their ferment. Such arguments are enough to choke the voice of God calling within us in the depths of our souls and penetrating to all worlds: Seek Me and live.

At a time such as this we must address ourselves to the most serious of our defects. I am not now concerned with detailed programs, how to arrange systems of study, systems of thought, a schedule of books, of schools, that by focusing primarily on the development of the simple meaning of the Torah will serve as a stronghold for the spirit of God, from which will come forth champions of God, as in the past. All the particular strategies will emerge, once the main principle is recognized, once the only question to deal with will be concerning the means and the strategies....

May it be the will of our heavenly Father to encourage those who labor with the public for the sake of heaven and to strengthen the spirit of all in whose hearts there bums a spark of divine light, that they may join in one fellowship to illumine His people with the light of God. The mission of *Erets Yisrael* as the land of vision will emerge only in such context from the many obscurities that surround it....

Poems

MY HEART RAGES

My heart rages
Like a boiling pot,
Like a stormy sea.
I aspire for the heights,
For lofty visions
Fed by divine lights,
By souls hidden in the realms above.
I will not be bound in chains,
But I will bear a yoke;
I am a servant of God
But not a slave of slaves.

I AM FILLED WITH LOVE FOR GOD

I am filled with love for God,
I know that what I seek, what I love,
Cannot be called by a name.
That which is greater than all,
Greater than the good,
Greater than reality,
Greater than existence?
I love, I say, I love God.
Light infinite abides
In the utterance of the name,
In the invocation of God,
And in all the names and designations
The human heart has conceived and spoken,
When the soul soars upward.
I cannot satisfy my soul
With the love sustained by the web of logic,
Through the quest for light

Revealed by the world, by existence,
As it parades itself before our eyes.
Divine lights are born in our souls,
Many gods according to our perception—
Before we know Him
In the fullness of His mystery
God reveals
Intimations of Himself.
He commands all our being
The life of the universe.
Wherever there is thought, feeling, will,
Wherever there is refined, spiritual life,
A light divine reigns,
It reigns and dies,
For it is a finite sovereignty—
As long as it is an inference
From the world, from existence,
The light eternal at times overpowers,
We seek a purer light, more inward,
More of the truth as it is in itself.
The light outruns the vessel,
Thought soars beyond existence,
The ordered world breaks down,
The vessels are broken,
The kings are dead,
The gods are dead.
The world stands naked, lovely, broken,
Stirred by a hidden longing
For higher light.
In His eternal mercy
God left in the broken vessels residues of His light.
In every life pulse,
In all existence,
There is a spark, a spark of a spark,
Faint and fainter than faint.
The inner light,
The light of God supreme,
Builds and establishes,

Assembles what is scattered,
Perfects worlds without end,
Orders and binds together; God's eternal realm is disclosed
Through the light unbounded within the soul,
From God to the world
A new light is born,
A light emanating from the splendor of God's face.

HOW GREAT IS MY INNER STRUGGLE

How great is my inner struggle,
My heart is filled with an upward longing,
I crave that the divine delight
Spread through my being,
Not because I seek its delights,
But because this is as it should be.
Because this is the true state of existence,
Because this is the true content of life.
And I am continually astir,
I cry in my inwardness with a loud voice,
Give me the light of God,
The delight of the living God,
The grandeur of visiting
The palace of the eternal king,
The God of my fathers,
To whose love I am committed
With my whole being
By whose awe I am uplifted.
And my soul continues to soar,
To rise above lowliness, smallness,
Above boundaries
With which nature, the body,
The environment, conformity,
Surround it, confine it in bonds.
A stream of duties comes,
Studies and inferences without end,
Complicated thoughts and deductive dialectics
Derived from letters and words—

It comes and surrounds my soul,
Which is pure, free, light as a cherub
That is immersed in a sea of light
But I have not yet come to the point
Of staying in my shelter from beginning to end,
To conceive the delight of tradition,
To feel the line of every inference, to perceive light in the
world's dark.
I am filled with anguish
And hope for deliverance and for light,
For higher exaltation,
For the dawn of knowledge and illumination,
And for the inpouring of the dew of life.
Even through these narrow channels
Whence I am nourished
And find delight in the pleasantness of the Lord,
I shall discern the purity of the ideal will,
The hidden grandeur, the strength supreme,
Which fills every letter and dot,
Every chain of dialectic.
And I shall play with your commandments
I have loved
And I shall expound Your precepts.

THE WHISPERS OF EXISTENCE[27]

All existence whispers to me a secret:
I have life to offer, take it, take it—
If you have a heart and in the heart red blood courses,
Which despair has not soiled.

But if your heart is dulled
And beauty holds no spell to you—existence whispers—
Leave me, leave,
I am forbidden to you.
If every gentle sound,
Every living beauty,
Stir you not to a holy song,

But to some alien thought,
Then leave me, leave, I am forbidden to you.

And a generation will yet arise
And sing to beauty and to life
And draw delight unending
From the dew of heaven.

And a people returned to life will hear
The wealth of life's secretes
From the vistas of the Carmel and the Sharon,
And from the delight of song and life's beauty
A holy light will abound.
And all existence will whisper,
My beloved, I am permitted to you.

The Writings of Hillel Zeitlin

The Fundaments of Hasidism

BEING AND NOTHINGNESS[28]

"The blessed Creator's life-energy is everywhere. Each thing that exists surely has some taste, smell, appearance, attractiveness, or some other qualities. But when we strip away the physical aspect of that thing and consider it only spiritually—considering, for example, the taste or smell without the physical object itself—we will understand that we are dealing with something that cannot be held in our hands or seen with the eyes of flesh. It is in fact grasped only by our life-force, our human soul. It therefore must indeed be something spiritual, the life-force of our blessed Creator, dwelling within that corporeal thing like the soul within the body."[29]

The meaning: Consider a fruit. Take delight and rejoice in it. What you have before you is a real physical object. But when you think about that fruit, raising it up in your memory, imagining it—that is a spiritual process. Concrete reality has been set aside; only the image remains. Of course that image too can be seen as a product of the senses. But now you analyze that image, keeping in mind its physical form, its species, appearance, size, quality, smell, and taste. When you consider any one of these specifics and go deeply into it, grasping at its very essence, there will be nothing concrete left before you, but only abstraction itself. This is something felt and fully grasped only by the soul, for this is the Nothing within each thing, the divine spark within it.

The Nothing is the spiritual essence of that which is conceived and the spiritual essence of the soul that conceives it.

"There are several rungs within Mind, namely consciousness, intellect, and speech, all of which receive from one another. Speech exists within time. So too does thought, for today you may have one thought and tomorrow another. But there is a quality that connects consciousness to mind, and that quality cannot be grasped.[30] It is the Nothing, the *hyle*, like the way an egg becomes a chicken. There is a moment when it is neither egg nor chick. No one can grab hold of that moment, for it is Nothing. So too when consciousness becomes intellect or when thought is formed into word, you can't grasp that which joins them."[31]

The Nothing is present in each person at that point where the rational intellect, that which is linked to the senses, ends, and higher mind, the divine within, begins. Thus it varies from person to person and from thought to thought.

"*Hokhmah* [Wisdom] is called Being, but the life-force within *hokhmah*, that which illumines it, is called Nothing (as scripture teaches, 'Wisdom derives from Nothing'—Job 28:12).[32] 'Nothing' is that which remains beyond the intellect and is not grasped. It sustains and enlightens the soul. All this is in accord with the person's intellect, whether greater or lesser. That which you grasp is considered 'being' to you, while that which remains beyond your intellect is called Infinity, that which gives life to the mind."[33]

Such is the measure of the Nothing in the soul of the one who grasps it and such is its measure within everything that is grasped. The Nothing is the innermost aspect of creation, the flowing Spring, that which exists beyond the border of what can be grasped by the senses or by ordinary mind. Intellect has a limit. The inward glance—or, more properly, the brilliant flash, the innermost exultation of the spirit, mysterious and hidden—is infinite.

The Nothing is the moment of wonder in creation, a moment that you cannot call by any name. Hence you call it Nothing. This wondrous moment, precisely because it is so wondrous, cannot be defined, regulated, or placed within bounds of space or time. Thus it constantly unifies opposites. Separations and oppositions have their place within Being, while the Nothing is always the One of equanimity.

"*Hokhmah* links things, making peace even between opposites like the elements. Were *hokhmah* not between them, fire and water could not dwell together. Yet we know that they exist in composite form. That is only because *hokhmah* links them, each of them perceiving the Nothing within it...."[34]

"Each thing in the world, when you take it to its root, can be transformed from what it previously was. Take, for example, the kernel of wheat. When you want to change it, bringing forth from it many more kernels, you need to take it to its root, which lies in the generative power in the soil. Therefore, it can grow in the ground, but nowhere else. But there too it will not grow unless rain falls and causes its original form to be disfigured [rotted] and lost. It is reduced to Nothing, to the *hyle*, which is the category of *hokhmah*. Thus scripture says: 'You made them all in wisdom' (Ps 104:24)."[35]

"Everything that exists passes from one nature into another. The linking of these natures is called Wonder. In the language of the Kabbalists it was known as *keter,* the power that links opposites and joins them in a wondrous unity."[36]

"Hylic matter is neither potential nor actual, but lies between the two. It is the starting point of all existent beings. Everything, from *keter 'elyon* downward, exists only because of it. Hyle does not pass away or go in and out of existence, since it is the beginning of existence itself."[37]

Because the Nothing is the essence of Creation and its innermost soul, it—the Nothing—is in fact the real Being, true existence, essential reality. That which we call Being—revealed existence, the sensory, visible to the eyes of flesh and grasped by the rational mind—is in fact naught but the blindness of the senses, illusory existence. It is a cosmic error that we must recognize and negate in order to be free of it.

All that we call existence, with all its charming and entrapping attractions: the blue heavens over our heads, the earth beneath our feet, endless stars, light and radiance, joy and pleasure, beautiful textures, plays of color, sorrow and tears, the roar of the sea and the whisper of springs, all that we pursue and seek out until flesh and spirit are wearied, all that we delight in attaining and all that we moan for when we lack—all of it is naught but illusion.

The more you reach the Nothing that lies within all being, the divine inwardness, the closer you are to truth, to the Godly, to the essence of creation. You reveal the mask and see before you the King in His glory, the endless light.

"There was a certain king who created an optical illusion consisting of walls, towers, and gates. He commanded that those who came in to him would have to pass through these gates and towers. Then he had the royal treasures scattered about at each gate. Some only came up to the first gate, gathered up some coins, and went back. Others—and so on. Along came the king's only son; he struggled hard to get to his father the king. Then he saw that there was no real separation between him and his father, that it was all illusion. The blessed Holy One hides behind various garments and partitions. Yet it is known that God fills all the world, that every movement and thought come from His blessed self. So all the angels and all the palaces are formed of God's own self, like the locust who spins his cocoon out of himself. In fact there is no partition that separates man from God."[38]

"God emanated the worlds and created Being out of Nothingness. The main purpose was so that the *tsaddik* could make Nothingness out of Being."[39]

"If you want to prepare to have God dwell upon you, the main thing is to understand deeply that you contain nothing but life-giving divinity. Without this you are truly nothing. That is the proper preparation for the indwelling of divinity. This 'dwelling' is as in 'Like an eagle rouses his nest, hovering over his chicks'—touching and not touching. If you grasp this (constantly and with all its power) you will be negated from 'reality.'"[40]

"Everything you see with your eyes, heaven and earth and all within them, are the outer garments of the King, the blessed Holy One. Through them you will come to take constant note of their inner selves, the life-force within them."[41]

Tsimtsum

The world was created *ex nihilo*, being out of nothingness. But just how did the Nothing become being? There is no place for this question when we understand the "Nothing" as the essence of being, when we see it as *keter 'elyon* [supreme crown, the highest of the divine emanations], the force of "Wonder" within all of Creation.

But there is still room for *this* question: Since all that exists is only illusion, being at its core the divine Nothing, how does Being come to be a separate entity? Why do we see the world as we ordinarily do, rather than always perceiving the divine power that courses through it?

In other words, the world is nothing but an optical illusion. But how did that illusion come about? The king's son breaks down all the partitions and comes to the king. But how did the partitions get there in the first place?

The Kabbalists' answer to this is *tsimtsum*. What do they mean by it?

In the school of Rabbi Isaac Luria we learned: "When it arose in the Emanator's will to create the worlds, there was no empty place in which they might stand. The Emanator's light flowed without limit. So He withdrew His own light, like that insect who spins his cocoon out of his own self.[42] He lifts the lights out of that space at the center and removes them to the sides. In this way a void is created in which the worlds can stand."

But this is still not enough. God is—all; "there is no place devoid of Him." Then it is still hard to understand how the lights were removed to the sides. How did that place become empty?

Furthermore, even if we accept that there came to be an "empty space," by what power did it exist? In the end it too relied on the power of God (since "there is no place devoid of Him!"). But in that case, everything is back where we started, and the question still stands: How did existence come to be imagined? How is it that we can think the world to be separate from God? How did that cosmic error come to be?

Hasidism thus explains *tsimtsum* in a different way. *Tsimtsum* is only from our point of view, that of the receivers, the created. *Tsimtsum* exists only in thought. The supreme Emanator sought to bring about diverse and separate entities, displaying His light before all creatures. Everything was thus created in a limited way, in accord with each recipient's power. Just like a father, when explaining some deep concept to his young child, reduces his own profound mind to the limits of that of the child, so does Mind—which is One[43]—descend from its high rung to a lower one.

Another explanation, by way of "king and servants":

"The Zohar says that when the King is in His castle, He is called the great King. But when He goes down among his servants, he is the little King. This was what they meant: The letters of Thought [the unspoken language of the mind] are large, since they transcend the letters of Speech. The King on His own has no need to speak. But for the sake of those who receive from Him, He has to reduce Himself from Thought to Sound and from Sound to Speech. Even though all is a simple unity and all is the King Himself, the vessels [i.e., the recipients of His light] are divided. 'When He is in His castle'—in Thought—[He is the great King.] 'But when He goes down'—into speech, so that His servants can grasp Him—He is called the little King."[44]

The act of cosmic illusion takes place in this way: the young child, as the great thought of the father flows into him, grasps the thought in his own small-minded way. When creatures see the world and its fullness, they grasp only its external nature, the outer garb of things, imagining that is all there is.

But all of these are only examples to offer the ear what it is capable of hearing, making analogy between the spiritual quality of humans and that of the cosmos. Thus we try to understand divine *tsimtsum* based on the reduction of the mind and its going down from expanded to ordinary consciousness, from thought to verbalization to speech. But we still do not know how the One became many. How did such varied and differentiated things come to be, each having its own existence and unique nature?

Tsimtsum is nothing other than the imaging forth of being, the act by which it became possible for being itself to appear as a distinct entity, separate from God. But that still does not give us the key to understand multiplicity, distinction, and the unique "personality" of each thing. We see not only a world, but also endless particular entities, each one (from the archangel Michael down to the smallest urchin in the sea) appearing as its very own world, a living reality all enclosed in its own microcosm. The question remains: How did the "All" split apart into all these tiny pieces?

The Hasidic answer to this is "the breaking of the vessels." This doctrine, taken from Kabbalah, has a distinct meaning in Hasidism. The best of the Kabbalists explained the breaking this way: the vessels were not able to withstand the intensity of the light that flowed ceaselessly into them, and they were broken. This is like a person unable to withstand a sudden burst of joy that overwhelms him. But the *hasidim* explain the breaking of the vessels in a more inward and deeper way. The essence of their idea will best be understood by comparison with more recent modes of thought.

What is the innermost, most natural and instinctive desire of each thing that is? The desire to exist. But what is the nature of that desire for existence? "Each thing tries as much as it can to continue forever in its own existence...since by that force of being it will continue to exist, so long as it is not destroyed by some external force,"[45] says Spinoza. The desire for existence is thus an inherent power, the force of eternity. Because the thing exists, because it is filled with the feeling of its own reality, it fears being lost.

Schopenhauer added that the desire to live is the absolute inner essence of all existence, realized in each in an individualized way. This cosmic desire, which creates the illusion of being as a whole, also creates the illusion of particular existence. The one who exists also thinks he can attain some understanding—and comes up with crumbs. The desire for life is no longer an inherent force, one that makes for eternity, but rather an active force, a power that spreads forth, flows, bears fruit, and fructifies.

Nietzsche came along and taught that the innermost nature of each thing is not the desire to live, but to rule. What is this "will to power"? It should not be understood in a popular and vulgar sense. Nietzsche's will to power is really the desire to reveal the "I," to manifest one's full inner powers, to have them rule and master the powers of others.

"The tree by my window—and this is its very nature—reveals its 'I,'" says Oscar Wilde.[46]

The desire to rule, that is the desire for self-manifestation, the feeling of being, is the heritage of everything that exists. This is the secret of personhood, of individuality.

Here we come to the true meaning of *malkhut* ["kingship" of God; the tenth *sefirah*], according to the *hasidim*. *Malkhut* is the manifestation of that which is, the spreading forth [of the self], the feeling of power, utterance, imperative, spiritual rule.

Now we come to the Hasidic understanding of the "breaking of the vessels." These vessels are what the modern philosophers and poets see as the beauty of creation, the individual identity of each creature. To the *hasidim* this is cosmic sin, the fall, the descent, the brokenness. *Malkhut* belongs only to the One who truly exists, the Creator. But since the creatures also rose up to seek rule, it was smashed into the tiniest fragments, each of them saying, "I will rule!"

"The brokenness comes about because each one says: 'I will rule.' The term *malkhut* (kingship) applies to each thing insofar as it is a thing in itself, with no need for anyone or anything else. But in truth this term properly applies only to God, because all others are needy, requiring nourishment from their divine Source. Each quality [or 'being'] has within it, from the moment it flows forth from that source, the inherent claim of 'I will rule,' which it had as part of its original Source. There in the Root the claim was appropriate; all of them were raised up there within that Root. In this way they came to have that natural sense about themselves even when it was no longer accurate, after they had been cut off from the Root and had their own force of life."[47]

Letters

Divinity has *hidden* itself in the world. But since the power of the Maker resides within the made, hints and signs are to be found within existing things and the revealed world that point to a more inward, elevated, holy, and pure reality.... The God who hides in the bastion of His strength sends His word to every person, calling them aloud, arousing their ears, speaking to their hearts, warning, reproving, teaching. God from afar whispers to the person: "Seek Me, for I am close, within your own mouth and heart...."[48]

Everything contains a pointer toward the most high God; it is there in every movement, feeling, desire, echo, in all that you feel, see, and hear. When you walk outside and hear people talking, go deeply into the meaning of their words. Join them together in a different accounting, purify them of their mundane afflictions, remove their coarse outer garments, raise them up to their essential cosmic spirituality—and you will see God within them....

In the moment when you suddenly feel the flow of the most delicate, most spiritual, of thoughts, thoughts so pure that your heart cannot grasp them; when your inner eye so sharpens its glance as to embrace all generations, all that has ever taken place—it is your God calling to you. You then feel with your whole being that there is an inner dimension to reality. All those things that you usually see as fleeting and low in value exist for a purpose—they have come to teach you about the most hidden level of being....

But the main revelation of God, according to Hasidism, is in Torah. The entire Torah, from beginning to end, is nothing other than God, garbed in earthly matters, human stories, human laws and statutes. Torah is divine not only in a general sense, but every single letter within it is a special revelation of the Deity. The combinations of letters found in Torah are those same combinations by which heaven and earth were made.

When you immerse yourself in Torah, you not only fulfill the commandment of studying Torah, but you are enrobed in the divine Self. God surrounds you from all sides, is taken up and grasped by you, since "Torah and God are one."

The twenty-two letters of Torah are twenty-two ways in which divinity flows forth, twenty-two cosmic forces. In the links among those flows and forces you find the combination that lies behind everything in creation. Everything in the world, big and small, has some sort of voice, expression, revelation, and the twenty-two letters represent all of these in combination. The complex interlinking of these letters fills cosmic space. The wisdom of all these linkages is found in Torah, since "Torah emerges from sublime Wisdom."

"When it arose in the blessed One's desire to create the world, in order to do good to His creatures, He reduced Himself. Into what was He concentrated? Into the letters of Torah, through which He created the world."[49]

"Torah is the imprint of the world, and the world is the imprint of Torah. One who is aware of his Maker can find the letters of Torah in everything in the world. It all depends upon the strength of your awareness and your grasp of the multi-colored garb of Torah. The upbuilding of *shekhinah* depends on this."[50]

"A person's mind is his soul, and it is a part of the *shekhinah*, as it were. The 'Torah of light' is the blessed Holy One. Therefore a person who links his own mind and good consciousness to matters of Torah is bringing about the union of the blessed Holy God and His *shekhinah*!"[51]...

The main difference between any ordinary religious viewpoint and that of Hasidism with regard to the divine origin of Torah lies in this: others may view Torah as coming from heaven, derived from God. Hasidism sees Torah as "heaven" itself; Torah is not only divine in origin. In its most innermost sense it is God, divinity itself.

Just as, according to Hasidism, "God is world and world is God," referring to their deeply hidden roots, so too is Torah world, and world is Torah. Not only are "Israel and Torah one," but world and Torah are one as well.

Just as the entire world, in the Hasidic view, is naught but the outer garment of God, so too is Torah nothing other than God's outer garb. In both of them—world and Torah—you have to discover God, seeking out the secret hidden within them. To see this way is to gaze with the inner eye, with a love so pure and a joy so divine that it is tasted only by a few in each generation.

"The secret is a matter that no one can truly explain to another. Just as the taste of a food cannot be communicated to one who has never tasted it, the same is true with regard to the Creator's love. It is impossible to describe to anyone this quality of love within the heart. That is why it is called 'secret.' But those things that most people consider 'secret'—like the wisdom of Kabbalah—how are they secret? The books are open for anyone who wants to study!"[52]...

Raising Up Sparks

The vessels, not able to bear the intensity of the light, were broken. Some of them broke into pieces, others into tiny fragments. Some fell, others sank down, some sank into the deepest maw of subterranean chaos. They were all scattered in every direction, with no one to gather them up. These castaways, wherever they are, sigh in longing for the sublime beauty of their original home. Holy sparks are bound up in matter, in nature, in coarseness, in body and—worse than all these—in evil, impurity, ugliness, pettiness.

They call out to God with all their strength: Please save us from captivity, from heaviness, from sin, and from our scattered state! The vessels sinned when each proclaimed, "I will rule!" As those divine lights came to dwell below, their own inner godly essence, as it were, hid its face from them for a moment, so that every world and each creature came to see itself as a separate being, set off and able to stand on its own without the entire divine Self, that which dwells within all worlds and that which hides in a secret realm all its own.

Then, when everything scattered and fell apart, the sparks were beset by a powerful longing. They understood their sin and how it had alienated them from the light of God's face. They moan all their days, looking toward their salvation, seeking to be redeemed.

Wherein lies their redemption? In the human soul. It is within our power to recognize God in each thing, the holiness and sublime beauty that lies everywhere. We can perceive the absolute oneness that lies within all this separation and scatteredness and understand the error of being. We can see through the cosmic optical illusion to perceive the God-of-world, breaking through all the partitions that separate us. When you know and see this, living within the Deity, you are able to uplift everything you see, hear, or encounter, restoring it to its root in the divine will. Everything you use or enjoy, the food you eat and the clothes you wear, every person or object with which you come into contact—all of them strip off their profane, weekday garments and are dressed in holy raiment. They come forth from the deepest depths and rise to the greatest heights. They shed all vulgarity and defilement, are purified to become their most noble selves....

The opposite is also true: when you forget the source from which you come, get all wrapped up within yourself and consider yourself a separate being, you become a world destroyer instead of a redeemer. Not only do you fail to uplift those holy sparks that have already fallen into the depths; you actively bring down new bits of light from the shining heavens into realms of filth and ugliness, the "deepest shells." The human being, a creature of mind, consciousness, and choice, can both uplift all with which he comes in contact, joining it to oneness, or bring it down, defile it, separate it ever further from its root, sinking it into the depths....

Uplifting the *Middot*[53]

Hasidism, like Kabbalah, its mother, sees duality in everything: good and evil, purity and defilement, truth and falsehood, beauty and ugliness, the *sefirot* of holiness and those of the impure realm. Hasidic sources, like the Kabbalah from which they stem, frequently quote the verse: "God made this opposite that" (Eccl 7:14). Both try to show that everything found in the holy world exists also in that of the impure, and vice versa.

All this frequent talk of duality within Hasidism is, however, superficial rather than essential to it. I mean to say that all this came to Hasidism by inheritance from earlier Kabbalah and does not reflect its essential spirit. Hasidism believes in this duality in the same way it believes in all that it received in written transmission; it does not take it upon itself to contradict anything that had been set forth by the earlier Kabbalists. But this principle of duality does not proceed from the essence of Hasidism, from its hidden soul. Had Hasidism built its house on virgin ground, rather than on the foundations of Kabbalah, it surely would not have spoken at all of holiness and defilement or any other duality in oppositional terms. It would rather have portrayed them as a single unity, one that descends from the highest rungs down to the very lowest. From there it rises back up to its source, ever richer and ever clearer.

With regard to evil in general, the disciples of the BeSHT have reported in his name: Evil is just the lowest level of the good.[54] When it is redeemed, it is transformed into pure goodness. This means that good and evil are not opposites; they are a single reality. In its lowliest manifestations we call that reality evil; in its highest, we call it good. Thus when evil is transformed it becomes pure goodness.

Since the *hasidim* do not distinguish between natural and moral senses of good and evil, and since "the good is that which is close to God" and "evil is that which is far from God," it rationally must follow from the BeSHT's teaching that the whole issue of holiness versus the "other side," so much discussed by Hasidic and Kabbalistic sources, is really just an allegory.

This allegory, so widely accepted for thousands of years, teaches something very deep, not easily grasped by most human minds. Because a superficial reading of it points toward an absolute duality within existence, many people have gradually transformed that into a depiction of reality. They have come to think that this reflects the true nature of things.

That is why you find many passages even in the Hasidic writings that speak of the holy and the "other side" as two creations standing in absolute opposition to one another, both created by the single God, made to fight and struggle constantly with one another until the holy wins its final victory.

In seeking to present the essential teachings of Hasidism in consistent fashion, we have only the statement by the BeSHT and that which necessarily proceeds from it. On this basis we say that Hasidism recognizes no duality in creation, just as it knows none in the Creator. Hasidism sees only a single unified divine force, giving life in an absolutely equal way to all that is, both good and evil. Divinity, descending from "the Hidden of all Hiddens," is a force that proceeds from rung to rung, becoming ever coarser and more sensate. Only as it reaches the very end is it so hidden that it can barely be detected. When we contemplate those lower rungs, where no divine clarity can be perceived, we call them evil. The person who is attached only to them (their outer, not their inner qualities) we call an evildoer or a sinner. But when that very person abandons those lowly rungs and reaches higher, or when he begins to see divinity within those lowly rungs themselves, he is engaged in redeeming and uplifting evil. To say it differently: he is raising up God's own Self, hidden within the coarseness of material existence, restoring it to its Source.

When you raise up all corporeal and lowly things, you are uplifting sparks. When in this way you raise up your lowly and material thoughts, you are uplifting distracting thoughts. When you apply the same uplifting to your own *middot* [your emotions and your patterns of behavior], feelings, and desires, you are "breaking" all those *middot* and raising them all to God.

There is thus no essential difference between good and bad human traits. Every *quality* a person has, when it is stuck in coarseness and small-mindedness, may be called evil. When it is purified and elevated, we call it good....

The same is true of any matter or want, anything a person contemplates or desires greatly. It applies whether you are cruel or compassionate, angry or gracious, cursing or speaking softly. You may hate or love, feel pride or be lowly in your own eyes, you may isolate yourself or live among people, be a lonely ascetic or a family person, swear off the world or enjoy everything you see. All of it can be good, and all of it can be evil. When your spirit is pure, elevated, living within God, and everything is in harmony with the divine life—it is all good. If your spirit turns downward, sinking, forgetting the God who bore you, caring only for your own desire and private pleasure—it is all bad.

Therefore, the *hasidim* understand the moral good not as decreed from without, not as commandment or statute, but rather as a stream of inspiration flowing from the Source of the person's divine soul. In that stream we purify and refine all of our emotions, until they become heavenly. The emotional teachings of Hasidism are an alchemy of the soul. Just as the alchemists labored to transform base metals into gold, so do the *hasidim* labor to transform every human quality within their souls into a godly one....

The *hasidim* reveal to us all the methods by which this holy work is done. They know various and sundry ways to raise up each *middah*, not just a single one. All depends on the traits of the particular quality and its nature, varying also with the person's character, the conditions in which he finds himself, the social setting, and the time and place in which he lives.

The *hasidim* understand that a person's character today is not necessarily what it was yesterday. Your mood when stirred by all sorts of activities is not the same as that which you feel when you are all alone, living true to yourself, sunken into your most undisturbed inner places, without desires or distractions that cloud your consciousness. There you perform your own inner judgments, take account of your own self.

The *hasidim* know how the essential character of people varies, sometimes even in strange ways. They are also aware of the various odd circumstances that affect people, how different people's feelings are when they do either good or bad. Following the lines of these feelings, there is good that is evil and evil that is good.... They know the power of desire, all the charms of sin, the natural and compelling power of things considered evil. They understand all the difficulty and bitterness, even the near impossibility, of the "battle against one's inclination...."

They also know this: the more you struggle against your desires, the stronger those desires grow. When you struggle for victory over your urges, those urges bring forth their strongest weapons, sending poison into the heart of the God-fearing person in order to defeat him. This is like two people fighting in fierce anger. The more one is winning, the harder the other struggles to knock him out....

"A person should always be cunning in the fear of God" (b. Berakhot 17a). This statement of the Talmud is parent to endless prescriptions found in Hasidic literature. The main point is not the *power* to make war, but the proper *strategy*. You have to know how to conquer the enemy within his own *stronghold*, how to steal his own sword and defeat him with it. The *hasid* battles with the evil urge not only by using the good urge, but by means of the evil urge's own powers.

You can only do battle with the evil urge by *looking* and *contemplation*....

Aramaic Chapters from *Sifran Shel Yehidim*

Editor's introduction: Zeitlin wrote these poignant and revealing essays in the Aramaic of the *Zohar*. Together with the *Admonitions*, which follow, they represent his address to the imaginary Yavneh community of mystics.

A SINGLE UNITY, THAT OF THE ANCIENT ONE

I now reveal to you, members of this holy assembly, a unification of God's name.[55] It is as old as that wine preserved with its grapes from the six days of Creation, yet as fresh as this morning's dawn. It is as bright as the sun shining through your window, like water drawn this very day, like the flight of birds just going by above my head. Yet you could also say that it is the most primal of all antiquities, the first thought of all, the primal will, the beginning point of all. So too is it the final act, the end of days, conclusion and fulfillment of all. It is the most hidden of all hidden things, secret of secrets, depth of depths, sealed up with a thousand seals. It is locked away in a cave as obscure as the very depths, a huge boulder set at its mouth, surrounded by a great snake. And yet it is the simplest of all simple things, the most revealed of revelations, known to all who study Torah, pronounced each day in blessings and readings, in prayers and supplications.

This unification, even though it is both ancient and known to all, has never been so clearly and distinctly revealed as it is now, in these days when messiah's footsteps can be heard.

Receive it from me, O holy assembly! When any one of you is aroused to study, to pray, to give alms, to recite a blessing, when putting on your fringed garment or your *tefillin*, or fulfilling any other commandment, intend with all the desire of your heart: "For the sake of uniting the blessed Holy One *and Israel*."

For those who are used to reciting the formula "For the sake of uniting the blessed Holy One and His *shekhinah*...," the most mysterious unification passed down to us by those holy angels, the teachers of yore, you must now add to it this formula I have mentioned. This refers to the union and attachment of the blessed Holy One and Israel of the World of *'Asiyah*, meaning Israel below, each and every Jew, those who work and strive and toil, suffering the yoke of exile. They utter sighs that could break any heart, yet their lives are so weighed down by heavy burdens that they lack the clarity of mind to set forth their prayers as they should. She [*shekhinah*] carries their inner cry upward, blasting through the air, breaking through all the heavens, smashing all the iron fences.

Come and see. Love for every single Jew is the beginning of everything. Anyone who does not have this love—all his good deeds remain within his own narrow space, bearing no fruit either above or below. Those good deeds have no vitality, no power to spread forth or bring about birth. But the one who does have love for every Jew in his heart—the good deeds he does do bear that holy life-force, the dedication and strength, the fiery flame from below that parallels the fire from above. (Of this it is said that "even though fire comes down from the heavens, it is better to have it brought from a human source."[56]) All of such a person's good deeds become a spring out of which the Tree of Life is fed, seeds that will sprout forth in the grasses of Eden. Holy trees! Beautiful flowers! Birds whose wings will protect everyone in the world! Mighty high-flying eagles, carrying all of Israel on their wings as they journey from the darkness of Egypt to *shekhinah*'s shining light!

Come and see! All the great ones among our nation attained the high rung they did only out of their abundant love for every Jew, even those who had sinned greatly against the blessed Holy One, including those who rebelled against Him. The Faithful Shepherd [Moses] handed himself over to death, saying "You, if You would, bear their sin! But if not, wipe me out of Your book that You have written." Who were those for whom he was willing to risk death? Those who had sinned greatly, as he says: "Please! This people has committed a grave sin" (Ex 32:31–32)! Of King Messiah it also is written: "He bears the sins of many, defending the transgressors" (Isa 53:12).

All those who have prepared the way for King Messiah, such as the holy ARI [Rabbi Isaac Luria], the holy Rabbi Moshe Hayyim Luzzatto, the holy Ba'al Shem Tov, the holy brothers Reb Elimelekh and Reb Zusia, the holy Rabbi Levi Yitshak, the holy Rabbi Nahman of Bratslav, and all who have labored in the field in every generation—all of these have attained what they did only because they preserved the flame of love for every Jew. Not only for every Jew, but for every human being![57] Indeed for all that God created! This is not because all those faces are the same—surely their love for those who dwell in the holy King's own palace and for all of Israel, children of the King, differs from their love for those who stand outside that holy palace until messiah comes. Of that day Scripture says: "Until Shiloh comes and the people assemble to Him" (Gen 49:10). This verse is translated to read: "Until the messiah's kingdom comes and all peoples will obey him." So too does it say: "Then I will change all nations to have clear speech, so that they all may call upon the name of God" (Zeph 3:9).

Yet their love was so strong that it poured forth like a mighty river flowing in every direction. They gave to all people and every nation to drink of their love, even the most distant of nations and creatures of God.

Come and see. "One who separates one of these ten *sefirot* from another is like one who brings about separation within You."[58] Whoever separates any one of the Children of Israel from the others is also like one who causes separation within the ten *sefirot*. There are "six hundred thousand letters in the Torah" and "six hundred thousand souls in Israel."[59] Anyone who says: "This one among the Children of Israel is pleasing to me, but that one is not" is like the "whisperer who separates familiar friends (Prov 16:28)."[60]

If the Children of Israel have sinned, let us bring them close to *shekhinah*. Let us pray and supplicate for them until they repent. Let us awaken the merit of the holy patriarchs, of the faithful shepherd, of all the generations. Let us seek compassion *for* them and *from* them, arousing the love hidden within their hearts. Let us blow on the holy spark within their souls until it bursts forth into a mighty flame. But let us not say to any Israelite, even to a sinner, "You have no place in the God of Israel." Surely we should not say to the many who have strayed from the path: "You have no place in the God of Israel."

[We are taught that] "All Israel have a place in the World to Come."[61] If so, they surely have a place in the God of Israel. Even those of whom that text says: "These have no place in the World to Come" can be purified and uplifted. Thus taught the great and holy priest Rabbi Tsadok[62] about those who "seek out the imprints," revealing the deeply hidden things and knowing that in the concealed heart of every Jew, even those who turn from the ways of faith and do every evil deed in the world, there remains a hidden point that is never separated from God. Because of that hidden point, such a person can return at the end of life, whether in this incarnation or another, to the Source of life. When King Messiah comes, he will reveal all those points of goodness within each Jew, uncovering that which is most hidden within their hearts. Then all the evil within them, even in those called "the sinners within Israel," (even though they will be punished, for how could judgment not be rendered?) will be shown to belong only to their outer selves, but not to that which lies within, and surely not to their innermost holy of holies.

For that reason, one who seeks to pray or do any good deed must join together with all the souls of Israel that have ever existed in the world, those that are present now, and those that are yet to be, linking all those souls to the one God. This is the secret meaning of "[The angel] Michael is the high priest who offers up the souls of Israel on the altar above."[63]

This is the revealed and secret meaning of *shema' yisra'el*.

"Listen"—behold.

"Israel"—all the souls of Israel in every generation, all those that were present in the first man—whether in mind, heart, heel, or any other limb.

"Y-H-W-H our God"—I and all the souls of Israel! I join myself to them with all the desire of my heart and the power of my love. Together we all take upon ourselves the yoke of heaven's kingdom. We cleave in complete union, with no hint of separation or blemish, to

"Y-H-W-H is One!"

THE MYSTERY OF THOUGHT

Thought is a person's inward palace; the innermost of thoughts is that person's holy of holies. That innermost point cleaves to the Endless with a love that never ceases. This is a "link that joins one to the blessed Holy One." But even if the person does not have the strength to rise to such a rung, but has only longings, passionate and painful desire—as in "Their heart cried out to God" (Lam 2:18)—that longing itself becomes God's dwelling, and this person too dwells within God. They are "One within one"—the Endless within the person; the person within the Endless.

If you, O child of the palace, do not yet have the strength to stand firmly on the rung of the "link that joins one" to God, be then on the rung of "his heart is troubled within him." Let your eyes fill with tears—like the "lower waters" that cried out, "We too want to be before the King!"[64]

At this time of messiah's approaching footsteps, especially in these final years when the imprint of those steps is revealed in the sands of "nations' desert" (Ezek 20:35),[65] overwhelming darkness surrounds us. Darkness perceives that its final hour has arrived; it rushes to send forth all its hosts and forces, both above and below. Seeing the kingdom of light drawing nearer, darkness trembles in terror and sets out to do battle with the light. It sends forth its shadow to swallow up all of light's forces, to consume all the world's goodness, to wreck, ruin, and demolish all that the "light sown for the righteous" (Ps 97:11) has planted.

Sometimes darkness sees that it cannot defeat a person, one who stands up like a firm pillar and does not allow evil desires or passions of the flesh to rule. Then the darkness appears in the form of a good angel, stealing its way into your heart and distancing you from God by way of sadness, a state of melancholy or small-mindedness that derives from the evil side.

Child of the palace, do not let that thief enter your heart! Keep your heart always both "broken" and "joyous." It was taught in Rabbi Simeon ben Yohai's name: "Have weeping firmly rooted in one side of your heart, while joy is in the other" (*Zohar* 3:75a). Sadness and brokenheartedness are not the same. The holy lion Rabbi Shneur Zalman taught that "sadness is having a heart as dull as stone with no life-energy within it, while a certain acidity and a broken heart, on the contrary, show there is enough life in that heart to turn it sour!"

When your heart is broken so that it has the energy to weep and plead before God, the "palace opened only by tears" will be revealed to you. Once the wellsprings of your heart are opened, a melody of attachment to God will burst forth on its own. Then a "palace opened only by melody" will become accessible to you. As your holy melody spreads through the upper worlds, a "palace attained only by joy" will open before you. As that palace opens, all forces of judgment and negativity will pass away, all accusing [or "guilt-producing"] forces will be hidden in the rocks, and the "shells" will be hidden in the cavity of the great deep. Then holy angels will come down among humans to hear words of Torah spoken by the faithful shepherd and all the other sages of that generation. They will rejoice and exult, dancing as at a festival of bride and groom. Forces of love will be revealed throughout the world, great blessings from above. Abundant love, desire, and grace will pour forth from before our Father in Heaven upon the holy people and upon all who live.

Remember, O child of the palace, what the pious of old have taught: "All the gates are sealed except those of tears" (b. Berakhot 32b). "Tears *open* the gates—but joy *smashes* all the gates." You, child of the palace, must not forget even for a moment that "God is your shadow" (Ps 121:5)—the blessed Holy One is your shadow, being and acting toward you as you are toward Him. If you desire God, God will desire you. The whole world knows this, but people do not grasp it in an *inner* way. Even if they know it deeply, they do not *live* in accord with that knowing. Knowledge and life remain separate from one another. Even when their knowledge is enlightening, that light shines around them but not through them. For you, child of the palace, your awareness that "God is your shadow" must be your life, both within and without. It must be your inner light, your inner and even your innermost desire, your soul and the soul within your soul.

When this simple awareness becomes your inner light, an aura from above will descend and surround you. Your life of holiness and good deeds will allow you to absorb that light until it shines from within you. Then another light will descend, surrounding you again, and it too will be absorbed and united with your soul. And so onward, to the highest of rungs!

The most important rule: Let the blessed Holy One in every single moment be your *life*, the very *air* that gives you life. Let every breath you take be in God. There is no quick way to achieve this, but only that of lengthy service and ceaseless prayer, an inward prayer of the very simplest words, yet penetrating down into the very depths.

Pray like this:

> My beloved Father, desire of my soul! You have sent me into this world. What have You sent me for? Surely to bear Your message! Teach me, beloved Father, what I am supposed to do this day and every day to fulfill Your will. What should I be saying to people—all of them my brothers and Your children? What should I be doing—right now and at all times—to make my life pure and holy, as You desire?
>
> My Father, my Heart! Grant me all those sublime lights and all that contains them. May I have the brilliance of soul, bodily health, clarity of mind, and clear awareness—all the abilities and powers needed to do that with which You have entrusted me.
>
> And you, holy souls of each generation! You who have fulfilled God's will throughout your lives, in holiness and purity, accompany me on my path! Help me in my actions! Pray with me and be with me in all the good I seek to do.
>
> Light of lights! Soul of all souls! Send me all those holy souls who are close to my own soul-root! Let them hold fast to me, and I to them. Raise us all up and carry us on the wings of endless love.

This is the sort of inward prayer that a child of the palace should offer every day. It may be prayed with these words and phrases or others; the main thing is that it be *constant*. It is the prayer of the poor and brokenhearted, yet at the same time the burning desire of a child to see his Father's smiling face.

ADMONITIONS FOR EVERY TRUE MEMBER OF *YAVNEH*[66]

(Fifteen Principles)

1. Support yourself only from your own work! Try as hard as you can to support yourself from simple physical labor and not from trade. Trade is based primarily on the deception of customers, and this means lies. And lies completely oppose what the blessed Holy One, who is

Absolute Truth, demands of us ("God, our Sovereign, is truth." And, "the signet of the God is truth.").

If you are, brother, a worker, try to become an expert in your craft. Don't look forward, as so many do today, to leaving this work so that you can support yourself more easily through business. If you are not yet a worker, make the effort to become one. If you have not yet been given the opportunity to join a labor union for religious or moral reasons, try to establish, together with a few of the members of *Yavneh*, cooperative workshops, and the like.

If you cannot work as a physical worker because of old age or infirmity, try at least to choose for yourself a type of livelihood that succeeds with a minimum of commerce in it, and help your friends who work with their hands in every way you can.

2. Keep away from luxuries! Luxuries throttle the mind and the strength of a person. Luxuries bring on acts of constant deceit, leading from there to thievery and robbery. Striving for the true Jewish life, and at the same time for a life of luxuries, is like dipping in a purifying pool while holding a defiling abomination in your hand.

   Therefore, choose a life of modesty, simplicity, keeping yourself far away from all external luxuries. Refrain as much as you can from various habits that cost you money, that do not benefit your body, and harm your soul. My friend, turn your steps away from the theater and from parties. Guard yourself from smoking, from liquor, from expensive clothes, from adorning yourself with rings, and the like. Seek not to adorn your dwelling with costly decorations. It would be better if you would purify and adorn your soul, my dear friend.

3. Do not exploit anyone! If you support yourself solely by the work of your hands, the length of your days will be surrounded by modesty, calm, and humility, by abstention from indulgence, luxury, and pleasure seeking. It will simplify your task if you fulfill the great and holy commandment to every pure mortal: do not exploit anyone! Do not "use" people, seeking your own benefit without their agree-

ment, or even with their agreement, if a full exchange of value is not received. Every person is a complete world. From the standpoint of morality and pure religion, every business abuse, in any form whatsoever, is robbery and murder.

A factory boss or supervisor who takes advantage of workers by paying them the lowest wage acceptable on the market, and not the full and proper sum for value received, is exploiting those workers. The merchant who takes unfair advantage in buying or selling exploits the people that merchant is dealing with.

Abuses are to be found today also among politicians, journalists, doctors, and the rest of the people involved in the free professions. Every pressing of advantage that is not the result of the complete, considered, free, and serious agreement of the person involved is a sin. Protect yourself from all this as you protect yourself from fire, my dear brother!

4. Purify your family life. The family has always been a stronghold for the Jew. In the face of work, persecution, and daily troubles, the Jew found rest and comfort in quiet, pleasant, and pure family life. The family has always been the Jew's sanctuary. Even Balaam saw this, and against his will declared: "How good are your dwelling places, O Jacob" (Num 24:5).

   Today, to our disaster, the anarchy of the street has broken into the Jewish family. This bulwark, the pure and pleasant Jewish family of Poland, has started to disintegrate since the time of the German conquest [World War I]. Now, this fall is deepening more and more. Further, this decline is abetted by the general moral ruin of the street, the theater, the movies, the pulp journals, and obscene literature. And a good bit of the so-called better and more serious literature abets this. Knowingly and unknowingly, many of those who declare themselves artists contribute to this decline.

   Protect your soul from this catastrophe, my dear

brother! Strengthen yourself to protect the quiet, the peace, and the love in your family!

5. Sanctify your sex life altogether! The preservation and sanctification of the covenant, these are the exalted bases of both interior and exterior holiness. Concerning this, we are charged: "Be holy" and "One who sanctifies oneself a little here below, will be greatly sanctified from above." "The sexual organ is the fundament of the body, sign of the holy covenant." One who is pure in this matter is holy; one who is impure in this area is defiled. In this one must be guarded not only from actual sin but also from sinful thoughts. And the proven ways to this are—always to be occupied with work (at best, physical work), and also with the learning of *Torah*, with concentration and depth. "There is no room for sin except in a heart that is void of wisdom," says the RaMBaM. "*Torah* is good when joined to work; the exertion of both cause sin to be forgotten" (m. Avot 2:2). Actual work—on no account idleness. Idleness brings on all misfortune.
6. Guard yourself from forbidden foods! "You will be defiled by them" (Lev 11:43). Read this as, "You will be *blocked* by them." Forbidden foods defile the body and soul; forbidden foods create vile and impure blood in the human body. If some of today's Jewish youth have a tendency to go toward evil, this is mainly an outcome of not protecting themselves against forbidden foods. Be careful, my brother, of forbidden foods, and thus you will save yourself from impurity, evil, and quick temper.
7. Sanctify your *Shabbos*! The Sabbath is not just an ordinary commandment, but the basic foundation. One who weakens the Sabbath, Heaven forbid, desecrates the God of Israel. A person who doesn't sanctify the Sabbath is like one who worships idols. "Keep" and "remember," the single God uttered at once. Unite with the holiness of the Sabbath, and in this way, commune with the blessed Holy One. The Sabbath, however, must be kept not only on the outside, but also within. This means prayer, learning, a basic stocktaking of the soul, concentration of the mind

on holy and pure matters. *Shabbat* upholds the entire Jewish people. The Community of Israel and *Shabbat* are truly a pair, and in them resides the Holy Ancient of Days.

8. Keep your home holy! Not only the synagogue, the house of learning, the prayer room, but also every Jewish house is a small-scale sanctuary. When can this be said? When the house abounds with words of *Torah*, prayers, blessings, *Kiddush,* and *Havdalah*, and when these are expressed seriously, truthfully, with profound and intent sincerity! When a mother and a father, a brother and a sister, live in calm and true peace (for in a peaceful place, there is the blessing of the Father of Peace); when the children are educated in the spirit of the serious and pure *Torah*; when all the children of the house speak the Jewish tongue and are full of love, honor, and recognition for every Jewish thing.

   But what is today the structure of a house of an average Jewish merchant? Mostly, it is a place of selling and buying, sometimes a feverish stock market, sometimes a club for a game of cards, and sometimes a hall for parties. The father goes out in search of "pleasures," and the mother seeks her own. In the house—a constant ill will, continual arguments behind the backs of others, or worse, to their face. The daughters no longer speak Yiddish; the sons are being prepared for empty careers. Even where *Shabbat* is kept in an exterior way, it is without joyous celebration, without soul, without life. They pray, and when they have the opportunity, they fulfill commandments and customs, but everything is mechanical. In a place where there is no light and no fire, no love or devotion—there is no resting place for the almighty God.

   Yavnehite! Don't allow your house to become secular and commercial. Let your house be suitable for a Jew—a small sanctuary of the Lord! See that the Jewish language is heard in your house, allow the voice of *Torah*, words of peace, heartfelt prayers, taking part in the immense and tragic mystery of Israel, and silent hopes for redemption.

9. Live always amid the whole Jewish people and for the

whole Jewish people. Don't be concerned about yourself, but about all of Israel. The pain of all should be your pain; Israel's joy, your joy. Every single Jewish soul is a part of the *shekhinah,* called *kenesset yisra'el* because She is the totality of Jewish souls. The Community of Israel is the lower *shekhinah*, the kingdom of heaven on earth. The suffering of a Jewish soul is distress to the *shekhinah*, as it were. So how can you, Yavnehite, cause pain to any Jew? Whoever works honestly and wholeheartedly for the redemption of Israel—as he understands it—is working to redeem *shekhinah*. Blessings to anyone who does something good for the Jewish people—even if his views are far from our own! Blessings to any hand that is stretched out to bring help to Jewry!

Yavnehite! In all your thoughts, all your longings, all your words and deeds, do not have yourself and only those close to you in mind, but rather the entire great holy Jewish people. Bring yourself and your loved ones into that whole. The salvation of the whole will be yours as well.

10. Remove yourself from party politics. Though you are bound to live as a part of the general society, and work especially for the community, do not join any particular party, be it ever so close to your heart. As long as the party is occupied with politics, it is bound for the furtherance of those politics to transgress the limits of justice and communion of all of *Yisrael*. If you are a member of a party, and you find it difficult to leave it, especially if the main purpose of the party is the building up of the nation—set your heart to scrutinize every act and deed of the party. Your humanity, your Judaism, your hidden treasure, is a thousandfold more important than even the best and loftiest party.

Whether you are a member of a party or not, you can and ought to participate in the work of any party, to the extent that it directs deeds to the building of the whole nation, and to the unification of the nation, and you are bound to remove yourself from it, when it divides Jews, or when, to achieve its purpose, it uses means that are contrary to the Jewish spirit, which is that of love, justice, and holiness.

11. Remember and never forget the three loves! The Yavnehite is bound to seek religious perfection, meaning avoidance of sin and the fulfillment of commandments in actual deeds. But we are especially bound to awareness of the three loves—the love of God, the love of *Yisrael*, and the love of *Torah*.
12. Subdue pride! Pride is the most profound and strongest idol. Pride is the "strange god" within one's own body. Pride has deeply rooted itself in us, and in order to uproot it, concerted effort over decades is necessary. We must combat it all the days of our life. As long as it rests in us, it hides God, it hides others, and it hides the world outside ourselves. We cannot reach the light of truth as long as pride rests in us. "Pay attention to this cursed one—and bury it!"
13. Sanctify speech! Speech is the expression of the soul. Guard the covenant of the tongue; the holiness of the tongue. Not one word of evil speech! Not one round of gossip! No idle words at all; and it goes without saying, not to defile your tongue with filth. Do not think that there is no damage from speech. What difference does it make? A vulgar joke? Whom does it hurt? No, dear brother! A word has the power to build and destroy worlds. It is your duty, Yavnehite, to be a builder, a creator, repairing lives that have been destroyed. Therefore, let your words be holy.
14. Sanctify your inner life! Let not a day in life pass without taking stock of your soul. Learn or hear *mussar* [moral teachings] every day. Books like *The Duties of the Hearts, The Path of the Upright, The Way of the Righteous, Tanya, Select Counsels,*[67] should always be your companions.

    Even if you are busy and cannot afford more time, separate yourself for five to ten minutes every day, in your chosen corner, for a short and precise tally of your soul. And at this same time, let there be a short silent prayer in your heart:

"Sovereign of the world, set me on the right path, on the path of light."

NOTE: Any reader who has firmly decided to start living in accord with the fourteen principles outlined above, even if gradually, in steps, may turn in this regard either orally or in writing to Hillel Zeitlin, Szliska 60, Warsaw.

15.[68] Broaden and deepen the activity of "Benei Yavneh." Wherever you encounter a person who is prepared to accept the views offered in this book and to seek to live by them, hold fast to him. Teach him, enlighten him, guide him. When you find a few people in your city ready to live in accord with everything said in this book, cleave to them. Enlighten and guide them; proceed together up the pathway that leads toward God. If the way is too far for you and you find it hard to fulfill everything said here, do not turn back. Fulfill first what is *possible* for you. Afterward try to go further. The God of heaven and earth will be there to help you.

Let one small gathering extend its hand to a second, the second to a third, until there is firmly established a whole assemblage of Jews returning to God in truth and wholeness, "doing His word in order to hear the voice of His word" (Ps 103:20).

Prayers (*Tefillot*)

MIDNIGHT

In the depths of night. All silent. All asleep. My heart remains awake.

I am awake. You are awake. Let us dwell together!

I pour my meditation out to You, You pour out Yours to me. We listen to each other's voice. Come, let's cling together for all time!

This time, I don't cry out to You. I don't ask anything of You. I am with You. You, with me.

Shall I sing my song to You? Shall I trumpet all that roars aloud
inside me?
My song and call You haven't wanted. My tears and sighing You
haven't sought.
Why should You need my tears? Why should You need my sigh?
All of me is Yours already.
Why should You need my petitions? Why should You need my
pleas? All of me is Yours already.
Why should You need my longings? Why should You need my
desires? All of me is Yours already.
Why would You need words? Why would You need utterances?
Come to me here. Enter me without a word being said.

"MY DISTRESS I SHALL TELL IN YOUR PRESENCE..."

When the news arrived of the riots in Jaffa and the deaths of pioneer builders, including [writer] Yosef Hayim Brenner.

My Creator, my Creator!
It is very bad for me. I am very much in pain. The burden of my
suffering is very great.
I cannot bear it. I have no one to turn to. None to help. None to
give support.
Yet You stay silent. You give help to our foes. You wipe out Your
children.
How long? Until when?
We run to our house. We run to our mother. We run to our Holy
Land.
We've said: Our mother will console us. We've said: she will
wipe off the tears from our face.
We have come to our house. We have come to our mother. And
there, too, we find our foes. We go from slaughter to slaugh-
ter. And where is our rescue? Where is our salvation?
From the land of slaughter, from Ukraine, our children ran to
You, ran to Your Holy Land.

By the sweat of their brows, they sought to water it, but You have watered with their blood the thirst for murder in our cruel foes.

Shall I pour out before You my torments and my troubles? Where shall I find words to express all this?
But what need have You of my words? What can I express to You that You don't know already, without a thing being said?
You know everything. But as for us, we know nothing. We don't know why for many centuries You have allowed Your children to fall victim to the knives of legions in the lands of exile. And for those who fled back to You, only to fall, they too, beneath the knives of Arabs in our Holy Land.
And even *he*? He who sought You out through sufferings so frightful and could not reach
You, given that he saw only the afflictions of his brethren, but Your compassion he never saw; he who walked about with such great truth before You, even though, from the weight of his despair and pain, he sometimes forgot Your Name, and even fought mightily, sometimes misguidedly, with those who spoke Your Name; he whose heart never did know joy, being ever filled with the sorrow and trouble of Your children—this man, Yosef Hayim, who so much loved, who so abounded in the power of love, why have You cast away his life? Why have You handed him over to forest beasts of men to tear him apart? Why have You let merciless wild asses quench his lamp? Why was that skull shattered, which had been so filled with light?

No! No, I cannot any longer bear all this. Your words provide no bandage for my wounds.
"Your words of consolation"—but how can Your words of holiness console me?
They shall surely say: "There is no birth without blood." Why must the blood of innocents be shed and shed again? While the polluted blood, the blood of murderers, will reign throughout the generations?

God great! God holy! Let a new thing be heard from Your mouth!
Let a new light gild the mountaintops of Zion!
Let it suddenly be revealed! Let it unexpectedly be seen! "Let the redeemer quickly come into the palace—the master we have waited for" (Mal 3:1).
May a great lightning bolt flash suddenly in the world! May a great rain of blessing come to Your servants, to them who yearn and thirst.
In one hour, in one moment—suddenly—
Let Your Name be made great and holy in the world!

Yitgaddal ve-yitkaddash shemeyh rabba…

ATTACHMENT TO GOD

From the song of Simon the Theologian found in Martin Buber's book Ecstatic Confessions*—with changes and abridgments and removal of passages based on Christian dogma.*

Come, now, to me, You whom my soul has desired, and desires still.
Come, now, solitary One, the solitary God, for I am alone, as surely Your eyes can see.
Come, now, to me, You who've made me alone, despised and abandoned in Your world.
Come, now, to me, sole desire of my life, You who have strengthened my yearning for You, the like of which has never been seen.
Come, now, to me, my breath, my very life, come, now, O solace of my soul. Come, now, to me, sole beauty or joy that I've ever known in my life.
I thank You for this, that without transformation, without any change or reversal, You have remained one with my soul, and that in being the God Most High over all, You are to me all, and in all.
Your spirit, a bread hidden and concealed, but never consumed—how much it will cling, truly does cling, to the lips of my soul, and cross all the banks of my heart.

I thank You, my God, that You are to me a day without night, a sun without dusk.

You have no place to hide, for Your glorious Presence fills all worlds.

You have no place to hide, for what sort of place could contain You?

But what ten thousands of ten thousands worlds can't contain, the human heart can hold.

Let, now, my heart be a place open to You. Let, now, my heart be Your palace of holiness.

Come, now, into Your royal palace. Come, now, into my heart. Dwell within me, and I within You.

Please do not separate from me, even for a moment, all of the days of my life. And when the day of my death shall arrive, let me remain within You, O life of all life, You who rule over all.

Please don't forsake me for even a moment, lest while we're apart my enemies find me and fall on my spirit to swallow it up.

Be, now, my refuge, a source of all strength, Your tabernacle placed within me forever. May I be fulfilled with the happiness of it, even when I am in torment, and saturated with Your life, even as I die.

Place, now, in me Your abode, and I'll be enabled to defeat any king. For You are my bread and my drink. When I'm wrapped up in You, I experience hours of rapture no human tongue can express.

My tongue has no word. What happens in me, my soul may behold, but it's something it cannot pronounce.

It comprehends fully the things that it sees and even may try to express it. But the words for it fail, they remain inaccessible. One truly beholds what cannot be seen, something that hasn't an image. It has no complexity, it is most elemental: the greatness of boundless divine.

The soul beholds fully what has no beginning, what has no end, and what has no realm in between. And whatever it sees, it knows not how to express.

You are the fire by which all lamps are kindled from one end of the world to the other. And the fire is never exhausted.

You are the single, primordial lamp. Your light cannot be divided.

All the world's separate lamps draw their strength from Your
light, and by Your light they are guided.
Behold You are here, O great, primal light. You are eagerly seized
by my naked heart, and I cannot provide it a name.
I have chosen for myself to keep silent. But the wonder of You,
awesome in splendor, gives emphatic command to my
mouth and my pen, telling me: Speak! And write!
Here He is, in my abode. Here He is, within me. Here He is, in
His palace. Here He is, in my heart. The One who inhabits
all worlds!
I am resting upon my bed. Because God is in me, behold, even
me, I'm transported beyond all worlds.
To the One to whom all belongs, the One who endures forever, I
dare to declare: "I love
You, O God," and I can do so, because God loves me.
I am sated to the full with expectation. I am wrapped and covered in its shawl. And when I am one with my God, I soar
up above the skies.
I know so well, and for sure, that the matter is true in this way,
but it is beyond my comprehension: where goes my inner
world at such times?
I know that I surely have seen what no mortal being can see.
I know that the One who is hidden, exalted above every creature, has taken me into itself, into the shelter of its hand,
and behold, I'm beyond all worlds.
I, an ephemeral being, see within me my eternal Creator, the
life that never goes astray.
At such a time, the thing comes alive, in my heart and also in
heaven: the light is One, both here and beyond.

From *Songs to the Boundless One*

Translations from the Yiddish

THE MOTHER

Based on strophes in Rabbi Moshe Alshekh's Midnight Song. *A free poetic rendering—rhythm, sound, and certain images wholly my own.*

Where has your companion gone away?
Has he vanished in the sky?
Exile's captive, on foreign ground,
He languishes, in shackles bound.

His princely crown has fallen down,
His purple garment now is torn,
Stolen from his palace site,
His army struck by serpent's bite.

A cry arises over woodland trees,
The angels sighing bitterly,
The sheep are straying in the field,
Oh, where is their protector's shield?

What does God's Presence say?
Oh, my head, O, my crown!
And there is One who says:
I'm going down, I'm going down!

I'm going where my children go,
Into exile, to the dark below,
I'm going where the sinners go,
To mitigate their exile's woe.

Now clothe yourself in sackcloth black,
Run through the streets and marketplace.
Father, father, what's this you do?
Mother, mother, where are you?

I am with you, I am with you,
What you are suffering I suffer, too.
For your misdeeds is Mother banished
For your misdeeds, Her voice has vanished.

DEEPEST WISH

Based on the first and last part of [Moses] Ibn Ezra's Bakkashah *(Prayer), with modifications of form and content.*

For You my flesh, for You my blood,
for You my love, for You passion's flood,
for You my staying, for You my going,
for You my being, for You my life outflowing,
for You my seeing, for You my hearing.
for You my turning, for You my appearing,
for You my today, for You my tomorrow,
for You my joy, for You my sorrow,
for You my thanks, for You my song,
for You my sound, for You my clang,
for You my cry, for You my shout,
for You my speech, for You my being mute.
From You my shape, from You my form,
from You my longing, from You my storm,
from You my breath, from You my embrace,
from You my build, from You my face.
I am the altar, I am the bull,
I am the sacrifice for my sins to the full.
You are mine while I live, You are mine when I die,
to You my suffering calls, to You my needs cry.
As from a woman in childbirth does my pain to You pour,
like an unhappy pauper, I knock on Your door.
May You be my stronghold, be my embankment,
Bring near to You my prayer, behold my lament.
I without You—all mine are the woes,
I without You—a straw the wind blows.
Press through a wall to the place where I stand,
stretch out to me Your loving right hand,
give light to where I walk on the way,
give renewal of spirit to my night and day.
Drown my misdeeds in the sea of my tears,
raise my prayers up, above heavens' tiers.
When You read of my sins, please render them null,

When my repentance arrives, please accept it in full.
And when my last hour in the end presses in,
let me not flog myself long because of my sin.
And when I shall from this world's gates depart,
may Your angels greet me with an open heart.
May they escort me into Your palaces sublime,
and set my soul free from exile's grime.
When my spirit shall enter into Eden's blissful space,
let there flow upon me *shekhinah*'s light and grace.
And may my shelter be inside Your hidden light,
my spirit drenched in awe as I behold Your Face's sight.

Afterword

The Contemporary Renaissance of Jewish Mysticism

Gershom Scholem, the pioneer of modern scholarship on Kabbalah, famously claimed that early Hasidism was the "latest phase" of Jewish mysticism. He took the scholars of the nineteenth-century Jewish *Wissenschaft* to task for their analytical dissection of Judaism and their embarrassed rejection of Kabbalah, but he too denied the existence of any true religious forms of Jewish mysticism in his day.[1] The events of the late twentieth and early twenty-first centuries demonstrate the error of this assessment. Jewish mysticism has neither vanished nor become irrelevant. In the past fifty years, Kabbalah has undergone a profound revival and transformation, finding new expressions as a vital part of Jewish life in both Israel and America. This volume concludes with the writings of two extraordinary mystics who died in the first half of the twentieth century, but the story of Jewish mysticism does not end with them. Let us close by exploring some of the important developments that have taken place since the end of the Second World War. We cannot hope to predict the directions in which Jewish mysticism will grow in the coming decades, but surveying its renaissance in the second half of the last century and the opening years of this one will surely disprove the illusion that Kabbalah has reached the end of its road.

A clear example of the sustained continuity of the mystical tradition is found in Sephardic and Middle Eastern Jewish communities, where it has remained an important source of inspiration for both intellectual elites and the general public. Kabbalah first bloomed on the soil of the Iberian Peninsula, and in addition to the well-known

Kabbalists of sixteenth-century Safed, the great Jewish centers of the Turkish Empire, Northern Africa, Yemen, and Iraq have produced many important mystical figures in the past few centuries.[2] These include Rabbi Hayyim ibn Attar (1696–1743), a Moroccan sage who moved throughout the Mediterranean before settling in Israel in the early 1740s. His commentary on the Torah (*Or ha-Hayyim*, 1742) was extremely popular and enjoyed considerable status in Hasidic circles.[3] Rabbi Shalom Sharabi (RaSHaSH, 1720–77) was born in Yemen, and, after moving to Jerusalem, he served as the leader of the important kabbalistic *yeshivah* Beit El.[4] His prayer book with mystical *kavvanot* ("intentions") in the style of Lurianic Kabbalah is used to this day. Rabbi Yosef Hayyim of Baghdad (1835–1909), known by the title of his book *Ben Ish Hai*, was a more recent Kabbalist of great importance. The works of this legal scholar and communal leader, some of which are clearly intended for a general readership, are filled with kabbalistic material.[5] Rabbi Yitshak Kaduri (d. 2006), who was born in Baghdad and moved to Israel in the 1920s, embodies the more popular legacy of Sephardic Kabbalah. His devotional piety and prowess for practical Kabbalah, such as healing with amulets, working miracles, and bestowing blessings, were legendary. Rabbi Kaduri became associated with the Shas political party in the 1990s, further incorporating his particular flavor of popular mysticism into the cultural mainstream.[6] The influence of such North African and Middle Eastern mystics in modern Israel is still quite strong.

Small, insulated circles of Kabbalists such as Beit El have continued to study and pray together in Jerusalem without attracting much attention.[7] But Rabbi Yehudah Ashlag (1885–1954), an important Jerusalemite scholar, broke with the general attitude of seclusion and became involved in public efforts to spread the teachings of Kabbalah. Trained in Europe, Rabbi Ashlag immigrated to the land of Israel in the 1920s and became a member of Jerusalem's traditional mystical community. He was the author of a translation and commentary to the *Zohar* known as *Ha-Sulam* ("the ladder") as well as a systematic recasting of Lurianic Kabbalah. Two important elements distinguish his path from that of his more reclusive kabbalistic associates. First, Rabbi Ashlag believed that he lived at the dawn of the messianic age and that the time had therefore arrived for Jewish mysticism to be taught to the masses. Second, he did not see Kabbalah primarily as a body of recondite knowledge to be memorized (theosophy for its own sake), but rather as an intensive guide for mystical self-improvement and empowerment. Rabbi Ashlag was a Kabbalist with one foot firmly planted in each world, fusing an authentic tradition with elements of modernity and an interest in using mysticism to transform both individuals and society.[8]

Two of Rabbi Ashlag's intellectual descendants have continued his quest of making Kabbalah accessible to the broader public, and in particular to seekers interested in New Age spirituality. Rabbi Michael Leitman was a student of Rabbi Ashlag's eldest son. He is the founder of Benei Barukh, an Israeli organization for the popularization and spread of Kabbalah that now has followers around the world, largely through Internet teaching. The enormous popularity of New Age spirituality has even allowed Kabbalah to spill over into the general American culture. The explicit goal of The Kabbalah Center, a for-profit institution founded by the late Philip Berg, is to bring the teachings of Jewish mysticism to non-Jews as well as Jews, including a number of high-profile celebrities. The Kabbalah Center treats Kabbalah as universal wisdom decontextualized from the Jewish religious tradition.[9] Rabbi Ashlag's approach was controversial in his day, and the even more radical openness espoused by his students has inspired severe condemnations from leaders of traditional kabbalistic circles.[10] Modern Jewish observers have also raised questions about cult-like aspects of these groups.

Jewish mysticism in Eastern Europe was consumed by the fires of the Holocaust. The Nazis and their helpers slaughtered tens of thousands of Hasidim together with their *rebbes*, and the Jewish communities of the Hasidic heartland were completely destroyed. Many unwritten traditions of personal devotional praxis and manuscripts were surely lost in this great conflagration, not to mention the great number of spiritual masters who were murdered. However, some Hasidic leaders either escaped or survived the war, and they succeeded in rebuilding their lost world in Israel and America. Their Hasidic communities, such as Ger, Belz, Vizhnitz, and Satmar, have fiercely guarded their traditional ways of observance, language, and dress. Indeed, they have continued the pre-War trend toward insularity and rejection of modernity, now exacerbated by their collective trauma during the Holocaust. This social and religious conservatism is particularly true of Hasidic groups in the state of Israel, where draft exceptions and monetary aid granted to *yeshivah* students enable an entire subculture that refuses to integrate into general society on both ideological and worldly grounds. Despite their success in replenishing the numbers of the faithful, the actual study of mystical texts in most contemporary Hasidic communities plays a very small role. As was already true in the days of Hillel Zeitlin, Hasidism is more focused on communal loyalty, external style, and devotion to a certain *rebbe* than the cultivation of a rich mystical life.

Two contemporary Hasidic groups are notable exceptions to these norms, and both have readily incorporated elements of modernity in their quest to recruit in new members. The Habad dynasty was founded by Rabbi Shne'ur Zalman of Lyady (1745–1812), a prodigious scholar and disciple of the Maggid of Mezritch. He and his followers developed a mystical path of great profundity. Also known as Lubavitch Hasidism, Habad was an important force in White Russia, but never became a numerically or politically significant voice in the greater Hasidic world of Poland and Galicia. Since their arrival in the United States in the 1940s, however, they have become increasingly interested in reaching out to nonobservant or unaffiliated Jews. Continuing a program developed under the leadership of their last *rebbe*, Rabbi Menahem Mendel Schneerson (1902–94),[11] Habad now sends "emissary" families all over the world in order to spread the teachings of Hasidism and promote religious observance.[12] Women accompany their husbands on these missions, and the education opportunities and status of women in Lubavitch is considerably higher than in other Hasidic groups. Marriages are very much considered a partnership, and both the rabbi and his wife have important, if traditionally defined, roles in establishing their new community.[13]

Bratslav Hasidism has also undergone a transformation in recent years. Rabbi Nahman of Bratslav founded a demanding spiritual path with a relatively small following. Some communities of Bratslav Hasidim still continue in this elitist vein, but, in the past few decades, a number of "neo-Bratslav" schools have emerged. These new groups, most of which are found in Israel, are often composed of *ba'alei teshuvah* ("newly-observant individuals") and led by charismatics who were themselves not raised in a Bratslav community. The neo-Bratslav groups are inspired by Rabbi Nahman's teachings and see themselves as authentic representations of his religious message, but they reject many of the strictures and traditions of Hasidic life. This is made possible by the fact that Bratslav Hasidism has been without centralized leadership ever since Rabbi Nahman's death in 1810, and the community lacks any clearly defined hierarchy or norms of behavior. Like Lubavitch Hasidim, the neo-Bratslav groups have started to reach out to secular Jews and unaffiliated spiritual seekers in the hopes of bringing them into the religious community.[14]

The study of mystical texts forms a crucial part of the religious identity and spiritual lives of Bratslav and Habad Hasidim, far more so than in any other contemporary Hasidic community. First and foremost, devotional study of the texts written by their founding *rebbes* offers Hasidim an opportunity to connect to their spiritual masters even long after their deaths. The central work of Habad thought is Rabbi Shne'ur Zalman's *Sefer shel Beinonim-Tanya* (1796), and in Bratslav it is Rabbi Nahman's *Likkutei Moharan* (1811/12). These books are seen as authentic representations of their *rebbes*' teachings, allowing present-day Hasidim to meet their deceased teachers through the timeless portal of the written word.[15]

The study of Hasidic texts is also intended to facilitate personal spiritual growth. Habad Hasidism, in particular, emphasizes that it is not enough for the community to rely vicariously on its *rebbe*'s mystical achievements and that the obligation for intense contemplative prayer and inner transformation is incumbent on each and every Hasid. Bratslav too demands that Hasidim devote much time to regular meditation and personal nonliturgical prayer (*hitbodedut*), a skill learned from books as well as absorbed from living spiritual mentors. Habad and Bratslav also regard the study of Hasidic writings as an essential part of their outreach efforts. They make them widely available at little or no cost in both Hebrew and translation, and, in order to do so, they make extensive use of modern technology, including the Internet and other mass media. Finally, their emphasis on the study of Hasidic theology has an important messianic undertone: both groups believe that redemption will come when their teachings have been spread throughout the world.[16]

With the exception of the Hasidic community, most Orthodox Judaism in the United States has marginalized or ignored Jewish mysticism. The descendants of the Lithuanian tradition have intensified in their opposition to mysticism, and most of their seminaries now focus almost exclusively on the study of Talmud; only a small amount of time is given to the ethical teachings of *musar*. Exceptions to this rule include Rabbi Yitshak Hutner (1906–81), a graduate of a Lithuanian *musar yeshivah* and founder of an important school in Brooklyn. His unusually broad education consisted of rabbinic thought, modern philosophy, and Jewish mysticism (for a time he was a student of Rav Kook), which he wove together in his own lectures.[17] A similar blend of sources is found in the works of Rabbi Eliyahu Dessler (1892–1953), a prominent leader of Lithuanian communities in England and Israel. Their teachings have become popular and influential, but are not typical of Lithuanian ultra-orthodoxy.

Modern Orthodoxy in America has been dominated by the personality of Rabbi Joseph B. Soloveitchik (1903–93). While by no means a hardline *mithnagged* (opponent of the teachings of Hasidism), in many ways, this extraordinary scholar and creative thinker was true to his Lithuanian roots.[18] Soloveitchik trained several generations of American Orthodox rabbis in a religious philosophy that unambiguously prides the study of Jewish law above all else, leaving little room for Kabbalah and Hasidic thought.[19] This lacuna in American Jewish theology is made more pronounced by the fact that Rav Kook's writings are scarcely known in the United States outside of academic circles. This has changed of late, as more of his teachings are being translated into English, but Rav Kook's thought has had relatively little direct impact on most American Jews.

The revival of Jewish mysticism in the United States has taken place in liberal circles. Rabbi Shlomo Carlebach (1925–94) and Rabbi Zalman Schachter-Shalomi (b. 1924) contributed significantly to this renaissance. These two charismatic European-born leaders started out together as some of the very first Habad emissaries sent out to work with college students in the 1950s, but after being exposed to the new cultural currents of the 1960s, they found the restrictions of traditional Hasidism (even in a community as open as Lubavitch) too great. At this point their paths diverged from each other. Zalman Schachter-Shalomi founded the Jewish Renewal movement, a nondenominational group that incorporates the teachings of Hasidism and Kabbalah as well as the lessons of New Age spirituality. He is a prolific author, and his numerous popular books are widely read in America.[20] Rabbi Schachter-Shalomi has also been a vocal proponent of interfaith dialogue, and he believes in bringing wisdom and rituals from other religious traditions (particularly mystical ones) into contemporary Jewish practice.[21]

Rabbi Shlomo Carlebach, who remained closer to some (but not all) aspects of Orthodox practice, is undoubtedly best remembered for his popular devotional music and enthusiastic prayer services. But he was also a skilled teacher and gifted storyteller with a particular flair for Hasidic tales.[22] He reinterpreted traditional mystical sources so that they would speak to the contemporary generation and, in particular, to the "flower children" of the 1960s and 1970s.[23] He also popularized the written works of once well-known Hasidic masters who had fallen into obscurity after the War, including Rabbi Mordecai Joseph Leiner (the "*Mei ha-Shiloah*," 1800–54) and Rabbi Kalonymous Kalman Shapiro (the "*Esh Kodesh*," 1889–1943). The fact that Rabbi Carlebach was not affiliated with any major Jewish institution allowed him to transcend denominational lines and reach people all the way from the Orthodox to the unaffiliated.[24] Throughout his career Rabbi Carlebach composed and released a great many songs but wrote no formal theology. Numerous recordings of his teachings are now being transcribed, and only recently have written collections begun to be published.[25]

Two other American Jewish theologians deserve special mention for their importance in the revival of interest in the mystical tradition. Rabbi Abraham Joshua Heschel (1907–72), the direct descendent of Hasidic *rebbes* and a professor at the Jewish Theological Seminary, felt that the symbolical language of Hasidism and Kabbalah could speak to both Jewish and non-Jewish seekers.[26] Heschel's writings, including *The Sabbath* and *God in Search of Man*, are considered modern spiritual classics and remain popular and influential in both Jewish and Christian circles. Heschel emphasized the spiritual importance of social and ethical justice, tirelessly campaigning for civil rights and against the war in Vietnam. The embrace of *tikkun 'olam* by liberal Judaism is in no small part the result of his efforts.[27] But the revival of mysticism that he envisioned only truly began toward the end of his life. Rabbi Arthur Green (b. 1941) was a close student of Heschel and has continued his teacher's project despite some theological differences. Throughout his career Green has served as both a professor of

Jewish studies and a leader of several rabbinical schools, and his writings integrate modern theology and academic scholarship.[28] Indeed, he describes his theology as "neo-Hasidic," maintaining that Jewish mysticism has much to offer those who live outside of the cloistered boundaries of Hasidic society. However, Green insists that mystical texts must be reinterpreted in light of modern values. He downplays the Jewish mystics' radical claims to metaphysical truth and instead emphasizes their insights into human psychology and spiritual life.[29] He has trained many disciples, rabbinic as well as academic, who continue to carry his approach forward.[30]

Hillel Zeitlin never succeeded in establishing Yavneh in Poland, but his dream of an intense spiritual fellowship inspired the *havurah* movement. Some American Jews, particularly among the younger generation, were alienated by the hyperinstitutionalization of American synagogue life that reached its peak in the 1950s. The seekers who started the *havurah* dreamed of a creative new style of Jewish experience that would be meaningful for the individual, not just for rabbis and professional clergy, and they promoted Jewish education among the laity. They felt guided by (but not bound to) Jewish law and tradition, and new versions of Hasidic and kabbalistic rituals formed an important part of their spiritual practice. Both Arthur Green and, to a lesser degree, Zalman Schachter-Shalomi were founding members of the first *havurah* in the late 1960s in Somerville, Massachusetts. This prototype inspired a wave of others across the United States. The *havurah* movement has had a profound effect on American Jewry, and for many it is still an attractive alternative (or complement) to the traditional synagogue.[31]

Religion occupies a very different place in modern Israeli life from its place in the United States. The state-sanctioned monopoly on all matters pertaining to Judaism held by the Orthodox has restricted the growth of liberal movements. The resulting lack of denominational pluralism means that groups with a wide spectrum of theologies and levels of observance all identify as "Orthodox," many of which incorporate elements of Jewish mysticism. Large Hasidic centers are thriving in Jerusalem and Benei Berak, but these groups show little interest in Jewish mystical texts. A notable exception is the charismatic Rabbi Yitshak Meir Morgenstern, a self-fashioned Hasidic *rebbe* with an eclectic following in Jerusalem. Rabbi Morgenstern is an original mystical thinker, and his works combine an extremely wide range of Hasidic and kabbalistic sources with modern meditation techniques and popular psychology.[32]

The writings of Rav Kook have had considerable lasting impact in religious Zionist circles. The theology of the controversial Settlement movement is in large part based in Rav Tsevi Yehudah Kook's messianic interpretation of his father's ideas. Indeed, Rav Kook's works have provided the mystical groundwork for many later Israeli theologians. Rabbi Yitshak Ginsburgh (b. 1944), a radical Zionist and follower of the Habad movement, has taken Rav Kook's nationalistic reading of Kabbalah to the extreme.[33] A very different side of Rav Kook's teachings was carried forward by the late Rabbi Menachem Froman (1945–2013), a noted peacemaker and spiritual leader of the community in Tekoa. He was also a devoted student of the *Zohar* and the teachings of Rabbi Nahman of Bratslav, and Rabbi Froman's struggle for rapprochement with the Palestinians was deeply informed by his mystical worldview.[34] Rabbi Shim'on Gershon Rosenberg (Rav Shagar, 1949–2007) has also continued Rav Kook's quest for a creative new approach to theology. His teachings weave together Jewish mysticism, traditional rabbinic thought, romantic poetry, and postmodern philosophy. His innovative method appeals to many religious Zionist youth not satisfied with the myopic canon of traditional orthodoxy.[35] Neo-Hasidic approaches are an important part of the Israeli religious landscape, and are found in *yeshivot* such as Otniel, Ramat Gan, and Bat Ayin.

The Orthodox claim to absolute religious authority has not stopped a blossoming of spirituality in Israel. Indeed, as noted above, the current renewal of Jewish mysticism in both Israel and America has some important elements in common with New Age religion.[36] This connection has been much expanded by the post-army journeys of many young Israelis to the Far East,[37] which have inspired an openness to the spiritual quest that was closed to them by the seeming monopoly of politicized Orthodoxy over the sources of Judaism. In recent years there has been some breakdown of borders between North American and Israeli approaches to the religious quest. New Age groups in Israel are influenced by Jewish Renewal, and Heschel is being widely read in Hebrew translation. These circles embrace the notion that we are standing at the dawn of a new type of human consciousness and the reframing of Kabbalah as a method for self-transformation and personal healing.[38] A great number of spiritual seekers who once looked for inspiration in Eastern traditions have later turned to the study and practice of Jewish mysticism in some form or another.

The study of Jewish mysticism has continued to thrive in Israeli, European, and American universities over the past fifty years. Of course, the diversity and vibrancy of this field is indicative of a healthy academic discipline, but it also reveals something important about the centrality of Kabbalah and mysticism within modern Jewish life. Scholem's project was also one of cultural restoration, in which he hoped to revive the forgotten mystical heart of the Jewish people through academic research. The generations of scholars of Kabbalah who have followed in his footsteps, both expanding and challenging his work, are a testament to his success.[39]

In the introduction to this volume, I suggested that mysticism may be understood as the quest for a direct or immediate experience of God's presence and the longing to grasp the mysteries of the human soul and know the inner dynamics of the divine realm. Jewish mystics are united by their common religious heritage, which is grounded in the Hebrew Bible and the layers of religious literature surrounding it. This has allowed them to express themselves in a unique symbolic language developed over more than a thousand years. We have seen that mystics who yearn to dwell in the presence of the One have described their longings and experiences in a great many ways over the centuries. This vitality and creativity continues unabated in our own day. Nobody can predict how the course of this mighty river will change in the future, but we should have no doubt that new inspiration will continue to cascade forth from the depth of the Well.

Further Reading

Garb, Jonathan. *The Chosen Will Become Herds: Studies in Twentieth-Century Kabbalah*. Translated by Yaffah Berkovits-Murciano. New Haven: Yale University Press, 2009.

Green, Arthur. *Radical Judaism: Rethinking God and Tradition*. New Haven: Yale University Press, 2010.

Heschel, Abraham Joshua. *God in Search of Man: A Philosophy of Judaism*. New York: Farrar, Straus and Giroux, 1976.

Huss, Boaz, ed. *Kabbalah and Contemporary Spiritual Revival*. Beer Sheva: Ben Gurion University of the Negev Press, 2011.

Schachter-Shalomi, Zalman. *Paradigm Shift: From the Jewish Renewal Teachings of Reb Zalman Schachter-Shalomi*. Edited by Ellen Singer. Northvale, NJ: Jason Aronson, 1993.

Notes

Introduction

1. For a selection of programmatic writings by important members of the Wissenschaft, see "Modern Jewish Studies" in *The Jew in the Modern World: A Documentary History*, ed. Paul Mendes-Flohr and Jehuda Reinharz (New York: Oxford University Press, 2011), 233–75.

2. An example of Scholem's indictment of the Wissenschaft scholars is his "Reflections on Modern Jewish Studies," in *On the Possibility of Jewish Mysticism in Our Time & Other Essays*, ed. Avraham Shapira, trans. Jonathan Chipman (Philadelphia: The Jewish Publication Society, 1997), 51–71.

3. Among Scholem's most lasting contributions to the study of Jewish mysticism in English is his monumental historical overview entitled *Major Trends in Jewish Mysticism* (New York: Schocken Books, 1995). It was first published in 1941, and has been reprinted countless times since.

4. The scholarship *about* Scholem and his methodology is quickly becoming a field of its own. See David Biale's exemplary intellectual biography *Gershom Scholem: Kabbalah and Counter-History* (Cambridge, MA: Harvard University Press, 1982); and the collection of essays in *Gershom Scholem: The Man and His Work*, ed. Paul Mendes-Flohr (Albany: State University of New York Press, 1994). For a somewhat different reading of Scholem's role in the academic study of Jewish mysticism, see Daniel Abrams, "Defining Modern Academic Scholarship: Gershom Scholem and the Establishment of a New (?) Discipline," *The Journal of Jewish Thought and Philosophy* 9 (2000): 267–302

5. See Moshe Idel, *Kabbalah: New Perspectives* (New Haven: Yale University Press, 1988), esp. 1–34. On Idel's contribution to the field of Jewish mysticism, see Daniel Abrams, "Phenomenology of Jewish Mysticism: Moshe Idel's Methodology in Perspective," *Kabbalah* 20 (2009): 7–146.

6. Of course, the study of Jewish mysticism is informed by the work of a great number of other learned American and Israeli academics. References to their books and articles are to be found throughout the notes to the texts and introductions.

7. In the early twentieth century some argued that all "mysticism" had a universal core shared by mystics from different religious backgrounds.

However, so much ink has now been spilled on qualifying and debunking this assumption that it is impossible to offer a full biography. For a survey of different positions on the relationship between mysticism and religion, see the studies collected in *Mysticism and Philosophical Analysis*, ed. Steven T. Katz (New York: Oxford University Press, 1978); and *Mysticism and Religious Traditions*, ed. Steven T. Katz (New York: Oxford University Press, 1983). For an extensive and insightful summary of the scholarly literature, see Bernard McGinn, "Theoretical Foundations: The Modern Study of Mysticism," in *The Foundations of Mysticism* (New York: Crossroad, 1992), 265–343.

8. On the origins of the term mysticism and the history of its academic study, see Leigh Eric Schmidt, "The Making of Modern Mysticism," *Journal of the American Academy of Religion* 71 (2003): 273–302.

9. Moshe Idel has addressed the question of how Jewish mystics relate to Scripture in great detail in his *Absorbing Perfections: Kabbalah and Interpretation* (New Haven: Yale University Press, 2002).

10. See Arthur Green's discussion of the symbolic language of Jewish mysticism in *A Guide to the* Zohar (Stanford: Stanford University Press, 2004), esp. 55–59.

11. Thus Maimonides, the great apophatic thinker of Judaism, is not generally seen as a mystic and his works are not considered here. For a different perspective, see David R. Blumenthal, *Philosophic Mysticism: Studies in Rational Religion* (Ramat Gan: Bar Ilan University Press, 2007); and José Faur, *Homo Mysticus: A Guide to Maimonides's Guide for the Perplexed* (Syracuse, NY: Syracuse University Press, 1999). Jewish mystics did read the works of Maimonides, and, as Elliot Wolfson has argued, his theology influenced the development of Kabbalah; see his "'Via Negativa' in Maimonides and its Impact on Thirteenth-Century Kabbalah," *Maimonidean Studies* 5 (2008): 393–442.

12. For a foundational study on the place of language in Jewish mysticism, see Gershom Scholem's two-part article "The Name of God and the Linguistic Theory of the Kabbala," *Diogenes* 79 (1972): 59–80, and 80 (1972): 164–94. See also Moshe Idel, "Reification of Language in Jewish Mysticism," in *Mysticism and Language*, ed. Steven T. Katz (New York and Oxford: Oxford University Press, 1992), 42–79; and for a more philosophical meditation on this subject, Elliot R. Wolfson, *Language, Eros, Being: Kabbalistic Hermeneutics and Poetic Imagination* (New York: Fordham University Press, 2005).

13. Daniel Matt, "The Mystic and the Mizwot," in *Jewish Spirituality: From the Bible Through the Middle Ages*, ed. Arthur Green (New York: Crossroad, 1986), 367–404.

14. Morris M. Faierstein, "'God's Need for the Commandments' in Medieval Kabbalah," *Conservative Judaism* 36 (1982): 45–59. In this way mystical religion is sometimes difficult to distinguish from magic, and there are indeed magical elements in Jewish mysticism. However, both the goals and the means of mysticism and magic are different: the Jewish mystic seeks primarily to heal the fractures within God (as well as between God and man), whereas it is the goal of magic to exert control over reality by manipulating it through ritual in disregard of the divine will. See Valerie I. J. Flint, *The Rise of Magic in Early Medieval Europe* (Princeton, NJ: Princeton University Press, 1991).

15. See Gershom Scholem, "Religious Authority and Mysticism," in *On the Kabbalah and Its Symbolism*, trans. Ralph Manheim (New York: Schocken Books, 1965), 5–31.

16. Steven Katz has articulated the most extreme position against the tendency toward homogenization in the comparative study of mystical texts; see his "The 'Conservative' Character of Mystical Experience," in *Mysticism and Religious Traditions*, ed. Steven T. Katz (Oxford: Oxford University Press, 1983), 3–60. However, a number of prominent scholars have taken issue with this formulation, instead arguing for a comparative approach without the naïve assumption of a shared universal core. See Jonathan Z. Smith, "In Comparison a Magic Dwells," in *Imagining Religion: From Babylon to Jonestown* (Chicago: University of Chicago Press, 1982), 19–35; Wayne Proudfoot, *Religious Experience* (Berkeley, CA: University of California Press, 1985); and Kimberly Patton, "Juggling Torches: Why We Still Need Comparative Religion" in *A Magic Still Dwells: Comparative Religion in the Postmodern Age*, ed. Kimberley C. Patton and Benjamin C. Ray (Berkeley, CA: University of California Press, 2000), 153–71. For a case study demonstrating the merits of such comparisons, see *Mystical Union and Monotheistic Faith: An Ecumenical Dialogue*, ed. Moshe Idel and Bernard McGinn (New York: Macmillan Publishing Company, 1989).

17. Two resources for the study of mysticism in world religions have recently been published; see *Comparative Mysticism: An Anthology of Original Sources*, ed. Steven Katz (Oxford: Oxford University Press, 2013); and *Teaching Mysticism*, ed. William B. Parsons (Oxford: Oxford University Press, 2011).

18. On the centrality of anthropomorphic images in biblical theology, see Yochanan Muffs, *The Personhood of God: Biblical Theology, Human Faith and the Divine Image* (Woodstock, VT: Jewish Lights Publishing, 2005). For a treatment of these visionary accounts and their later repercussions, see Elliot Wolfson, "'Israel: The One Who Sees God'—Visualization of God in Biblical, Apocalyptic, and Rabbinic Sources," in *Through a Speculum That*

Shines: Vision and Imagination in Medieval Jewish Mysticism (Princeton: Princeton University Press, 1994), 13–51.

19. See George W. Savran, *Encountering the Divine: Theophany in Biblical Narrative* (London and New York: T & T Clark International, 2005); and Steven D. Fraade, "Hearing and Seeing at Sinai: Interpretive Trajectories," in *The Significance of Sinai: Traditions about Sinai and Divine Revelation in Judaism and Christianity*, ed. George J. Brooke, Hindy Najman, and Loren T. Stuckenbruck (Leiden: Brill, 2008), 247–68.

20. For a survey of biblical anthropomorphism, its sexual imagery and development in Jewish thought, see Charles Mopsik, "The Body of Engenderment in the Hebrew Bible, the Rabbinic Tradition and the Kabbalah," in *Fragments for a History of the Human Body*, ed. Michel Feher with Ramona Naddaff and Nadia Tazi (New York: Zone, 1989), 49–73.

21. Scholem, *Kabbalah*, 10; Ithamar Gruenwald, *Apocalyptic and Merkavah Mysticism* (Leiden: Brill, 1980), 3–72. For an overview of these texts and their broader historical context, see Michael E. Stone, "Apocalyptic Literature," in *Jewish Writings of the Second Temple Period*, ed. Michael E. Stone (Philadelphia: Fortress, 1984), 383–422; and Martha Himmelfarb, *Ascent to Heaven in Jewish and Christian Apocalypses* (New York and Oxford: Oxford University Press, 1993).

22. See *The Early Enoch Literature*, ed. Gabriele Boccaccini and John J. Collins (Leiden and Boston: Brill, 2007).

23. See Himmelfarb's discussion in *Ascent to Heaven*, 94–114.

24. Rachel Elior argues that later Jewish mysticism grew out of a priestly tradition preserved in the Scrolls. See her controversial *The Three Temples: On the Emergence of Jewish Mysticism*, trans. David Louvish (Oxford and Portland, OR: Littman Library of Jewish Civilization, 2004). See also Philip Alexander, *Mystical Texts: Songs of the Sabbath Sacrifice and Related Manuscripts* (London and New York: T & T Clark, 2006). For a very different perspective, see Peter Schaefer, *The Origins of Jewish Mysticism* (Princeton, NJ: Princeton University Press, 2009), esp. 27–33.

25. See Risa Levitt Kohn and Rebecca Moore, "Where is God? Divine Presence in the Absence of the Temple," in *Milk and Honey* (Winona Lake, IN: Eisenbrauns, 2007), 133–53; and Ephraim E. Urbach, *The Sages: Their Concepts and Beliefs*, trans. Israel Abrahams (Cambridge, MA: Harvard University Press, 1987), 36–96.

26. This transition began in the Diaspora after the First Temple was destroyed in 586 BCE, but accelerated after the destruction of the Second Temple. On Judaism as a scriptural religion and its interpretive tradition more generally, see Moshe Halbertal, *People of the Book: Canon, Meaning, and Authority* (Cambridge, MA: Harvard University Press, 1997); and

Michael Fishbane, *The Exegetical Imagination: On Jewish Thought and Theology* (Cambridge, MA: Harvard University Press, 1998).

27. See Robert Goldenberg's excellent study "Law and Spirit in Talmudic Religion," in *Jewish Spirituality: From the Bible Through the Middle Ages*, ed. Arthur Green (New York: Crossroad, 1986), 232–52.

28. Scholem, *Major Trends*, 7–8; David J. Halperin, *The Faces of the Chariot: Early Jewish Reponses to Ezekiel's Vision* (Tuebingen: Mohr, 1988). For an analysis of Scholem's claim, see Moshe Idel, "Rabbinism versus Kabbalism: On G. Scholem's Phenomenology of Judaism," *Modern Judaism* 11 (1991): 281–96.

29. See the texts collected in Ira Chernus, *Mysticism in Rabbinic Judaism* (Berlin and New York: Walter de Gruyter, 1982). See also Alon Goshen-Gottstein, "Is *Ma'aseh Bereshit* Part of Ancient Jewish Mysticism," *The Journal of Jewish Thought and Philosophy* 4 (1995): 185–201.

30. On Song of Songs in rabbinic literature, see Judith Kates, "Entering the Holy of Holies: Rabbinic Midrash and the Language of Intimacy," *Scrolls of Love: Ruth and the Song of Songs*, ed. Peter S. Hawkins and Lesleigh Cushing Stahlberg (New York: Fordham University Press, 2006), 201–13; and Reuven Kimelman, "Rabbi Yokhanan and Origen on the Song of Songs: A Third-Century Jewish-Christian Disputation," *The Harvard Theological Review* 73 (1980): 567–95.

31. See Nehemia Polen, "*Derashah* as Performative Exegesis in Tosefta and Mishnah," in *Midrash and the Exegetical Mind*, ed. Lieve Tuegels and Rivka Ulmer (Piscataway, NJ: Gorgias Press, 2010), 123–53, and his forthcoming "Rabbis in Paradise: Law and Holy Spirit in Early Rabbinic Judaism."

32. *Sefer Yetsirah* in its current form has been heavily edited, and several distinct recensions have been passed down. For a study of the different versions of this work and a critical edition of the earliest recoverable text, see A. Peter Hayman, *Sefer Yesira: Edition, Translation and Text-Critical Commentary* (Tuebingen: Mohr Siebeck, 2004).

33. Scholem, *Kabbalah*, 26–28; Yehuda Liebes, *Ars Poetica in Sefer Yetsirah* (Tel Aviv: Schocken Books, 2000), 229–37 [Hebrew]; Peter Hayman, "Some Observations on Sefer Yesira: (1) Its Use of Scripture," *Journal of Jewish Studies* 35 (1984): 181–83. For an alternate view that pushes forward *Sefer Yetsirah*'s redaction into the Islamic period, see Elliot R. Wolfson, "Text, Context, and Pretext: Review Essay of Yehuda Liebes's *Ars Poetica in Sefer Yetsira*," *The Studia Philonica Annual XVI* (2004): 226–27.

34. Scholem, *Kabbalah*, 23–26.

35. See Liebes, *Ars Poetica*, esp. 31–71.

36. Joseph Dan, "The Language of Creation and Its Grammar," in *Jewish Mysticism: Late Antiquity* (Northvale, NJ: Jason Aronson, Inc., 1998), 129–54.

37. Liebes, *Ars Poetica*, 16–17, 53.

38. Liebes, *Ars Poetica*, 118–20.

39. Peter Hayman, "Some Observations on Sefer Yesira: (2) The Temple at the Centre of the Universe," *Journal of Jewish Studies* 37 (1986): 176–82.

40. Hayman, "Observations on Sefer Yesira (1)," 168–84.

41. Liebes, *Ars Poetica*, 64–66, 73–75. For a different perspective, see Peter Hayman, "Was God a Magician? Sefer Yesira and Jewish Magic," *Journal of Jewish Studies* 40 (1989): 225–37, esp. 233–34.

42. Scholem, *Kabbalah*, 350–51; Moshe Idel, *Golem: Jewish Magical and Mystical Traditions on the Artificial Anthropoid* (Albany: State University of New York Press, 1990), esp. 9–26.

43. For some possible Talmudic references, see b. Berakhot 55a and b. Sanhedrin 65a.

44. See Efraim Gottlieb, "The Meaning and Purpose of Commentaries on the 'Works of Creation' in Early Kabbalah," in *Mehkarim be-Sifrut ha-Kabbalah*, ed. Joseph Hacker (Tel Aviv: Chaim Rosenberg School for Jewish Studies at Tel Aviv University, 1976) [Hebrew].

45. James Tabor's work uses the notion of heavenly ascent as a case study for cultural interchange at this time; see his *Things Unutterable: Paul's Ascent to Paradise in Its Greco-Roman, Judaic, and Early Christian Contexts* (Lanham: University Press of America, 1986).

46. See Philip S. Alexander, "Jewish Elements in Gnosticism and Magic c. CE 70–c. CE 270," in *The Cambridge History of Judaism*, vol. 3 (Cambridge: Cambridge University Press, 2008), 1052–78; and Joseph Dan, "Jewish Gnosticism?," in *Jewish Mysticism: Late Antiquity* (Northvale, NJ: Jason Aronson, Inc., 1998), 1–25.

47. See Scholem, "*Merkabah* Mysticism and Jewish Gnosticism," in *Major Trends*, 40–79; and Gruenwald, *Apocalyptic and Merkavah Mysticism*, 9–123. For a learned summary of the modern scholarship, see Ra'anan Boustan, "The Study of *Heikhalot* Literature: Between Mystical Experience and Textual Artifact," *Currents in Biblical Research* 6 (2007): 130–60. For a comprehensive study of the theological landscape of this literature, see Peter Schafer, *The Hidden and Manifest God: Some Major Themes in Early Jewish Mysticism*, trans. Aubrey Pomerance (Albany: State University of New York Press, 1992). For a new translation of many of the important works, see James R. Davila: *Hekhalot Literature in Translation: Major Texts of Merkavah Mysticism* (Leiden: Brill, 2013).

48. The distinction between these two genres is not always clear, especially given that late apocalypses and early *heikhalot* works could very well have overlapped. For an analysis of *heikhalot* and *merkavah* texts within the broader context of Late Antiquity apocalypses and early Christianity, see Naomi Janowitz, *Icons of Power: Ritual Practices in Late Antiquity* (University Park, PA: Pennsylvania State University Press, 2002), esp. 63–84. See also Philip S. Alexander, "Comparing *Merkavah* Mysticism and Gnosticism: An Essay in Method," *Journal of Jewish Studies* 35 (1984): 1–18.

49. For a broader study of ascent texts in later Jewish thought, see Moshe Idel, *Ascensions on High in Jewish Mysticism: Pillars, Lines, Ladders* (Budapest: Central European University Press, 2005).

50. The history and analysis of this work is fraught with textual difficulties. See the issues raised in Daniel Abrams, "The Dimensions of the Creator—Contradiction or Paradox? Corruptions and Accretions to the Manuscript Witness," *Kabbalah* 5 (2000): 35–54.

51. Scholem suggested that *heikhalot* mystics could never achieve a vision of God, but Chernus argued that the visions were accompanied by warnings precisely because such experiences could the mystic; see Ira Chernus, "Visions of God in Merkabah Mysticism," *Journal for the Study of Judaism* 13 (1982): 129–30; Wolfson, *Through a Speculum*, 91.

52. On the evolution of this symbol, see Arthur Green, *Keter: The Crown of God in Early Jewish Mysticism* (Princeton, NJ: Princeton University Press, 1997), esp. 12–19, 33–41.

53. Gershom Scholem, *Jewish Gnosticism, Merkabah Mysticism, and Talmudic Tradition* (New York: Jewish Theological Seminary of America, 1960), 12–13; David Halperin, *The Faces of the Chariot: Early Jewish Responses to Ezekiel's Vision* (Tuebingen: Mohr, 1988), 366–87; Michael Swartz, *Scholastic Magic: Ritual and Revelation in Early Jewish Mysticism* (Princeton, NJ: Princeton University Press, 1996); Daphna V. Arbel, "'Understanding of the Heart:' Spiritual Transformation and Divine Revelations in the Hekhalot and Merkavah Literature," *Jewish Studies Quarterly* 6 (1999): 320–44.

54. Scholem, *Jewish Gnosticism*, 65–74.

55. See the compelling arguments laid out by Peter Schaefer in *The Origins of Jewish Mysticism* (Princeton, NJ: Princeton University Press, 2009); and Ra'anan S. Boustan, "Rabbinization and the Making of Early Jewish Mysticism," *The Jewish Quarterly Review* 101 (2011): 482–501.

56. Peter Schaefer's synoptic edition of some of the most important *heikhalot* manuscripts is now the standard text for the study of this literature. See his *Synopse zur Hekhalot-Literatur*, with Margaret Schlueter and Hans Georg von Mutius (Tuebingen: Mohr Siebeck, 1981).

57. Robert Brody, *The Geonim of Babylonia and the Shaping of Medieval Jewish Culture* (New Haven: Yale University Press, 1998), 142–47. For a description of an authentic mystical text traceable to the Geonic period, see Klaus Hermann, "Jewish Mysticism in the Geonic Period: The Prayer of Rav Hamnuna Sava," in *Officina Magica: Essays on the Practice of Magic in Antiquity* (Leiden: Brill, 2005), 171–212.

58. Scholem, *Major Trends*, 84; Moshe Idel, "From Italy to Ashkenaz and Back: On the Circulation of Jewish Mystical Traditions," *Kabbalah* 14 (2006): 47–94. On the place of Italy in medieval Jewish mysticism, see Moshe Idel, *Kabbalah in Italy: 1280–1510: A Survey* (New Haven: Yale University Press, 2011).

59. On the textual problems and reception history of this work, see Yitzhak Fritz Baer, "The Socio-religious Orientation of *Sefer Hasidim*," *Binah* 2 (1989): 57–95; and Haym Soloveitchik, "Piety, Pietism and German Pietism: '*Sefer Hasidim* I' and the Influence of *Hasidei Ashkenaz*," *The Jewish Quarterly Review* 92 (2002): 455–93.

60. On the place of *Hasidei Ashkenaz* in the greater spectrum of Jewish and Christian pietism, see Ivan Marcus, *Piety and Society: The Jewish Pietists of Medieval Germany* (Leiden: Brill, 1981).

61. See Scholem, "Hasidism in Medieval Germany," in *Major Trends*, 80–118. The most comprehensive summary of their mystical theology is Joseph Dan, *The Esoteric Theology of Ashkenazi Hasidism* (Jerusalem: Mossad Bialik, 1968) [Hebrew].

62. Haym Soloveitchik, "Three Themes in *Sefer Hasidim*," *AJS Review* 1 (1976): 315–17.

63. See Ronald C. Kiener, "The Hebrew Paraphrase of Saadiah Gaon's *Kitab al-Amanat wa'l-I'tiqadat*," *AJS Review* 11 (1986): 1–25; and Scholem, *Major Trends*, 107–18.

64. Soloveitchik, "Three Themes," 311–25.

65. Scholem, *Major Trends*, 90.

66. See Elliot R. Wolfson, "The Mystical Significance of Torah Study in German Pietism," *The Jewish Quarterly Review* 84 (1993): 43–78.

67. Scholem, *Major Trends*, 100–3; Talya Fishman, "Rhineland Pietist Approaches to Prayer and the Textualization of Rabbinic Culture," *Jewish Studies Quarterly* 11 (2004): 313–31.

68. Scholem, *Major Trends*, 91–95. Regarding the relationship between the Pietists, the Tosafot, and Jewish mysticism, see Soloveitchik, "Three Themes," 339–57; and Ephraim Kanarfogel, *"Peering through the Lattices:" Mystical, Magical, and Pietistic Dimensions in the Tosafist Period* (Detroit: Wayne State University Press, 2000).

69. Soloveitchik, "Three Themes," 322–24.

70. Scholem and Soloveitchik strongly disagree regarding the impact and influence of the German Pietists. See Scholem, *Major Trends*, 80–84; and Soloveitchik, "Piety, Pietism and German Pietism," esp. 46–482.

Chapter 1

1. For a general introduction of kabbalistic theology, including (but not limited to) the mysticism of the thirteenth century, see Gershom Scholem, "The Basic Ideas of Kabbalah," *Kabbalah* (Jerusalem: Keter Publishing House, 1974), 87–189.

2. On the subject of *Devekut* as a central goal of the religious life in early Kabbalah, see Idel, *New Perspectives*, 35–58; and Adam Afterman, *Devequt: Mystical Intimacy in Medieval Jewish Thought* (Los Angeles: Cherub Press, 2011) [Hebrew].

3. For an overview of this period, see Gershom Scholem, *Origins of the Kabbalah*, ed. R. J. Zwi Werblowsky, trans. Allan Arkush (Philadelphia: Jewish Publication Society, 1987).

4. See the work of Joseph Dan in his *The First Kabbalistic Circles* (Jerusalem: Academon, 1985) [Hebrew].

5. Idel, *New Perspectives*, 20–21, 253; Elliot Wolfson, "Beyond the Spoken Word: Oral Tradition and Written Transmission in Medieval Jewish Mysticism," *Transmitting Jewish Traditions: Orality, Textuality and Cultural Diffusion*, ed. Yaakov Elman and Israel Gershoni (New Haven: Yale University Press, 2000), 166–224.

6. On the cultural world of Provence, see Charles Homer Haskins, *The Renaissance of the Twelfth Century* (Cambridge, MA: Harvard University Press, 1979).

7. Moshe Idel, "On European Cultural Renaissances and Jewish Mysticism," *Kabbalah* 13 (2005): 43–78.

8. Jonathan Dauber, *Knowledge of God and the Development of Early Kabbalah* (Leiden and Boston: Brill, 2012).

9. Scholem argues that an ancient nucleus of the *Bahir* arrived in Europe from the East, to which other textual layers were then added; see Scholem, *Origins*, 106–23; and Ronit Meroz, "On the Time and Place of Some of *Sefer ha-Bahir*," *Da'at* 49 (2002): 137–80 [Hebrew].

10. Joseph Dan and Daniel Abrams have suggested that the *Bahir* should be considered primarily the work of German Pietists, and that there is no concrete evidence linking it to tradition from the Middle East. See Abrams, *The Book Bahir: An Edition Based on the Earliest Manuscripts* (Los Angeles: Cherub Press, 1994), 4–20 [Hebrew]; and Dan's remarks in the

introduction to his *Jewish Mysticism: The Middle Ages* (Northvale, NJ: Jason Aronson, 1998).

11. See Abrams, *The Book Bahir*, 13–14n* [English abstract]; and Haviva Pedaya, "The Provençal Stratum in the Redaction of *Sefer ha-Bahir*," *Jerusalem Studies in Jewish Thought* 9 (1990): 139–64 [Hebrew].

12. Scholem, *Origins*, 68–97.

13. As noted in the introduction, the appearance of Talmudic sages is also common in the earlier *Heikhalot* texts.

14. Scholem, *Origins*, 53–54.

15. See Joseph Dan, "Midrash and the Dawn of Kabbalah," in *Jewish Mysticism Volume Two: The Middle Ages* (Northvale, NJ: Jason Aronson, 1998), 1–18.

16. Scholem, *Origins*, 68–80. Elliot Wolfson has suggested that instead of assuming that the cosmic tree represents a Jewish version of the gnostic *pleroma*, as did Scholem, it should be understood as a symbol for the manner in which mundane reality blossoms forth from a divine origin. See his "The Tree That Is All: Jewish-Christian Roots of a Kabbalistic Symbol in *Sefer ha-Bahir*," *Journal of Jewish Thought and Philosophy* 3 (1993): 31–76.

17. Elliot Wolfson, "Hebraic and Hellenic Conceptions of Wisdom in *Sefer ha-Bahir*," *Poetics Today* 19 (1998): 147–76.

18. It should be noted that *Sefer ha-Bahir* portrays evil as a very real part of the created world but *not* a power of its own, as it will become in later Kabbalah. See Dan, "Introduction," *Jewish Mysticism Volume Two: The Middle Ages*, xx–xlviii.

19. Arthur Green, "*Shekhinah*, the Virgin Mary and the Song of Songs: Reflections on a Kabbalistic Symbol in Its Historical Context," in *AJS Review* 26 (2002): 1–52.

20. An overview of the diverse *'Iyyun* group and its literature may be found in Scholem, *Origins*, 309–64. Their writings have recently been reissued as Oded Porat, *The Writings of 'Iyyun: Critical Edition* (Los Angeles: Cherub Press, 2013) [Hebrew].

21. Scholem's findings have been challenged by the research of Mark Verman. He argues that because all citations before the late thirteenth century come from Castilian Kabbalists, we may assume that the *'Iyyun* Circle immediately post-dates the Gerona school and was active in Castile rather than Provence. Indeed, Verman suggests that the writings of Rabbi 'Azriel of Gerona influenced the *'Iyyun* Circle. See Mark Verman, *The Books of Contemplation: Medieval Jewish Mystical Sources* (Albany: State University of New York Press, 1992), esp. 179–99.

22. Verman, *Books of Contemplation*, 2. For an excellent introduction to Christian Kabbalah, see Allison P. Coudert, "Christian Kabbalah," in *Jewish*

Mysticism and Kabbalah: New Insights and Scholarship, ed. Frederick E. Greenspahn (New York: New York University Press, 2011), 159–72.

23. For a survey of Yitshak the Blind's life and teachings, see Scholem, *Origins*, 249–309. His work is complemented and challenged by that of Haviva Pedaya in her *Name and Sanctuary in the Teaching of R. Isaac the Blind: A Comparative Study in the Writings of the Earliest Kabbalists* (Jerusalem: Magnes Press, 2001) [Hebrew]. Mark Sendor's unpublished dissertation provides an illuminating analysis of Yitshak the Blind's mystical thought in addition to a translation of his commentary to *Sefer Yetsirah*. See Mark Brian Sendor, "The Emergence of Provençal Kabbalah: Rabbi Isaac the Blind's Commentary on Sefer Yezirah," PhD diss., Harvard University, 1994.

24. Rabbi Yitshak's students may have actually penned this work, but scholars agree that it is an authentic representation of his mystical thought. Pedaya, *Name and Sanctuary*, 55–57; Scholem, *Origins*, 257; Sendor, "Provençal Kabbalah," 45–50.

25. See Isadore Twersky, *Rabad of Posquières: A Twelfth-century Talmudist* (Cambridge, MA: Harvard University Press, 1962), 286–300; Scholem, *Origins*, 200, 205–26; and Pedaya, *Name and Sanctuary*, 42–55.

26. See Scholem, *Origins*, 365–465, esp. 365–70.

27. RaMBaN's Kabbalah has been the subject of a number of important studies. See Daniel Abrams, "Orality in the Kabbalistic School of Nahmanides: Preserving and Interpreting Esoteric Traditions and Texts," in *Jewish Studies Quarterly* 3 (1996): 85–102; Moshe Halbertal, *By Way of Truth: Nahmanides and the Creation of Tradition* (Jerusalem: Shalom Hartman Institute, 2005) [Hebrew]; Moshe Idel, "We Have No Kabbalistic Tradition on This," in *Rabbi Moses Nahmanides (Ramban): Explorations in His Religious and Literary Virtuosity*, ed. Isadore Twersky (Cambridge, MA: Harvard University Press, 1993), 11–34; Haviva Pedaya, *Nachmanides: Cyclical Time and Holy Text* (Tel Aviv: Am 'Oved, 2003) [Hebrew]; and Elliot Wolfson, "By Way of Truth: Aspects of Nahmanides' Kabbalistic Hermeneutic," in *AJS Review* 14 (1989):103–78. See also Idel's claim that RaMBaN was not actually a member of this group in "Nahmanides: Kabbalah, Halakhah, and Spiritual Leadership," in *Jewish Mystical Leaders*, ed. Moshe Idel and Mortimer Oslow (Northvale, NJ: Jason Aronson, 1998), 15–96.

28. On Rabbi Asher's mystical thought, see Scholem, *Origins*, 252–53, 393, 401–3, 431–33; Daniel Abrams, *R. Asher ben David: His Complete Works and Studies in His Kabbalistic Thought* (Los Angeles: Cherub Press, 1996) [Hebrew]; and Eitan Fishbane, "The Speech of Being, the Voice of God: Phonetic Mysticism in the Kabbalah of Asher ben David and His Contemporaries," *The Jewish Quarterly Review* 98 (2008): 485–521.

29. See Scholem, *Origins*, 394–95.

30. See Moshe Halbertal, *Concealment and Revelation: Esotericism in Jewish Thought and Its Philosophical Implications*, trans. Jackie Feldman (Princeton: Princeton University Press, 2007).

31. Scholem, *Origins*, 398–400; Dauber, *Knowledge of God*, 33–34; Jacob Katz, "Halakhah and Kabbalah as Competing Disciplines of Study," in *Divine Law in Human Hands: Case Studies in Halakhic Flexibility* (Jerusalem: Magnes Press, 1998), 56–86.

32. Scholem, *Origins*, 371–74; Verman, *Books of Contemplation*, 123. On the Song of Songs in later Jewish mysticism, see Arthur Green, "Intradivine Romance: The Song of Songs in the *Zohar*," in *Scrolls of Love: Ruth and the Song of Songs*, ed. Peter S. Hawkins and Lesleigh Cushing Stahlberg, 214–27.

33. Scholem, *Origins*, 272–76.

34. Scholem, *Origins*, 414–30; Daniel Matt, "*Ayin*: The Concept of Nothingness in Jewish Mysticism," in *Essential Papers on Kabbalah*, ed. Lawrence Fine (New York: New York University Press, 1995), 67–108.

35. On the fruitful dialectic between creativity and the authority of tradition in Kabbalah, see Gershom Scholem, "Revelation and Tradition as Religious Categories in Judaism," in *The Messianic Idea in Judaism and Other Essays on Jewish Spirituality* (New York: Schocken Books, 1971), 282–303.

36. For more on the Castilian surroundings of this circle, see Hartley Lachter, "The Politics of Secrets: Thirteenth-Century Kabbalah in Context," *The Jewish Quarterly Review* 101/4 (2011): 502–10.

37. Though the works of Abulafia and Gikatilla have not been included in this volume, they represent important contributions to the development of kabbalistic thought. See Moshe Idel, *The Mystical Experience in Abraham Abulafia*, trans. Jonathan Chipman (Albany, NY: State University of New York Press, 1988); Moshe Idel, *Language, Torah and Hermeneutics in Abraham Abulafia*, trans. Menahem Kallus (Albany, NY: State University of New York Press, 1989); and Elke Morlok, *Rabbi Joseph Gikatilla's Hermeneutics* (Tübingen: Mohr Siebeck, 2011). For an English translation of one of Rabbi Gikatilla's most interesting works, see *Gates of Light*, trans. Avi Weinstein (San Francisco: HarperCollins, 1994).

38. Idel, *New Perspectives*, 210–11.

39. The text of the *Bahir* remained unstable even after its initial appearance, as is clear from the divergent quotations by early Kabbalists and misattributions by later authors of passages that do not appear in our version of the text. The following translation is based on the popular edition prepared by Reuven Margoliot (Jerusalem: Mossad ha-Rav Kook, 1951). Margoliot's is an eclectic fusion of various versions of the *Bahir*, and Daniel Abrams' annotated critical edition of the *Bahir* based on the Munich 1298 manuscript is

now the standard text for scholarly work. The following passages appear in Abrams, *The Book Bahir*, 87–94, 173–81.

40. This section continues the homily in the previous section on the verse in Lev 9:22, concerning the priest's benediction: "And Aaron raised his hand and blessed the people." This verse is connected with Num 6:24–26, which constitute the actual text of the benediction, part of the daily liturgy.

41. The *sefirot* here refer to the ten dimensions of the cosmos found in the *Sefer Yetsirah*: up, down, east, west, north, south, beginning, end, good, and evil.

42. The term "sealed" is used both in *Sefer Yetsirah* and in ancient Jewish mystical literature to denote God's actions in the universe using His holy name or attributes.

43. In the Hebrew text of the Decalogue there are 613 letters. The number 613 is the classic representation of the sum total of Jewish commandments, composed of 248 negative and 365 positive commandments.

44. The ninth letter, *tet*, is absent from the text of the Decalogue. The reason given by the *Bahir* is unclear. Is it because it denotes an unclean part of the body? Cf. *Bahir* #84.

45. The mystical homilist uses the threefold connection, based on the *Sefer Yetsirah*, between *sefirot* and *misparim* (numbers), to which he now adds "declare" (*mesaprim*), to express the new idea that the heavens express the Glory of God by the ten *sefirot*.

46. The mystic author presents an intentional paradox: The ten *sefirot* are indeed three, and they represent three celestial forces. Thus he moves from the framework of ten, which governed the previous sections, to the number three, which is the basis of the revelations to come.

47. Only two realms are explained here. The first is quite obscure, probably based on the system of the emanation of the *sefirot* in the *Sefer Yetsirah*. The first is *ruah Elohim hayyim* (Spirit of the Living God), which is hinted here by the substitution of "light" for "spirit." In *Sefer Yetsirah* the third is the water, which comes from the spirit.

48. The second realm is that of the divine chariot described by Ezekiel in the first chapter of his book. The description here follows the terminology current in *hekhalot* mysticism.

49. The next sections are a mystical homily on the third benediction of the daily *'amidah* ("standing") prayer, the *kedushah* ("sanctification").

50. The first example is a nonexistent verse, but a formula that was accepted into the prayers: God's kingdom in the past, present, and future. This formula was used to explain the meaning of the vocalization of the name Y-H-V-H in the Bible, understood to mean "God will be, He is, and He will be."

51. The second example is the priest's benediction itself, which is comprised of three elements in three subsequent verses.

52. The third example is the names of God in the verse in Exodus, which was understood in rabbinic tradition to denote the thirteen divine attributes of mercy. This verse includes God's name three times.

53. In this section the full forces of the mystical symbolism of the *Bahir* is revealed, when the divine world is divided into the three categories corresponding to the triad of "holy's" in the *kedushah*.

54. The highest part is the Supreme Crown (*keter 'elyon*), which in subsequent Kabbalah was regarded as the first and highest of the divine emanations. This is an original *Bahir*ic symbol (as far as we know) and in the list of the ten divine powers in the *Bahir* #141, it also appears first.

55. The second is based on the *Bahir*ic symbolism (probably based on Gnostic sources) that pictures the divine powers as an enormous divine tree, whose roots come from above and whose branches reach downwards. The root, therefore, is the highest part of the divine tree.

56. The third, which is the most important one for the interpretation of the *kedushah*, is described by two conflicting terms (see below, #133). It is both united with the others and separate from them.

57. This section is intended to explain the paradox of "united" and "special" (meaning here "separated"). How can He be both simultaneously?

58. The parable, based on the theurgic element in *Bahir*ic mysticism, explains that when the people of Israel (the "grandsons") fulfill God's wishes, the celestial powers and the people on earth are amply provided for by God and He is "united" with them. But if they do not, God gives the celestial powers (the "sons") the minimum they need, and the earthly people are punished by God's being "special," remote and separated.

59. According to the verse from Proverbs, the "Glory" is the lot of the wise (using the double meaning of the Hebrew *kavod*: both "honor" and "Glory," therefore the essence of the Glory is wisdom, and it fills up the celestial Land of Israel).

60. The author introduces here the verse from Ezekiel, which is part of the *kedushah*, probably to denote that the remote place of the Glory ("from Its place") is the celestial Land of Israel.

61. The *matronita*, "great lady," is the divine Glory. It is doubtful whether this parable can be understood to hint at the feminine nature of the *kavod*.

62. The distinction between knights and sons refers to the belief that the *kedushah* is said both by angels (as attested by Isaiah) and by the praying Jews (b. Hullin 91b). The first are the knights, while the sons are the people praying in the synagogue.

63. This parable explains the traditional interpretation of the verse from Ezekiel (found also in b. Hagigah 14b). The angels and the people do not know the place of the Glory, and they praise it wherever it is.

64. The meaning of "from Its place" in this parable is exactly the opposite of that in the previous one. Here the Glory itself is known and present among the people (unlike the hiding *matronita*), only her place of origin is hidden. They bless the princess in her presence, and they refer to her origin by "wherever she comes from." [Tolerance of two different, even mutually exclusive interpretations of the same verse is a foundational principle in rabbinic midrash. See Dan, "Midrash," 14–15.]

65. While the feminine description of the *kavod* in the previous section does not necessarily denote a specific symbol, here it seems that the use of a princess instead of a prince (especially as she is not described as a mother) seems to convey a notion of the feminine nature of the *kavod/shekhinah*.

66. The Gnostic character of the *Bahir*ic symbolism is apparent here more than in almost all other sections of the book. The picture of the "daughter of light," in exile in the material world, representing her hidden, unknowable place of origin "on the side of the light" is a stark gnostic one.

67. The question here is: Why do we include in the prayers Ezekiel's verse, and thus give a separate blessing, to the Glory? Is the Glory not united with God, and does not the blessing to God (of Isaiah 6:3) include the Glory as well?

68. The garden is the fullness of the divine powers, symbolized by the Supreme Crown and the root of the Tree, while the third part is united, but outside, this framework, and therefore needs the separate blessing of Ezekiel 3:12.

69. The term "from Its place" receives its third explanation: From the special place God opened to provide for the Glory independently from the other powers in the garden.

70. The numerical value of the Hebrew letters of these two words, *kavod* (K-B-V-D) and *lev* (L-B; "heart"), is the same: 32. This denotes that they must represent the same secret.

71. The Glory is, therefore, the celestial counterpart of the "heart" in the lower realms of creation. It seems that the author refers to the opening paragraph of the *Sefer Yetsirah*, which describes the creation by 32 "paths," often called *lev*.

72. The homilist returns here, after dedicating a detailed discussion to the *kedushah*, to his original theme—the priest's benediction.

73. The term "Israel" here is clearly symbolic, referring to a divine force that was awarded to Jacob when his name was changed.

74. The author uses here the term *middah*, which has many meanings. It is an ethical characteristic, but also a measurement, and a divine attribute. In Kabbalistic literature the term is sometimes used for the divine emanations more often than the term *sefirot*.

75. The author emphasizes the correspondence between what Abraham did and what he received. Abraham, like Isaac and Jacob, is treated here as both the ancient father with his specific personal characteristics, and as a manifestation of divine attributes that were given to him and that he comes to represent, following the *Bahir*, throughout Jewish mystical literature. Abraham, Isaac, and Jacob are consistently described in Kabbalistic literature as the symbols of the three divine emanations, the fourth—Lovingkindess; the fifth—Justice or Fear; and the sixth—Truth or Mercy.

76. Abraham not only won the *middah* for himself, but because of his righteous deeds Isaac and Jacob became worthy to receive theirs.

77. The term *tohu* is explained in the *Bahir* as the material realm from which evil emerges. In #2 it is described as that which is nothing, probably referring to the Aristotelian description of the relationship between form and matter, when matter does not exist by its own right, only in combination with specific from. It is probable that the *Bahir* derived this homiletical interpretation of Gen 1:2 from Rabbi Abraham bar Hiyya, a twelfth-century philosopher and scientist in Spain.

78. After explaining the essence of Isaac's fear, the mystical homilist identifies Abraham's charity with the Torah.

79. Lovingkindness is generally the fourth emanation, coming before Fear, which is the fifth. Since the order is reversed in the verse, the homilist must explain the changing of the order.

80. The interrelationship between the patriarchs is presented here, symbolically, as the process of emanation from the fourth down to the sixth divine manifestation. The symbols of Torah, Truth, Peace, and Justice are the basic ones in the *Bahir* and in later Kabbalah for the sixth and central divine power (called *tif'eret*, "beauty," by the Kabbalists in Provence and Spain). Jacob and Israel are its biblical names in this tradition.

81. The true Torah, probably still referring to the sixth *sefirah*, is in the center of existence and governs all the divine powers, using the force of Thought, which is the supreme divine emanation.

82. The theme of the Ten Utterances was originally presented in rabbinic literature as the ten occurrences in Genesis 1:1 in which God created by speech ("Let there be light," etc.), and by these ten the whole world was created. See m. Avot 5:1 and b. Megillah 21b. In the *Bahir*, as in later Kabbalah, these Utterances were identified with the ten divine emanations.

83. Regarding these two important *'Iyyun* texts, see Scholem, *Origins*, 310–330; and Verman, *Books of Contemplation*, 87–89, 121–64.

84. A pseudepigraphic attribution to a legendary rabbi. [Verman suggests that the very name *Hamai* implies one who is engaged in visionary activity. See Verman, *Books of Contemplation*, 1.]

85. Much of the terminology used to designate the emanations is taken from the visions of Ezekiel.

86. An image earlier employed by Solomon ibn Gabirol (c. 1021–58), the great Hebrew poet of Spain, to describe the act of Creation.

87. Kabbalistic operations by which mystics performed quasi-magical transformations of nature, also mentioned in the *Fountain of Wisdom*. Other recensions of the *Sefer ha-'Iyyun* make no mention of these operations.

88. [*Sefer Ma'aseh Bereshit*. The identity of this work is unknown. See Verman, *Books of Contemplation*, 83n144.]

89. See Isaiah 25:1. In other circles, this term designated the first and most concealed *sefirah*, *keter* or Crown.

90. Mystical knowledge and insight penetrate deeper than "scientific" investigation.

91. See *Sefer Yetsirah* 1:7.

92. A similar motif of emanations as a result of hammer blows can be found in *Zohar* 1:15a.

93. Lit. "the Lord God is Truth."

94. Lit. "death." Now the statement on the forehead reads, "The Lord God is dead."

95. The attribution of these works to Rabbi Yitshak is complicated. The Kabbalists of Provence and Gerona wrote a great many commentaries to Creation in the late twelfth and early thirteenth centuries. The authorship of these different texts is easily confused, and many were infused with later kabbalistic ideas by the scribes who copied them. See Abrams, *Writings of R. Asher*, 15–16n* [English] and 301–53 [Hebrew]. Scholem, *Origins*, 260, and Dan confirm the authenticity of *The Mystical Torah* as the work of Rabbi Yitshak the blind, but this has been challenged by Sendor, "Provençal Kabbalah," 45; and Moshe Idel, *Absorbing Perfections* (New Haven: Yale University Press, 2002), 503n36. The manuscript refers to "R. Yitshak the Elder," who may in fact be Rabbi Yitshak of Acre (thirteenth–fourteenth centuries). Lacking conclusive evidence, these works are reprinted here as representative of Rabbi Yitshak's school of thought, if not the words of the master himself.

96. See *Bereshit Rabbah* 1:1. For explorations of how this concept was treated in later Jewish literature, see Idel, *Absorbing Perfections*, 31–34,

44–53; and Barbara Holdrege, *Veda and Torah: Transcending the Textuality of Scripture* (Albany: State University of New York Press, 1996), 131–212.

97. The letter *bet* is the first letter of the word *be-reshit* and hence the first letter of the Torah scroll. It is a traditional orthographic feature of the written scroll that this *bet* be larger than all other *bets*, and its unique size is seized on by Rabbi Yitshak as an allusion to the first *sefirah*, called by him either Crown or Thought.

98. Preceding the words "the heavens" and "the earth" in the Hebrew text is the accusative preposition *et*, which is untranslatable. Each *et* is taken by Rabbi Yitshak as a symbol for two further *sefirot*: Lovingkindess and Fear. The latter is subsequently referred to in the later Spanish Kabbalah as Strength or Severity.

99. Source unknown. For the "foundation stone," see b. Yoma 54b; Sanhedrin 26b.

100. See *Sefer Yetsirah* 1:5.

101. Wisdom is situated directly over Lovingkindess, which here is likened to water. It is the "summit of five *sefirot*," first to receive emanation among the five *sefirot* that constitute the Beauty and its retinue.

102. Repentance is a designation for the third *sefirah*.

103. Cf. *Bereshit Rabbah* 3:4, ed. Albeck, p. 20.

104. Beauty is often linked with the Torah, especially the written Torah.

105. R. Yitshak's work is a commentary to *Midrash Konen*, a mystical account of Creation from the eleventh or twelfth century.

106. The Jewish tradition posits that there are 613 commandments in the Torah. The four letters of the Hebrew word (T-V-R-H) have the numerical value of 611. By adding to this sum two outstanding commandments, it becomes possible to link the word *Torah* to the 613 commandments.

107. The sefirotic world is often described vertically as right ride, left side, and middle pillar. The right side is linked with the *sefirah* Lovingkindness (*hesed*), the left side, as we shall see, is linked with Strength/Severity (*gevurah/din*), and the middle pillar is associated with Beauty or Mercy (*tif'eret* or *rahamim*).

108. Yitshak the Blind uses the term Thought for the most supernal *sefirah*, which in later Kabbalistic traditions became known as Crown (*keter*). R. Yitshak employs the word "crown" as a synonym for degree, attribute, and *sefirah*.

109. *Mahtsev ha-teshuvah,* a reference to the *sefirah* Understanding (*binah*).

110. The first name was drawn from Lovingkindness. From the antithesis of Lovingkindness—Strength—a second name was drawn forth. Strength

is on the left side, and, in accordance with the imagery of severity, is associated with fire. (The more gentle Lovingkindness is associated with water.)

111. These angelic names are permutations of two words: "light" ('-V-R) and "face" (P-N).

112. These three lights correspond to three levels of creation. The first light brings forth a throne, resting on the *sefirot* Lovingkindness, Strength, and Mercy. This throne is in all likelihood *binah*, "Understanding." The second light brings forth the world to come, usually Foundation, here linked to Kingdom. The third light brings forth the physical "this-world" of creation.

113. The Written Torah is usually associated with Beauty/Mercy. From it a light was emanated, which formed the three "crowns" of Foundation, Endurance, and Majesty. The Oral Torah is linked with Kingdom, and secondarily with Severity and the world to come. The two Torahs, both juridically and mystically, are intertwined.

114. Here we see the release and freedom that the divine flow exerts on the lower, entrapped *sefirot*.

115. The sun is associated with Mercy, and the Moon with Kingdom. Also, Mercy is known as "the unreflecting mirror"; while Kingdom/Moon, reflecting the light of the sun, is called "the reflecting mirror." Prophecy comes through being illuminated by these spiritual lights.

116. Of course, this "Rabbi Yitshak" is none other than Rabbi Yitshak the Blind. [From this caveat it is clear that the copyist lacks clarity regarding the identity of the text's author.]

117. Usually understood by Kabbalists as referring to *malkhut*, the tenth *sefirah*, the feminine-receptive aspect of the Godhead.

118. *Shir ha-Shirim Rabbah* 6:12. The Song is thus sung by *tif'eret* and *malkhut*, bridegroom and bride within the Godhead.

119. The Glory is *tif'eret*, the masculine pole of creative energy in the realm of divine emanation.

120. Source of life (*mekor ha-hayyim*) and holy spirit (*ruah ha-kodesh*) generally symbolize *hokhmah* in Geronan sources.

121. Lit. *sibah* or cause.

122. The word *tovim* is plural: your love is an improvement upon the wine of *hokhmah* as it flows in multiple directions.

123. "Goodness" is the ongoing flow of light from lamp to lamp, the ceaseless flow of divine life, through the *sefirot* and into the world.

124. Points or students (*nekudot*). The term is used as well to designate the vowel signs that are placed above and below the consonants of the Hebrew alphabet and look very much like points (*nekudot*). R. Ezra will construct an elaborate exegetic pun on the multiple meanings of the term in which the studs (*nekudot*) of silver—the teachings of written Torah—will

serve as the animating force of the wreaths of gold—oral Torah—just as the vowels (*nekudot*) transform inert consonants into pliable words and living discourse.

125. See *Kohelet Rabbah* 8:11, where Rabbi Haninah interprets Zechariah 12:1 "God created (*yatsar*) humanity's spirit within it" as meaning that the spirit has been tied or bound up within the body in order to animate.

126. Concerning this verse, the Midrash states: "As for the Holy One, blessed be He, His name and might, when He declaims in enunciated speech, the sound is divided into seven voices." Divine speech creates the cosmogenerative septet ranging from *hesed* to *shekhinah*. However, it only becomes audible, giving rise to the differentiated cosmos and producing prophetic discourse through the aegis of *shekhinah*, the final rung in the chain of divine being.

127. Prayer shawl, a rectangular garment bearing fringes at its four corners.

128. The two versions of the Decalogue (Ex 20 and Deut 5) differ in the wordings of the Sabbath command. Exodus says "remember the Sabbath Day" and Deuteronomy says "keep." These are taken to refer to positive and prohibitive aspects of Sabbath observance, and then generalized to refer to positive and negative commandments altogether. For Kabbalists they also refer to the two *sefirot yesod* and *malkhut*.

129. [Rabbi Ezra follows with a list of all six hundred and thirteen commandments as they emerge from the Decalogue].

130. Or: from the mouth of *gevurah*, the God of power.

131. Perhaps we should read: "hewn out of"; *mi-shemo* rather than *bi-shemo*.

132. [The first verse of the *Shema'*.]

133. "Full" and "lacking," two ways of spelling Hebrew words.

134. *Tsaddik* or "the righteous" is *yesod*, the source of sefirotic energy as it flows into *shekhinah*.

135. No such interpretation is found in the extant rabbinic sources. It is also found, however, in *Zohar* 1:135b, a passage possibly dependent upon Ezra.

136. The three patriarchs represent *hesed*, *gevurah*, and *tif'eret*, the way-stations in the flow of life from Wisdom, the primal sefirotic font, to *shekhinah*.

137. Return to your safe haven of *halakhik* expertise.

138. Here the light imagery becomes that of wine. The primal flow is as perfect and undiminished as it was before creation, before flow through the seven primal "days."

139. A radically different and ironic reading. At the time of exile, the omnipresent divine "descends" as it were back into its recesses—the source

of creative manifestation—divine Wisdom, from whence it must be reinvoked through prayer and the performance of the commandments.

140. *Tif'eret*, the Beloved, "descends" from *hokhmah*, bringing sustenance for Himself and *shekhinah*, his garden.

141. Because of the cosmic exile, the *sefirot* turn "upward" and the *tsaddik*, the righteous one [*yesod*] is not nourished by them.

142. *Hesed, gevurah, tif'eret*, symbolized by the Patriarchs.

143. See Maimonides, *The Guide of the Perplexed*, I:58.

144. *Sefer Yetsirah* 1:4.

145. *Sefer Yetsirah* 1:4.

146. *Sefer Yetsirah* 1:4.

147. m. Avot 5:1. The word "statement" (*ma'amar*) also signifies *sefirah*.

148. Traditionally a very dark blue associated with sky-blue.

149. The twelfth and final question seeks to establish biblical and rabbinic proof texts for the positions taken in the answers to the first eleven questions. Much of what presently constitutes the published answer to the twelfth question was added to Rabbi 'Azriel's original composition.

150. A phrase from *Sefer Yetsirah* 1:6.

151. I.e., committing the heresy of separating between the *sefirot*.

152. *Yalkut Tehilm* 843; [cf. *Midrash Tehilim* 91].

153. [See b. Ketubot 110b–11a.]

154. b. Rosh ha-Shanah 17b.

155. Gershom Scholem discovered the writings of the Kohen brothers and published their works for the first time in 1926; see Scholem, "The *Kabbalot* of R. Jacob and R. Isaac," *Mada'ey ha-Yahadut* 1 (1926): 165–293 [Hebrew].

156. The demonic entity Sama'el figures prominently in Hekhalot literature. *The Alphabet of Ben Sira* (date uncertain, but pre-medieval) refers to Lilith as the rebellious first wife of Adam who transforms into a demon that harms infants. See Joseph Dan, "Sama'el, Lilith and the Concept of Evil in the Early Kabbalah," *AJS Review* 5 (1980): 17–40, esp. 19–21; and Gershom Scholem, "*Sitra Ahra*: Good and Evil in the Kabbalah," in *On the Mystical Shape of the Godhead*, trans. Joachim Neugroschel (Schocken Books: New York, 1991), 56–87, esp. 62–64.

157. y. Hagigah 2:1. This theme is found in the *Shi'ur Komah* literature and in *Sefer ha-Bahir* #142.

158. [*Bereshit Rabbah* 68:9.]

159. Cf. *Pesikta de-Rav Kahana* 145b. [See Alexander Altmann's discussion of this midrashic theme in "A Note on the Rabbinic Doctrine of Creation," *Journal of Jewish Studies* 7 (1956): 196–97.]

160. [Idel, *Absorbing Perfections*, 50–53.]

161. [Elsewhere Rabbi Yitshak has explained that evil worlds were emanated and subsequently destroyed, a kabbalistic expansion of *Bereshit Rabbah* 9:2. Afterward, the divine Will brought forth princes and angels, essentially pure but destructive and full of enmity. Sama'el is the first among them.]

162. [I.e., evil forces have been unleashed in the world.] See Dan, "Sama'el," 18–19.

163. [Earlier Rabbi Yitshak claims that Rabbi Sherira and Rabbi Hai Gaon, as well as some early Spanish rabbis, had a tradition going back all the way to Talmudic times that the earliest emanations, including the angels, are only spiritual forms and not corporeal entities. He says this is the argument of the philosophers, but that some other sages disagreed.

164. [See *Bereshit Rabbah* 8:1.]

165. [The work *Hekhalot Zutartei* as preserved makes no mention of this account of Lilith and Sama'el, and it is therefore likely that Rabbi Yitshak's chain of tradition is largely apocryphal. See Dan, "Sama'el," 25; and Verman, *Books of Contemplation*, 172–78.]

Chapter 2

1. For two excellent overviews of the *Zohar*'s mystical thought, see Scholem's chapter "The *Zohar*: The Theosophic Doctrine of the *Zohar*," in *Major Trends in Jewish Mysticism* (New York: Schocken Books, 1995), 205–43; and Arthur Green, *A Guide to the* Zohar (Stanford: Stanford University Press, 2004).

2. Yehuda Liebes, "Myth versus Symbol in the *Zohar* and Lurianic Kabbalah," in *Essential Papers on Kabbalah*, ed. Lawrence Fine (NYU Press: New York, 1995), 212–42; Michael Fishbane, *Biblical Myth and Rabbinic Mythmaking* (Oxford University Press: New York, 2003), esp. 253–305.

3. Yehuda Liebes, "*Zohar* and Eros," *Alpayyim* 9 (1994): 67–119 [Hebrew]; Melila Hellner-Eshed, *A River Flows from Eden: The Language of Mystical Experience in the* Zohar, trans. Nathan Wolski (Stanford: Stanford University Press, 2009), esp. 204–28; Green, "Intradivine Romance." On the broader question of erotic love, gender imagery, and power dynamics in Jewish mysticism, see the differing evaluations of Idel and Wolfson: Moshe Idel, *Kabbalah and Eros* (New Haven: Yale University Press, 2005); and Elliot R. Wolfson, *Circle in the Square: Studies in the Use of Gender in Kabbalistic Symbolism* (Albany: SUNY Press, 1995).

4. Eitan Fishbane, "Tears of Disclosure: The Role of Weeping in Zoharic Narrative," *The Journal of Jewish Thought and Philosophy* 11 (2002):

25–47; Aryeh Wineman, *Mystical Tales from the* Zohar (Philadelphia: Jewish Publication Society, 1997).

5. Jacob Katz, "Halakhic Statements in the *Zohar*," in *Divine Law in Human Hands: Case Studies in Halakhic Flexibility* (Jerusalem: Magnes Press, 1998), 9–30; Israel Ta-Shma, *Ha-Nigleh she'-ba-Nistar* (Tel Aviv: Hakibbutz Hameuchad, 1995) [Hebrew].

6. See Isaiah Tishby, "Prayer and Devotion in the *Zohar*," in *Essential Papers on Kabbalah*, 341–99; and Seth Brody, "Human Hands Dwell in Heavenly Heights: Contemplative Ascent and Theurgic Power in Thirteenth-Century Kabbalah," in *Mystics of the Book: Themes, Topics, and Typologies*, ed. Robert A. Herrera (New York: Peter Lang, 1993), 123–58.

7. Idel, *New Perspectives*, 212–18; Liebes, "*Zohar* as Renaissance," *Da'at* 46 (2001): 5–11 [Hebrew]; Wolfson, "The Hermeneutics of Visionary Experience: Revelation and Interpretation in the *Zohar*," in *Through a Speculum that Shines: Vision and Imagination in Medieval Jewish Mysticism* (Princeton: Princeton University Press, 1994), 326–92. The creativity at the heart of the *Zohar*'s mystical world is the theme of Hellner-Eshed's exemplary study, *A River Flows from Eden*.

8. Hellner-Eshed, *River Flows from Eden*, 202–3.

9. Rabbi Moshe de Leon wrote a number of less theologically creative mystical works in Hebrew. See Asi Farber-Ginat, "On the Sources of Rabbi Moses de Leon's Early Kabbalistic System," in *Jerusalem Studies in Jewish Thought* 3 (1983–84): 67–96 [Hebrew]; Eitan Fishbane, "Mystical Contemplation and the Limits of the Mind: The Case of 'Sheqel ha-Qodesh'," *The Jewish Quarterly Review* 93 (2002): 1–27; and Elliot Wolfson, *The Book of the Pomegranate: Moses de Leon's Sefer ha-Rimmon* (Atlanta: Scholars Press, 1988).

10. Gershom Scholem discussed the authorship of the *Zohar* at great length in *Major Trends*, 156–204. Scholem supported the antiquity of the *Zohar* at the beginning of his career, a position that he later retracted. See Scholem, "Did R. Moses de Leon Write the *Zohar*?," *Mada'ey ha-Yahadut* 1 (1926): 16–29 [Hebrew].

11. Liebes, "How the *Zohar* was Written," in *Studies in the* Zohar, trans. Arnold Schwartz, Stephanie Nakache, Penina Peli (Albany: State University of New York Press, 1993), 85–138.

12. For an exhaustive study of the history of the redaction and printing of the Zoharic literature and its implications, see Daniel Abrams, "The Invention of the *Zohar* as a Book," in *Kabbalistic Manuscripts and Textual Theory: Methodologies of Textual Scholarship and Editorial Practice in the Study of Jewish Mysticism* (Jerusalem and Los Angeles: Magnes Press and Cherub Press, 2010), 224–428.

13. See Boaz Huss, "*Sefer ha-Zohar* as a Canonical, Sacred, and Holy Text: Changing Perspectives on the Book of Splendor Between the Thirteenth and Eighteenth Centuries," *The Journal of Jewish Thought and Philosophy* 7 (1998): 257–307.

14. Aram. *millin de-hedyotei*. *Millin* has several meanings in this passage: words, things, matters. *Hedyotei* means "common, popular, ignoble." The phrase may be translated: "everyday matters." Cf. *Zohar* 3:149b, where the phrase refers to secular, ignoble stories of the Torah, in contrast to *millin kaddishin*, "holy words, holy matters."

15. A basic exegetical principle of the *Zohar*; cf. 2:55b: "There is no word in the Torah that does not contain many secrets, many reasons, many roots, many branches"; cf. 3:79b, 174b.

16. Heb. *gufei Torah*, "bodies of Torah." In the Mishnah this term denotes the essential teachings of Torah; See m. Hagigah 1:8: "Judgments and the laws of sacrifices, what is pure and impure, sexual immorality... these are gufei Torah"; cf. Tosefta Shabbat 2:10; m. Avot 3:23. Here the category is broadened to include all the commandments; cf. *Zohar* 2:85b.

17. According to the Midrash, the souls of all those not yet born were present at Sinai; see Shemot Rabbah 28:4; Tanhuma Yitro #11, Pirkei de-Rabbi Eli'ezer Ch. 41; cf. *Zohar* 1:91a. Here the *Zohar* implies that only the souls of mystics were actually present; perhaps only mystics are aware that they were present at Sinai.

18. The mystics see through the outer, physical layers of Torah, both her garments of stories and her body of commandments, into her soul. Real Torah, orayta mammash, is their sole object of study and contemplation. What this soul is becomes clear below.

19. Heb. *keneset yisra'el*, "Community of Israel." In earlier rabbinic literature this phrase denotes the people of Israel, the Ecclesia of Israel. In the *Zohar keneset yisra'el* refers to *shekhinah*, the divine counterpart of the people, that aspect of God most intimately connected with them. Here *shekhinah* is described as a divine body clothed by the heavens who receives the soul, a higher *sefirah*.

20. The masculine aspect of God is called *tif'eret yisra'el*, "the Beauty of Israel" (cf. Lam 2:1). *Shekhinah* receives Him as the body receives the soul.

21. This is not merely redundant. b. Yevamot 62a speaks of a cosmic body that contains all souls cf. Rashi, ad loc. Moses de Leon identifies this body with *shekhinah*; see his *Sefer ha-Mishkal*, 93; cf. *Zohar* 2:142a, 157a. *Shekhinah* receives the soul of *tif'eret* and thereby carries all human souls, which are engendered by the union of these two *sefirot*; see 1:13a 197a, 209a.

22. This refers not only to the immediately preceding lines but also to the preceding passage: "The wise ones...look only at the soul." The mystics gaze into the soul of Torah, which is none other than the *sefirah* of *tif'eret*. One of the names of this *sefirah* is the Written Torah, while *shekhinah* is called the Oral Torah. The hidden essence of Torah is God. The ultimate purpose of study is direct experience of the divine, who is real Torah; the search for meaning culminates in revelation. Cf. *Zohar* 2:60a, 90b; 3:9b; Scholem, *On the Kabbalah and Its Symbolism*, trans. Ralph Manheim (New York: Schocken Books, 1969), 37–50.

23. *Attika kaddisha*, the Holy Ancient One, is the primal, most ancient manifestation of *Ein Sof*, the Infinite, through *keter*, Its Crown, beyond both *shekhinah* and *tif'eret*. The phrase "soul of the soul" derives from Solomon ibn Gabirol (eleventh century: "You are soul of the soul" (*Keter Malkhut*); cf. *Zohar* 145a, 79a (Sitrei Torah), 103b, 245a; 2:156b; Zohar Hadash, Ruth 75a, 82c (Midrash ha-Ne'elam).

24. The literalists are not merely fools; they are wicked sinners, hayyavayya. The Zohar is referring here to radical rationalists who read the Torah critically and question its divine origin, thus undermining its authority.

25. The brilliance of the first *sefirah*, *keter*, the Crown. *Keter* is coeternal with *Ein Sof*.

26. Aram. *Botsina de-kardinuta*. *Botsina* means "lamp," but in the *Zohar* also "light" and "spark." *Kardinuta* offers a good example of the author's linguistic method. In conveying mystical secrets, he fashions words that conceal more than they reveal. *Kardinuta* is intended to evoke an image of darkness, *kadrut*. The spark is overwhelming, so bright and powerful that it cannot be seen. This blinding spark is the first impulse of emanation proceeding from *Ein Sof*, the Infinite, through keter. The goal of meditation is to attain this spark and participate in the flow of being; see Zohar Hadash, *Va-Ethanan*, 57d–58a.

27. The spark that is a vapor is also a band or cord (Aram. *meshiha*), referred to elsewhere in the *Zohar* as kav ha-middah, "the line of measure."

28. It is impossible to describe the spiritual nature of the breakthrough, so the act is stated and immediately denied; see Scholem's remarks on expressions of this kind in *Major Trends*, 166–177. The aura (or "ether" or "air"; Aram. *Avira*) is *Keter*; cf. *Zohar* 1:16b; 3:135b (Idra Rabba).

29. The flow of emanation manifests as a point of light. This is the second *sefirah*: *hokhmah*, Wisdom.

30. The Mishnah states that God created the world with ten commands. Only nine explicit commands appear in Genesis 1, but the decade is completed by counting the phrase "In the Beginning." See m. Avot 5:1, b. Rosh ha-Shanah 32a, Megillah 21b.

31. Heb. *Ha-Maskilim.* On the following pages of the *Zohar*, this term is applied to secret aspects of the alphabet and the *sefirot*; see 1:15b–16a. Elsewhere the *Zohar* employs the term to designate Kabbalists, masters of mediation. The citation of this verse here, at the beginning of the *Zohar* on Genesis, may also refer to them.

32. In the verse *Zohar* means "splendor, brilliance." Here the word designates the hidden power of emanation (see below) and suggests the title of the book; cf. *Zohar* 3:124b, 153b (Ra'aya Meheimna).

33. The purpose of emanation is to display the glory of the hidden God. This is achieved through a rhythm of revelation and concealment. The point expands into a circle, a palace; cf. Bereshit Rabbah 1:1. This palace is the third *sefirah*: *binah*, Understanding. She is the divine womb; the seed of holiness, another name for *hokhmah*, is sown inside Her. *Binah* will give birth to the seven lower *sefirot*, which bring about the rest of creation.

34. As the silkworm spins a cocoon out of its substance, so *hokhmah*, the point of Beginning, expands into the palace of *binah*. Cf. Bereshit Rabbah 21:5: "like the locust whose garment is of itself."

35. The human being mirrors the structure of divinity, the ten *sefirot*, in which masculine and feminine are balanced. The *sefirot* constitute the mystery of faith, *raza di-meimanuta*, the belief system of Kabbalah. See Bahir #82, *Zohar* 1:101b; 3:117a, 141b (Idra Rabba).

36. Cf. b. Bava Batra 74b: Rabbi Yehudah said in the name of Rav, "Everything that the Blessed Holy One created in His world He created male and female"; cf. *Zohar* 2:144b. Rabbi Shim'on's formulation does not appear in the Mishnah or the Talmud; he is referring to a secret, mystical Mishnah known only to him and his fellow Kabbalists.

37. Cf. b. Yevamot 62b: Rabbi Tanhum said in the name of Rabbi Hanilai, "Any man who does not have a wife is without joy, without blessing, without goodness." Cf. *Zohar* 1:165a; 3:74b.

38. Cf. b. Yevamot 63a. Rabbi Shim'on is also alluding to the original androgynous nature of Adam, a theme that informs the *Zohar*'s psychology and theosophy; see Bereshit Rabbah 8:1. The *Zohar* refers to this myth frequently; see *Zohar* 1:34b–35a, 37b. An essential component of the "mystery of faith" is that the *sefirot* realm is androgynous. *Tif'eret* and *shekhinah* are the masculine and feminine aspects of God, and the language of this myth is applied to them. From their union all souls are born, and these souls too, in their original nature, are androgynous. It is only because of Adam's sin that our androgynous nature has been lost. By joining together and engendering new life, each couple extends the chain of being. The inner purpose of human sexuality is to regain wholeness and manifest the oneness of God.

39. Cf. b. Hagigah 13b, and Bahir #130-31 [p. 8 Above].

40. Proverbs 31:10–31, which describes the "woman of valor," is understood by the *Zohar* as a hymn to *shekhinah*, the feminine aspect of God. Her husband is *tif'eret*, the Blessed Holy One, a more transcendent *sefirah*.

41. Imagination provides the human being access to God, though, as Rabbi Yehudah goes on to say, all imaginative representations fall short of God's true being.

42. Aram. *be-libbeih*. *Lev*, usually translated "heart," also means "mind" in the Bible.

43. The soul-breath, the spiritual essence of the human being.

44. The human *neshamah* is of divine origin: the Blessed Holy One is the essence of this essence. Here "Blessed Holy One" refers not to *tif'eret* but to *Ein Sof*, the Infinite, who becomes known through the *sefirot*.

45. *Shekhinah* is the opening of the divine tent, the first *sefirah* one encounters upon entering the divine realm. She is also called *tsedek*, Righteousness or Justice.

46. Cf. b. Sukkah 52b, Kiddushin 30b.

47. The demonic is the opposite of the holy. It is both masculine and feminine, Sama'el and Lilit. It moves back and forth between heaven and earth, demanding strict judgment from God and tempting human beings to sin.

48. The *shofar*, a ram's horn, is a device given to confound Satan. Cf. b. Rosh ha-Shanah 16a–b.

49. See Leviticus 16:7–22. The late Midrash Pirkei de-Rabbi Eli'ezer (Chap. 46) says: "They gave him [Satan] a bribe on Yom Kippur so that he would not interfere with Israel's sacrifice." Rabbi El'azar draws on the midrashic passage here and then alludes to his source with the formula: "This has been established." The *Zohar* returns to the same motif frequently. In several passages it suggest that by means of this device the demonic accuser is transformed into an advocate of Israel (1:174b, 3:102a; 203a).

50. The realm of the *sefirot*, the content of mystical faith and experience, the goal of Torah study.

51. From a mystical perspective, the holy and the demonic are the two sides of existence.

52. There is abundant erotic imagery in the *Zohar*, but this passage is unusual and daring. The feminine aspect of the demonic, Lilit, attempts to seduce God into lying with her so that she can obtain power (or "authority"; Aram. *reshu*). In the *Zohar* Joseph represents the *sefirah* of *yesod*, Foundation, which corresponds to the phallus in the human body (*Zohar* 2:258a, 3:296a). Joseph attained *yesod* as a result of his model behavior in this biblical narrative. By withstanding sexual temptation, he became the archetype of righteous conduct and self-control: Joseph the *tsaddik*, the Righteous (cf. b. Yoma 35b, and Prov 10:25: "the *tsaddik* is the *yesod* (foundation) of the world)."

Normally, the *sefirah* of *yesod* channels all divine energy to *shekhinah* (also called *malkhut*, "Kingdom"); it is through *yesod* that the union between *tif'eret* and *shekhinah* is consummated. Since *yesod*, i.e., Joseph, is the conveyor of power, Lilit tries to seduce Him. If she is successful, she will take the place of *shekhinah*, receive the potency of *Yesod* herself, and tyrannize the world (cf. 3:69a).

53. Rabbi Abba indicates that his own interpretation is not in conflict with that just offered by Rabbi El'azar. He is about to speak about psychological evil, the Deviser of Evil who works within the human being, rather than mythological evil, Lilit, who attempts to seduce man and God. But "it is all one path," above and below, Lilit and the Deviser of Evil.

54. Cf. Bereshit Rabbah 87:6, b. Yoma 35b.

55. Cf. b. Gittin 57a. Here Moses de Leon lashes out at the unbelievers of this time.

56. "To turn in *teshuvah*." *Teshuvah* means turning back to God, reorienting one's life to focus on the divine.

57. Cf. Bereshit Rabbah 22:6, 85:7.

58. m. Avot 6:2. While alluding to this tradition, Rabbi Yehudah goes on to create a new ancient tradition: "It has been taught..."

59. When one is about to die, as indicated in the verse: "The days of Israel drew near to die" (Gen 47:29).

60. To enter and experience higher dimensions of reality, one's soul must be clothed in a garment of splendor. Such a garment is woven out of days lived in goodness or out of the good deeds themselves (cf. *Zohar* 1:66a, 226b; 2:229b; 3:69a). Parallels appear in Islamic and Iranian eschatology and also in Mahayana Buddhism, where it is said of Buddha that upon attaining Nirvana "he has, as it were, a special body created from his good deeds." See Gershom Scholem, "The Paradisic Garb of Souls and the Origin of the Concept of Haluka de-Rabbanan," *Tarbiz* 24 (1955), 305 [Hebrew]; [see also Gershom Scholem, "Tselem: The Concept of the Astral Body," in *On the Mystical Shape of the Godhead*, trans. Joachim Neugroschel (Schocken Books: New York, 1991), 251–73.

61. What follows is a kabbalistic homily with no basis in the Mishnah. The *Zohar* employs this formula to conceal the recent character of the teaching and present it as ancient tradition.

62. Adam and Eve's sin was so great that their entire fabric of days was ruined.

63. According to the *Zohar*, Adam and Eve were originally clothed in garments of "light" (*or*, spelled with an *alef*), befitting their high spiritual nature. As a result of the primordial sin, they fell into a lower, physical form

and were clothed in garments of skin (*'or*, spelled with an *'ayin*). Cf. Bereshit Rabbah 20:12, *Zohar* 1:36b; 2:229b; 3:261b).

64. Heb. *ba ba-yamim*. The phrase is usually translated "advanced in days," "advanced in years." Literally, however, it means "came into days."

65. Job is a target of criticism in the *Zohar* because he denied resurrection and dared to question God's justice.

66. Jacob's life was the culmination of the days and lives of the Patriarchs. Upon his death, he was arrayed in the *sefirah* of *tif'eret*, Beauty, which harmonizes the *sefirot* of Abraham and Isaac, *hesed* and *gevurah*.

67. The primal, most ancient manifestation of *Ein Sof*, the Infinite, through *keter*, Its Crown.

68. Aram. *ze'eir anpin*, lit. "short faced," but meaning "short-tempered, impatient" (cf. Pro 14:17). The term designates the *sefirot* from *hokhmah* to *yesod*. *Keter*, the highest *sefirah*, is pure compassion and therefore described as *arikh anpin*, "long-faced, long-suffering, slow to anger" (cf. Ex 34:6). The lower *sefirot* are characterized by a tension between different aspects of the divine: right and left, love and rigor. Relative to *keter*, they are impatient.

69. *Shekhinah*. The apple trees are the *sefirot* from *hesed* to *yesod*, which fill Her. The image originates in the Talmud (b. Ta'anit 29b) as a midrashic comment on Genesis 27:27.

70. See b. Yoma 75b and RaMBaN on Exodus 16:6.

71. By being circumcised. Circumcision is a sign of the covenant with God, and according to the *Zohar*, the Jewish male who undergoes this rite achieves a mystical bond with the *sefirah* of *yesod* (*Zohar* 1:216a).

72. See Exodus 12:8, 34, 39. Matsah is a symbol of *shekhinah*, the first taste of the world of *sefirot*.

73. Heaven is a name of *tif'eret*, the divine partner of *shekhinah*.

74. The mystical Comrades, striving to attain wisdom, are nourished from the *sefirah* of Wisdom, *hokhmah*, which is even higher than Heaven (*tif'eret*), the source of manna. Now the meaning of the phrase above, "two balancing one," becomes surprisingly clear: the food of the comrades is twice as holy (not half as holy) as manna!

75. The Comrades penetrate to the essence of Torah, the roots of the Tree of Life. Climbing the ladder of *sefirot*, they contact the source of revelation, Primordial Torah: *hokhmah*, the *sefirah* of Wisdom.

76. The spark is the first impulse of emanation and revelation. See Exodus 32:16: "The tables were the work of God; the writing was the writing of God, engraved upon the tablets."

77. The numbers derive from the *gimatriyya* (numerical value) of the letters of *anokhi*. *Yod*, the final letter, is equal to ten; the other three letters (*alef*, *nun*, *khaf*) add up to seventy-one.

78. Cf. y. Shekalim 6:1: "The Torah that the Blessed Holy One gave to Moses was given to him thus: white fire engraved with black fire..." Cf. Mekhilta ba-Hodesh #9, Shir ha-Shirim Rabbah 1:13.

79. Silver and gold are often symbols of *hesed* and *gevurah*, the love and power of God. These two *sefirot* are balanced and refined in *tif'eret*, the voice of Y-H-V-H. This voice is transformed into speech through *shekhinah*, the mouth of the *sefirot*. The entire process can be imagined as the birth of divine language. At Creation, and again at Sinai, God manifests through the alchemy of letters.

80. The *Zohar* transforms the Talmudic simile, "One who receives the face of his friend (*havero*), it is as if he receives the face of *shekhinah*" (y. 'Eruvin 5:1), into a synonym for the *havrayya*, the mystical Comrades, who "are called the face of *shekhinah* because *shekhinah* is hidden within them. She is concealed and they are revealed" (*Zohar* 2:163b).

81. The rabbis of the *Zohar* often encounter donkey drivers who amaze them; see *Zohar* 1:5a–7a; 2:145b; 155b–157a; 3:21a–23a.

82. These riddles confuse not only Rabbi Yose; the cryptic language is intended to mystify the reader as well. Most of the images in the first two riddles allude to various stages in the process of *gilgul*, reincarnation, one of the most esoteric doctrines of the *Zohar*; see 2:99b–100a, 105b–106a; Scholem, *Kabbalah*, 344–50.

83. The bell appears as a symbol for divine inspiration in b. Sotah 9b.

84. The Old Man plus the two rabbis make a group of three who are joined together. This is one meaning of the Old Man's riddle. On another level, the riddle refers to three parts of the soul described later by the Old Man; see *Zohar* 2:100a.

85. The Old Man is about to reveal secrets of Torah; he begins by invoking divine protection and help. In the presence of the rabbis who have not proved themselves, he has some misgivings about the venture. The quotation also reflects Moses de Leon's own hesitancy to publish the secrets. For him, the human threat is posed by opponents of Kabbalah or by other Kabbalists who might disapprove of his undertaking.

86. The four adjectives allude to the four levels of meaning in Torah, which the Old Man describes below.

87. *Shekhinah*, the Rainbow, takes off her garment, the cloud, and gives it to Moses. Shielded by this cloud, he ascends the mountain and encounters the beyond. Cf. *Zohar* 1:66a, 2:229a; and b. Yoma 4a.

88. The "search" for meaning and interpretation. *Derashah* (or midrash) is the second level of meaning in Torah, after the literal sense. Through applying certain hermeneutical rules and with the help of imagination, the

midrashic method expands the meaning of the Bible. The rabbis of the Talmud employ midrash constantly to discover/invent new interpretations.

89. Aram. *millin de-hidah*, "words of riddle," e.g., the Old Man's riddles. *Hidah* also means "allegory" in medieval Hebrew, and the Old Man is referring to the allegorical method of interpretation prevalent among Jewish and Christian philosophers and sometimes to be found in the *Zohar*. Scholem, *On the Kabbalah*, 50–62. Here this method is called *haggadah*, "telling," expounding the Torah through allegory.

90. According to several rabbinic traditions, Torah existed before the creation of the world (Bereshit Rabbah 1:1, Va-Yikra Rabbah 19:1). "Primordial days" also alludes to the six *sefirot* from *hesed* to *yesod*, who are the six Days of Creation (*Zohar* 3:94b). They flow into *shekhinah* and transmit to Her the emanation of the "hidden ways," the thirty-two hidden paths of Wisdom.

91. One who is in love with Torah and has received her secret teachings is called her Husband (*ba'al torah vadda'i*). The phrase "master of the house" (*mar'ei de-veita*) elsewhere designates Moses (*Zohar* 1:236b), husband of *shekhinah*. Here it is applied to any mystic who has mastered the secrets of Torah.

92. The *peshat* is the plain meaning and is sometimes contrasted with deeper layers of meaning; see above, "How to Look at Torah." Here, instead of making contrasts, the Old Man points to the paradox of mystical study. The *peshat* is the starting point, the word on the page. As meaning unfolds, layer by layer, one encounters the face of Torah. This is revelation, enlightenment. But in Kabbalah, enlightenment leads back to the word; the *peshat* reappears as the upshot. One emerges from the mystical experience of the Torah with a profound appreciation of her form. Cf. the Zen koan: "First there is a mountain; then there is no mountain; then there is." By employing this hermeneutic of mystical literalness, Kabbalah bolstered tradition and resanctified the text, while simultaneously uncovering the countless interfaces between word and imagination.

93. Yeiva the Elder, who appears in b. Pesahim 103b; Bava Kama 49b.

94. Aram. *le-it'ara millin illein*. Heb. *hit'orer* means "to wake up." In medieval usage it means "to discuss, explain, deal with." The *Zohar* sometimes plays with the two meanings.

95. *Shekhinah* is the Sabbath Queen entering the palace of time on Friday evening at sunset. As the seventh *sefirah* below *binah*, *shekhinah* is the primordial seventh day, the hypostatization of the seventh day of the week. This secret of One is *tif'eret*, the Holy King, joined together with the *sefirot* surrounding Him. *Shekhinah* and *tif'eret* must each be whole before their union.

96. *Sitra ahra*, the demonic real, which threatens *shekhinah* on the weekdays. Once the Sabbath begins, however, She is safe and provides blessing openly to the world.

97. Once Sabbath has entered, the power of strict judgment disappears. According to b. Sanhedrin 65b, even the wicked in hell are granted rest on the Sabbath.

98. In the *Zohar*'s mythical drama, Israel helps prepare the Queen for union with the King.

99. According to b. Beitsah 16a, "The Blessed Holy One gives an extra soul to a human being on the eve of Sabbath. When Sabbath leaves, it is taken from him." The Jewish philosophers of the Middle Ages disregarded this teaching or reinterpreted it rationalistically. The *Zohar* revels in the literalness of the image and embellishes it. The extra soul enables Israel to leave behind the turmoil of the week and experience the joy of Sabbath.

100. In the *Zohar et* is a name for *shekhinah*, who expresses the fullness of divine speech, *alef* to *tav*: *et*. Here this interpretation is applied to the opening words of the Sabbath evening prayer, the *barekhu*. The mystical meaning is that Israel is blessing *shekhinah* first, and then Y-H-V-H. Crowning the Queen from below, Israel proclaims and initiates her union with the King, Y-H-V-H. This passage from the *Zohar* is recited in the Sephardic liturgy on Sabbath Eve as an introduction to the *barekhu*.

101. The *korban* is a sacrament, unifying all aspects of divinity and symbolizing the ascent of the human soul on the ladder of the sefirot.

102. Y-H-V-H, whose letters symbolize the entire range of *sefirot*. By drawing near all the *sefirot*, the *korban* unifies and spells out God's being. The *Zohar*'s emphasis on the cosmic role of *korban* is directed implicitly against Maimonides, who stated that the sacrifices were not pure divine service but rather a concession to Israel's idolatrous habits and environment (Guide of the Perplexed 3:32). The Kabbalists reacted strongly against his position, perceiving it as a rationalistic attack on tradition.

103. Y-H-V-H denotes the *sefirah* of *rahamim* (*tif'eret*), Compassion, while *Elohim* refers to *din*, Judgment. Rabbi Shim'on moves from exegesis to an impassioned plea to God and a directive to the Comrades on where to focus their meditation: on the name Y-H-V-H. This will ensure harmony and compassion, whereas contemplation on the name *Elohim* will draw down strict judgment.

104. *'Olah*, that which goes up, is a specific type of offering that is totally consumed by fire, producing "a pleasing aroma for Y-H-V-H." The *'olah* symbolizes *shekhinah*, who rises up to *binah*, the Holy of Holies, and thereby connects all the lower *sefirot* to their source.

105. The pure desire of one who engages in the ritual of *'olah* is joined to *shekhinah*. The three groups also represent three *sefirot*: *hesed*, *gevurah*, and *tif'eret*, who are elevated by the ritual.

106. And *Ein Sof*. The phrase can also be translated "infinitely." *Ein Sof* (lit. "there is no end") is the designation of the Absolute, God as infinite Being beyond the specific qualities of the sefirot. Rabbi Shim'on states that the bond of *'olah*, *shekhinah* encompassing the desire of those down below and the *sefirot*, ascends to *Ein Sof*.

107. *Keter*, the highest *sefirah*, borders on infinity and "cannot be counted." It is often referred to as Nothingness (*ayin*), through which all other *sefirot* emanate.

108. The second *sefirah*, the first that can in any way be perceived: *hokhmah*, Wisdom, the highest point.

109. The rabbinic concept of *'olam ha-ba* (Aram. *'alma de-atei*) is often understood as referring to the hereafter; it is usually translated as "the world to come." However, another interpretation is that "the world that is coming" is already in existence, occupying another dimension. The *Zohar* identifies *'alma de-atei* with the *sefirah* of *binah*, the Divine Mother, the Who of meditation. She is "the world that is coming, constantly coming and never stopping" (3:290b, Idra Zuta).

110. Both words have the same root: *shkhn*, "to dwell." *Shekhinah* is God's Indwelling Presence who accompanied Israel through the desert in the *mishkan*.

111. The Midrash invents this play on words. The Tabernacle constructed by Israel in the desert and the Temple in Jerusalem are both referred to as a *mishkan*, the dwelling place of God. But each is also a *mashkon*, a "pledge" offered by the people as a guarantee of their loyalty and observance of God's commands (Shemot Rabbah 31:9, 35:4; Tanhuma Pekudei #2). The *Zohar* adds the identification of *mishkan* with *shekhinah*. She is seized on account of Israel's sins and banished into exile.

112. We posses part of God's own being: His feminine half; this is his ultimate guarantee.

113. Cf. b. Megillah 29a: Rabbi Shim'on son of Yohai says, "Come and see how beloved Israel is to the Blessed Holy One: Wherever they went in exile, *shekhinah* was with them." This teaching is cited numerous times in the *Zohar* (1:211a, 2:2b, 82a, 3:66a, 90b, 297b).

114. The bed is a symbol of both intimacy and stability. *Shekhinah* is called Bed in the *Zohar*, indicating Her intimate relationship with *tif'eret*, the Blessed Holy One (2:48b, 51a, 3:118b).

115. In the *Zohar* a talmudic legend (see b. Berakhot 3b) is expanded into a ritual: all Kabbalists are expected to rise at midnight and adorn *shekhi-*

nah with words of Torah and song; see Scholem, *On the Kabbalah*, 146–50. This parallels the midnight vigil, common among Christian monks from early medieval times. *Zohar* 3:119a alludes to the Christian practice: "I have seen something similar among the nations of the world."

116. Cf. b. Bava Batra 75a. In the *Zohar* the moon is a symbol of *shekhinah*, and Joshua shares that symbol with her (*Zohar* 1:241b; 2:215a).

117. The parable and the analogy do not correspond. In the parable the pledge is the son, who guarantees the king's faithfulness and love for the queen. In the analogy the pledge is *shekhinah*, the Queen, who guarantees God's love for Israel, the son.

118. *Shir ha-Shirim Rabbah* 2:20–22.

119. b. Berakhot 34b.

120. Rabbi Shim'on urges the Comrades to deepen and stabilize their understanding of the secrets.

121. Maimonides cites this verse in the Introduction to Guide of the Perplexed as justification for his plan to reveal "concealed things." Here Rabbi Shim'on is about to reveal some of the deepest secrets of Kabbalah, and he opens with the same verse. The threat to tradition posed by unbelievers and radical rationalists demands a bold response.

122. Cf. m. Avot 2:20; m. Avot 6:2.

123. The Comrades are called Reapers of the Field frequently in the *Zohar*. Cordovero offers the following explanation of the name (*Or ha-Hammah* on 3:106a): "The Reapers of the Field are the Comrades, masters of this wisdom, because *malkhut* (*shekhinah*) is called the Apple Field, and She grows sprouts of secrets and new flowerings of Torah. Those who constantly create new interpretations of Torah are harvesting Her." *Shekhinah* is the source of inspiration and kabbalistic creativity. Yet even the Comrades have not succeeded in penetrating the secrets. They need the guidance of the Master, Rabbi Shim'on. For an analysis of the Idras, see Yehuda Liebes, "The Messiah of the *Zohar*," in *Studies in the* Zohar, trans. Arnold Schwartz, Stephanie Nakache, Penina Peli (Albany: State University of New York Press, 1993), 1–84.

124. Aram. *bei idra*. In Shir ha-Shirim Rabbah 5:7 the phrase "threshing floor (*idra*) of Torah" refers to an intensive study session. In the *Zohar idra* has a wide range of meanings: "threshing floor, room, assembly"; it is also a symbol of *shekhinah* and other *sefirot*. The *Zohar* refers to this particular section (3:127b–145a) or to the event as *Idra*, Holy *Idra*, Idra of Rabbi Shim'on. Later copyists and editors called it *Idra Rabba*, "The Great *Idra*," to distinguish it from another section (3:287b–296b) that they called *Idra Zuta*, "The Small *Idra*." [See "The Wedding Celebration," 70–74]

125. The Comrades are summoned to engage in the battle of Torah (cf. b. Shabbat 63a, Ta'anit 7a, *Zohar* 2:110a–b, 3:188a–189b).

126. The words indicate various *sefirot*. Design, *eita*, is associated with the highest *sefirah keter* (*Zohar* 3:133b). Wisdom Intellect and Knowledge appear in Exodus 35:31. They correspond to *hokhmah* and *binah*, the second and third *sefirot*, and *da'at*, which represents the hidden balancing power of the *sefirot*. Vision, *heizu*, refers to *shekhinah*, who reflects all the *sefirot*. The two Hands are *hesed* and *gevurah*, the arms of God; the two feet, *netsah* and *hod*, the legs of God. The Comrades are instructed to equip themselves with sefirotic powers in preparation for the battle of Torah.

127. Early rabbinic literature speaks of four rabbis who entered pardes ("orchard" and Paradise"), i.e., engaged in mystical contemplation on the divine chariot. Only Rabbi Akiva "entered in peace and emerged in peace" (t. Hagigah 2:4). The *Zohar* employs the phrase "one who has entered and emerged" to designate the Kabbalist who has entered the realm of the divine, discovered wisdom, and come out unscathed.

128. Before beginning to reveal the secrets of Divinity, Rabbi Shim'on cites this verse as a warning against taking his words and symbolic images literally. Such a misunderstanding would be tantamount to idolatry.

129. The Name Y-H-V-H must be recited with the proper *kavvanot* ("intentions," mystical awareness and focus). Otherwise, *tif'eret* (the Torah up above, the *sefirah* corresponding to Y-H-VH) is rendered incomplete.

130. *Atik yomin* (Dan 7:9) is a name of *keter*.

131. By means of a selective citation, Rabbi Shim'on begins to draw an analogy between his own circle and God. This is spelled out as he proceeds.

132. Cf. b. Sukkah 45b, Yerushalmi 9:3.

133. Rabbi Shim'on and his two close Comrades embody the three pillars of the sefirotic world: right, left and center. The seven other Comrades fill out the decade. By joining together to engage in secrets of Torah, Rabbi Shim'on and the Comrades correct the instability of the pillar (see above).

134. These words reflect Habakkuk's revelation of the stern manifestation of God, *ze'ir anpin*, the Impatient One, the realm of *sefirot* from *hokhmah* to *yesod*.

135. Rabbi Shim'on's revelation, now being introduced, derives from a higher aspect of Divinity, the realm of *keter*, above *ze'ir anpin*. Here there is nothing but love (*Zohar* 3:138b, 140b). There is no need to be afraid of revealing the secrets of this high realm; fear does not pertain. These verses are from Leviticus 19:18; Deuteronomy 6:5, 7:8, Malachi 1:2.

136. The White Head is *keter*, who is pure love and compassion, unattained by judgment (cf. Dan 7:9).

137. The blinding flash (*botsina de-kardinuta*) is the *Zohar*'s name for the first impulse of emanation proceeding from *Ein Sof*, the Infinite, through *keter*. The flash directs the entire process of emanation, providing its rhythm and measure. The goal of mediation is to attain this flash and participate in the flow of being. The spark is the first point, *hokhmah* (wisdom).

138. From *keter*, who is called *avira*, the "aura" of *Ein Sof*.

139. *Binah*, who proceeds from the spark of *hokhmah*.

140. The four sides (north, south, east, and west) symbolize four *sefirot* that emanate from *binah*: *din*, *hesed*, *tif'eret*, and *shekhinah*.

141. *Hokhmah* is absorbed by its source. It does not dissolve there but rather remains hidden and transmits the power of further emanation to *binah*.

142. *Din*, *gevurah*, the *sefirah* of Judgment.

143. *Hesed*, Love.

144. How can there be first above *Din*? The highest *sefirot* are not characterized by Judgment. *Binah*, the product of the spark of *hokhmah*, is the compassionate Divine Mother. However, she includes within Herself the roots of Judgment and gives birth to *din*, the *sefirah* of Judgment. 270 may be an allusion to *ra'*, "evil," which has the numerical equivalent of 270. According to Yitshak ben Ya'akov ha-Kohen, a contemporary of Moses de Leon, evil proceeds from *binah*. If 270 is an allusion to evil, then the number 370 above may allude to the 270 evil realms plus the 100 holy realms of the *sefirot*.

145. See b. Shabbat 88b; Pirkei de-Rabbi Eli'ezer, Ch. 34; *Zohar* 1:130b, 232a, 3:128b.

146. Pure love and compassion.

147. *Binah*, the skull. The *sefirot* below *keter*, from *hokhmah* to *yesod*, are referred to as the Impatient One (*ze'ir anpin*, lit. "short-faced" but meaning "short-tempered, impatient"). *Keter*, the White head, the highest *sefirah*, is pure compassion and therefore described as *arikh anpin*, "long-faced, long-suffering, slow to anger" (cf. Ex 34:6). The lower *sefirot* are characterized by a tension between different aspects of the divine: right and left, love and rigor. Relative to *keter*, they are impatient. Red is the color of Judgment.

148. The first part of the verse is pertinent: "Your dead will live! Corpses will arise! Awaken and shout for joy, you who dwell in the dust!"

149. *Shekhinah*.

150. When Judgment looms and the world needs compassion...

151. The Ancient of Days, *keter*, called *arikh anpin* ("long-suffering"). Looking back to His source, the Impatient One is soothed and manifests the compassion overflowing from *keter*.

152. The secrets disclosed here are divine revelation.

153. On the Sabbath 250 worlds are filled with joyous song (*Zohar* 2:88b).

154. According to rabbinic sources, Moses, Aaron, Miriam, and the three Patriarchs all died by a kiss from God, not through the Angel of Death (Shir ha-Shirim Rabbah 1:16, b. Bava Batra 17a; cf. Maimonides, Guide of the Perplexed 3:51, *Zohar* 1:125a). Here the *Zohar* confers this honor upon the three Comrades who died.

155. Their *devekut*, "cleaving" to God, assures the departed Comrades eternal life. The verse also applies to Rabbi Shim'on and the Comrades still with him who strive for *devekut*.

156. The chambers of the Heavenly Academy, where secrets are studied by angels and departed souls.

157. Thirteen rivers of Balsam await the righteous in the world that is coming.

158. The seven Comrades represent the seven divine powers that conduct the world and watch over it.

159. The six symbolize the *sefirot* from *hesed* to *yesod*. The seventh corresponds to *binah*, the Divine Mother, who sustains all seven lower *sefirot* and is called Seven.

160. The declaration of God's oneness that opens with the words: "Hear O Israel! Y-H-V-H is our God; Y-H-V-H is one" (Deut 6:4). Traditionally it is recited every morning and evening. The *Zohar* attaches cosmic significance to the *Shema'*.

161. The proper time to recite the morning *Shema'* is from the first traces of dawn until a quarter of the day has passed (m. Berakhot 1:2). In rabbinic law a ban, *niddui*, involves isolation from, and enforced contempt by, the community at large. Various offences are punishable by *niddui*, but failure to recite *Shema'* is not specified as one of them.

162. Cf. Avot de-Rabbi Natan Ch. 4, b. Ketubbot 17a. The rabbis may also be alluding to their mystical preoccupation with the union of the divine bride and groom, *shekhinah* and *tif'eret*. According to the *Zohar*, this union is the mystical purpose of reciting *Shema'* (*Zohar* 2:133b–134b).

163. b. Sukkah 26a.

164. He said the blessing for washing the hands before washing them (cf. b. Pesahim 7b). The accepted practice is to first wash and then bless.

165. Rabbi Shim'on, Master of the Comrades, who is occasionally referred to as Hasid, "pious one, devotee" (*Zohar* 3:166a–b, 169b).

166. Cf. b. Berakhot 53b, Sotah 4b.

167. Aram. *yanuka*, "suckling, infant, child." There are children like this one running throughout the *Zohar*, catching the rabbis unawares with their startling wisdom.

168. The ten fingers of the human hand symbolize the ten *sefirot*. Cf. Sefer Yetsirah 1:3, Bahir #124 [See p. 7 above].

169. When Moses held up his hands to defeat the Amalekites (Ex 17:8–16). That Moses raised his middle finger seems to be an invention of the child. The sefirotic symbolism is spelled out below: the middle finger corresponds to *tif'eret*, the *sefirah* of Moses. Thus by raising his middle finger, he invoked that *sefirah*.

170. The *mishkan*, the Tabernacle, in the desert, which for the *Zohar* is a symbol of the *sefirot* (2:221a); Tishby, *Wisdom of the* Zohar, 909–40.

171. The five bars represent the five *sefirot* from *hesed* to *hod*. The two on the right symbolize *hesed* and *netsah*; the two on the left, *gevurah* and *hod*. *Tif'eret* is the Center Bar, balancing the two sides. This central *sefirah* is associated with Jacob and Moses.

172. Cf. Bereshit Rabbah 15:6. Here the *Zohar* identifies the Tree of Life with *yesod*, and the five hundred years with the five *sefirot* referred to above, which provide *yesod* with the flow of emanation.

173. The Holy Covenant is *yesod*, which corresponds to the phallus and the covenant of circumcision.

174. The fingers transmit the blessing from the *sefirot*.

175. The Other Side, the Demonic, feeds on whatever is unclean.

176. [The child later reveals that he is the son of Rav Hamnuna Sava.] Rabbi Hamnuna the Elder was a Babylonia sage of the third century. In the *Zohar* he is frequently referred to as a great authority, and several original ritual acts are attributed to him; see 1:6a, 7b, 250a; 2:88a; 3:87b.

177. The account of Rabbi Shim'on's earlier illness is found in *Zohar Hadash*, *Bereshit*, 18d–19a (Midrash ha-Ne'elam).

178. Ahiyah was the prophet who revealed to Jeroboam that Solomon's kingdom would be divided (1 Kings 11:29–39). According to rabbinic tradition, he was a master of the secrets of Torah (b. Sanhedrin 102a) and the teacher of Elijah (y. Eruvin 5:1). Later, Hasidic legend portrays him as the mentor of Yisra'el Ba'al Shem Tov, the founder of Hasidism.

179. This phrase appears frequently in the *Zohar* in the context of mystical or prophetic vision. Here it conveys he image of seeing *shekhinah* before one's death. See *Zohar* 1:65b, 79a, 226a, 245a; 3:88a.

180. When it was decreed that Rabbi Yitshak was to die, Rabbi Shim'on interceded with God and saved his life, pledging himself as surety (1:217b–218b). Now it is time for Rabbi Yitshak to depart along with Rabbi Shim'on.

181. During the assembly at the threshing house, six of the Comrades proved their mystical ability and stamina. Three others died from the over-

whelming power of the revelations. Now the experienced Comrades are invited to hear Rabbi Shim'on's final words.

182. Lit. "Silence," the silence of death (Ps 94:17). In the Talmud Dumah is the name of the angel of souls after death (b. Berakhot 18b, Shabbat 152b, Sanhedrin 94a). In the *Zohar* he sometimes retains this function but also appears as the Prince of Hell.

183. *Tif'eret*, the central *sefirah*, less concealed than the Holy Ancient One.

184. The primal and most ancient manifestation of *Ein Sof*, the Infinite, through *keter*, Its Crown.

185. Aram. *hillula*. In the Talmud the word means "wedding celebration" (b. Berakhot 30b–31a). In the *Zohar* this literal meaning recurs (3:94b). The word is also applied to a circumcision celebration (1:93a), perhaps because circumcision initiates the male into an intimate relationship with *shekhinah* (1:8a–8b, 216a). In a number of passages *hillula* describes the *hieros gamos*, the sacred marriage between *tif'eret* and *shekhinah* (inter alia, 1:10a, 3:66b). The occasion of Rabbi Shim'on's death is also a wedding celebration: his soul is about to ascend and unite with *shekhinah*. By the sixteenth century, it was customary to visit the grave of Rabbi Shim'on at Meron in the Galilee on Lag ba-'Omer [the thirty-third day of the period between Passover and Shavu'ot.]. This was a ritual of celebration, not mourning, and became known as Hillula de-Rabbi Shim 'on bar Yohai. See Morris M. Faierstein, "The Kabbalistic Background of Some Lag ba-Omer Customs," *Conservative Judaism* 63 (2012): 73–77; and Boaz Huss, "Holy Place, Holy Time, Holy Book: The Influence of the *Zohar* on Pilgrimage Rituals to Meron and the Lag be-Omer Festival," *Kabbalah* 7 (2002): 237–56 [Hebrew].

186. Both of these verses appear elsewhere in the *Zohar* to describe the flow of emanation. The first one is cited over fifty times (inter alia, 1:34a, 35b, 2:83a, 3:65b).

187. Aram. *botsina 'ila'ah*. Above, this phrase denotes Rabbi Shim'on. Here it denotes the Holy Ancient One, the primal manifestation of *Ein Sof* through *keter*, the highest *sefirah*.

188. The *Zohar* carefully avoids the common kabbalistic term *sefirot*; see Scholem, *Kabbalah*, 229.

189. The *sefirot* are God's Name, the expression of Its being.

190. Through meditation, one discovers the ultimate reality of the High Spark. The *sefirot*, levels of enlightenment, are stages on the path to this realization and are finally seen to have no independent existence.

191. Rabbi Shim'on's death has thrown all of nature into chaos (cf. *Zohar* 3:296a). Rabbi El'azar may also be alluding to the holy animals carry-

ing the divine throne and the birdlike angels who will flee to the Great Sea of *shekhinah* (2:48b–49a).

192. This bizarre image is apparently meant to convey the Comrade's misery. An allusion to Christian beliefs should also be considered; the doctrine of transubstantiation had been defined at the Fourth Lateran Council in 1215.

193. The root TaRaQ means "to sting, bite"; in the *Zohar* it usually describes powers of harsh judgment (2:244a; 3:291b). The shield-bearing warriors are of a similar nature. Here the warriors are not powers from beyond but mighty Torah scholars from Sepphoris who want Rabbi Shim'on buried in their city, famed for its learning.

194. Reading *kol be-Ramah* ("a voice in Ramah") as *kol be-ruma* ("a voice in the heights").

195. Referring to the mixed multitude, held responsible for the sins of Israel in the wilderness. See Proverbs 30:23.

Chapter 3

1. The best single-volume study of the mystical world of Safed is Lawrence Fine, *Physician of the Soul, Healer of the Cosmos: Isaac Luria and his Kabbalistic Fellowship* (Stanford: Stanford University Press, 2003). For a dated but still useful article describing the unique spiritual atmosphere of this period, see Solomon Schechter, "Safed in the Sixteenth Century," *Studies in Judaism* 2 (Philadelphia: Jewish Publication Society of America, 1908), 202–306. On the connections between the Sephardic exile and Safed renaissance, see Morris M. Faierstein, "Safed Kabbalah and the Sephardic Heritage," in *Sephardic and Mizrahi Jewry: From the Golden Age of Spain to Modern Times,* ed. Zion Zohar (New York: New York University Press, 2005), 196–215.

2. There are two excellent overviews of the technical aspects of the kabbalistic systems of Safed in English. See Gershom Scholem, "Isaac Luria and His School," in *Major Trends in Jewish Mysticism* (New York: Schocken Books, 1995), 244–86; and Fine, *Physician of the Soul,* esp. 41–77, 124–49.

3. See Mordechai Pachter, "*Devequt* in Sixteenth Century Safed," in *Roots of Faith and Devequt: Studies in the History of Kabbalistic Ideas* (Los Angeles: Cherub Press, 2004), 235–316.

4. See Gershom Scholem, "Tradition and New Creation in the Ritual of the Kabbalists," in *On the Kabbalah and Its Symbolism,* trans. Raphael Manheim (New York: Schocken Books, 1969), 118–57. For a recent study of the spread of these mystical rituals, see Morris M. Faierstein, *Jewish Customs*

of Kabbalistic Origin: Their History and Practice (Boston: Academic Studies Press, 2013).

5. See Arthur Green, "Some Aspects of Qabbalat Shabbat," in *Sabbath—Idea, History, Reality*, ed. Gerald J. Blidstein (Beer Sheva: Ben Gurion University of the Negev Press, 2004), 95–118.

6. On the *hanhagot* literature and its importance in the diffusion of Kabbalah, see Zeev Gries, "The Fashioning of *Hanhagot* (Regimen Vitae) Literature at the End of the Sixteenth Century and During the Seventeenth Century and its Historical Significance," *Tarbiz* 56 (1986–87): 527–81 [Hebrew].

7. See Rabbi J. Zwi Werblowsky's study of Rabbi Karo's spiritual life *Joseph Karo, Lawyer and Mystic* (Philadelphia: Jewish Publication Society of America, 1977).

8. On the phenomenon of spirit possessions in Jewish history, see J. H. Chajes, *Between Worlds: Dybbuks, Exorcists, and Early Modern Judaism* (Philadelphia: University of Pennsylvania Press, 2003).

9. On Cordovero's life and teachings, see Bracha Sack, *Be-Sha'arei ha-Kabbalah shel Rabbi Moshe Kordovero* (Be'er Sheva: Ben Gurion University Press, 1995) [Hebrew]. For a study of Cordovero in English, see Zohar Raviv, *Decoding the Enigma: The Life, Works, Mystical Piety and Systematic Thought of Rabbi Moses Cordoeiro* (Saarbruecken: VDM, Verlag Dr. Mueller, 2008).

10. Several of Cordovero's smaller works are now available in English: Ira Robinson, *Moses Cordovero's Introduction to Kabbalah: An Annotated Translation of His Or Ne'erav* (Hoboken, NJ: KTAV Publishing House Inc., 1994); and *The Palm Tree of Deborah*, trans. Louis Jacobs (New York: Sepher-Hermon Press, 1981).

11. Bracha Sack, "The Influence of Cordovero on 17th-century Jewish Thought," in *Jewish Thought in the Seventeenth Century*, ed. Isadore Twersky and Bernard Septimus (Cambridge, MA: Harvard Univeristy Press, 1987), 365–79.

12. An exemplary study of the blend of kabbalistic allusions and rabbinic motifs found in the hymn is Reuven Kimelman's *Kabbalat Shabbat ve-Lekha Dodi: Ha-Mashma'ut ha-Mistit* (Jerusalem and Los Angeles: Magnes Press and Cherub Press, 2003) [Hebrew]; forthcoming English translation: *The Mystical Meaning of Lekha Dodi and Kabbalat Shabbat* (Littman Library of Jewish Civilization, July 2015).

13. On this understudied yet highly influential figure, see Kalman P. Bland, "Issues in Sixteenth-Century Jewish Exegesis," in *The Bible in the Sixteenth Century*, ed. David C. Steinmetz (Durham, NC: Duke University Press, 1990), 50–67. This article also discusses the sermons of Rabbi Yosef Karo and Rabbi Moshe Cordovero.

14. On Luria's self-image as a kabbalistic leader in the style of Rabbi Shim'on bar Yohai, see Yehuda Liebes, "'Two Young Roes of a Doe': The Secret Sermon of Isaac Luria Before His Death," *Jerusalem Studies in Jewish Thought* 10 (1992): 113–69 [Hebrew]; and Fine, *Physician of the Soul,* 322–30.

15. For an analysis of these interesting hagiographical traditions, see Eitan P. Fishbane, "Perceptions of Greatness: Constructions of the Holy Man in *Shivhei ha-Ari,*" *Kabbalah* 27 (2012): 195–222.

16. See Scholem, *Major Trends*, 260–64; Fine, *Physician of the Soul*, 128–31. See also Idel, "On the Concept of *Zimzum* in Kabbalah and its Research," *Jerusalem Studies in Jewish Thought* 10 (1992): 59–112 [Hebrew].

17. Fine, *Physician of the Soul*, 151–68.

18. Rabbi Yisra'el Sarug and Rabbi Yosef ibn Tabul were also important students of Luria who wrote down their master's teachings. Sarug was an Italian Kabbalist active in the 1590s; see Fine, *Physician of the Soul*, 361n1; and Sharron Shatil, "The Kabbalah of R. Israel Sarug: A Lurianic-Cordoverian Encounter," *Review of Rabbinic Judaism* 14 (2011): 158–87. Ibn Tabul was one of Luria's closest disciples, and Vital saw him as a rival and sought to suppress his writings from becoming part of the Lurianic corpus. See Fine, *Physician of the Soul*, 126–28, 342–45, and 391n2.

19. See Michael Oron, "Dream, Vision and Reality in Hayyim Vital's *Sefer ha-Hezyonot,*" *Jerusalem Studies in Jewish Thought* 10 (1992): 299–309; and J. H. Chajes, "Accounting for the Self: Preliminary Generic-Historical Reflections on Early Modern Jewish Egodocuments," *The Jewish Quarterly Review* 95 (2005): 1–15.

20. On the various summaries of *Reshit Hokhmah*, see Mordecai Pachter, "Elijah de Vidas' *Beginning of Wisdom* and Its Abbreviated Versions," *Kiryat Sefer* 47 (1972): 686–710 [Hebrew].

21. The idea that the mystic's heart is God's true dwelling place is a typically Sufi notion. R. J. Zwi Werblowsky suggests that "it is quite obvious that those among the Safed authors who used this language drew heavily upon such writings of earlier Kabbalists as have, in fact, absorbed Sufi influence." See his *Joseph Karo, Lawyer and Mystic* (Philadelphia: Jewish Publication Society of America, 1977), 58.

22. The *'amidah* (lit. "standing prayer") refers to the "Eighteen Benedictions," the central part of Jewish prayer.

23. This is a typical rabbinic sentiment. Cf. Bava Batra 10a.

24. This custom appears to foreshadow an important characteristic of spirituality associated with the Hasidic movement. This is the idea known as *'avodah be-gashmiyut*, according to which a person is called upon to transform material or physical activities, such as eating and drinking, into con-

templative moments. Drink-offering refers to many kinds of scripturally enjoined Temple offerings.

25. R. Avraham Galante (dates unknown) was a prominent disciple of Moses Cordovero.

26. [This rule is one of the earliest witnesses to the practice of treating the day before the New Moon as *yom kippur katan*, a minor Day of Atonement. The language Galante employs makes it clear that his proscription is addressed to the greater Safed community, not just an elite mystical fellowship.]

27. According to rabbinic law, there are four different means of administering capital punishment, dependent on the nature of the transgression involved: stoning, burning, decapitation, and strangulation, the details of which may be found in m. Sanhedrin 7:1.

28. Cf. b. Yoma 19b.

29. The injunction concerning the Sabbath found in Exodus 20:8 begins, "*Remember* the Sabbath day to keep it holy," while in Deuteronomy 5:12 it reads, "*Observe* the Sabbath day...." According to rabbinic tradition (b. Shevu'ot 20b) both forms were miraculously communicated by God simultaneously.

30. "Beloved" refers, according to some commentators, to the *sefirah tif'eret*.

31. According to Jewish tradition, the Messiah will be a descendant of King David, the son of Jesse, of Bethlehem.

32. The imagery and wording in this and the following stanzas draw on the second part of Isaiah.

33. King David was descended from Perez through the biblical character Boaz (Ruth 4:18–22).

34. This moral obligation is based on an injunction in Deuteronomy 24:15 that requires one to pay a hired servant what he is owed before sundown.

35. This appears to reflect the Talmudic teaching: "A man should always eat and drink less than his means allow, clothe himself in accordance with his means, and honor his wife and children more than his means allow..." (b. Hullin 84b).

36. The figure of supernal Adam, or primordial man (*adam kadmon*), refers to that initial configuration of divine light which flowed from within the deepest recesses of the Godhead into the space left after *tsimtsum*. *Tikkun* can be conceived of as the restoration of this first and highest form to its original state of being.

37. b. Kiddushin 30a teaches that one should divide his study into three parts: Scripture, Mishnah, and Talmud, that is, Gemara. [It is of note here that Kabbalah has been entered into the daily curriculum.]

38. [Rabbi Avraham ben Eliezer ha-Levi Berukhim was a Moroccan-born Kabbalist who became a close disciple of Luria. He was an associate of both Eliyahu de Vidas and Hayyim Vital.]

39. The term *kelippah* is a technical one in Lurianic Kabbalah, referring to the realm of the material in which the fallen sparks of divine life have become trapped. This text, along with the next two, suggests a highly interesting theory concerning the role played by the logical puzzle (*kushia*) characteristics of rabbinic legal discourse. It serves as a mask or barrier separating an individual from the holy light which lies at the heart of all things. In this case, the hidden inner core is defined as the esoteric or kabbalistic interpretation of the Torah. Far from rejecting the study of Jewish law, the mystic Luria virtually transforms the study of *halakhah* into an esoteric activity.

40. The custom of reading the Torah portion in Hebrew and Aramaic in anticipation of the coming Sabbath is mentioned in b. Berakhot 8a.

41. The "extra holiness" refers to the notion that every individual is invested with an additional soul on the Sabbath.

42. Aram. *hakal tappuhin kaddishin*, alluding to *shekhinah*.

43. The use of myrtles on the Sabbath drew its inspiration from a Talmudic story (b. Shabbat 33b).

44. Rabbinic custom requires making a blessing over two Sabbath loaves known as *hallah* at the festive meal. Luria deviated from this tradition out of desire to have his table resemble "the table of show-bread" in the Temple on which twelve loaves were arranged in two rows of six. [The passage not included here gives their precise arrangement.]

45. Meron is a short distance from Safed and is held to be the gravesite of R. Shim'on bar Yohai and his son El'azar. [See above, "The Wedding Celebration," 70–74]. It is also believed that Lag be-Omer, the thirty-third day of the *'Omer*, is the date of R. Shim'on bar Yohai's death, helping to account for the custom of visiting Meron on this day. It is customary not to have the hair cut during the *'Omer* except on Lag be-'Omer because of its festive character. Even today, in Israel, a great celebration is held at Meron on this holiday.

46. This invocation points to the sacred action that is represented by the meal, and calls for *shekhinah* to share the meal with Her Bridegroom *tif'eret* as well as the Holy Ancient One. The Sabbath morning meal, celebrated following the morning prayers, focuses on the "Holy Ancient One." The final meal, celebrated in the late afternoon as the Sabbath begins to wane, focuses on the "Impatient."

47. The Sabbath table is prepared for *shekhinah*.

48. Her Husband *tif'eret* (or "Impatient") embraces her.

49. The unification of Bride and Bridegroom causes the forces of impurity to depart and the power of holiness to emerge; the Sabbath revitalizes the soul.

50. The union of Bride and Bridegroom results in the creation of new souls. The thirty-two paths refer to the thirty-two paths of Wisdom mentioned in *Sefer Yetsirah*. The three branches are *hesed, din* and *tif'eret*, the three main pillars of the sefirotic realm.

51. That is, six on each side.

52. The sacred action carried out on the Sabbath incapacitates all evil.

53. Many of the footnotes are based on the notes in the Hebrew edition edited by A. Z. Aescoli. There are indicated by [A].

54. Soniadora means female dreamer in Spanish. [Fine points out that the example of Soniadora suggests that there may have been other such charismatic and spiritually talented women in sixteenth-century Safed; see *Physician of the Soul*, 120–23.]

55. [A] This passage is related to *Shir ha-Shirim Rabbah* 1:8. However, it is a different version.

56. On witchcraft and impotence, see Idel, *Kabbalah*, 81n43.

57. See Idel's analysis of the relationship of crying and revelation, as it relates to this dream in *Kabbalah*, 81–88. [See also Eitan Fishbane, "Tears of Disclosure; The Role of Weeping in Zoharic Narrative," *The Journal of Jewish Thought and Philosophy* 11 (2002): 25–47.]

58. This refers to the practice started by the Kabbalists of Safed to go out into the field to welcome the "Sabbath Queen" at the beginning of the Sabbath.

59. The concept of wool extinguishing heavenly fire is found in *Tanhuma*, Va-Yishlah #2.

60. This is a technical term found in earlier kabbalistic literature referring to exoteric scholars who are not Kabbalists. See Pinhas Giller, *The Enlightened Will Shine: Symbolization and Theurgy in the Later Strata of the* Zohar (Albany, NY: State University of New York Press, 1993), 71–74.

61. This term can be understood in two ways. Normally, it means "men of sublime spirituality" or spiritual elite. However, it can also be translated literally as "sons of the attic" or "upper story." In both cases it refers to Kabbalists.

62. b. Sanhedrin 92b; see also *Zohar* 1:12b.

63. A paraphrase of the prayer of R. Alexanderai in b. Berakhot 17a.

64. [On the circumstances of Luria's death, see Fine, *Physician of the Soul*, 340–53.]

65. [It is telling that in Vital's vision even Cordovero admits that Luria's kabbalistic teachings are the highest order of mystical knowledge.]

66. [A] The intention is clear. Luria would repair Vital alone and Vital would repair the others.

67. *Aravot* is the seventh heaven.

68. [A] Vital is the Italian and Vidal the Spanish translation of the name "Hayyim," meaning "life." The *Maggid Mishneh* is one of the important commentaries on Maimonides' legal compendium *Mishneh Torah*.

69. Animus, Spirit, and Soul are the three parts of the Soul. I have consistently used these terms for their Hebrew equivalents. This tripartite division of the Soul is already found in the *Zohar*. See Tishby, *Wisdom of the* Zohar, vol. 2, 684–98.

70. Lit. "great assembly," the section of the *Zohar* which records a gathering of Rabbi Shim'on bar Yohai and his disciples.

71. [Communing with departed sages by prostrating at their graves was an important ritual for the Safed mystics. See Jonathan Garb, "The Cult of the Saints in Lurianic Kabbalah," *The Jewish Quarterly Review* 98 (2008): 203–29.]

72. The number 613 refers to the number of biblical commandments. According to R. Simlai, "613 commandments were revealed to Moses on Sinai, 365 prohibitions equal in number to the solar year and 248 positive commandments equal to the limbs of the human body" (b. Makkot 23a). Later the meaning of the number 365 was changed to refer to the number of sinews and blood vessels in the human body.

73. 600,000 is the traditional rabbinic number for the Israelites present at Sinai.

74. [Cain and Abel are the shoulders of *adam kadmon*. To some extent they represent good and evil, but each one is an admixture of both positive and negative forces. Cain is paradoxically the greater of the two, since although his source possesses less goodness, it is of a superior quality and it is from his source that the Davidic Messiah will arise. See Fine, *Physician of the Soul,* 333–41.]

75. The age at which one becomes an adult in the Jewish tradition.

76. Vital-soul (*nefesh*), spirit (*ruah*), and super-soul (*neshamah*) are three aspects of the soul. The lowest grade of the soul is the *nefesh*; every individual is inherently endowed with this quality of soul. The other two aspects, however, *ruah* and *neshamah*, are latent within a person and need to be activated. The *neshamah* is aroused and enlivened when a person prays with appropriate kabbalistic intention, studies Torah, and observes the commandments properly. The activities assist in the development of the higher intuitive powers of cognition and represent the fullest maturation of the soul. See *Zohar* 1:83b; 2:141b.

77. According to kabbalistic tradition, Adam and Eve wore "garments of light" (*kotnot or*) prior to their commission of sin. It is this garment, "woven" by one's righteous deeds, that the soul wears once again following death.

78. Evil shells, *kelippot*, refer to the realm of materiality and evil.

79. That is, the evil forces, the powers of strict judgment are placated or overpowered by virtue of the study of Torah. At the same time such devotion constitutes a means of repentance.

80. [De Vidas later writes the *keter* shows humility before its Source (*Ein Sof*) by descending in order to sustain the worlds.]

81. Rabbinic tradition understands these as thirteen attributes of divine compassion that are to be recalled during prayer (b. Rosh ha-Shanah 17b). The Kabbalists also speak of thirteen higher attributes that belong to the *sefirah keter*, in which there is no element of divine judgment whatsoever.

82. Generally, *neshamah*, the highest part of the soul, is considered to derive from *binah*, although some Kabbalists taught that its source is *hokhmah*.

83. The Tree of Life corresponds to the right side of the sefirotic structure, the side of divine mercy. According to the *Ra'aya Mehemna* and *Tikkunei Zohar*, whereas during the period of exile the world is dominated by the Tree of Good and Evil, in the time of the redemption dominion will pass over to the Tree of Life.

84. This refers to a technique of calculating the numerical value of Hebrew words and discounting the tens or hundreds.

85. The situations in which *shekhinah* and the individual find themselves are parallel to one another; each must be divested of evil and impurity.

86. These two rabbinic phrases are intended to teach that a person must not have in mind a woman other than the one with whom he is making love. Similarly, a person must have only *shekhinah* in mind so as to cleave to Her.

87. [Rabbi Yitshak of Akko was an important thirteenth and fourteenth century Kabbalist. Born in the land of Israel, he traveled to Spain in search of the origins of the *Zohar*. Rabbi Yitshak studied with some of the greatest Talmudic scholars and mystics in Iberia and North Africa, and his works bring together and preserve an array of different mystical traditions. While he often tries to harmonize disparate teachings, Rabbi Yitshak's are a valuable window into the transmission of early Kabbalah. See Eitan P. Fishbane, *As a Light Before Dawn: The Inner World of a Medieval Kabbalist* (Stanford: Stanford University Press, 2009).]

88. According to the *Zohar*, when a man is with his wife, her presence ensures his attachment to *shekhinah*. During time of separation from his

wife, the study of Torah suffices to sustain his relationship to *shekhinah* See, for example, *Zohar* 1:49b. [Cf. b. Ketubot 62b].

89. De Vidas is almost certainly referring to Yitshak Luria, who was well known for having such abilities.

90. "Practical" Kabbalah refers to purely motivated "white" magic, usually having to do with the manipulation of various esoteric names of God. The Kabbalists were wary of engaging in such activity, except in the case of the most pure and highly qualified persons.

91. The "Verses of Praise" (*pesukei de-zimra*) are biblical verses that are recited prior to the beginning of the formal prayer service.

92. [According to b. Gittin 7a and Sotah 48a, music was forbidden after the destruction of the Temple.]

93. Of course, Europe and the Mediterranean were home to a number of prominent Kabbalists even before the arrival of Cordovero's and Luria's teachings. For example, Rabbi Yehudah Leib of Prague (MaHaRaL, 1520–1609) was a towering rabbinic figure well versed in Jewish mysticism, but there is no clear evidence that he was influenced by Safed Kabbalah. On his relationship to Jewish mysticism, see Roland Goetschel, "The Maharal of Prague and the Kabbalah" in *Mysticism, Magic and Kabbalah in Ashkenazi Judaism*, ed. K. E. Grözinger and J. Dan (Berlin and New York: Walter de Gruyter, 1995), 172–80.

94. See Rabbi Menahem 'Azaria's *Peleh ha-Rimon* (1600), a digest of Cordovero's theology often printed together with *Pardes Rimmonim*, and Rabbi Avraham Azulai's widely-read *Hesed le-Avraham* (1685).

95. In the past twenty years, scholars have made significant progress in charting the evolution and dissemination of Lurianic Kabbalah. See Yosef Avivi, *Kabbala Luriana*, 3 vols. (Jerusalem: Ben Zvi Institute, 2008) [Hebrew]; Gershon Hundert, *Jews in Poland-Lithuania in the Eighteenth Century* (Berkeley and Los Angeles: University of California Press, 2004), 119–59; Moshe Idel, "'One from a Town, Two from a Clan': The Diffusion of Lurianic Kabbala and Sabbateanism: A Reexamination," *Jewish History* 7, no. 2 (1993): 79–104; and Ronit Meroz, *Torat ha-Ge'ulah be-Kabbalat ha-Ari*, PhD diss., Hebrew University, Jerusalem, 1988 [Hebrew].

96. For example, see the works *Emek ha-Melekh* by Rabbi Naftali Bachrach (seventeenth century), and *Megaleh 'Amukot* by Rabbi Natan Nata Spira (1585–1633). See also Sharron Shatil, "The Doctrine of Secrets of *Emeq Ha-Melech*," *Jewish Studies Quarterly* 17 (2010): 358–95.

97. It is rather curious that, despite his obvious importance and influence, Horowitz's life and teachings have been the subject of rather few recent studies. For a biography, see Eugene Newman, *Life and Teachings of Isaiah Horowitz* (London: E. Newman, 1972).

98. On the tension between and synthesis of different mystical systems in the *SheLaH*, see Sack, "Influence of Cordovero," esp. 365–72; and Elliot R. Wolfson, "The Influence of the *Ari* on the *SheLaH*," *Jerusalem Studies in Jewish Thought* 10 (1992): 423–48 [Hebrew].

99. See *Kitsur Shelah* (1683) by Rabbi Yehiel Mikhel Epstein. This work, which circulated in a number of different versions, was accused of containing heretical Sabbatean ideas. See Bezalel Naor, *Post-Sabbatian Sabbatianism: Study of an Underground Messianic Movement* (Spring Valley, NY: Orot, 1999), 46–48; and Jean Baumgarten, "The Printing of Yiddish Books in Frankfurt-on-the-Main (17th and 18th Centuries)," *Bulletin du Centre de Recherche Français à Jérusalem* 20 (2009).

100. On the biography and career of Shabbatai Tsevi, see Gershom Scholem, *Sabbatai Sevi: The Mystical Messiah*, trans. R. J. Zwi Werblowsky (Princeton: Princeton University Press, 1975); Matt Goldish, *The Sabbatean Prophets* (Cambridge, MA: Harvard University Press, 2004); and David J. Halperin, *Sabbatai Zevi: Testimonies to a Fallen Messiah* (Oxford and Portland, OR: The Littman Library of Jewish Civilization, 2007), 1–19. See also the classic studies by Isaiah Tishby, *Paths of Faith and Heresy: Essays in Kabbalah and Sabbateanism* (Jerusalem: Magnes Press, 1994) [Hebrew]; and Yehuda Liebes, *On Sabbateanism and its Kabbalah: Collected Essays* (Jerusaelm: Mossad Bialik, 1995) [Hebrew].

101. This date was long heralded as the advent of messianic era. See Scholem, *Sabbatai Sevi*, 88–90; and Halperin, *Sabbatai Zevi*, 5.

102. On Natan of Gaza's life and prophetic teachings, see Scholem, *Sabbatai Sevi*, 199–325; Goldish, *Sabbatean Prophets*, 56–88; Tishby, *Paths of Faith and Heresy*, 30–51 [Hebrew]; and Liebes, *Sabbateanism and its Kabbalah*, 15–17 [Hebrew].

103. Scholem, *Sabbatai Sevi*, 214–15; Halperin, *Testimonies*, 4–5.

104. It is interesting to note that Rabbi Nathan's father owned part of the manuscript of Yosef Karo's mystical diary, which he published for the first time in 1649. See Werblowsky, *Joseph Karo*, 26; and Goldish, *Sabbatean Prophets*, 67.

105. The role of women in the Sabbatean movement is the subject of Ada Rapoport-Albert's book *Women and the Messianic Heresy of Sabbatai Zevi 1666–1816*, trans. Deborah Greniman (Oxford and Portland, OR: The Littman Library of Jewish Civilization, 2011).

106. Goldish, *Sabbatean Prophets*, 122.

107. It remains unclear if Shabbatai Tsevi hoped that his followers would convert along with him. See Scholem, *Sabbatai Sevi*, 668–93; and Halperin, *Testimonies*, 11.

108. Scholem, *Sabbatai Sevi*, 566–71; Goldish, *Sabbatean Prophets*, 130–61.

109. See Shnayer Z. Leiman, "When a Rabbi Is Accused of Heresy," in *From Ancient Israel to Modern Judaism*, ed. Jacob Neusner, Ernest S. Frerichs, and Nahum M. Sarna, vol. 3 (Atlanta, 1989), 179–94.

110. Goldish, *Sabbatean Prophets*, 110–12.

111. For the importance of the context of the messianic elements in the surrounding dominant cultures, see Goldish, *Sabbatean Prophets*, 12–40.

112. See David B. Ruderman, *Early Modern Jewry: A New Cultural History* (Princeton: Princeton University Press, 2010), 133–89.

113. This point is one of the central theses of Abraham Elqayam's dissertation, "The Mystery of Faith in the Writings of Nathan of Gaza," PhD diss., Hebrew University, 1993 [Hebrew].

114. On the Donmeh, see Paul F. Bessemer, "Who is a Crypto-Jew? A Historical Survey of the Sabbataean Debate in Turkey," *Kabbalah* 9 (2003): 109–52.

115. See Gershom Scholem, "Redemption Through Sin," in *The Messianic Idea in Judaism and Other Essays on Jewish Spirituality* (New York: Schocken Books, 1971), 78–141; and Pawel Maciejko, *The Mixed Multitude: Jacob Frank and the Frankist Movement, 1755–1816* (Philadelphia: University of Pennsylvania Press, 2011). Regarding the Donmeh and their connection to the Frankists, see Harris Lenowitz, "Leaving Turkey: The Donme Comes to Poland," *Kabbalah* 8 (2003): 65–113.

116. [For an extensive discussion of this medieval mystical term and its implications in later Kabbalah, see Moshe Idel, *Hasidism: Between Ecstasy and Magic* (Albany: State University of New York Press, 1995), 66–67, 77, 156–77.] A possible translation would be "spiritual energy."

117. See *Tanhuma*, Va-Yakhel #7.

118. *Vav* alludes to *tif'eret* and the five *sefirot* located around it: *hesed*, *gevurah*, *netsah*, *hod*, *yesod*.

119. Lit. "the act of creation," more especially the section in Genesis that describes the stages of creation.

120. I.e., the divine creative speech.

121. I.e., it would not have had a corporeal effect.

122. This is an important midrash that is often found in Hasidic texts.

123. The idea of fulfilling commandments in a more spiritual way had great meaning for the early Hasidic masters. See Arthur Green, *Devotion and Commandment* (Cincinnati: Hebrew Union College Press, 1989).

124. Lit. "orchard."

125. The "material" commandments allude to the spiritual entities which are their name in Holy Language above.

126. Although Yitshak Luria is not cited explicitly and the characteristic components of his system are not utilized, Yeshaya Horowitz seems to be presenting a point of view here that may have been strongly influenced by the Lurianic outlook.

127. This section on spiritual transformation, rather than suppression of evil, is one of the most influential teachings of our author. [This idea is developed by R. Menahem Nahum of Chernobyl, a later Hasidic master, in his homily for *parashat lekh lekha* in *Me'or 'Eynayim*, 165–69].

128. The literal meaning is probably, "according to the exposed region." However, the rabbis explained it as I have translated. See b. Yoma 54a–b, and see RaSHI's comment there.

129. [In the first part of this letter Cardozo offers six arguments in favor of Shabbatai Tsevi's messianic claims.]

130. This suggests that "exile" is for Cardozo less a matter of locality than of mode of life. [Earlier in the letter he describes his excellent material situation and comfortable living quarters.]

131. Cardozo is obviously drawing on Daniel 7:1, and probably 7:28 as well, but it is not wholly clear what he is trying to say.

132. "Lunatic," *meshugga'* is a common Jewish polemic term for the Prophet Muhammad. I am not aware of its being used elsewhere for a muezzin.

133. That is, the Sabbath before Passover.

134. We here see Cardozo making pious use of his youthful talent for poetry. Scholem, *On the Kabbalah and Its Symbolism*, 146–53.

135. b. Berakhot 6a refers to God's phylacteries, 7a to His prayers. God's studying Torah is mentioned in b. 'Avodah Zarah 3b, His fringed garment in *Midrash Pesikta Rabbati* 15:17.

136. See *Bereshit Rabbah* 19:4. Cardozo apparently thinks that the "Tree" in question is the sefirotic structure (often envisioned as a tree) and that the midrash hints at the doctrine that Cardozo will presently state explicitly: "Making use of the *sefirot*, and drawing upon the power of the Infinite [First Cause], [God] created and administers everything that exists."

137. b. Hullin 60b; cf. *Bereshit Rabbah* 6:3. According to the Talmud, God "diminished the moon" in punishment for her having tried to aggrandize herself at the sun's expense, and afterward regretted it. The Kabbalists, whom Cardozo follows, understood the "moon" to be symbolic of *shekhinah* and the moon's diminution to refer to *shekhinah*'s exile, or, in the Lurianic system, the loss of the nine *sefirot* that She had received from the Irascible One (*ze'ir anpin*), in order to build Her up as a complete Female Person. To "atone" for this loss—that is, to "mend" it—God requires human assistance.

138. Cardozo is referring to Deistic critics of the Jewish God, as well as Christian opponents of the Talmud.

139. *Bereshit Rabbah* 8:9, quoted in *Yalkut* (a medieval compilation of midrashim) to Genesis #14. Cardozo has added the words "but rather like Us" to the text and suppressed its original conclusion ("nor the two of them without *shekhinah*") in order to make it support his argument more convincingly.

140. [See "Openings," 49–51.]

141. *Berit Menuhah* is a fourteenth-century Kabbalistic text.

142. Cardozo here alludes, in very vague and general terms, to his difficult and complex doctrine of *shekhinah*. See Elliot R. Wolfson, "Constructions of the *Shekhinah* in the Messianic Theosophy of Abraham Cardoso with an Annotated Edition of *Derush ha-Shekhinah*," *Kabbalah* 3 (1998): 11–143.

143. The *sefirah hokhmah* is often equated in the *Zohar* with the "Eden" of Genesis 2:10, which is the source of the "river" of divine effluence. Cardozo uses *hokhmah* to describe Shabbatai Tsevi's sefirotic source of inspiration, which withdrew itself from him when he appeared on earth.

144. [Cardozo means to say that in exile the flow of divine vitality into *keter*, *hokhmah*, *binah*, *ze'ir anpin*, and *malkhut* has been disrupted.]

145. See b. Hagigah 12a.

Chapter 4

1. See the work of Mendel Piekarz, who underscored the impact that the works of popular kabbalistic ethical and homiletical literature had on Hasidism; see his *The Beginning of Hasidism: Ideological Trends in* Derush *and* Musar *Literature* (Jerusalem: Mossad Bialik, 1998) [Hebrew].

2. On the state of Kabbalah in Eastern Europe, see Gershon Hundert, *Jews in Poland-Lithuania in the Eighteenth Century: A Genealogy of Modernity* (Berkeley and Los Angeles: University of California Press, 2004), esp. 119–85; and Moshe Idel, *Hasidism: Between Ecstasy and Magic* (Albany: State University of New York Press, 1995), 33–44.

3. For two important biographies of Rabbi Israel by foremost scholars in this field, see Moshe Rosman, *Founder of Hasidism: A Quest for the Historical Ba'al Shem Tov* (Berkeley: University of California Press, 1996); and Immanuel Etkes, *The Besht: Magician, Mystic, and Leader*, trans. Saadya Sternberg (Waltham: Brandeis University Press, 2005).

4. See Etkes, *The Besht*, 113–51. Scholars have noted the similarity between the Ba'al Shem Tov's emphasis on religious ecstasy and the devotional attitudes of some Christian mystics living in this same region. For a recent study, see Moshe Idel, "R. Israel Ba'al Shem Tov 'in the State of Walachia': Widening the Besht's Cultural Panorama," in *Holy Dissent: Jewish*

and Christian Mystics in Eastern Europe, ed. Glenn Dynner (Detroit: Wayne State University Press, 2011), 69–103.

5. Gershom Scholem, "*Devekut*, or Communion with God," in *The Messianic Idea in Judaism and Other Essays on Jewish Spirituality* (New York: Schocken Books, 1971), 203–27. For a very different perspective, see Mendel Piekarz, "Hasidism as a Socio-religious Movement on the Evidence of 'Devekut'," in *Hasidism Reappraised*, ed. Ada Rapoport-Albert (London: Valentine Mitchell & Co. Ltd, 1996), 225–48.

6. Martin Buber and Gershom Scholem debated Hasidism's complicated relationship with the material world for many years. Buber underscored the Hasidic masters' positive attitude to physicality, while Scholem emphasized texts that articulate the movement's more other-worldly, even ascetic, impulse. See Martin Buber, *Hasidism and Modern Man*, trans. and ed. Maurice Friedman (New York: Horizon Press, 1958), esp. 126–81; Martin Buber, *Origin and Meanings of Hasidism*, trans. and ed. Maurice Friedman (New York: Horizon Press, 1960); and Gershom Scholem, "Martin Buber's Interpretation of Hasidism," in *The Messianic Idea in Judaism and Other Essays on Jewish Spirituality* (New York: Schocken Books, 1971), 228–50. For a nuanced analysis of this controversy and an insightful new reading of the Hasidic sources, see Seth Brody, "'Open to Me the Gates of Righteousness': The Pursuit of Holiness and Non-Duality in Early Hasidic Teaching," *The Jewish Quarterly Review* 89 (1998): 3–44.

7. For a recent study of the origins and evolution of this concept, see Moshe Idel, "The *Tsadik* and His Soul's Sparks: From Kabbalah to Hasidism," *The Jewish Quarterly Review* 103 (2013): 196–240.

8. Jonathan Dauber has provided an excellent summary of the scholarship on this epistle; see his "The Baal Shem Tov and the Messiah: A Reappraisal of the Baal Shem Tov's Letter to R. Gershon of Kutov" in *Jewish Studies Quarterly* 15 (2008): 210–41. For an English translation of the different versions of the letter, see Etkes, *The Besht*, 272–88. The BeSHT's other letters have been translated in Rosman, *Founder of Hasidism*, 114–22.

9. For a recent translation of an important collection of teachings on prayer attributed to the BeSHT and other early Hasidic masters, see Menachem Kallus, *Pillar of Prayer: Teachings of Contemplative Guidance in Prayer, Sacred study, and the Spiritual life from the Ba'al Shem Tov and his Circle* (Louisville, KY: Fons Vitae, 2011).

10. See Gershom Scholem, "The Neutralization of the Messianic Element in Early Hasidism," in *The Messianic Idea in Judaism and Other Essays on Jewish Spirituality* (New York: Schocken Books, 1971), 176–202; and Moshe Idel, *Messianic Mystics* (New Haven: Yale University Press, 1998), 212–47.

11. See Rivka Schatz-Uffenheimer, *Hasidism as Mysticism: Quetistic Elements in Eighteenth Century Hasidic Thought*, trans. Jonathan Chipman (Princeton: Princeton University Press, 1993); Ron Margolin, *The Human Temple: Religious Interiorization and the Structuring of Inner Life in Early Hasidism* (Jerusalem: Hebrew University Magnes Press, 2005); and Haviva Pedaya, "The Ba'al Shem Tov, R. Jacob Joseph of Polonoy and the Maggid of Miedzyrzecz: Guidelines Toward a Religious Typology," *Daat* 45 (2000): 25–73 [Hebrew].

12. For a study of the debate in early Hasidism regarding the ideal form of spiritual leadership, see Arthur Green, "Around the Maggid's Table: *Tsaddik*, Leadership, and Popularization in the Circle of R. Dov Baer of Mezritch," in *The Heart of the Matter* (forthcoming).

13. For a fuller accounting of these shared beliefs, as well as a comprehensive overview of the history and theology of the first three generations of Hasidism, see the introduction to Arthur Green, *Speaking Torah: Spiritual Teachings from Around Maggid's Table*, vol. 1, with Ebn Leader, Ariel Evan Mayse and Or N. Rose (Woodstock, VT: Jewish Lights, 2013), 1–74.

14. Arthur Green has published extensively on the subject of Hasidic leadership. See his "The Zaddiq as Axis Mundi in Later Judaism," *Journal of the American Academy of Religion* 45, no. 3 (1977): 327–47; and "Typologies of Leadership and the Hasidic Zaddiq," in *Jewish Spirituality: From the Sixteenth-Century Revival to the Present* (New York: Crossroad Publishing Company, 1987), 127–56.

15. Idel, *Hasidism*, 117–38.

16. On the spread of Hasidism, see Ada Rapoport-Albert, "Hasidism after 1772: Structural Continuity and Change," in *Hasidism Reappraised*, ed. Ada Rapoport-Albert (London: Valentine Mitchell & Co. Ltd, 1996), 76–140; and Glen Dynner, *Men of Silk: The Hasidic Conquest of Polish Jewish Society* (Oxford: Oxford University Press, 2006).

17. Alan Brill, "The Mystical Path of the Vilna Gaon," *Journal of Jewish Thought & Philosophy* 3 (1994): 131–51.

18. See Immanuel Etkes, *The Gaon of Vilna: The Man and His Image*, trans. Jeffrey M. Green (Berkeley: University of California Press, 2002). Eliyahu Stern's new intellectual biography explores this thinker's rather complicated relationship to tradition and modernity; see his *The Genius: Elijah of Vilna and the Making of Modern Judaism* (New Haven: Yale University Press, 2013).

19. For a summary of these bitter polemics, see Mordecai L. Wilensky, "Hasidic-Mitnaggedic Polemics in the Jewish Communities of Eastern Europe: The Hostile Phase," in *Essential Papers On Hasidism: Origins to*

Present, ed. Gershon David Hundert (New York: New York University Press, 1991), 244–71.

20. Scholem, *Major Trends*, 330–34.

21. Idel, *Hasidism*, 12–29, 45–50.

22. See Joseph Weiss, "The Kavvanoth of Prayer in Early Hasidism," in *Studies in East European Jewish Mysticism and Hasidism*, ed. David Goldstein (Oxford: The Littman Library of Jewish Civilization, 1997), 95–125. For a different perspective, see Menachem Kallus, "The Relation of the Baal Shem Tov to the Practice of Lurianic Kavvanot in Light of His Comments on the Siddur Rashkov," *Kabbalah* 2 (1997): 151–67.

23. On the oral nature of early Hasidic homilies and the relationship between the Hebrew transcriptions and the Yiddish original, see Arthur Green, "On Translating Hasidic Homilies," *Prooftexts* 3 (1983): 63–72; Moshe Idel, *Absorbing Perfections: Kabbalah and Interpretation*, (New Haven, CT: Yale University Press, 2002), 470–81; and Daniel Reiser and Ariel Evan Mayse, "The Last Sermon of R. Judah Leib Alter of Gur and the Role of Yiddish in the Study of Hasidic Sermons," *Kabbalah* 30 (2013): 127–60 [Hebrew].

24. On the bibliography and purpose of this literature, see Ze'ev Gries, *Sifrut ha-Hanhagot* (Jerusalem: Mossad Bialik, 1989) [Hebrew].

25. Buber and Scholem also debated whether Hasidic thought is better defined by the tales or the homilies. Buber argued that the stories represent Hasidism's vital core, whereas Scholem preferred the movement's more abstract theological literature. See Scholem, "Buber's Interpretation," esp. 233–41; and Moshe Idel, "Martin Buber and Gershom Scholem on Hasidism: A Critical Appraisal," in *Hasidism Reappraised*, ed. Ada Rapoport-Albert (London: Valentine Mitchell & Co. Ltd, 1996), 389–403.

26. Rosman and Etkes have debated the validity of using this compendium as a source for authentic traditions about the BeSHT's life and times. For a summary of their arguments and some broader observations, see Glenn Dynner, "The Hasidic Tale as a Historical Source: Historiography and Methodology," *Religion Compass* 3/4 (2009): 655–75. *Shivhei ha-BesSHT* has been translated into English as *In Praise of the Baal Shem Tov*, trans. Dan Ben-Amos and Jerome R. Mintz (Bloomington: Indiana University Press, 1970).

27. On the importance of stories in Hasidic culture, see Gedalyah Nigal, *The Hasidic Tale*, trans. Edward Levin (Oxford: Littman Library of Jewish Civilization, 2008); and Justin Jaron Lewis, *Imagining Holiness: Classic Hasidic Tales in Modern Times* (Montreal: McGill-Queen's University Press, 2009).

28. Nicham Ross, "'I.L. Peretz's Between Two Mountains': Neo-Hasidism and Jewish Literary Modernity," in *Modern Jewish Literatures*, ed. Sheila E. Jelen, Michael P. Kramer, and L. Scott Lerner (Philadelphia: University of Pennsylvania Press, 2011), 104–26; S. Daniel Breslauer, "The Hasidic Anecdote in Martin Buber and Shmuel Yosef Agnon," in *Hebrew Studies* 19 (1978): 8–15.

29. For a spiritual biography of this remarkable Hasidic teacher, see Arthur Green, *Tormented Master: The Life and Spiritual Quest of Rabbi Nahman of Bratslav* (Woodstock, VT: Jewish Lights, 1992).

30. Rabbi Nahman's tales have been the subject of extensive scholarly attention. See, inter alia, Ora Wiskind-Elper, *Tradition and Fantasy in the Tales of Reb Nahman of Bratslav* (Albany, NY: State University of New York Press, 1998); and Marianne Schleicher, *Intertextuality in the Tales of Rabbi Nahman of Bratslav: A Close Reading of Sippurey Ma'asiyot* (Leiden and Boston: Brill, 2007).

31. See Arthur Green, "Hasidism-Discovery and Retreat," in *The Other Side of God: A Polarity in World Religions*, ed. Peter L. Berger (Garden City, NY: Anchor Press/Doubleday, 1981), 104–30.

32. See Marcin Wilenski, *Haskalah and Hasidism in the Kingdom of Poland: A History of Conflict* (Oxford and Portland, OR: Littman Library of Jewish Civilization, 2005).

33. Rabbi Israel Salanter (1810–83) introduced the study of *musar*, a new form of moralistic literature, as a non-mystical complement to Talmud study in Lithuanian *yeshivot*. On Israel Salanter's stance regarding the study of Kabbalah, see Benjamin Brown, "'It Does Not Relate to Me': Rabbi Israel Salanter and the Kabbalah," in *Ve-Zot li-Yehudah*, ed. Maren R. Niehoff, Ronit Meroz, Jonathan Garb (Jerusalem: Mossad Bialik, 2012), 420–39 [Hebrew].

34. On the emergence of these dynasties, see Nehemia Polen, "Rebbetzins, Wonder-Children, and the Emergence of the Dynastic Principle in Hasidism," in *The Shtetl: New Evaluations*, ed. S. Katz (New York: New York University Press, 2007), 53–84.

35. See Shaul Magid, *Hasidism on the Margin: Reconciliation, Antinomianism, and Messianism in Izbica/Radzin Hasidism* (Madison: University of Wisconsin Press, 2003). For a recent evaluation of his teachings, see Herzl Hefter, "'In God's Hands': The Religious Phenomenoogy of R. Mordechai Yosef of Izbica," *Tradition* 46 (2013): 43–65.

36. Alan Brill, *Thinking God: The Mysticism of Rabbi Zadok of Lublin* (New York and Jersey City: Michael Scharf Publication Trust of the Yeshiva University Press, 2002).

37. For a selection of translations of Rabbi Yehudah Aryeh Leib's teachings, see Arthur Green, *The Language of Truth: The Torah Commentary of the Sefat Emet* (Philadelphia: Jewish Publication Society, 1998).

38. On the political involvement of Hasidic leaders in the nineteenth and twentieth centuries, see Marcin Wodzinski, *Hasidism and Politics: the Kingdom of Poland, 1815–1864* (Oxford and Portland, Oregon: The Littman Library of Jewish Civilization, 2013); and Gershon Bacon, *The Politics of Tradition: Agudat Yisrael in Poland, 1916–1939* (Jerusalem: Magnes Press, 1996).

39. "Shame" (*bushah*) as spoken of here has the sense of "embarrassment" rather than "guilt." The sense of *bushah* as described in Hebrew ethical literature is usually the result of awareness of God's greatness, rather than response to a particular sin.

40. Do not limit yourself to literal observance of the law that forbids, but add to holiness of your own accord by the way you do that which is permitted.

41. *The Gates of Zion* is a collection of penitential prayers and supplications edited by Nathan Hanover and first printed in 1662. It contains a prayer for this occasion ascribed to Nahmanides. The *Shulhan 'Arukh*, Joseph Caro's law code of the sixteenth century, serves as the basic guide to Jewish religious practice. "For the sake of the union..." is the formula of kabbalistic intent to be recited before the fulfilling of each religious commandment. The commandment to be performed is thereby dedicated to the union of the upper divinity with the *shekhinah*, symbolically represented as the male and female potencies within God. The point that the sex act is the fulfillment of a biblical commandment ("be fruitful and multiply," (Gen 1:28) is here overshadowed by the vision of human coupling as evocative of the great union above.

42. The Ba'al Shem Tov taught that excessive brooding over sin left a dangerous opening for the evil forces that abound in the human mind to become dominant and keep one from further religious devotion. He taught rather the uplifting of sins or, as the author here suggests, quick and full resolve to depart from them, followed by an immediate turn to worship of a more positive character. Brooding over sin, as can be seen from the language of the following sentence, keeps one from that wholeness of heart required for true worship.

43. The rabbis' willingness to render a legal decision in this way shows how much stock they put even in a single thought of repentance.

44. Fear and love, held in their proper balance, are taken to be the central emotions of the religious life. This is commonplace in later Jewish liter-

ature, particularly that written under the influence of the *Zohar*. See further discussion in the homily for *parashat va-yetse* in *Me'or 'Eynayim*.

45. The verse may also be translated: "It is pleasant to listen to the words of the wise."

46. Heb. *middot tovot*. The popular and Yiddish usage refers to decency of character and proper human values: generosity, concern for others, respect, etc. In Hasidic usage these "qualities" refer specifically to the seven qualities of the emotional life parallel to the seven *sefirot*.

47. Eliyahu De Vidas' *Reshit Hokhmah* was frequently reprinted and exercised great influence in the later devotional life of Judaism, both in Hasidim and elsewhere. [See above, 108–18.]

48. The rabbis' statement here plays on *me'od* ("might") and *middah* ("portion").

49. Thank God even for that which seems to you a curse rather than a blessing; in some way that you cannot presently understand, it is given you for the ultimate healing of your soul.

50. [b. Pesahim; Nazir 23b, inter alia].

51. "Not for its own sake" is here interpreted to refer to religious actions performed without those "wings" of emotional intensity that will enable it to rise upward. The word of study or prayer, even if spoken in an offhand manner, will ultimately communicate its own inner fire to the speaker and will lead him to the higher form of religious life; "continue to *do*" is the constant Hasidic counsel, "and the spirit will inevitably follow."

52. Along with Torah and worship. The author refers to m. Avot 1:2.

53. [*Toledot Ya'akov Yosef*, Hukat (Jerusalem: 2011), 1056; *Ben Porat Yosef*, Va-Yigash (Jerusalem: 2011), 416.]

54. [*Degel Mahaneh Ephrayim*, Va-Yikra (Jerusalem, 1994), 138.]

55. The Hasidic masters followed the Kabbalists in viewing Torah study not only as a religious obligation but as a *ritual* act. The structure of one's daily regimen of studies took on a great importance for the mystics, who saw correspondences between the order of materials studied and the divisions of the human soul.

56. The phrase *ehad yahid u-meyuhad* has its origins in the philosophical poetry of the Middle Ages. It is not intended as a precise theological formulation, and should not be read as such. "United" is in fact quite inadequate for *meyuhad*, the meaning of which is not clearly distinguishable from *yahid* in this formulation.

57. The terms "fills" and "surrounds" to describe God's immanence and transcendence originate in the *Zohar*. See *Zohar* 3:225a (R.M.). In the spirit of mysticism, Hasidic authors seek an end to this duality, a way to point out that *sovev* and *memale* are in fact one.

58. [This phrase, found in *Tikkunei Zohar* (#70, 122b) was particularly beloved by the Hasidic masters and often cited together with Isaiah 6:3].

59. [This is similar to the BeSHT's quite literal interpretation of Psalm 121:5 "He is your shadow"—God's actions reciprocally shadow those of people. See *Kedushat Levi*, Be-Shalah (Brooklyn: 1995), 178.]

60. In these sentences lies the essential core of distinctively Hasidic teaching. "Know Him in all your ways" (Prov 3:6), for all things and all moments, no matter how seemingly ordinary, are but "garb" for the all-pervading presence of God.

61. Many sorts of meditation on the names of God have characterized Jewish mysticism in every period of its history. From the time of the *Zohar*, the association of particular names with the various *sefirot* became a commonplace. Here the point seems to be that Eheyeh represents the upper triad, the world of pure contemplation; Y-H-V-H refers to God as Being, the God of theistic religion; and Adonay refers to the God who dwells within the human self. It is the union of these three, the God of theism serving as a bridge between the other two, that forms the content of mystical contemplation.

62. The ritual bath, originally ordained for purification from states of bodily taboo, but used by Hasidim especially as preparation for the Sabbath, holidays, or daily morning prayer. It is to this latter usage that the passage here refers: *mikveh* as a purification from sin before the daily prayers. [In the eyes of the early Hasidic masters, the immersion itself took on importance as a spiritual experience of being entirely surrounded by God's immanent Presence; see Tsippi Kauffman, "Ritual Immersion at the Beginning of Hasidism," *Tarbiz* 80 (2012): 409–25 [Hebrew].]

63. While incorporating a desire to retain the power of meditation on the names, Hasidism also wants to claim that the unification of names is effected of its own accord in the person who is morally pious and upright. This renders the abstruse science of such meditation accessible to the ordinary Jew.

64. The Psalms play a particular role in Jewish popular devotion; recitation of Psalms was an avenue of religious expression open to even the simplest and most unlearned of the community.

65. These are both metaphors for the final redemption, and a certain urgent messianic note is heard in their employment.

66. [b. Nedarim 39b. For a slightly different listing of the elements which preceded creation, see *Bereshit Rabbah* 1:4].

67. God and the *shekhinah*, or the transcendent God and His indwelling presence.

68. The two hundred forty-eight words of the *Shema'* are said to correspond to the number of limbs in the human body, fulfilling the Scripture, "All of my bones shall say: 'Lord, who is like You?'" (Ps 35:10). [See *Zohar Hadash* 77b; *Zohar* 3:263a].

69. b. Shabbat 118b. The generation of Enosh was that in which idolatry originated. See Midrashim and Targum Y. to Gen. 4:26.

70. The double play involves three words derived from the root TSDK. The union of the last two of the ten *sefirot*, often described particularly in conjugal terms, is sometimes called that of *tsedek* and *tsedakah*, masculine and feminine forms of the same word but that often translate "justice" and "righteousness" or "almsgiving." The ninth *sefirah*, *tsedek*, is also frequently associated with *tsadik*, the one who performs just acts of goodness.

71. The inner mathematical relationship between the single one, the decade, and the hundred is often discussed in kabbalistic sources concerned with number. This is here associated with a play on the word *TSeDaKaH*, but in a somewhat obscure fashion.

72. *Zohar* 1:65b.

73. *Zohar* 1:1b. As the most revealed revel of divinity is called "I," for there God presents Himself as one available to human search, the most hidden reaches are referred to as "Who?", the place of the transcendent and unanswerable questions.

74. [*Zohar* 2:128b, 200a. See Isaiah Tishby, "Prayer and Devotion in the *Zohar*," in *Essential Papers On Kabbalah*, ed. Lawrence Fine (New York: New York University Press, 1995), 341–99, esp. 377–82.]

75. The passage is built around the prayer of thanksgiving for restoration of the soul to life, an early part of the daily morning service. [See b. Berakhot 60b].

76. The Ba'al Shem Tov was said to have spoken of the possibility that a person might die due to the intensity of prayer. It was he who originally offered the counsel of preparing for death before each prayer of the day. See the sources quoted in Arthur Green and Barry Holtz, *Your Word is Fire: The Hasidic Masters on Contemplative Prayer* (Woodstock, VT: Jewish Lights, 1993), 33.

77. Here begins a list of the seven lower *sefirot*, each of them referred to as some aspect of the spiritual/emotional life. The sefirotic references are here italicized to help the reader remain aware of the list.

78. Note how the language of theism and that of emanation are combined with one another: God is at once Master and Source!

79. "Attachment" is a somewhat unusual way to refer to *yesod*, the sixth of the seven lower *sefirot*. The point is that it joins together with *malkhut* and the forces above it; it is the instrument of attachment.

80. [b. Sanhedrin 37a. See also Rabbi Abraham ben David's comments to Maimonides, *Hilkhot Teshuvah* 5:5].

81. To the rung of *binah*, beyond the differentiation between good and evil and hence beyond the origin of the *dinim*.

82. A period of eight weeks (the name is formed by an acronym of eight Torah portions, beginning with *shemot*) during the winter set aside by the Kabbalists as a time of penitence, particularly for sexual misdeeds.

83. The designation of the eve of the new moon as a lesser Yom Kippur is also a kabbalistic custom.

84. "All the worlds" is derived from the kabbalistic notion that there exist several levels of Creation, one above the other. Here it is used in a broader sense of "throughout the universe."

85. He takes the root *HaNaT* here to refer to "bear fruit" rather than "embalm." Both meanings are possible; such plays on words will be found frequently in the text and are common to most Hasidic writings.

86. As Joseph, representing the Tree of Life in broken or fallen form, was placed in an *aron*, so were the broken tablets, again Torah in broken pieces, in the days of Moses.

87. *Bereshit Rabbah* 1:14.

88. Psalm 16:8 was used by the Kabbalists as support for the practice of constant mediation on the letters of the name. Here our author suggests, in typically Hasidic fashion, that he who finds God in all things is in fact also carrying on this venerable practice. Note how even the most spiritual practices can be yet again "spiritualized."

89. The divine name *Elohim* used in this verse is often taken to refer to judgment or negative forces within divinity.

90. The rabbis' point is that Abraham observed even the finest details of the law, including matters nowhere mentioned in Scripture but added only in later times. [For a study of this rabbinic teaching in Hasidic thought more broadly, see Arthur Green, *Devotion and Commandment: The Faith of Abraham in the Hasidic Imagination* (Cincinnati, OH: Hebrew Union College Press, 1989].

91. The seven lower *sefirot*.

92. He who treats guests as did Abraham brings other to feel the presence of God, an act of greater merit than simply being aware of that presence oneself.

93. *Hesed* in this verse is usually translated "abomination"; this is a case in which the original meaning of "love" has been reversed, possibly for euphemistic purposes. The author plays on this reversal of meaning, seeing in the text an indication that even this *hesed* is in fact derived from divine love. Abraham in Egypt refers to Sarah as his sister; this apparently is the act

of descent to the level of the Egyptians, resulting in the uplifting of their fallen or abused love.

94. I.e., between husband and wife and at the proper time in the menstrual cycle.

95. The awkwardness of persons in the text of Genesis 18:1–3 leads the rabbis to so interpret it that Abraham is speaking with God when they are interrupted by the three angelic visitors. Abraham asks God, who is paying him a sick call as he recuperates from circumcision, to wait for him until the guests have been properly welcomed.

96. b. Berakhot 18b.

97. *Sifre 'Ekev* #38.

98. Even though God is everywhere, man may often feel himself to be cut off from God's presence. This seems to be the subject of Abraham's request.

99. Moses, as *da'at*, is the channel of revelation that brings language and expression to that which had formerly been beyond speech.

100. *Tikkunei Zohar* t. 10, 25b.

101. He has now reversed the process, showing that *da'at* is crucial to both directions of the flow. In the transmission of Torah from God to man, *da'at* represents conscious mind, the level of understanding to which speech is first appropriate and where speech may not enter. As we turn to God in prayer, *da'at* represents our religious awareness of presence of mind; only with this mind, composed first of love and fear, can prayer ascend to God. Even with proper prayer and inwardness, however, true understanding of *hokhmah* and *binah* is beyond human reach.

102. Conventionally translated: "I am understanding and power is mine," but here meaning that *binah*, the second of the *sefirot*, stands at the head of the left column and is thus the ultimate source of judgment, even of the demonic.

103. b. Berakhot 26b.

104. True liberation is found in the boundlessness of the fully contemplative life, set loose from those attachments to corporeal things that necessarily keep one within a world of limitation. The World of Thought, identified with *binah*, is associated with freedom or liberation by a long kabbalistic tradition in the exegesis of the Jubilees command (Lev 25:10).

105. [The word *va-yishkav* may be read as *yesh kav,* or "here are the twenty-two letters."]

106. Faith is often a name for the *shekhinah*, seventh among the seven lower *sefirot*.

107. Based on Midrashic interpretation. Literally "For in *Yah* the Lord you have an everlasting rock."

108. b. Menahot 29b.

109. *Binah* is beyond voice; one may listen to and be instructed by its silence, but there is as yet no word. The purely contemplative may instruct, but only in silence. It is there that "evil" forces are transformed.

110. [For a comprehensive treatment of this story, see Yoav Elstein, *In the Footsteps of a Lost Princess: A Structural Analysis of the First Tale by Rabbi Nachman of Braslav* (Jerusalem: Bat Hen Press, 1984) [Hebrew].]

111. For more lengthy interpretations of this story, see Joseph Dan, *The Hasidic Story: Its History and Development* (Jerusalem: Keter, 1975), esp. 132–88 [Hebrew].

112. Rabbi Safrin's life and teachings await proper scholarly analysis. For some insightful remarks regarding his mystical theology and experiences, see "Safrin, Yitzhaq Yehiel of Komarno" in the index to Jonathan Garb, *Shamanic Trance in Modern Kabbalah* (Chicago and London: University of Chicago Press, 2011).

113. Cf. b. Hagigah 12a.

114. R. Yitshak Yehiel was raised by his uncle R. Tsevi Hirsh of Zidachov after the death of his father when he was twelve.

115. R. El'azer (c. 1165–c. 1230) was the last major figure in the medieval Ashkenazi Pietist movement.

116. R. Solomon ibn Adret (c. 1235–c. 1310) was a Spanish rabbi and one of the most influential medieval halakhic authorities. [A disciple of Rabbi Yonah Gerondi and RaMBaN, it is clear that Adret was well-versed in Kabbalah. He was fiercely critical of the both hyper-rationalism of the Jewish philosophers and the prophetic mysticism of Rabbi Avraham Abulafia.]

117. Cf. b. Ketubot 17a.

118. The term *katnut* has a variety of meanings in ethical and kabbalistic literature. In the ethical literature it means humility, in contrast to *gadlut* or arrogance. In Lurianic Kabbalah it acquired the meaning of distance from God. In Hasidic literature, it is used in both senses at different times.

119. Adorning the *shekhinah* through the study of Torah is a motif found in rabbinic and mystical sources. See Yehuda Liebes, "The Messiah of the *Zohar*," in *Studies in the* Zohar, trans. Arnold Schwartz, Stephanie Nakache, Penina Peli (Albany: SUNY Press, 1993), 5, 63, 75–78, 192n2.

120. This is an exact parallel to the description of what happened when the Ba'al Shem Tov studied. Cf. *In Praise of the Baal Shem Tov*, ed. and trans. J. Mintz and D. Ben Amos (Bloomington: Indiana University Press, 1970), 45–46.

121. A town in central Poland.

122. *Zohar* 3:115b.

123. R. Elimelekh of Lyzhansk (1717–87) was a disciple of the Maggid of Mezritch and one of the founders of Hasidism in Galicia.

124. R. Moshe Hayyim Ephrayim of Sudylkow (c. 1740–1800).

125. A similar story is found in *In Praise of the Baal Shem Tov*, 18.

126. [*Degel Mahaneh Ephrayim*, Va-Yishlah, 44. This note appears in Naftali Ben Menahem's Hebrew edition of *Megillat Setarim* (Jerusalem: Mossad ha-Rav Kook, 1944).]

127. See *In Praise of the Baal Shem Tov*, 23–24.

128. An allusion to the belief that the messiah was expected in 1575. See David Tamar, "The Expectations in Italy for the Year of Redemption—1575," in *Studies in the History of the Jewish People in Eretz Israel and in Italy* (Jerusalem: Reuven Mas, 1970), 11–38 [Hebrew].

129. [The text reads R.M., most likely a reference to Moses, the "Faithful Shepherd" (*ra'aya mehmna*) of the later strata of the *Zohar*.]

Chapter 5

1. See Zvi Y. Gitelman, *A Century of Ambivalence: The Jews of Russia and the Soviet Union, 1881 to the Present* (Bloomington: Indiana University Press, 2001); Benjamin Nathans, *Beyond the Pale: The Jewish Encounter with Late Imperial Russia* (Berkeley: University of California Press, 2002); and the second two volumes of Antony Polonsky's series *The Jews in Poland and Russia* (London and Portland, OR: The Littman Library of Jewish Civilization, 2010 and 2012).

2. Rabbi Kalonymous Kalman Shapira of Piazecna (1889–1943) was also aware of the deep internal spiritual crisis and numerical attrition brought on by a purely reactionary stance toward modernity. His writings represent a similar attempt to reformulate Jewish mysticism as an intelligent, mature, and holistic spiritual discipline capable of engaging with enduring human questions. See Nehemia Polen, *The Holy Fire: The Teachings of Rabbi Kalonymus Kalman Shapira, the Rebbe of the Warsaw Ghetto* (Northvale, NJ: Jason Aronson, Inc., 1999).

3. Rav Kook has been the subject of a great number of academic studies, primarily in Hebrew. For an intellectual biography of Rav Kook in English, see Benjamin Ish-Shalom, *Rav Avraham Itzhak ha-Cohen Kook: Between Rationalism and Mysticism*, trans. Ora Wiskind-Elper (Albany, NY: State University of New York Press, 1993). There are two collections of essays in English on Rav Kook's mystical thought, legal writings, and religio-political philosophy; see *Rabbi Abraham Isaac Kook and Jewish Spirituality*, ed. Lawrence J. Kaplan and David Shatz (New York and London: New York University Press, 1995); and *Essays on the Thought and Philosophy of Rabbi*

Kook, ed. Ezra Gellman (Rutherford: Fairleigh Dickenson University Press, 1991). For a recent biography analyzing Rav Kook's relationship to tradition and modernity, see Yehudah Mirsky, *Rav Kook: Mystic in an Age of Revolution* (New Haven: Yale University Press, 2013).

4. See Eliezer Goldman, "Rav Kook's Relation to European Thought," in *The World of Rav Kook's Thought*, ed. Benjamin Ish-Shalom and Shalom Rosenberg, trans. Shalom Carmy and Bernard Casper (Jerusalem: Avi Chai, 1991), 139–48.

5. See Benjamin Ish-Shalom's essay "Tolerance and its Theoretical Basis," in *Rabbi Abraham Isaac Kook and Jewish Spirituality*, ed. Lawrence J. Kaplan and David Shatz (New York and London: New York University Press, 1995), 178–204.

6. *Iggerot ha-Re'ayah* (Jerusalem: Mossad ha-Rav Kook, 1985), 1:164, 214 [Hebrew].

7. Avinoam Rosenak, "Hidden Diaries and New Discoveries: The Life and Thought of Rabbi A. I. Kook," *Shofar: An Interdisciplinary Journal of Jewish Studies* 25 (2007): 111–47.

8. On the nationalistic thought of Rav Kook and his interpreters, see Aviezer Ravitzky, *Messianism, Zionism, and Jewish Religious Radicalism*, trans. Michael Swirsky and Jonathan Chipman (Chicago: University of Chicago Press, 1996); and Jonathan Garb, "Rabbi Kook and His Sources: From Kabbalistic Historiosophy to National Mysticism," in *Studies in Modern Religions, Religious Movements and the Babi-Baha'i Faiths*, ed. Moshe Sharon (Leiden: Brill, 2004), 77–96.

9. Aside from Arthur Green's volume in this series, at present there is still very little scholarship on Zeitlin in English. See Moshe Waldoks' unpublished dissertation "Hillel Zeitlin: The Early Years (1894–1919)," PhD diss., Brandeis University, 1984. For a comprehensive biography in Hebrew, see Shraga Bar Sella, *Between the Storm and the Quiet: The Life and Works of Hillel Zeitlin* (Tel Aviv: Hakibbutz Hameuchad, 1999) [Hebrew].

10. For a comparative study of Hillel Zeitlin and two other important Jewish thinkers in early twentieth-century Warsaw, see Arthur Green, "Three Warsaw Mystics," in *Rivkah Shatz-Uffenheimer Memorial Volume*, vol. 2, ed. Rachel Elior and Joseph Dan, (Jerusalem: 1996), 1–58.

11. *Yesodot ha-Hasidut* was republished in a posthumous collection of Zeitlin's writings entitled *Be-Fardes ha-Hasidut va'ha-Kabbalah* (Tel Aviv: Yavneh, 1960), 11–52.

12. Zeitlin's revolutionary program was undoubtedly influenced by the writer Micha Josef Berdychewski (1865–1921), who also hoped to radically refashion Jewish intellectual life.

13. Arthur Green, "Hillel Zeitlin and Neo-Hasidic Readings of the *Zohar*," *Kabbalah* 22 (2010): 59–78.

14. A similar return to prophecy is found in the writings of a remarkable number of modern mystics. See Eliezer Schweid's analysis of this phenomenon in "'Prophetic Mysticism' in Twentieth-Century Jewish Thought," *Modern Judaism* 14 (1994): 139–74.

15. Shraga Bar Sella, "On the Brink of Disaster: Hillel Zeitlin's Struggle for Jewish Survival in Poland," in *Polin* 11 (London and Portland, Oregon: The Littman Library of Jewish Civilization, 1998), 77–93.

16. Zeitlin's elder son Aaron survived the War in the United States, where he had been lecturing when the conflict broke out in 1939.

17. Hillel Seidman's testimony was first published in the New York *Morgen Zhurnal*, January 26, 1947, 7.

18. On the relationship between Zeitlin and Rav Kook, see Bar Sella, *Between the Storm and the Quiet*, 208, 214–16; and Jonatan Meir, "Longing of Souls for the *Shekhina*: Relations between Rabbi Kook, Zeitlin and Brenner," *The Path of the Spirit: The Eliezer Schweid Jubilee*, vol. 2, ed. Yehoyada Amir (Jerusalem: Mandel Institute of Jewish Studies at the Hebrew University and the Van Leer Institute, 2005), 771–818 [Hebrew]. See also Hillel Zeitlin, "The Basic Line of Rabbi Kook's Kabbalah," in *Sifran shel Yehidim* (Jerusalem: Mossad ha-Rav Kook, 1980), 235–37 [Hebrew]. In this short but astute essay Zeitlin suggests that Rav Kook's national and psychological understanding of Kabbalah was deeply influenced by the BeSHT's Hasidism.

19. *Keter 'elyon*, the highest of the ten *sefirot* that emanate directly from God.

20. The Hebrew name for Israel is a composite of the two Hebrew words *shir el*, the song of God. The identification of Solomon in the Song of Songs with God and the correspondence of God's four-letter name with the four levels of song is found, inter alia, in *Shir ha-Shirim Rabbah* 1:11; *Zohar* 3:27b; *Tikkunei Zohar* 10, 13.

21. The reference is to Abraham.

22. *Zohar* 2:227b.

23. An allusion to Ezekiel's vision of the chariot, in chapter 1, in which Rabbi Kook sees exemplified one of his basic positions, that man can identify with the forces through which God acts, but not with God as He is in Himself.

24. For Rabbi Kook these holy sparks are elements embodying the divine purpose.

25. The original speaks of a woman's temptations.

26. [See Bezalel Naor's study of Rav Kook's correspondence: *The Limit of Intellectual Freedom: The Letters of Rav Kook* (Spring Valley, NY: Orot, Inc., 2011).]

27. [For a phenomenological study of this poem and its kabbalistic background, see Jerome I. Gellman, "Poetry of Spirituality," in *Rabbi Abraham Isaac Kook and Jewish Spirituality*, ed. Lawrence J. Kaplan and David Shatz (New York University Press, 1995), 88–119, esp. 103–16.]

28. Editor's note: most notes in this section are Zeitlin's own. Those appearing in square brackets belong to Arthur Green.

29. R. Dov Baer ["the Maggid"] of Midzyrzec, *Likkutei Amarim*, "Introduction." [This book is also called *Maggid Devarav le-Ya'akov*. The critical edition is by Rivka Schatz-Uffenheimer (Jerusalem: Magnes Press, 1976). The passage is by R. Shlomoh of Lutsk's, and is found on p. 5]. I will bring quotations from Hasidic literature *as they are*, except when wording needs to be changed due to improper usage.

30. He means to say that it cannot be grasped by the outer soul, but only the soul within, its innermost part, its godliness.

31. *Likkutei Amarim* #56, p. 83f.

32. [Based on a widespread play on words already found in the earliest Kabbalistic sources, intentionally misreading *me-ayin* to mean "from Nothing" instead of "from where?"]

33. R. Menahem Mendel of Vitebsk, *Peri ha-Arets*, *Tetsaveh* (Kopyst, 1814), 11a.

34. *Likkutei Amarim* #60, p. 91.

35. *Likkutei Amarim* #78, p. 134. That which the author of *Peri ha-Arets* calls "being," his master, writing in *Likkutei Amarim*, calls "Nothing." This will come as no surprise to one familiar with Hasidic writings. There are often contradictions in the use of terms, and not always even between different authors. For our purpose, however, the idea is essentially the same.

36. *Sha'arei ha-Yihud ve'ha-Emunah* by R. Aaron of Starroselye (disciple of R. Shne'ur Zalman of Liadai), *Kelalut ha-Yihud*, 27b. [*Pel'e* or "wonder" is *aleph* spelled backward; *aleph* is frequently taken to represent *keter*, the primal One behind the process of emanation.]

37. R. Avraham ben David of Posquieres, in the introduction to his commentary on *Sefer Yetsirah*. I have joined his words to those of the *Hasidim*, even though he preceded them by many generations sine the Hasidim based themselves on him with regard to Being and Nothingness.

38. R. Yisra'el Ba'al Shem Tov, *Keter Shem Tov* (Brooklyn: Kehot, 1972), #51, p. 31 and elsewhere.

39. *Peri ha-Arets*, *Bereshit*, 9.

40. *Likkutei Amarim* #120, p. 197.

41. *Sefer ha-Tanya*, Chapter 42. [This is the foundational work of Habad Hasidism, authored by R. Shne'ur Zalman of Liadai. A.E.M.].

42. [He can withdraw it back into himself.]

43. See *Kitvei Kodesh* 5b, and many other sources. A distinctive explanation of *tsimtsum* is found in Habad writings, but that will have to be elaborated elsewhere. Here we offer only general headings, fundaments accepted by all Hasidic systems.

44. *Likkutei Amarim* #60, p. 89f., quoting *Zohar* 1:234b.

45. *Ethics* #4–5.

46. *De Profundis*.

47. *Or Torah*, (Printed with *Likkutei Amarim*), p. 192.

48. [Based on Deuteronomy 30:14].

49. *No'am Elimelekh, Va-Yera*, ed. G. Nigal (Jerusaelm, 1978), 40, in the name of the Maggid of Mezritch. [This work represents the collected teachings of Rabbi Elimelekh of Lizhensk (1717–1786/87). A.E.M.]

50. *Or ha-Me'ir, Hayyei Sarah*, 39. [By Rabbi Ze'ev Wolf of Zhitomir (d. 1797).]

51. R. Avraham ha-Mal'akh, *Hesed le-Avraham, Lekh Lekha*, 32. [Rabbi Avraham was the son of the Maggid of Mezritch.]

52. *Likkutim Yekarim*, 20b.

53. [*Middot* (sing. *middah*) is an extremely difficult term to translate. Literally "measures," it often refers to ethics or ethical conduct—in Yiddish a *bal mides* (= *middot*) is an ethical person—but in the Hasidic context it can also mean "emotions," based on associations with the seven lower *sefirot* and their human emotional counterparts. "Qualities" or "attributes" are also frequently appropriate renditions.]

54. *Keter Shem Tov*, p. 38, absed on "Pharaoh drew near" (Exod 14:10) and elsewhere.

55. *Yihudim*, or "unifications," are the essential secret practices of Kabbalah. Usually they involve the joining of the *sefirot* or *partsufim* in a particular configuration, often having to do with a particular spelling out of the letters of the divine name Y-H-V-H. Bringing them together in a contemplative exercise thus forms a particular "unification" of God's name and affects the related cosmic forces.

56. B. Yoma 21b, referring to the fire on the Temple altar.

57. This is Zeitlin's wishful extension and universalization of *ahavat yisra'el*, although he has recognized above that it belongs more to the future than the past.

58. From *Patah Eliyahu*, a passage from *Tikkunei Zohar* recited in the Sephardic and Hasidic prayer services.

59. This and other structural and numerical parallels between the inner divine self, the Torah, and the souls of Israel, are widespread in Jewish mystical sources. The point is that each of these three dimensions must be kept whole if the others are to be preserved.

60. The obscure phrase *mafrid aluf* in this verse is widely interpreted as *mafrid alef*, bringing about separation within the One.

61. m. Sanhedrin 10:1.

62. Rabbi Tsadok ha-Kohen of Lublin (1823–1900), Hasidic master and original thinker and author. See his *Takkanat ha-Shavin* (Jerusalem: Mekor ha-Sefarim, 2002), 14a and elsewhere.

63. Tosafot to b. Menahot 110a.

64. Referring to an ancient legend that the "lower waters" of the second day of Creation called out against the injustice of their being farther from God. [See *Bereshit Rabbah* 5:4; *Tikkunei Zohar* T. 40, 80a.]

65. I.e., a time when the political situation reveals that the End is near.

66. Revision of a translation first made by Rabbi Zalman Schachter-Shalomi.

67. *Likkutei 'Etsot* by Rabbi Nahman of Bratslav.

68. The fifteenth principle was added by Zeitlin in the Hebrew version in *Sifran shel Yehidim* (1928), 57–63.

Afterword

1. See his remarks in "Reflections on the Possibility of Jewish Mysticism in Our Time," in *On the Possibility of Jewish Mysticism in Our Time & Other Essays*, ed. Avraham Shapira, trans. Jonathan Chipman (Philadelphia: The Jewish Publication Society, 1997), 6–19. Scholem himself seems to have been conflicted on this point. He repeatedly denies that there were any important developments in Kabbalah after the early nineteenth century, but in the closing paragraphs of *Major Trends* Scholem predicts that Jewish mysticism will indeed find some new manifestation in the future. In his later writings Scholem makes explicit his belief that the next great revival will take place within the religious anarchy of modern secularism. See Boaz Huss and Joel A. Linsider, "Ask No Questions: Gershom Scholem and the Study of Contemporary Jewish Mysticism," *Modern Judaism* 25 (2005): 141–58.

2. For a survey of Kabbalah in North Africa, see Moshe Idel, "Jewish Mysticism Among the Jews of Arab/Moslem Lands," *Journal for the Study of Sephardic and Mizrahi Jewry* 1 (2007): 14–38.

3. See Ariel Evan Mayse, "'Or ha-Hayyim': Creativity, Tradition and Mysticism in the Torah Commentary of R. Hayyim ibn Attar," *Conversations* 13 (2012): 68–89; and David Assaf, "'A Heretic Who Has No Faith in the Great Ones of the Age': The Clash Over the Honor of 'Or ha-Hayyim,'" *Modern Judaism* 29 (2009): 194–225.

4. On the significance of Rabbi Shalom Sharabi and his *yeshivah*, see Pinchas Giller, *Shalom Shar'abi and the Kabbalists of Beit El* (Oxford and New York: Oxford University Press, 2008).

5. Jonatan Meir, "Toward the Popularization of Kabbalah: R. Yosef Hayyim of Baghdad and the Kabbalists of Jerusalem," *Modern Judaism* 33 (2013): 148–72.

6. J. H. Chajes, "'Too Holy to Print': Taboo Anxiety and the Publishing of Practical Hebrew Esoterica," Jewish History 26 (2012): 247–62.

7. Jonatan Meir has contributed much to the study of kabbalistic circles of Jerusalem; see his "The Imagined Decline of Kabbalah: The Kabbalistic Yeshiva *Sha'ar ha-Shamayim* and the Kabbalah in Jerusalem in the Beginning of the Twentieth Century," in *Kabbalah and Modernity: Interpretations, Transformations, Adaptations*, ed. Boaz Huss, Marco Pasi and Kocku von Stuckrad (Leiden and Boston: Brill, 2010), 197–210; and *Rehovot ha-Nahar: Kabbalah ve-Ekzoteriyut bi-Yerushalayim* (Jerusalem: Yad Yitshaak ben Tsevi, 2011) [Hebrew].

8. Jonathan Garb, *The Chosen Will Become Herds: Studies in Twentieth-Century Kabbalah*, trans. Yaffah Berkovits-Murciano (New Haven, CT: Yale University Press, 2009), 29–32. See Jonatan Meir's comparison between Rabbi Ashlag and Hillel Zeitlin in his "Wrestling with the Esoteric: Hillel Zeitlin, Yehudah Ashlag, and Kabbalah in the Land of Israel," *Judaism, Topics, Fragments, Faces, Identities: Jubilee Volume in Honor of Rivka Horowitz*, ed. Haviva Pedaya and Ephraim Meir (Beer Sheva: Ben Gurion University of the Negev Press, 2007), 585–648 [Hebrew].

9. On this turn toward universalism, see Jody Myers, "Kabbalah for the Gentiles: Diverse Souls and Universalism in Contemporary Kabbalah," in *Kabbalah and Contemporary Spiritual Revival*, ed. Boaz Huss (Beer Sheva: Ben Gurion University of the Negev Press, 2011), 181–211; and Jody Myers, *Kabbalah and the Spiritual Quest: The Kabbalah Centre in America (Religion, Health, and Healing)* (Westport, Conn: Praeger, 2007).

10. See Jonatan Meir, "The Boundaries of the Kabbalah: R. Yaakov Moshe Hillel and the Kabbalah in Jerusalem," in *Kabbalah and Contemporary Spiritual Revival*, ed. Boaz Huss (Beer Sheva: Ben Gurion University of the Negev Press, 2011), 163–80.

11. For two very different studies of this remarkable leader and thinker, see Elliot Wolfson, *Open Secret: Postmessianic Messianism and the Mystical*

Revision of Menahem Mendel Schneerson (New York: Columbia University Press, 2012); and Samuel C. Heilman and Menachem M. Friedman, *The Rebbe: The Life and Afterlife of Menachem Mendel Schneerson* (Princeton and Oxford: Princeton University Press, 2012).

12. These emissaries have experienced a surprisingly low rate of attrition and have been successful in their mission of inspiring Jews to be more observant. See Elise Berman, "Voices of Outreach: The Construction of Identity and Maintenance of Social Ties Among Chabad-Lubavitch Emissaries," *Journal for the Scientific Study of Religion* 48 (2009): 69–85; and Sue Fishkoff, *The Rebbe's Army: Inside the World of Chabad-Lubavitch* (New York: Schocken, 2005).

13. On the status of women in Habad as reflective of modern values, see Bonnie J. Morris, *Lubavitcher Women in America: Identity and Activism in the Postwar Era* (Albany: State University of New York Press, 1998); Susan Handelman, "Women and the Study of Torah in the Thought of the Lubavitcher Rebbe," in *Jewish Legal Writings by Women*, ed. Micah D. Halpern and Chana Safrai (Jerusalem: Urim Publications, 1998), 143–78; and Naftali Loewenthal, "From 'Ladies' Auxiliary' to 'Shluhot Network': Women's Activism in Twentieth-century Habad," in *A Touch of Grace: Studies in Ashkenazi Culture, Women's History, and the Languages of the Jews Presented to Chava Turniansky*, ed. I. Bartal (Jerusalem: The Zalman Shazar Center for Jewish History, 2013), 69–93.

14. For a survey of the various neo-Bratslav groups, see Zvi Mark, "Contemporary Renaissance of Braslav Hasidism: Ritual, *Tiqqun* and Messianism," in *Kabbalah and Contemporary Spiritual Revival*, ed. Boaz Huss (Beer Sheva: Ben Gurion University of the Negev Press, 2011), 101–16.

15. On the study of *Tanya* see Naftali Loewenthal, Communicating the Infinite: The Emergence of the Habad School (Chicago: University of Chicago Press, 1990), 45–63; and Nehemia Polen, "Charisma, Miracles and Leadership in Habad Lubavitch Hasidism," paper delivered at the conference "Reaching for the Infinite: The Lubavitcher Rebbe—Life, Teachings and Impact," New York University, November 7, 2005 (unpublished). On the place of *Likkutei Moharan* in Bratslav, see David B. Siff, "Shifting Ideologies of Orality and Literacy in Their Historical Context: Rebbe Nahman of Bratslav's Embrace of the Book as a Means for Redemption," *Prooftexts* 30 (2010): 238–62.

16. For a comparison of the modern revival in Habad and Bratslav Hasidism, see Yoram Bilu and Zvi Mark, "Between Tsaddiq and Messiah: A Comparative Analysis of Chabad and Breslav Hasidic Groups," in *After Spirituality: Studies in Mystical Traditions*, ed. Philip Wexler and Jonathan Garb (New York: Peter Lang, 2012). On the messianic thrust of their out-

reach efforts, see Wolfson, *Open Secret*, 33–38; Naftali Loewenthal, "The Baal Shem Tov's *Iggeret ha-Kodesh* and Contemporary Habad 'Outreach,'" in *Let the Old Make Way for the New: Studies in the Social and Cultural History of Eastern European Jewry Presented to Immanuel Etkes*, ed. David Assaf and Ada Rapoport-Albert, vol. 1 (Jerusalem: Zalman Shazar Center for Jewish History, 2009), 69–101; and Mark, "Contemporary Renaissance," 103–7.

17. Steven S. Schwarzschild, "An Introduction to the Thought of R. Isaac Hutner," *Modern Judaism* 5 (1985): 235–77.

18. See Allan Nadler, "Soloveitchik's Halakhic Man: Not a *Mithnagged*," *Modern Judaism* 13 (1993): 119–47.

19. The influence of Jewish mystical texts on Rabbi Soloveichik's own religious philosophy is a rather complicated question. See Dov Schwartz, *From Phenomenology to Existentialism: The Philosophy of Rabbi Joseph B. Soloveitchik, Volume 2* (Leiden: Brill, 2013), 89–114.

20. The most systematic treatment of Rabbi Schachter-Shalomi's approach to Jewish spirituality is found in his *Paradigm Shift: From the Jewish Renewal Teachings of Reb Zalman Schachter-Shalomi*, ed. Ellen Singer (Northvale, N.J.: Jason Aronson, 1993). For an example of his more popular mystical writings, see Zalman M. Schachter-Shalomi, *Credo of a Modern Kabbalist*, with Daniel Siegel (Victoria, BC: Trafford, 2005).

21. For an interesting evaluation of mysticism in American Jewish life, see Shaul Magid, *American Post-Judaism: Identity and Renewal in a Postethnic Society* (Bloomington and Indianapolis: Indiana University Press, 2013), esp. 74–132.

22. For a new biography of Rabbi Shlomo, see Natan Ophir (Offenbacher), *Rabbi Shlomo Carlebach: Life, Mission, and Legacy* (Jerusalem: Urim Publications, 2014). On Rabbi Shlomo's religious personality and innovative approach to Jewish devotion, see Alon Goshen-Gottstein, "Was Shlomo a Religious Genius?" (forthcoming).

23. See Yaakov Ariel, "Hasidism in the Age of Aquarius: The House of Love and Prayer in San Francisco, 1967–1977," *Religion and American Culture: A Journal of Interpretation* 13 (2003): 139–65; and Magid, *American-Post Judaism*, 132–39.

24. On Rabbi Carlebach's place within the greater renewal of Jewish spirituality, including the efforts of his one-time partner Rabbi Schachter-Shalomi, see Yaakov Ariel, "From Neo-Hasidism to Outreach Yeshivot: The Origins of the Movements of Renewal and Return to Tradition," in *Kabbalah and Contemporary Spiritual Revival*, ed. Boaz Huss (Beer Sheva: Ben Gurion University of the Negev Press, 2011), 181–211.

25. See the new series *The Torah Commentary of Rabbi Shlomo Carlebach*, ed. Shlomo Katz (Jerusalem: Urim, 2012).

26. Regarding Heschel's life, see the two-volume biography of Heschel: Edward K. Kaplan and Samuel H. Dresner, *Abraham Joshua Heschel: Prophetic Witness* (New Haven: Yale University Press, 1998); and Edward Kaplan, *Spiritual Radical: Abraham Joshua Heschel in America 1940–1972* (New Haven: Yale University Press, 2007). On his theological writings and his scholarship of Jewish mysticism, see Arthur Green, "Abraham Joshua Heschel: Recasting Hasidism for Moderns," *Modern Judaism* 29 (2009): 62–79; and Reuven R. Kimelman, "Abraham Joshua Heschel's Theology of Judaism and the Rewriting of Jewish Intellectual History," *The Journal of Jewish Thought & Philosophy* 17 (2009): 207–38.

27. In traditional Kabbalah, *tikkun* refers to restoring the fractured cosmos by uplifting sparks through acts of devotion both spiritual (prayer, study) and ethical (giving alms), but in modern parlance it has been redefined as repairing the world through social justice. On the history of this term, see Gilbert S. Rosenthal, "*Tikkun haOlam*: The Metamorphosis of a Concept," *The Journal of Religion* 85 (2005): 214–40.

28. See Ariel Evan Mayse, "Arthur Green: An Intellectual Portrait," in *Arthur Green (Living Jewish Philosophers Series)* (Boston and Leiden: Brill, 2014).

29. Arthur Green's most important contribution to modern Jewish theology is his three-part series: *Seek My Face: A Jewish Mystical Theology*, 2nd ed. (Woodstock, VT: Jewish Lights Publishing, 2003); *Ehyeh: Kabbalah for Tomorrow* (Woodstock, VT: Jewish Lights Publishing, 2003); and *Radical Judaism: Rethinking God and Tradition* (New Haven: Yale University Press, 2010).

30. See the recent work in Green's honor published by his students and colleagues: *Jewish Mysticism and the Spiritual Life: Classical Texts, Contemporary Reflections*, ed. Lawrence Fine, Eitan Fishbane, and Or N. Rose (Woodstock, VT: Jewish Lights, 2011).

31. Peter Margolis, "Seeds of Community: The Role of the Reconstructionist Movement in Creating Havurot in America," in *YIVO Annual of Jewish Social Science* 23 (1996): 319–64; Chava Weissler, "Worship in the Havura Movement," in *The Life of Judaism*, ed. Harvey E. Goldberg (Berkeley: University of California Press, 2001), 79–91; Joseph Reimer, "The 'Havurah' as a Context for Adult Jewish Education," in *The Uses of Tradition*, ed. Jack Wertheimer (New York: Jewish Theological Seminary of America, 1992), 393–410.

32. See Aubrey L. Glazer, "Touching God: Vertigo, Exactitude, and Degrees of *Devekut* in the Contemporary Nondual Jewish Mysticism of R. Yitzhaq Maier Morgenstern," *The Journal of Jewish Thought and Philosophy* 19 (2011): 147–92.

33. See Shlomo Fischer, "Radical Religious Zionism: From the Collective to the Individual," in *Kabbalah and Contemporary Spiritual Revival*, ed. Boaz Huss (Beer-Sheva: Ben-Gurion University of the Negev Press, 2011), 285–310.

34. See "The Settler Who Spoke with Arafat" in *Peacemakers in Action: Profiles of Religion in Conflict Resolution*, ed. David Little (Cambridge, UK: Cambridge University Press, 2007), 241–356.

35. Garb, *Chosen Will Become Herds*, 116–17. On Rav Shagar's thought, see Yair Dreyfuss, "Torah Study for Contemporary Times: Conservatism or Revolution?," *Tradition* 45 (2012): 31–47; and Alan Jotkowitz, "'And Now the Child Will Ask': The Post-modern Theology of Rav Shagar," *Tradition* 45 (2012): 49–66.

36. The popular "Yemima Method" of personal healing and development is an example of such a fusion between Jewish mysticism and New Age spirituality; see Tsippi Kauffman, "The Yemima Method as a Contemporary-Hasidic-Female Movement," *Modern Judaism* 32 (2012): 195–215.

37. On the Israeli pilgrimage to India, see Darya Maoz, "When Images Become 'True': The Israeli Backpacking Experience in India," in *Karmic Passages: Israeli Scholarship on India*, ed. David Shulman and Shalva Weil (New Delhi: Oxford University Press, 2008), 214–31.

38. See Boaz Huss, "The New Age of Kabbalah: Contemporary Kabbalah, the New Age and Postmodern Spirituality," *Journal of Modern Jewish Studies* 6 (2007): 107–25; and Rachel Werczberger, "Self-Identity and Healing in the Ritual of Jewish Spiritual Renewal in Israel," in *Kabbalah and Contemporary Spiritual Revival*, ed. Boaz Huss (Beer-Sheva: Ben-Gurion University of the Negev Press, 2011), 75–100.

39. On Jewish mysticism in the European academy, see Paul B. Fenton, "Qabbalah and Academia: The Critical Study of Jewish Mysticism in France," *Shofar: An Interdisciplinary Journal of Jewish Studies* 18 (2000): 45–69. For a study of the sometimes fraught relationship between modern scholarship and contemporary Jewish mysticism, see Boaz Huss, "'Authorized Guardians': The Polemics of Academic Scholars of Jewish Mysticism against Kabbalah Practitioners," in *Polemical Encounters: Esoteric Discourse and Its Others*, ed. Olav Hammer and Kocku Von Stuckrad (Leiden and Boston: Brill, 2007), 81–106.

Sources

We are grateful to the publishers for permission to use the following materials for this anthology:

Chapter 1: The Dawn of Kabbalah. From Joseph Dan, *The Early Kabbalah*, trans. Ronald C. Keiner. Classics of Western Spirituality. New York/Mahwah: Paulist Press, 1986. The Book *Bahir*, pp. 59–69; The *'Iyyun* Circle: The Book of Speculation, pp. 45–48; The Fountain of Wisdom, pp. 49–52; Explanation of the Four-Lettered Name, pp. 54–56; Rabbi Yitshak the Blind: The Process of Emanation, pp. 80–82, 85–86; The Mystical Torah—Kabbalistic Creation, pp. 73–79; Rabbi 'Azriel of Gerona, pp. 89–96; Rabbi Ya'akov ben Sheshet, pp. 128, 130–32; The Writings of the Kohen Brothers: Explanation of the Letters, pp. 153–56; Treatise on the Left Emanation, pp. 173, 179–82.

From Seth Brody, *Commentary on the Song of Songs: Ezra ben Solomon of Gerona and other Kabbalistic Commentaries*. Kalamazoo, MI: Medieval Institute Publications, Western Michigan University, 1999. Rabbi Ezra ben Shlomo of Gerona, pp. 38–40, 48–49, 77–86, 86–88, 105–6.

Chapter 2: The *Zohar*. From Daniel Matt, *Zohar: The Book of Enlightenment*. Classics of Western Spirituality. New York/Mahwah: Paulist Press, 1983. How to Look at Torah, pp. 43–45; The Creation of *Elohim*, pp. 49–50; Male and Female, pp. 55–56; Abram's Descent into Egypt, pp. 63–64; Openings, pp. 65–68; Seduction Above and Below, pp. 85–90; Jacob's Garment of Days, pp. 91–95; Manna and Wisdom, pp. 113–16; All of Israel Saw the Letters, pp. 119–20; The Old Man and the Beautiful Maiden, pp. 121–26; The Secret of Sabbath, pp. 132; *Korban* and *'Olah*, Drawing Near and Ascending, pp. 145–47; God, Israel, and *Shekhinah*, pp. 153–57; Threshing Out the Secrets, pp. 163–69; The Rabbis Encounter a Child, pp. 170–72; The Wedding Celebration, pp. 182–89.

From Seth Brody, *Commentary on the Song of Songs: Ezra ben Solomon of Gerona and other Kabbalistic Commentaries*. Kalamazoo, MI: Medieval Institute Publications, Western Michigan University, 1999. *Zohar Hadash*: The Hidden Midrash to the Book of Lamentations, pp. 153–55, 168–75, 178–88.

Chapter 3: The Safed Renaissance and Its Legacy. Part One: The Kabbalistic World of Safed. From Lawrence Fine, *Safed Spirituality:*

Rules of Mystical Piety, The Beginning of Wisdom. Classics of Western Spirituality. New York/Mahwah: Paulist Press, 1984. The Pious Customs of R. Moshe Cordovero, pp. 34–38; The Pious Customs of Rabbi Avraham Galante, pp. 42–44; Come, My Beloved, *Lekha Dodi*, pp. 38–40; The Pious Customs of R. Yitshak Luria, pp. 65–77; Rabbi Yitshak Luria's Aramaic Invocations for the Sabbath Eve, pp. 77–80; The Beginning of Wisdom, pp. 92–93, 95, 102–4, 106–7, 109–10, 112, 116, 118–19, 123–25, 126–28, 135, 137, 142–45, 151–56.

From Morris M. Faierstein, *Jewish Mystical Autobiographies: Book of Visions and Book of Secrets*. Classics of Western Spirituality. New York/Mahwah: Paulist Press, 1999. The Book of Visions, pp. 43–45, 78–82, 90, 94–95, 130–31, 156–57, 167, 170, 172, 195–99, 209, 216, 219–21.

Part Two: Lurianic Kabbalah and its Interpreters in the Seventeenth Century. From Miles Krassen, *Isaiah Horowitz: The Generations of Adam*. Classics of Western Spirituality. New York/Mahwah: Paulist Press, 1996. The Generations of Adam: The House of Y-H-V-H [I], pp. 65, 79, 81–82; The House of Israel [I], pp. 99–100, 114–15, 120; The House of David [I], pp. 231–33; The Faithful House [II], pp. 148–54. The House of Wisdom [II], pp. 175–79; The House of Wisdom [III], pp. 265–66, 269–70; The House of Choosing, pp. 292–94; The Great Gate, pp. 298–99.

From David J. Halperin, *Abraham Miguel Cardozo: Selected Writings*. Classics of Western Spirituality. New York/Mahwah: Paulist Press, 2001. Defending the Fallen Messiah, pp. 161–67; This Is My God and I Will Praise Him, pp. 237–42; Israel, Holiness to the Lord, pp. 255, 266–70.

Chapter 4: Hasidic Spirituality. From Arthur Green, *Menahem Nahum of Chernobyl: Upright Practices, The Light of the Eyes*. Classics of Western Spirituality. New York/Mahwah: Paulist Press, 1982. Upright Practices, pp. 31–43; The Light of the Eyes *(Me'or 'Eynayim)*: Parashat Bereshit, pp. 48–54; Parashat Noah, pp. 97–99, 93–94; Parashat Lekh Lekha, pp. 113–17; Parashat Va-Yera, pp. 135–37; Parashat Va-Yetse, pp. 216–14.

From Arnold J. Band, *Nahman of Bratslav: The Tales*. Classics of Western Spirituality. New York/Mahwah: Paulist Press, 1988. The Lost Princess, pp. 55–61; The Seven Beggars, pp. 255–62, 278–82.

From Morris M. Faierstein, *Jewish Mystical Autobiographies: Book of Visions and Book of Secrets*. Classics of Western Spirituality. New York/Mahwah: Paulist Press, 1999. Book of Visions, pp. 275–77, 279–81, 285–86, 291–92; The Deeds of the Lord, pp. 294–99, 301, 303, 305.

Chapter 5: Modern Mystics. From Ben Zion Bokser, *Abraham Isaac Kook: The Lights of Penitence, Lights of Holiness, the Moral Principles, Essays, Letters, and Poems*. Classics of Western Spirituality. New York/Mahwah: Paulist Press, 1978. Lights of Holiness: The Summons to the Mystical, pp. 192–93; The Mystical Dimension That Embraces Everything, pp. 194–95; Those Destined for the Mystical, pp. 201–3; The Doctrine of Evolution, pp. 220–21; The Perfection of the Spiritual through the Material, pp. 225–26; A Fourfold Song, pp. 228–29; Withdrawal and Sociability, pp. 233–34. Essays: The Sage is More Important than the Prophet, pp. 253–55; The Significance of the Revival, pp. 282–86. The Lights of Penitence: Chapter 4, pp. 49, 53; Chapter 5, pp. 55–56; Chapter 6, pp. 56–58; Chapter 8, pp. 63–64; Chapter 10, pp. 73–74, 77–78. The Moral Principles: Love, pp. 135–37; Faith, pp. 141, 146, 148; Linking Life to God, pp. 156–57; Bringing Up Holy Sparks, pp. 158–59; Freedom, p. 161; Fear of God, pp. 162, 165, 169–70; Tolerance, p. 175. Letters: Letter to R. Judah Leib Seltzer, pp. 354–58. Poems: My Heart Rages, p. 371; I Am Filled with Love for God, pp. 373–74; How Great is my Inner Struggle, pp. 377–78; The Whispers of Existence, p. 381.

From Arthur Green, *Hasidic Spirituality for a New Era: The Religious Writings of Hillel Zeitlin*. Classics of Western Spirituality. New York/Mahwah: Paulist Press, 2012. Fundaments of Hasidism: Being and Nothingness, pp. 73–77; *Tsimtsum*, pp. 77–80; Letters, pp. 83–87; Raising Up Sparks, pp. 88–89; Uplifting the *Middot*, pp. 97–101. Aramaic Chapters, pp. 51–58. Admonitions for Every True Member of Yavneh, pp. 43–49. Prayers: Midnight, pp. 199; My Distress I Shall Tell in You, pp. 211–13; Attachment to God, pp. 218–20; The Mother, pp. 226–27; Deepest Wish, pp. 228–29.

Primary Source References

The following is a list of the passages translated in this volume as they are found in relatively common printed editions of Jewish mystical books. It is intended as an aid to the scholar or seeker who wishes to explore the texts in the original Hebrew or Aramaic. The passages are listed in the order they appear within this volume. Pieces that already include clear references to a chapter and subsection within a widely available book, such as Hayyim Vital's *Book of Visions* or Menahem Nahum of Chernobyl's *Me'or 'Eynayim*, do not appear on this list. The Hebrew reader will doubtless be able to locate them with comparative ease. Translations based on unpublished manuscripts are not included below because of their inaccessibility.

Chapter 1: The Dawn of Kabbalah

Sefer ha-Bahir—Daniel Abrams, *The Book Bahir: An Edition Based on the Earliest Manuscripts* (Los Angeles: Cherub Press, 1994), 87–94, 173–81.

The Book of Speculation—*The Works of Iyyun: Critical Editions*, ed. Oded Porat (Los Angeles: Cherub Press, 2013), 103–5.

The Fountain of Wisdom—ibid., 66–69.

Explanation of the Four-Lettered Name—ibid., 193–94.

The Process of Emanation—Daniel Abrams, *R. Asher ben David: His Complete Works and Studies in His Kabbalistic Thought* (Los Angeles: Cherub Press, 1996), 325–26.

Commentary on the Song of Songs—*Kitvei RaMBaN*, ed. Hayyim Dov Chavel (Mossad Harav Kook: Jerusalem, 1963), 2:485, 487, 496–98, 504.

Explanation of the Ten *Sefirot*—*Bi'ur 'Eser Sefirot* (Jerusalem: 1997), 29–44.

The Book of Faith and Reliance—*Kitvei RaMBaN*, 2:368–70.

Explanation of the Letters—Gershom Scholem, *Kabbalot R. Ya'akov ve-R. Yitshak* (Jerusalem: 1926), 201–3.

Treatise on the Left Emanation—ibid., 251–52, 260–61.

Chapter 2: The *Zohar*

How to Look at Torah—*Sefer ha-Zohar*, ed. Reuven Margaliot (Jerusalem: Mossad Harav Kook, 1947), 3:152a.
The Creation of *Elohim*—*Zohar,* 1:15a.
Male and Female—ibid., 1:55b.
Openings—Ibid., 1:103a–b.
Seduction Above and Below—ibid., 1:189b–90b.
Jacob's Garment of Days—ibid., 1:224a–b.
Manna and Wisdom—ibid., 2:61b–62a.
All of Israel Saw the Letters—*Zohar Hadash*, ed. Reuven Margaliot (Jerusalem: Mossad Harav Kook, 1978), 41b–c.
The Old Man and the Beautiful Maiden—*Zohar*, 2:94b–95a, 99a–b, 114a (*Saba de-Mishpatim*).
The Secret of Sabbath—ibid., 2:135a–b.
Korban and *'Olah*, Drawing Near and Ascending—ibid., 3:4b–5a, 26b.
God, Israel, and *Shekhinah*—ibid., 3:114a–115b.
Threshing Out the Secrets—ibid., 3:127b–28a, 135b, 144a–b (*Idra Rabba*).
The Rabbis Encounter a Child—ibid., 3:186a–b (*Yanuka*).
The Wedding Celebration—ibid., 3:287b–88a, 291a–b (*Idra Zuta*).
Zohar Hadash: The Hidden Midrash to the Book of Lamentations—ibid., 91a, 92a–d.

Chapter 3: The Safed Renaissance and Its Legacy

Part One: The Kabbalistic World of Safed

The Pious Customs of Rabbi Moshe Cordovero—Solomon Schechter, "Safed in the Sixteenth Century: Appendix A," in *Studies in Judaism 2* (Philadelphia: Jewish Publication Society of America, 1908), 292–94.
The Pious Customs of Rabbi Avraham Galante—ibid., 294–96.
The Pious Customs of Rabbi Yitshak Luria—Meir Benayahu, *Toledoth ha-Ari* (Jerusalem: Ben Zvi Institute, 1967), 316–17, 319–21, 327–34.

Part Two: Lurianic Kabbalah and Its Interpreters in the Seventeenth Century

Epistle to the Judges of Izmir—Gershom Scholem, "Epistle of the Judges of Izmir," in *Studies and Texts Concerning the History of Sabbetianism and Its Metamorphoses* (Jerusalem: Bialik Institute, 1974), 319–24.

This Is My God and I Will Praise Him—Gershom Scholem, "Abraham Michael Cordozo: 'This is My God and I Will Praise Him,'" in *Studies and Texts Concerning the History of Sabbetianism and Its Metamorphoses* (Jerusalem: Bialik Institute, 1974), 365–67.

Israel, Holiness to the Lord—Gershom Scholem, "Abraham Michael Cordozo: 'Israel, Holiness to the Lord,'" in *Researches in Sabbateanism*, ed. Yehuda Liebes (Tel Aviv: Am Oved, 1991), 441, 449–51.

Chapter 4: Hasidic Spirituality

Book of Secrets: Book of Visions—*Megilat Setarim* (Jerusalem: 2001), 3–9, 14–15, 22–23.

Book of Secrets: The Deeds of the Lord—ibid., 25–28, 30–31, 33–34, 36, 38–39.

Chapter 5: Modern Mystics

The Summons to the Mystical—*Orot ha-Kodesh* (Jerusalem: Mossad Harav Kook, 1990), I:5–6.

The Mystical Dimension that Embraces Everything—ibid., I:9–10.

Those Destined for the Mystical—ibid., I:88–89.

The Doctrine of Evolution—ibid., II:555.

The Perfection of the Spiritual through the Material—Ibid., II:435.

A Fourfold Song—ibid., II:458–59.

Withdrawal and Sociability—ibid., III:271–72.

The Sage is More Important than the Prophet—Orot (Jerusalem: Mossad Harav Kook, 1950), 120–21.

The Significance of the Revival—ibid., 135–37.

Letter to R. Judah Leib Seltzer, 1913—*Iggerot ha-Re'iyah* (Jerusaelm: Mossad Harav Kook, 1946), II:483, 123–25.

My Heart Rages—A. M. Habermann, "Rav Kook's Poetry," *Sinai* 17 (1945): 8.
I Am Filled with Love for God—ibid., 8–10.
How Great Is My Inner Struggle—ibid., 12–13.
The Whispers of Existence—ibid., 15.
The Fundaments of Hasidism—*Be-Fardes ha-Hasidut ve'ha-Kabbalah* (Tel Aviv: Yavneh, 1960), 11–18, 20–26, 33–36.
Aramaic Chapters—*Sifran shel Yehidim* (Warsaw: 1928), 10–16.
Admonitions for Every True Member of *Yavneh*—ibid., 57–63.
Midnight—*'Al Gevul Shenei 'Olamot* (Tel Aviv: Yavneh, 1976), 219–20.
"My Distress I Shall Tell in Your Presence…"—ibid., 230–31.
Attachment to God—ibid., 236–38.
The Mother—*Gezangen tsum Ein Sof* (Warsaw: 1931), 103–4.
Deepest Wish—ibid., 81–82.